# NORFOLK CENTURY

# NORFOLK CENTURY

Edited by TREVOR HEATON

Eastern Daily Press

First published in 1999 by Eastern Counties Newspapers Group Ltd



ISBN 1 902729 02 1



Edited and designed by Trevor Heaton

Cover design by Richard Snowball

Film separations by Saxon Photolitho, Saxon House, Hellesdon Park Road, Norwich, NR6 5DR

Printed by Jarrolds Book Printing, 3 Fison Way, Thetford, Norfolk, IP24 1HT

Editorial consultant: Ian McIntyre, Parke Sutton, Orchard House, Grange Farm, Ashwellthorpe, Norfolk, NR16 1ET

Facing title page: Sunset over the River Chet near Langley Marshes (photograph: Simon Finlay)

*Dedicated to the memory of Trevor Westgate*

# Contents

# Introduction

Turning back to the Eastern Daily Press of January 1st 1901 - the date the paper insisted the new century properly started - the now-yellowed and fragile pages seem a world away from the computer-generated full-colour papers of today. Column after column were full to bursting with gloomy reports of the Boer War, a watershed in Britain's relations with its colonies.

That was, no doubt, the thought behind the first editorial of the twentieth century. *"The new century,"* the paper wrote, *"cannot be said to open very cheerfully. We are not enjoying peace or doing brilliant deeds in war."*

It went on to say how prophets of doom were predicting how Germany and America were fast overtaking Britain in commerce and influence and that the British people were *"given up to sport and money making and that a weight of scepticism in religion and politics is settling down upon us."*

Strong stuff - and a case of *plus ça change...*, one might say - but the editorial continued by saying there was much to look forward to in the new century and that Britain's ingenuity and spirit of scientific invention were undimmed.

Elsewhere there were reports of Kaiser Wilhelm giving a sabre-rattling speech to a special review of his troops. There were, no doubt, plenty of people who were already dreading the escalating commercial, political and industrial rivalry between Europe's two greatest nations spilling over into war.

Even the most optimistic of observers could see how the new century would promise massive change. For Norfolk, as for the rest of the world, change was what it received. And that change is the theme of Norfolk Century.

And on what a scale! As usual, it was the Bard who said it first. "Can this cockpit hold the vasty fields of France?" he bemoaned in the prologue to Henry V. And summarising a century of change in Norfolk's vasty fields has been scarcely less of a challenge.

Norfolk Century brings together more than twenty of the county's writers to reflect on a 100 years of different aspects of local life, from the county's natural heritage to its unique links with the Royal Family, from the changing face of our towns and villages to the upheaval of two world wars.

It is no coincidence that this book has been written under the banner of the Eastern Daily Press. No other local morning newspaper can claim as close a link with the county it serves as the EDP. The fact that the paper goes into the next century outselling all its rivals in its county - including national titles - is a measure of the respect and affection it continues to engender. The millions of words published this century have proved invaluable in providing source material for the contributors.

Many of the writers include some of the EDP's best-loved columnists, and the near-300 pictures in this book have drawn heavily on the extensive EDP photographic archive, although many have been taken especially for this volume. Some have already become classics in their own right, for example the famous image of the number 26 bus down a hole in a Norwich street - or Bill Smith's award-winning picture of boxer Herbie Hide celebrating a victory. But in compiling this book, I have also taken advantage of some fine material from elsewhere, notably Derek Edwards' marvellous aerial photographs of Norfolk's archaeological heritage.

Twentieth-century Norfolk was not simply

created at the turn of a page in a calendar, of course, and where appropriate writers have set their subjects against a relevant chronological background. This does not mean that Norfolk Century is a mere chronicle of events; although there is plenty of useful information for the researcher and interested reader, contributors have striven to deal with their subjects in a thematic fashion, looking to take an overview of events rather than simply list them.

This desire to set things within their proper context explains, for example, the decision to include a chapter on discovering the county's past. The way Norfolk is today has been shaped not only by modern events but by its past - and how significant, yet again, that the twentieth is the century that has provided more information about our ancestors than any other.

Even a work of this magnitude has had to be selective. An example of this selection at work can be seen in the discussion of Norfolk sport. The subjects have been whittled down to football, cricket, motor-racing, speedway, horseracing, boxing and - appropriately enough for the county containing the Broads - sailing. There have been many fine Norfolk performances in other sports, some of world class. The chapter as chosen does not seek to belittle their success but to provide a fair cross-section of the sporting life of the county.

Turning over the pages, it will be seen how certain themes have dominated Norfolk life over the past hundred years. For example, the changing nature of our villages; the decline of the agricultural workforce; the battle to preserve Norfolk culture against the multi-media onslaught of the outside world; the love-hate relationship with the sea which has brought so much prosperity - and so much heartache. Where the subject matter dictates it, I have included Lowestoft within the orbit of this book as its story has been bound up in Yarmouth's in many areas this century.

In editing this volume it is interesting to note how frequently the writers have found themselves referring to that appropriate Norfolk motto "dew diffrunt". The Norfolk way of doing things is not merely a question of imitating what has been done elsewhere. It is surprising how often the county's independent spirit shines through its story.

So please read, and savour, this look at Norfolk over the past 100 years. It is my sincere hope that this unique collection of essays will be dipped into again and again with enjoyment; a special book for a special county.

As a record of the past century in Norfolk I hope it will be valued; but as a feast of good writing and photography, I hope even more that it will be treasured.

**Trevor Heaton**
**Editor**
**Norfolk Century**

# Foreword

The Eastern Daily Press has occupied a unique position in the hearts of Norfolk people for almost 130 years. So when we posed the question: should we mark the ending of an eventful century in a special way, there could be really only one answer - of course we should.

And the fruit of that long-nurtured project is the Norfolk Century book you are holding in your hands.

It would have been tempting to opt for a simple year-by-year format. After all, what could be more natural for a newspaper, used to dealing with the news in daily bursts? But Norfolk's famous motto of "dewin' diffrent" applies to its daily paper too. By instead opting to approach the century in 16 chapters, we were able to give free rein to our writers to range backwards and forwards across the years to develop their themes.

And in any case, such an approach fits in with one of the consistent tenets of the EDP. Its layout, typefaces, staff, even its size, may have changed over the years but its commitment to fine writers and photographers remains undiminished.

From the days of Lilias Rider Haggard, Henry Williamson and Jonathan Mardle (Eric Fowler) to fine present-day writers of the calibre of Charles Roberts, Colin Chinery and Steve Snelling, our determination to bring our readers the excellence of the written word remains undimmed. Pictures too; fine photographers such as Les Gould - whose pictures of Yarmouth life remain classics - and Dick Jeeves have given way to a new and equally talented generation. Their work, as well as their predecessors, is represented here.

To ensure as rounded a picture of the county as possible we have also involved such well-regarded local experts as Dr Peter Wade-Martins and utilised picture resources from as far afield as the RAF's archive and the British Museum to make this volume as comprehensive as possible.

In his Postscript looking ahead to 2050, Trevor Heaton has observed that the only certain thing about the future is that it will be different. Well, that may be so - but the Eastern Daily Press plans to be Norfolk's favourite for our grandchildren and great-grandchildren, just as it was for our forefathers.

Peter Franzen
Editor
Eastern Daily Press

## CHAPTER 1

# Population

From his garden on Kett's Hill, Necton, 72-year-old Basil Bell sweeps an arm towards the far side of this residential road. "Up until the Sixties we could sit here and see right through to Holme Hale and Ashill. I remember the lovely trees."

The trees and the view have long gone. There are bungalows there now as in much of this mid-Norfolk village known to the motorist on the nearby A47 for the engaging two-tier lantern on the tower of the parish church.

Necton perhaps as much as any community symbolises the transforming late-twentieth century expansion of a category of Norfolk village, though Mattishall, Horsford, Mulbarton, Griston, Lyng, and the Woottons are among others that come immediately to mind.

For Norfolk the twentieth century is in part the story of a loss of isolation and a large and continuing inward migration, changes that were to come relatively late. Yet even now it might be said that the county remains predominantly little touched by urbanisation, relative to other and, may we say, less blessed counties.

In 1901 Norfolk's population was 476,500. By 1921 it had topped half a million, a figure that scarcely changed through the inter-war period. By 1951 it had risen to 552,300, reaching 694,600 by 1981. The most recent figure (1998) is 783,000, and from the 1991 Census the typical Norfolk dweller emerges as a car-owning thirty- to 44-year-old co-habiter, employed, living in an owner-occupied detached house.

From the nineteenth century right through to the Fifties, the county as a whole had been growing steadily, yet more than half of its parishes were declining in population, a reflection of the run-down in agricultural employment. The only ones to grow lay close to the major centres.

But then in the Sixties the rate of growth accelerated and the pattern of development changed dramatically. People began moving in increasing numbers into the rural areas, and new development was permitted in many small villages. Between 1961 and 1966, three times as many parishes were growing as in the Fifties, and over the decade annual inward migration rose from two to six thousand. By the early Seventies and again in the mid-Eighties it was to reach 8000.

This was the period, says Martin Shaw, Norfolk's director of planning and transportation, when it became clear that Norfolk was an integral part of a wider south east and eastern England economy. "Norfolk joined the South East about 1986."

The origins lay far beyond the county borders. In the post-war years there began in London an experimental social upheaval that was to have profound demographic consequences. Young people and retired couples began to move outwards, settling in the towns and villages of Hertfordshire, Bedfordshire and mid-Essex. Within a few years the wave had advanced into East Anglia, and by the late Sixties Norfolk, whose twentieth-century population had been expanding slower than the country as a whole, was suddenly growing at twice the national average. At its peak in the Seventies, the population was increasing at ten times this figure.

That which the historian Correlli Barnett scorned as 'The Middlesex Look' - repetitive, off-the-peg designs, frequently bungaloid - seemed all but de rigeur wherever

**COLIN CHINERY joined the Eastern Daily Press in 1965 from the weekly paper in his family home town of Bury St Edmunds. After working in King's Lynn and Norwich, he became leader writer of the East Anglian Daily Times in 1969. He later joined the BBC, working in radio in the Midlands, returning to the EDP in 1974 as leader writer and feature writer in succession to Eric Fowler. In 1992 he was named as the UK Press Gazette Feature Writer of the Year. He is married with a son and a daughter, and lives in a small South Norfolk village.**

**W Ellis Clarke, 81, joined Thetford Town Council as Clerk and Chief Financial Officer in 1949, intending "to stay five years and then move on to a bigger place after five years. But my wife and I liked the town and we are still here." With the 1974 local government re-organisation, he took early retirement – "I could see there would be urban and rural conflicts" – and joined a firm of solicitors, retiring eight years later.**
**Born in Luton, he says that in 1959 he was the only man within 100 miles of Norwich who wanted Luton to beat Norwich in the FA Cup semi-final. "I've been a supporter of Luton Town all my life. It has taught me to be cheerful in the face of perpetual disappointment."**

planners had consented to new rural housing. The reaction was both aesthetic - as in the case of Barnett's observation - and often instinctive; indigenous hands groping for the phantom levers of what was to become the sometimes mocked emblem of resistance, the Norfolk drawbridge. But by then something altogether bigger, a social revolution no less, had taken root among the spreading, brooding coniferous acres along Norfolk's border with Suffolk.

In the early Fifties, Thetford, the old Anglo-Saxon capital of East Anglia, was a small, rather inconsequential town in a thinly-populated area of modest agricultural value. Arriving from St Neots in 1949, the new Town Clerk and Chief Financial Officer to the Borough Council, 32-year-old W Ellis Clarke, was struck by its rather traumatised air. Since the closure in 1929 of the great Burrell's engineering works with the loss of 500 skilled jobs, Thetford had ceased to generate employment, new population or even hope, "waiting like Mr Micawber, for something to turn up" as one town councillor was to reflect. But within ten years Ellis Clarke had had a decisive hand in reviving all three.

After Swindon and Bletchley, Thetford became the third English town to pioneer a successful London-primed expansion scheme. But the beginnings were unpromising, "like getting an aircraft into the air in the early days of aviation," recalls Clarke.

Ellis Clarke must rank as one of the most influential men in twentieth-century Norfolk. Town Clerk and Chief Financial Officer of Thetford Borough Council from 1949 to 1974, he was first to see the potential of town expansion, thereafter driving and overseeing it throughout the formative years during which a 4000 population increased five-fold.

Fifty years ago the town was still without sewerage, and near the Bury Road where there are now houses, Clarke had been astonished to see acres of dumped night soil.

Thetford emerged from the war with little or no male employment opportunities, and five years on Clarke was noting the occasional show of feudal deference. "You walked down the street, and you might meet a council

**Dennis Mead, 78, and Mary Mead, 76, were among Thetford's first London "settlers", arriving in the Sweyn Close house where they still live, on August 8th 1959. Mr Mead moved up with Williams Engineering, the first factory to be set up under the town's expansion scheme, but only after Mrs Mead had pondered long and hard. "I'd lived in Willesden all my life and when we came here I felt lonely, missing my family back in London," said Mrs Mead." Some of their friends moved back to London.**
**But Dennis and their five children – a sixth was later born in Thetford – settled almost at once, and their four sons married local girls.**
**"I love it now," says Mary. Forty years on does she think of herself as a Londoner or a Thetfordian? "Oh I don't know. Once a Londoner always a Londoner isn't it?"**

workman who stepped off and touched his forelock."

One of his first moves was to write to the owners of derelict commercial property asking them to tidy their premises. But in 1951 the council went on the offensive, setting up an industrial development sub-committee. This was the era of planning controls, however, and the obligatory industrial development certificates were reserved almost exclusively for new towns and traditional jobless blackspots. "It soon became clear to me that we would never get anywhere."

But the following year brought the Town Development Act, a mechanism for decanting populations and industry from overcrowded London to communities desperate for economic regeneration. The London County Council wanted to re-settle 300,000, but many of the towns approached were hostile. Thetford, however, was not merely willing but eager. Eighty six miles from London however, it it seemed too distant to qualify.

Then while browsing through a morning paper, Clarke read that Ashford in Kent, sixty miles from London, was negotiating with the LCC. Would London he wondered, stretch the limits and consider Thetford?

In January 1953, backed by the council, he made contact. London was indeed interested. Three months later talks opened between Thetford, the LCC and Norfolk County Council, concluding in a town expansion agreement for a first-phase building of 1500 houses.

A straw poll in the EDP – strongly supportive from the outset – revealed general enthusiasm for the "overspill" scheme. In the early days this admittedly tactless word found cautious refuge in quotation marks, later to be removed. Subsequently the expression was dropped altogether in favour of "town expansion", but the initial term entered the popular vocabulary where it more or less remains.

Semantics aside, Thetford took to its dramatic new partnership with London with general enthusiasm. Mr F Duboc, a one-man storekeeper of Castle Street said Thetford was dying and here was a chance of revival. Mr E Bennett, secretary and manager of the town's Co-operative Society feared that without town expansion Thetford would become a second Lavenham, "a most depressing place".

Yet there were also fears that Thetford would prove uncongenial to Londoners missing the big city, and that the scheme would conclude in friction and tears. "During the war the evacuees from London had not adapted themselves to the methods of the country," noted one citizen darkly. Councillor George Kybird was more sanguine. "We should not be getting dyed-in-the-wool cockneys. We should get the young married couples." Mr G D Block, visiting the town from Conservative Central Office concurred, forecasting that Thetford would be attracting people "likely to be more the more industrious element rather than the sluggards".

At a British Industries Fair at Olympia, Thetford council distributed leaflets that made much of the level land and "pine-laden bracing air". But it was not until September 1958 that building began, and then on a magnitude scarcely reconcilable with the subsequent scale; just 22 houses.

Working with borough engineer Bill Jennings, the town expansion scheme became for Ellis Clarke "almost a personal challenge". Three factors weighed against it; finance, industrial procurement, and a lukewarm Government.

The logistics were indeed challenging. To begin the roads, which as Ellis Clarke remarks, while not brilliant even now, "were terrible" in the early- and mid-Fifties. "A lot of people you talked to about moving up, regarded Norfolk as one railway stop before Greenland."

As for finance, how was it possible for the slight resources of a small authority to rise to the millions required to finance new industry and the doubling or tripling of population?

Clarke encountered a joshing scepticism among the Norfolk council fraternity. "Still no industry yet?" he would be asked.

But early on the LCC gave Thetford some smart advice; buy land now rather than pay for the later and higher value that the borough council would have created.

NORWICH

# THETFORD MAY TAKE LONDON 'OVERSPILL'

## Negotiations for Transfer of People and Industry

IT WAS revealed yesterday that Thetford Borough Council is negotiating with the London County Council to take an "overspill" of people and industry under the Town Development Act of 1952. If successful the population of Thetford will rise from 4500—little more than that of the original Saxon town—to about 13,000.

The approach was made by the Borough Council to the L.C.C. after obtaining the approval of Norfolk County Council as town planning authority.

After earlier negotiations the local Industrial Development Sub-Committee last week met at Thetford Mr. Reginald Stamp, chairman of the L.C.C. Housing Committee, Mrs. Eveline Dennington, the vice-chairman, Lady Pepler and administrative and technical officials of the L.C.C.

### Essential Factors

Yesterday the Borough Council held a special meeting and unanimously approved the following recommendation of its sub-committee: "That as there appears to be a prima facie case for proceeding under the Town Development Act, the matter be referred to officers of the respective authorities which would enable them to prepare a scheme which could be submitted to the councils concerned for their consideration and, if desired, for ultimate submission to the Ministry of Housing and Local Government."

The Act is yet largely untried and the success of the negotiations depends on whether or not it can be made to work. Finance and the industrial development

### Deration Hopes for Fats, Bacon

Although nothing official is known, there is some hope in Government circles that Major Lloyd-George, the Minister of Food, may be able before the end of this year to deration bacon, butter, margarine and cooking fats. The freeing of sugar may be delayed a little but it should be off the ration by November. Shipments of Cuban sugar will begin next month, but this raw sugar will have to be refined before distribution.

**April 22nd 1953: The Eastern Daily Press reports the talks to bring overspill to Norfolk.**

Thetford duly complied; 220 acres on London Road, then a further 55, and finally Abbey Farm and a plot on the Mundford Road, 360 acres in all. London paid for the land, put in the roads and sewers, recovering the outlay as the ground rents began to roll into Thetford's account. The LCC and its successor, the Greater London Council, also extended loans at preferential rates. "I cannot speak too highly of them," says Clarke.

For its part, London must have been relieved to find a town which welcomed expansion and worked to make it succeed. As Ellis Clarke recalls, in the four or five municipal elections held between the first public announcement in 1953 and the signing of the agreement in 1958, pro-expansion candidates were regularly returned. By the time the expansion scheme had finished, 10,000 Londoners had settled (the opportunity to take a further 10,000 was rejected in the Seventies).

"People from outside sometimes wondered why Thetford wanted to have all these Londoners. But the people of the town knew all about the paucity of services and employment, and there was very little opposition."

More than forty years after the first expansion scheme homes were built, Ellis Clarke is still asked occasionally whether "overspill" ruined Thetford's character.

"My response is to ask what was the character of Thetford? It had the characteristics of a dying community." While accepting the town has "a number of bad eggs" he says its social problems receive a scale of publicity scarcely merited by its extent. "Integration was difficult at first, and it was unfortunate that the development had to be in large lumps and on the periphery. Overall however the newcomers settled in pretty well."

He remembers a common sight in the early Fifties, a crowd of men standing on the corner of the Bury and Brandon roads waiting for a truck to take them to the American bases, or to Brandon, which had rather more industry than Thetford. "Ever since town development got under way, it's been the reverse, and the number of people who live in Bury and surrounding villages to work here is quite tremendous. I met someone recently who put it all into perspective. He told me town expansion had kept his son and now his grandchildren in Thetford in decent jobs alongside him."

**Eddie Edgley: Wartime experiences led him to become one of the leading supporters of the Sixties King's Lynn-London overspill agreement.**

Over the West Suffolk border, Brandon, Mildenhall and Bury St Edmunds were to follow Thetford's example (Haverhill, a village of largely Victorian houses on the Essex border had been an early pioneer), but the old East Suffolk County Council declined to have anything to do with "overspill", despite pressure from towns such as Halesworth.

Meanwhile Thetford's expansion had been noted in King's Lynn. Lynn's population had grown in the late nineteenth century with the development of industries drawn by the new docks and railways, and by 1900 it was pushing out to Gaywood and North and South Lynn. In the inter-war years slum clearance accelerated this movement and by 1935 Gaywood was absorbed into the town.

But rather like Thetford, though on a different scale and with additional priorities, Lynn emerged from the Second World War with serious problems, above all a chronic shortage of housing. There had been slum clearance schemes in the Thirties, and by 1944 a campaign began to finish the job. In fact nothing was achieved until the mid-Fifties, the intervening period providing years of recurring frustration and occasional despair.

Sites had been bought for new homes around Lynn (ex-PoWs helping to lay kerbs on the new estates) but even so, by the end of 1947, housing committee chairman J W Raby, estimating that 900 families were on the waiting list and 150 living in overcrowded conditions, sighed that he wished he were a magician.

Among the streets and neighbourhoods singled out by their bad housing was Hillington Square, birthplace and home of Eddie Edgley, later chairman of the housing committee, Lynn mayor in 1964, and an early advocate of the town expansion scheme. "I hate to call them slums, but they were, two-up and two-down, some with no back ways and everything coming through the front door; coal, night soil, everything. When you think of families with eight, nine, ten children in a two-up and two-down, the amount of poverty was terrific."

Edgley, now 80, remembers the 1926 General Strike, "queues to the labour exchange five abreast all down New Conduit Street and into Broad Street." His father recalled an appearance before the Means Test board, and being told he could have tickets for milk, bread and flour. "My dad said 'I don't want them! I want a job.' So he was sent to the corporation depot the next morning and given a bag and a stick with a nail in, to pick up litter paper. As a kid you didn't think anything about it, but later you thought how degrading for an industrial blacksmith."

Demobbed in 1946 after four years in German PoW camps, Eddie Edgley returned to Hillington Square and to a Lynn with a housing crisis the despair of its council. But slums and shortages were not Lynn's only problem. A town rich in historic buildings and quarters was confronted with the reality of structural decay and the threat of demolition. Where were the resources with which to restore and maintain? The job market too was restricted to a handful of industries, businesses and occupations, a cheerless prospect for a returning war generation. "A lot of my pals worked at what we called the muck works, a few at the gas works, and there was Dodman's, the boiler makers," recalled Eddie Edgley. "A lot of them went as errand boys. No end of errand boys."

This was the background that was to lead to Lynn's October 1962 overspill agreement with the Greater London Council. From then until 1975, 4400 units, public and private, were added to Lynn's housing stock, sending the town's population up from 28,000 to 35,000 at one time. As was generally the case, initial population targets and predictions had been considerably higher, for example 54,000 by 1981 (Housing Minister Richard Crossman looking into his crystal ball in 1969). In fact the Lynn urban area approaches the 21st century with a population of around 40,000.

Unlike Thetford there had been considerable local opposition to overspill. On Christmas Eve 1961, the Lynn Overspill Prevention Committee was launched, Joan, Lady Evershed, a leading figure in the town's conservation movement warning there were many who feared the character of Lynn would change amid an overcrowded countryside. The first prediction was not long in its fulfilment, though this was an indirect result of expansion, and owed more to the destructive planning and re-development orthodoxy of the period. Others drew on their wartime experience and said it was far from certain that Londoners would settle.

Eddie Edgley's war experience led him to a very different conclusion. "When I was a PoW I was the only Norfolk Dumpling in a barrack room with an Australian and six cockneys. I

found them such good pals, and that stuck in my mind. So when during the expansion talks people started criticising Londoners, I'd tell them they didn't know what they were talking about."

Meanwhile local vox pops suggested that opinion was divided, although a poll taken six months before the signing of the agreement showed that three quarters of young people were in favour. By March 1963 Lynn's first overspill family arrived at Mayflower Avenue, North Lynn; Mr and Mrs Pocock. Not all newcomers settled of course. Clifford Walters, county council area planning officer from 1965 to 1974, and later chief planner for the Lynn and West Norfolk borough council, recalls many going back to London or the north east. "Some were saying 'My God, mate, is this what it's like living in the country?' By the mid-Seventies they were just packing up and going back in droves."

In retrospect Edgley believes there should have been integrated settlements and that it was a mistake to group Londoners on the Fairstead estate, which quickly gained a poor reputation. "Very sad," says Edgley. "It's a case of a lack of discipline. Everybody's done away with discipline." This is not his only regret.

**A late-Fifties EDP picture of Mrs Kitty Fayers in her home at 4 North Street in the heart of King's Lynn's doomed North End. Her granddaughter, Mrs Pamela Howard, recalls: "She kept it impeccably clean but it was always so cold and primitive." The North End, Lynn's ancient fishing quarter, was razed only a few months afterwards.**

**All change: These two views of Acle provide a striking illustration of the suburbanisation of Norfolk towns and villages in the later years of the twentieth century. The picture above was taken around 1954; the picture opposite in 1988.**

Together with the expansion of Lynn went the destruction of half its town centre to make way for car parks and supermarkets. Symbolic of this collective spasm of witless brutality was the surrender of the elegant curve on the north side of New Conduit Street, straightened and replaced in the spirit of Milton Keynes or Basildon. Thirty years on, it remains hard for anyone who knew the old Lynn not to be moved to anger. "When I look back, I'm sorry I was part of it," said Edgley. "I wonder how it happened."

Clifford Walters, now district councillor for North Gaywood, and borough mayor in 1997-98, says that almost everyone shares Edgley's sense of regret. "At the time there were many who thought this was the New Jerusalem. I came to Lynn in 1965 and I saw just in time the old Lynn. We have lost the magic of the 1939 town and I don't know what we are going to do to recover it.

"When I came here you could turn your head one way, and not be distant from the past. You could see old Lynn, old Norfolk, old Norwich. We were on the cusp as it were.

"Turning the other way it was difficult to know what our objective was. When I came into planning we were looking forward to a

better, brighter Britain. So many of the advertisements around the time of the Festival of Britain in 1951 were set against a rising sun. And we were still at it in the Sixties. But then things started to evaporate. There was something frenetic about the Sixties, and planning as a profession began to lose its way. Now I think planning exists in its own right, feeding on itself, and I'm not sure where we are going."

While Lynn and Thetford were occupied in induced expansion, natural growth was creating suburban settlement around Norwich and Yarmouth. Both had been severely bombed during the war, with historic buildings and quarters among the casualties.

Like Lynn, Norwich in the first half of the century was an imposing city riddled with slums. Before the First World War half its population - mostly the poorest - lived within the circuit of the medieval walls. Slum clearances in the inter-war years may have forfeited potential sources of enlightened restoration - more Elm Hills perhaps - but it removed along with the physical abominations, measureless human misery and degradation. The distinguished EDP journalist

Eric Fowler, writing as Jonathan Mardle, recalled the maze of courts and alleys of his boyhood around the end of the First World War, and the people who inhabited them. *"Women made shapeless and toothless by poverty and too much child bearing; women in rusty black dresses and grimy aprons, and men's caps skewered with hatpins on to their unkempt heads.*

*"There were pale and sometimes rickety children, playing with balls made of rags tied together with string, and there were children limping along, within irons on tubercular legs."*

In the late Fifties, Fowler received a letter from a man born and brought up in the slums of old Coslany, and by then – tellingly – a patient at the Kelling Sanatorium.

*"What a place this yard was!"* he wrote. *"Cobbled, and having a paved drain down the middle of it, it was common practice for the housewife to empty all and sundry of their pots and pans down this drain.*

*"Swarming with rats, and infested with fleas and bugs, Bagshaw's Yard was the playground of many kids, with their dirty feet, their sore eyes and runny noses. Bagshaw bought old rags, old bones, old bottles, all culled from the dustbins of other parishes where people could afford to throw things away. As the piles of old bones grew, so did the smell, but nobody seemed to mind...*

*"What was it to women who regularly sported black eyes, and gave birth to their children in slum attics, accompanied by some neighbour, or one of the old women in their shawls who professed to be midwives? How many thousands conveniently died at birth, or were stillborn, will never be known."*

Norwich's slum clearance and council house building programmes were a striking example of energetic municipal government, and it might be thought nothing could be regretted in the obliteration of those vile hovels. Yet in the post-war slum clearance programmes at any rate regrets there were.

With the approach in 1971 of a new phase of clearances, the Norwich City councillor Pat Hollis (now Baroness Hollis of Heigham) ran a small survey. She found that the destruction of a local community by wholesale clearance was seen as "little short of disastrous by those with roots in it". The loss of the old neighbourliness and stability was particularly mourned. Many indeed liked their former houses, citing in particular their cosiness and the pleasure afforded by a garden.

The introduction along with vandalism, of problem families into their new communities was widely resented, likewise flats, large estates and the mixing of the elderly and young children. What the re-housed wanted, revealed the survey, was private gardens, space for the keeping of pets, public parks and playgrounds separated from housing.

"Time and again," noted Hollis, "a fatalistic note came across in the interviews, a feeling of helplessness and resignation." If the survey was representative she added, "it raises extremely serious questions about the whole paternalistic justification of current slum clearance." If the ultimate test was to improve the quality both of housing and of life, by this sample, "it had failed".

Ellis Clarke, referring to the abandonment of "push-pull" expansion when it became clear it was inner London that needed jobs, has noted how wrong planners can be.

But the observation applies equally – and in terms of social damage perhaps more forcibly – in the re-housing assumptions and methods criticised by Patricia Hollis. And another series of miscalculations was the population increase forecasts bandied about in what Clifford Walters calls the "frenetic Sixties".

The Sixties, in fact, had seen the formulation of the county's first rural settlement policy. Until then the absence of housing development pressure in most rural areas had made this kind of approach unnecessary. But with unprecedented population growth came a threat to the open landscape, and this led to the designation of 300 "village envelopes". These were often drawn widely around villages and extended well into open countryside. They were intended to define the areas outside of which there was a very strong presumption against new housing. But the development pressures in rural Norfolk were such, that according to Martin Shaw, the

envelopes came to be seen as actually allocating land enclosed within them for housing. The result was that in the second half of the decade the rural population was growing three times faster than in the first. This could be seen not only in more distant villages, but in the enlarging commuter areas around the main towns, in places such as Hethersett, Wymondham, Taverham, the Woottons, Toftwood, Swanton Morley, the northern fringes of Norwich and the coastal and inland villages from north of Yarmouth down to Lowestoft.

Yarmouth's post-war population had actually fallen sharply from its inter-war figure, partly a result of bombing and subsequent dispersal, but more significantly by the movement across the constricting borough boundary, and out to places such as Bradwell, Belton, Caister and the Fleggs. In contrast by the early Sixties Lowestoft's population had overtaken its great rival, Oulton Broad and Pakefield having been absorbed within its boundaries. And throughout the Sixties, as the bricks were being laid in increasing volumes, so future population predictions suddenly took off into the stratosphere. In the summer of 1966, the then Norfolk County Planning Officer, Richard Maxwell, warned that the north east of East Anglia had to be prepared to take at least one million of the five to six million expected to move out of London under overspill plans. Norfolk, predicted Maxwell, might see its population rise by as much as fifty per cent.

Two years earlier the Government's "South East Study" had stated that by 1984 Norwich should receive a planned population increase of 30,000 over and above natural growth. Even so representative a figure of 'Old Norfolk' as County Council chairman Sir Bartle Edwards, dismissed as "futile" suggestions that this should be opposed. The same plan envisaged the doubling of the Ipswich population, and a new town of 150,000 linking it to Felixstowe. These and similar schemes, warned the

**The Burnhams – nicknamed "Chelsea-By-Sea" – illustrate the gentrification which has affected picturesque parts of Norfolk as affluent families for the South East search for second homes. But their arrival has pushed up house prices and affected grass-roots community services.**

**Edwin Gooch, MP for North Norfolk 1945-1959, president of the National Union of Agricultural Workers for 36 years, and a former chairman of the Labour Party, began work in his father's blacksmith shop in Wymondham. When he entered Parliament he was chief sub-editor of the Mercury series. "Tenacious and shrewd in advancing the principles he cherished," he served at every level of Norfolk local government, and was a former county council vice-chairman. He died in August 1964 aged 75. "A kindly soul," said Lord Wise, the former MP for King's Lynn, "When the history of Norfolk men and women of this century comes to be written his name will be remembered and revered."**

Bressingham horticulturist Alan Bloom were "frightening in their implications... a devastating folly".

Fortunately the folly was limited to the assumptions implicit in the projections. How could they have been so wrong? In retrospect they can be seen as part of the mania of the decade, along with tower blocks, the obliteration of town centres, and the destruction of remediable housing in settled neighbourhoods. Martin Shaw, Norfolk's director of planning and transportation, says these were part of a series of waves of predictions. "In the Fifties it was becoming clear that population forecasts were being under-estimated. By the Sixties forecasts went to the other extreme and were being over-estimated. These included extremely high car-ownership projections which envisaged Norfolk reaching Californian standards by the Eighties."

Although by then Norfolk's population was indeed increasing at an unprecedented – if by these earlier prophesies, sluggardly rate – it began to slow, with the overspill movement to Thetford and Lynn coming to an end by the decade's end, by which time 15,000 Londoners had made the planned move to Norfolk.

But by now the shifting pattern of rural population movement had led to a new strategy from the planners. For whereas in the Fifties only one per cent of new houses were built in villages with a population of less than 500, by the Seventies this figure had reached twenty per cent. But public expenditure arguments as well as the resolve to limit the further suburbanisation of villages, strongly favoured the limitation of most new development to towns and selected villages.

In 1976-77 Norfolk produced the first of its formal Structure Plans, taking the county to the year 2000. This argued that the next 15 years should be a period of consolidation, "of rather slower growth than in recent years, and of balanced development". House building was to be centred on Norwich, Yarmouth, Lynn, Thetford, Fakenham, Swaffham, Diss, Downham and Dereham. In villages beyond a 10-kilometre radius of these employment centres, housing was to be actively discouraged. The county wanted an annual growth rate target of 3500. District councils then – as now – favouring higher growth, wanted up to 6000. Environment Secretary Michael Heseltine, while supporting Norfolk's attempt to moderate growth, compromised at between 4-5000. Interestingly, County Hall's estimate of the 1991 population – 750,000 – was to fall short by only 4500.

One result was that speculative estate development in villages quickly fell to only half that seen in the early Seventies. If reasonable access to employment was one housing market, retirement migration and second home ownership defined the others, a feature significant in the Broads, the Waveney Valley, and above all the North Norfolk Coast.

In no part of rural Norfolk has the social change of the past forty years been so profound as in North Norfolk. Up till then it was largely synonymous with farm work, Methodism and a sitting Labour Member of Parliament. In Edwin Gooch, the area had a man who encapsulated the three.

Born in Wymondham, Gooch was MP for North Norfolk from 1945 to 1959, and for 36 years up to his death in 1964, president of the National Union of Agricultural Workers. His Parliamentary successor, Bert Hazell, was another Norfolk-born NUAW activist. But by the time Hazell had lost his seat to the Conservative Ralph Howell in 1970, farm work and Methodism (if not low wages and unemployment) had been disappearing from the North Norfolk scene.

An unspoilt coast of rare charm, a rolling landscape, and not least, comparatively cheap houses and cottages of pleasing aspect or potential, drew the affluent and discriminating from London to one of England's best-kept secrets. Throughout the Eighties and Nineties this retiree and holiday/ second home migration continued to move into North Norfolk, not only from the capital, but also from Cambridge, where micro-chip industrialisation had helped to send land values into a light blue sky. The market town of Holt was a symbol of this 'gentrification', while Burnham

**Geoffrey Leigh: "Advertisers portray a concept of country living completely different to reality. As a nation we seem obsessed by this romantic view, and as a result there is a wish to re-create that golden era that never was."**

Market became known as 'Chelsea-By-Sea.' By the mid-Eighties, Diana Cohen of the Wighton Gallery near Wells, noted that at least thirty per cent of the village comprised of holiday homes.

Clifford Walters recalls visiting villages within a five-mile band of the North Norfolk coast during the late Sixties and Seventies. "House after house was closed, except at weekends and during a fortnight in summer. As a result there was nobody to support a school or a bus."

By Spring 1999, it was estimated that there were more than 7600 second homes in Norfolk (excepting South Norfolk where the figures were not available), 4500 in North Norfolk alone. Walters, like some others, says the social consequences are serious. "I can understand why some Welsh have such a violent dislike of second homes. If I was a 'native' along the coast, I'd feel jolly hot under the collar too."

The farm worker-Methodism seam of a vanished Norfolk has been noted by Geoffrey Leigh, Field Manager for the Norfolk Rural Community Council. "Fifty years ago the largest single employer was agriculture. Now it's down to two per cent. In fact the rural working class has shrunk almost to next to nothing. And with it has gone many of the institutions that class supported. The Methodists are a good example. The chapel has disappeared from most villages."

Leigh says rural Norfolk, like rural England, has seen a "long, slow and steady decline in the facilities and services that would have been found fifty years ago". While villages have seen the arrival of newcomers, many of whom have sold well and bought cheaper and often superior housing, it is among the indigenous Norfolk people where the "rural poor" are to be found. Another group in this category consists of older people who have moved in, only to find the value of their pensions falling behind the cost of living. It is no coincidence that the first national conference on rural deprivation was held in Norwich in 1977, to be followed by a welter of academic analysis and surveys, often using East Anglia as a case study. "One of the difficulties in talking about rural poverty and deprivation," says Geoffrey Leigh, is that traditionally poverty is seen as an inner city phenomenon, large and easily defined. "You can't say that in rural areas because you have relative affluence and poverty almost side by side."

Leigh's office is in Hingham, home of Abraham Lincoln's forebears, and just 14 miles from Norwich, attractive to commuters. "People look around Hingham and think it's all hunky-dory. In fact it is a very divided village, a lot of large houses and a lot of very affluent people. But it also has a large number of people who live a very different life."

Leigh estimates that a quarter of the people in villages are living at or below the poverty level. "Driving around you don't see it. It's not visible and therefore it 'doesn't exist.' You don't see young people in cardboard boxes or in shop doorways. We argue that it is there, but you have to look for it and use different methods to measure it.

"In cities a lack of car ownership is included in the indices of deprivation. But in the country the less well-off can struggle to keep an old tin bucket on the road because it is essential to get them to work and the shops. We know there are a lot of young people who are homeless in rural areas, squatting on friends' floors or with a tent in a back garden."

The lack of affordable housing or property to rent – as with the shortage of local employment – strikes hard at many of the young who want to live in or close to their home village, a problem exacerbated by external demand driving up prices. While there will always be those who leave for positive reasons, Leigh points out that the victims are often those who in different circumstances would eventually run the village institutions. "Sometimes when you look at the demographic make-up of a community there's a gap, with very few people between the ages of 19 to forty. They are not there. As a result, the social composition and nature of villages is becoming distorted."

The NRCC was formed in 1986 – fifty years after Suffolk, and the last county to have a rural community council – with a brief to listen to local people and help in the solving of rural problems. Among its achievements has been a high-profile campaign for improvements to that totem of a rural community, the village hall.

But at the end of half a century of convulsive change, what is left of a distinctive village life? "This is a problem we have all the time," says Leigh. "Many people see life in the village and countryside through those splendid early post-war British films. Advertisers portray a concept of country living completely different to reality. As a nation we seem obsessed by this romantic view, and as a result there is a wish to re-create that golden era that never was."

He points to a vacuum "which for the best of intentions people have attempted to fill, but without the same functions, cannot do. Those organisations were part and parcel of the lives of the people who were then and there. It isn't there any more and can't be re-created." So farewell to whist drives in a draughty village hall, and forward new and multi-purposes and functions, a small community centre perhaps with a sub post-office, and a room where children can access the Net.

But while the village young await the communal website, Norfolk's population continues to have a relatively elderly age profile, with a higher than national average proportion of 45s and over, and fewer in the younger age groups. Leigh notes that the over sixties form a "disproportionate" number of those living along the coast from Dersingham to Yarmouth, and he has seen a "deliberate targeting" of older people by development companies. According to the 1991 Census, almost a quarter of those living in Norfolk were aged sixty and over, with 14 per cent of the inward migration of 22,900 being in this age group.

In 1995-6, 24,600 people settled in Norfolk (almost sixty per cent from Greater London and the South East), and 20,500 left, giving a ratio that has been more or less steady through the decade. Live births have been consistently less than deaths (in 1996-97, 8700 as against 9200).

**Johnny and Sandy Byrne: "Don't complain and don't start imposing your nice little Surrey or whatever suburban values. Such people probably should be driven out."**

Some at least of this inward migration has resulted from closely-focused targeting. The past two years have seen a phenomenal increase in the price of good country property, the rise in London house values and the quantities of money sloshing around the City causing eyes to lighten on Norfolk and Suffolk as desirable places for second homes and a different lifestyle. Johnny and Sandy Byrne, who settled in North Norfolk twenty years ago, indirectly from London, counsel a certain caution however.

"You cannot stress strongly enough that they must not come into these communities and start complaining," says Johnny Byrne, the writer whose television creations include All Creatures Great and Small and Heartbeat. "Don't complain and don't start imposing your nice little Surrey or whatever suburban values. Such people probably should be driven out. I think that the local councils and courts should, whenever possible, support the local people even if it's slightly prejudicial. It's their county, their land, their forefathers." Sandy, his wife, says good inner resources and self-motivation are very important. "It can be a tremendous culture shock if you give up your London life to live here."

The Byrnes came to Little Barney near Fakenham twenty years ago, moving to their present home, a former rectory at West Beckham near Holt ten years later. They seem model incomers; appreciative, open, non-judgmental, understanding of the ways of the community in which they have settled. "We are social people, but we don't push it, nor have we ever sought to impose ourselves. We've always accepted the thing as it is and made our own adjustments to it," says Byrne. "We've always felt welcome. There's a gentleness about Norfolk people, a consideration and a kindness."

One of the reasons why they came to Norfolk was that despite its relative proximity to London, there was an "otherness" about it. The 'Old' Norfolk then still existed, said Byrne and while it is less visible now it is still there. "The more we explored Norfolk, the more our sense of belonging increased, an appreciation of how different and unique it is."

He says anyone contemplating a move to the country has to make a comparison and a choice. "You can go down to places like Dorset and see what has become of an infinitely beautiful area where a kind of middle-class life has planted itself. The local life has virtually vanished.

"In Norfolk the great distinction – and it is a very vulnerable thing – is that are ordinary, working villages. Of course if you go over to the Brancaster area" (Sandy had noted that 'their' side of Holt is very different) "you find many professionals gathered into a kind of enclave where they have a self-sustaining way of life that could as easily be carried out in Hampstead; a mini-London situation. In Dorset they are virtually the majority."

This 'otherness' may even be giving Norfolk a certain voguishness. "When our eldest son comes back with a group of mates from Manchester," laughed Sandy, "he says 'you guys don't realise how lucky you are to be coming to the coolest place in England'."

Perhaps this is a further reason why North Norfolk in particular has attracted 'second home' London money, with estate agents putting this figure as high as seventy per cent of their country house market. Indeed so important is this sector that some agents have opened a 'shop window' presence in the capital offering Norfolk property on a continuous basis.

Norwich, with its finance, food, science and leisure industries has also drawn people in from outside the county, many on short-term contracts. This has led to an increase in demand for good-quality rented property, which in turn has forced up demand for letting-potential investment.

While Norfolk life has speeded up considerably – lamentably so to many a middle-aged native – for those contemplating it from a big city the significantly quieter-paced comparison is often seductive. Even so the reality can sometimes prove more than challenging. Location, to borrow the estate agent's dictum, can be everything. "If you come to a village with young children and then have to start ferrying them to a distant village or town, then that eats up part of the free time and involves the travel which was one of the reasons why you left London," said an ex-London professional woman. Not surprisingly sale boards are sometimes removed only to be re-erected.

Fifty years ago, says Geoffrey Leigh, the probability was that the vast majority in a Norfolk village would have either been born there, or that their family had come from a closely-defined part of the area. Clearly this has not been true for the past three decades.

At Bressingham west of Diss on the Norfolk/Suffolk border, Elizabeth Handy conducted a mid-Nineties survey of the village to which she and her husband Charles, the international business writer and authority, came in 1971.

The Handys also have a home in London, and are therefore effectively 'second-homers' though their stays in the village are frequent and prolonged and their attachment strong.

The view from their cottage has scarcely changed in a century. The school, pub, shop, mill, Hall, Rectory and Grange are still there, and the Handys can walk from home down a track to the thirteenth-century – and very much alive – village church.

But much else has changed. Farms have gone or been amalgamated, and old Bressingham names and occupations vanished, replaced in part by vogue-ish or other post-industrial occupations facilitated by tele-working and fast trains from Diss (1987 saw the electrification of the Norwich-Ipswich section of the London main line). Where there were once farm workers, grooms, a wheelwright or a knapper, there were now systems analysts, a psychotherapist, an au pair and nanny agency, an international banker and an editor of scientific books. Here as in other Norfolk villages, it is not difficult to set up a home office while maintaining a London presence or link.

A nice feature of Bressingham, said Elizabeth Handy, is an absence of hierarchy. "People around here have always been smallholders, and always been very independent, making a living off the land, creating something out of nothing. The new people who have come have this same kind of entrepreneurial or survival spirit."

Bressingham in fact seems to have moved from the Age of Agriculture to that of Information without the intervening industrial age, thus fulfilling an original insight and axiom of her husband Professor Charles Handy. "Like a well-darned sock," says Elizabeth, "Bressingham looks the same, still works as well, although much of the old wool has been replaced by newer stuff."

At Necton, Basil Bell and his wife Heather have seen almost all the wool replaced with enough stuff to make a drawerful of new socks. Looking back to 1948 when he was demobbed, he recalls a village with four pubs, a bakery, two butchers, four grocery shops and a post office. Now there is a post office and mini market, one pub, a butcher and a garden centre.

He remembers too the years before the massive Seventies development when "everybody knew everybody else, all very sociable. Now if you asked me where somebody Bloggs lived in Bengy's Walk couldn't begin to tell you."

On farmer Billy Larwood's field - now Larwood's Walk - he played cricket, "a lovely ground," and now recalls the Necton cricket sides of the Fifties, "when we had four or five bus loads of spectators going to see them play in the big local knock-out cups."

The majority of the 'New Nectonians' are Londoners, most of whom, says Basil Bell have settled. "One old boy, Harry, who's eighty-odd, comes into The Windmill on a Sunday lunchtime. He's lived here 18 years and says he's accepted now! I could be old fashioned, but we are the strangers." Absolutely, says Heather, "but it's moving with the times I suppose." Mr Bell looks across the road where

**Tom Cook of Sennowe Park, Guist, old Etonian, naturalist, landowner, and great-great grandson of the founder of mass tourism, was the 55-year-old High Sheriff of Norfolk when he delivered his "fly-by-night developers" speech. "I didn't say anything in it that I hadn't been saying for years. But it touched a chord. I think it helped to trigger people in coming forward." Might those in a less privileged position take a perhaps less hostile view of development? "Fair comment. But being fortunate enough to live in this situation, I could turn a blind eye to it all and commute in and out by helicopter and I wouldn't know anything about it. My concern is not for myself but for the county and its people."**

**Martin Shaw, 54, Norfolk's Director of Planning and Transportation since 1993, was born in Yorkshire and worked in the north west and West Midlands before coming to Norfolk as assistant county planning officer in 1971. He was appointed county planning officer in 1977. A past president of the County Planning Officers' Society, he is chairman of the County Surveyors' Society Strategic Transport Committee, Advisor to the Local Government Association, and lead advisor to the Standing Conference of East Anglian Local Authorities. Visiting Professor at Oxford Brookes University, in 1997 was awarded the OBE for services to local government. "I'd never been to Norfolk prior to the interview. I came for two years and have stayed for quarter of a century and do not intend to leave. Norfolk seemed to be an ideal place in which to bring up children, and that's what we did."**

once there had been those beautiful trees. "Necton will eventually join up with Holme Hale, won't it?"

In truth it should not, but the suspicion is part of a wider and growing apprehension. In June 1986 in a speech at Diss, John MacGregor, Conservative MP for South Norfolk and at the time Chief Secretary to the Treasury, warned of the possibility of a "carpet of concrete" spreading across Norfolk. The immediate response to his call for a debate was a fusillade from a number of county MPs and local authority leaders attacking him for espousing the Drawbridge Mentality. He replied that as someone who had worked hard to bring new industry to Diss, he rather resented the inference.

But MacGregor's anxieties attracted wide sympathy and support far from the margins of reaction. And five years later the High Sheriff of Norfolk, Tom Cook of Sennowe Park, told a church fete at Beeston Regis that "fly-by-night" developers were ruining Norfolk, and posed a greater threat to the countryside than either Saddam Hussein or global warming. His remarks received instant endorsement from former county council chairman, John Birkbeck, Norfolk traditionalist and scourge *par excellence* of the concreting invader. In an EDP phone poll, 94 per cent of 2669 callers backed the Cook analysis.

Geoffrey Leigh, travelling around the county in his NRCC role, says he is not aware of any great support for 'Drawbridge' proscriptions, and that in any case these tend to be favoured by the privileged. "What people are really afraid of is the speculative builder, a fear that mass house developers will simply apply for permission to build 300 houses here and another 500 there, and then just open them up for anyone with readies to buy."

Yet despite the ringing bark from the MacGregor-Cook rebellion, the developers' caravan continued to pass into Norfolk, sometimes with the wholehearted approval of Whitehall. In January 1995 for example, the planners' attempt to block a giant Downham Market housing development described as a "sea of bungalows" was overturned by a Government inspector. Paradoxically the go-ahead for the 323-bungalow estate was approved by Environment Minister John Gummer, Suffolk Coastal MP and the "greenest" member of the Major Cabinet.

Downham in this last decade of the century has become one of the county's "hot spots", its new (and historically, unexpected) popularity owing much to the electrification (London 88 minutes) of the Lynn main line in 1992. An observer from east Norfolk who lived there in the mid-Sixties recalls "a very sleepy place without any great vitality." But between 1971 and 1991, the town's population rose by 58.6 per cent from 3614 to 5733, the mid-1997 estimate taking it to 6300, an astonishing 74 per cent increase in 25 years.

While the population of the majority of Norfolk's 539 parishes increased between 1991 and 1997, in 29 per cent it actually fell. Among the latter are villages such as Helhoughton and Raynham which lost resident service personnel. At the other end of the scale, Taverham over this same period grew from 6875 to 9630, a forty per cent increase in six years. At Horsford it went up 45 per cent, from 2260 to 3285.

Sisland's 1991 population remained at forty for a further five years, then went up by five within a year. The village has doubtless taken this in its steady stride, but Leigh observes that "if you suddenly increased the population of London by say ten per cent it would be phenomenal. For a village of 100, another ten has the same sort of impact. It can distort a village quite considerably."

Eighteen months ago the Government delivered a national house-building blueprint that rocked conservationists and sent a tremor through the shires. In it ministers announced their intention to allow another 4.4 million homes to be built by 2016, equivalent to an area the size of Greater London. Of this 90,000 would be in Norfolk, with a quarter of a million in East Anglia as a whole. Quite how the figure of 4.4 million (since revised to 4.1 million) was arrived at has never been made clear. But while some regard it as fanciful, the implications are to say the least, challenging, Martin Shaw warning it would lead to the suburbanisation of a predominantly rural region. Shaw points out that despite the overall scale of population change, the settlement map of Norfolk at the end of the twentieth century is not very different from that of the eighteenth. Even so the "economic" argument for concentrating new housing in market towns and selected villages is frequently countered by the largely "social" claim that modest, easily assimilated development in small villages will strengthen communities and encourage services.

In fact the post-Fifties decline in rural services shows that even where a village has increased in population, services have still been lost. "Adding housing development to the vast majority of small villages would certainly cause a suburbanisation of character without any compensating advantages," says Martin Shaw. "What we have seen in recent decades is the increasing distancing of housing from jobs and services. We are trying to check this and ensure a greater degree of self-containment of towns and villages, and if we are serious about 'sustainable development' this must be a major objective of the first few decades of the next century. It would not be helped by a proliferation of development in villages where there is no real prospect of being served by public transport or attracting local services."

The strategy to which Shaw refers is "counter-urbanisation," a cause to which the Government's "brownfields" exhortations are notionally committed. Shaw says that while it is right that a focus on brownfield sites is at the heart of national and local policy, it has yet to be delivered.

"As a society we are setting ourselves nothing less than checking the trend towards de-centralisation from the major urban areas of Britain. But it involves massive investment in improved infrastructure, and in my view there will need to be some real fiscal incentives if we are to make cities and urban sites sufficiently attractive to attract developers at the expense of the easier greenfield option."

Geoffrey Leigh agrees. The strategy will work "only if cities are attractive places where people can walk at night without thinking they will be robbed, where public transport is of good quality, and culture and entertainment accessible to all."

As Martin Shaw remarks, the secret is to ensure that people are " 'happy to stay where they are.' The answer to the question 'why can't we stop developing in villages?' is that it isn't an issue about villages. It's a matter of making cities more attractive."

Estate agent David Bedford, involved in the Norfolk and Suffolk property business for forty years, suggests that over the next ten years not a single extra acre of greenfield should be released. "Developers and planners would then have to use a bit of imagination and, dare I say, common sense, to ensure that the hundreds (yes, hundreds) of sites within towns and villages are developed in a sensitive and practical manner."

Martin Shaw is less sanguine. For while the Government wants sixty per cent of new homes built on brownfield sites, he says that in East Anglia forty per cent would be a reasonably ambitious target. "That means sixty per cent of new housing may still end up on greenfield sites."

If so, much of this will be centred on or around Dereham, Wymondham, Fakenham, North Walsham and Downham, the principal areas of expansion in rural Norfolk. Whether population growth is good or bad is open to debate, he says. "What is beyond debate is that the relatively rapid rate of growth since the Sixties has led to a loss of distinctiveness in the individual character of towns and villages. And it will be a continuing challenge to retain that sense of place which makes Norfolk so special."

## CHAPTER 2

# *Nature*

*"As I passed through the countryside between here and the coast this evening, dark piles of clouds hung in the amber heights, the arc of a rainbow spread its broad ribbon of delight before me, the corn fields were white unto harvest, the very hedge banks were crested with the flaxen-gold of dry, unkempt grasses, the trees were bold and dark and in the far smudged horizon I saw the threshold of Valhalla, the coast of Thule, the kirtle of the Universe.*

*"The slowly-moving storms were steeds for the heroic figures of mythology. The world below lay like a bright and fertile kingdom, cherished and blessed with all the yearning and achievement of man and nature consummated in its beauty"*
Ted Ellis, EDP August 8th 1955.

**Writer and journalist MARTIN KIRBY was born and brought up on the North Norfolk coast and has been inspired throughout his career by his native county. Now deputy editor of the Eastern Daily Press, he has 21 years' experience covering Norfolk. His wider work has included features and short stories, and a book about the Norfolk Wherry and Broads which was published in 1998. He is married with a young daughter.**

To paint the face of Norfolk's century will take many colours, many shades. An exhausting 100 years have taken their toll, nowhere more so than upon her most beguiling feature, the natural beauty that for much of history had to contend only with the give and take of the North Sea or the vagaries of the seasons. This is the story of her greatest asset, where the losses have been the most painful and profound.

And yet, though much has gone, there are so many reasons to be thankful. For all her trials and tribulations the story of Norfolk's nature and environment is alive with achievement and commitment, resistance and recovery - reasons to look to the new millennium with hope. There remains a wealth of wildlife and habitats of international importance across the 2072 square miles that, in some small yet vital measure, have managed to survive the urgency and violations of the twentieth century.

One can imagine (guided by the joyous prose of people such as Arthur Patterson and William Dutt and others who were writing 100 years ago) the expansive woodlands, waterways and coastal wildernesses of this county's glorious, unfettered past. For me it is Meadow Dyke weaving its way to Horsey Mere, locked in by golden reeds; coastal creeks

and pools reflecting the drama of brooding skies where plover wheel and fall and geese fill the air with their cries; or the glorious colours and folds of Pretty Corner woods above Sheringham where I played as a boy.

Here in Norfolk, beyond the margins of man, lies a powerful magic that can bind people for life.

The wide horizons and dramatic skies crown the driest corner of the country where habitats vary from wetlands and fens to ancient woods, from mudflats and saltmarshes to soaring cliffs, from heath and brecks to meadows and meandering rivers.

Everyone who knows the county's true worth will cherish places that hold a timeless wonder across this broad, bright and richly varied landscape. These places survive because of a now powerful weave of societies, organisations and landowners who work

**Dr Sydney Long, the dedicated Norfolk physician and naturalist who worked tirelessly until his death in 1939 to preserve the county's wildlife sites. A memorial stands on East Wretham Heath in honour of the long-standing secretary of the Norfolk and Norwich Naturalists' Society and founder of the Norfolk Naturalists' Trust – and his ashes are scattered on the Scolt Head nature reserve which he was instrumental in establishing. His commitment and achievements make him one of Norfolk's men of the century.**

together to protect many miles of coastline and thousands of acres of reserves and Sites of Special Scientific Interest.

Here follow some of the milestones spanning 100 years of a changing world that has inspired some remarkable people.

Even by 1900 Norfolk's wildlife and countryside were suffering in the name of progress. The Victorian era had heralded new pressures and the serious decline of many habitats and species. Since that time change has been unrelenting, although in those early years it may have been barely perceptible to the masses.

The age of steam had fostered commerce and tourism, with grand hotels being built on clifftops around the coast while early adventures afloat heralded the huge Broads industry which was to dominate the five thousand acres of water and many miles of rivers in the years to come. As the wider world was waking up to the wonders of the great wetland, Norfolk was also in the forefront of the agricultural revolution. Steam pumps were used to drain wetland. Uncontrolled hunting and egg collecting, too, were pushing some species to the brink.

In 1866 Henry Stevenson (1833-88), publisher of the Norfolk Chronicle and author of the three-volume Birds of Norfolk, himself a keen wildfowler, was one of the first naturalists to set alarm bells ringing. Later he warned fellow enthusiasts that collectors and gunners were getting more demanding as the numbers of species diminished:

*"In one season alone, upward of seventy eggs of the beautiful little bearded tit were taken at Surlingham, solely for this purpose, though abundant there twenty years ago this bird is now rarely seen. The swallow-tailed butterfly, and amongst ferns the beautiful Lastraea cristata, may be classed in the same category; the latter, to my knowledge, having been all but exterminated in some localities through the wholesale orders of London florists."*

His audience were fellow members of the Norfolk & Norwich Naturalists' Society, the county's oldest-surviving natural history organisation and such a vital part - then and now - of Norfolk's story. So much is known, good and bad, because of the detailed and invaluable observations of its members.

Founded in 1869, the society's membership has included so many naturalists who have had a profound and lasting impact on the value we place on the county's gifts, people such as John Henry Gurney (1848-1922), the banker and MP, one of the first honorary members and three-time president; author Arthur Patterson (1857-1935) who wrote in the Yarmouth Mercury and also the EDP under the pseudonym John Knowlittle and also completed a shelf-full of natural history books on the East Coast and the Broads; renowned physician, ornithologist and naturalist Dr Sydney Long (1870-1939) the son of a Wells doctor who was key to the preservation of sites such as Scolt Head and Cley Marshes; Russell Colman (1861-1946), the Lord Lieutenant of Norfolk who was a member for 64 years and a major benefactor; Dr Joyce Lambert, whose research in 1953 revealed the man-made origins of the Norfolk Broads; Dick Bagnall-Oakeley (1908-1974), the school-master, naturalist, broadcaster and champion of the dialect; and celebrated naturalist Ted Ellis (1909-1986), Arthur Patterson's friend and student who achieved so much through his work at Norwich Castle Museum, through the media and at his beloved Wheatfen Broad.

The roll of society members is long and distinguished. So many of the great names of Norfolk feature through the generations.

The society, which followed on from earlier like-minded Norfolk groups, began to bring its members' knowledge and influence to bear on what it saw as the critical decline in wildlife. Henry Stevenson gave evidence that helped to frame the Wild Birds Protection Acts which were passed from 1880 onwards. But while a law was one thing, enforcement was another. Groups of ornithologists set up committees who appointed watchers to prevent the illicit shooting and taking of rare birds.

It was a start - and one of the first in the country was at Breydon Water, the great expanse of marshes and tidal flats where the Yare, Bure and Waveney rivers meet before their waters pour jointly out to sea through

**The beautiful shifting sands of Scolt Head, the North Norfolk spit that was bought for the National Trust for £600 in 1923 after an appeal run by Wells-born Dr Sydney Long.**

Yarmouth harbour. This was the domain of Arthur Patterson, the son of a poor shoemaker, who explored the area in the company of old punt-gunners and who soon became an authority on everything to be found there.

The new law was hard to apply as the wildfowlers and poachers supplemented their precarious earnings from game dealers by supplying rarities for collectors. One old saying was "A curlew, be she white or be she black, there's always a shilling on her back."

Some control, and certainly the efforts by the society to widen awareness did have an effect. From the members' notes we learn how the bittern, once so plentiful and now so threatened, was absent from England for forty-five years around the turn of the century. There was no evidence of the bittern in this country until a nest was discovered near Hickling Broad in 1910.

It was found and carefully protected on the Whiteslea Lodge estate of Lord Desborough, a sportsman whose care of his Broadland acres was an outstanding although by no means isolated example of the evolution of a sporting estate into a nature reserve.

The discovery was made by the estate's head keeper Jim Vincent (1883-1944) who took enormous pride in his conservation work. It was he, with bird photographer Miss E L Vincent, who also recorded the return of the Montagu's harrier to breed in Norfolk. Nearby another great sportsman/naturalist Major Anthony Buxton was doing similar work and the whole area soon saw rare breeds such as the bearded tit and swallowtail butterfly flourish there.

Norfolk's first publicly-owned reserve was established in 1912. Blakeney Point, the 1300 acres of shingle spit, sand dune and marram grass that sweeps westward along the North Norfolk coast, was bought for the National Trust following an appeal for funds. Now home to a large ternery, with many migrant birds - and ornithologists - making their way to its famous bird sanctuary, it was then under threat from uncontrolled use. Flat and remote from the rest of the country it had little to correspond to the Victorian and Edwardian idea of the picturesque and, like much of the county's coastline, was left to the part-agricultural, part-maritime population.

The Point was valued chiefly for its rabbits, wildfowling and eggs. But there were some

**A rich tapestry: from top, a marsh harrier, orchids (and caterpillar!) at Leziate, a bearded tit, and the swallowtail butterfly.**

who visited it for its wildlife, including the man who launched the appeal - Professor F W Oliver of University College London. The National Trust, founded in 1895, had been incorporated by an Act of Parliament in 1907 which set out its aims, including... *"as regards lands, the preservation (so far as practicable) of the natural aspect, features and animal and plant life"*. The professor, who took parties of students to Blakeney Point to study ornithology, botany and entomology, saw his chance to protect it, and the Norfolk and Norwich Naturalists' Society was quickly enlisted by the new owner to help manage the reserve.

It was a huge step forward for the county and for that twenty-mile stretch of ever-changing coastline between the chalk cliffs at Hunstanton and Sheringham which today is almost all under the care of wildlife bodies who look after the rich variety of species that live and grow there.

The dunes, mudflats and salt marshes which were once dismissed as bleak and uninteresting are now studied intently as a classic example of the phenomenon of long-shore drift, the action of waves in shifting shingle and sand along the coastline to give a completely different system of spits and creeks in only a few years.

Two years after Professor Oliver's achievement, however, the momentum for positive change was lost.

The Great War heralded major changes to the face of Norfolk, not least because of the wholesale loss of key rural skills as craftsmen enlisted to fight in the trenches. Previously well-managed reed beds, pastures and woodland were left until the men returned. But so many of those craftsmen did not come home and scrub started to became established on many important sites. It was a trend of semi-neglect that, to this day, presents organisations like the Norfolk Wildlife Trust with their biggest challenge. In later years the fight became focussed on the damage done by pesticides and other poisons, but today the biggest effort facing the trust and others is clearing scrub. Before the First World War the view from Ranworth Church north across the broad and river would have been of mostly water and reed, not the vast acres of scrub you see today.

Yet while the Great War years heralded unwanted trees it also saw huge losses in Norfolk's mature woodland. Between 1914 and a year after the conflict ended about a fifth of the county's woodland was felled. Then, in 1919 the pattern of ownership and policy changed as well with the setting up of the Forestry Commission, which set about acquiring and planting its own forest estate.

Much of what is known today as Thetford Forest, the vast Breckland estate covering more than eighty square miles across the border into Suffolk, was planted before war was again to grip Europe in 1939. Other far smaller plantations were established in North and West Norfolk.

Some of this land became available because agriculture was in serious depression, but former heathland was badly affected too. In 1880 the Brecks of Norfolk and Suffolk still contained more than 50,000 acres of heath; by 1968 this had declined by seventy per cent.

Today Norfolk's forestry is home to many rare species - a fifth of Britain's woodlark population, for example, can be found in Thetford Forest - and the commission manages its sites in coordination with wildlife bodies. Work goes on to protect and encourage populations like those of the red squirrel and nightjar, and there is a new project to re-create 750 acres of heathland within the forest.

Despite the First World War the work at the new Blakeney Point reserve went on, and one member of the committee which managed the site was later to be the driving force for more wildlife havens being protected. His name was Sydney Long, whose dedication to his work as house physician to the Norfolk and Norwich Hospital and his commitment and achievement in the sphere of nature conservation make him one of Norfolk's men of the century.

Away from his work he would venture forth from his tall Georgian terrace in Surrey Street in the heart of Norwich, scouring the county in all seasons in his open-top car pursuing his

**Thetford Forest was one of the great man-made changes on the Norfolk landscape this century. The forest is home to a wide variety of species, including one-fifth of the entire British woodlark population.**

great love of ornithology.

Born at Wells in 1870, Sydney Long was secretary of the Norfolk and Norwich Naturalists Society for 24 years and later was to be president. In the spirit of mid-Victorian naturalist Henry Stevenson he worked tirelessly to counter the trade in rare wildfowl and eggs, unafraid to pursue prosecutions of predatory collectors.

But this was not his only fear. As well as indiscriminate shooting and the rate of egg thefts he had the foresight to point to the new dangers of population spread and tourism, unmanaged trends that in time would destroy habitats and drive out the wildlife people had come to see.

In 1923 Dr Long took the first of several major steps to preserve areas of his beloved Norfolk. As a child he had grown to know well the shifting sands to the east and west of Wells. One isolated place close to his heart was Scolt Head between Burnham Overy

**Terns, rare but a familiar sight in Norfolk, have become synonymous with wildlife preservation and been adopted as the Norfolk Wildlife Trust's logo.**

Staithe and Brancaster – like Blakeney Point a rare and beautiful spit sheltering a harbour and valuable salt marshes. Building on his experience with Blakeney and seeing the merit in National Trust ownership he set about raising the £600 needed to buy three-mile-long Scolt Head.

Russell Colman headed the appeal and it was not long before Norfolk – and the National Trust – had a second, invaluable site protected as a nesting place for terns and other birds. Dr Long was elected secretary of the Scolt Head Committee and remained so for the rest of his life. Fittingly, the ashes of this tall, gentle man who died in 1939 are scattered there.

But Scolt Head is not his only memorial. His obituary in the EDP read:

*In 1926 Dr Long founded the Norfolk Naturalists' Trust. In his own name he purchased Cley Marshes on March 6th. On March 14th a lunch was held at The George at Cley to discuss future plans for the property and there Dr Long propounded an idea that had long been in his mind – the formation of a Norfolk Trust with powers similar to those of the National Trust, to be run by Norfolk people for the purpose of acquiring and holding for all time certain properties in the county.*

He told that meeting: "When one considers the changes in the face of the county that are being made or contemplated by Forestry Commissioners, Drainage Boards, speculative builders and the like, one is anxious to preserve for future generations areas of marsh, heath, woods and undrained fenland (of which there still remain a few acres in the county) with their natural wealth of flora and fauna.

"At the present time most of Broadland is in the hands of owners who can be relied upon not to interfere with the natural beauties of the district, but who can say what will happen in a hundred or even in ten years' time?"

It was an historic moment. Norfolk became the first county to form a trust that would acquire and manage nature reserves of its own. Dr Long's example was to have a profound effect on nature conservation nationwide.

After buying the 400 acres of Cley Marshes, just east of Blakeney and complementary to the Blakeney Point Reserve, the doctor was keen to highlight the need for such action and to unify local efforts under one banner. After his rousing words at The George Inn the Norfolk Naturalists' Trust was formally incorporated on November 5th 1926. Russell Colman was the first president and Dr Long was secretary, who also took on (in addition to the work he already did for the Norfolk Naturalists' Society) the supervision of the reserves and the payment of the watchers. His first appointment was the old Cley fisherman and wildfowler Bob Bishop, who was succeeded as watcher in 1936 by his son Billy. At that time the Naturalists' Trust had Watcher's Cottage built overlooking the reserve and latterly it has been home to Bernard Bishop, Bob's grandson, who was appointed warden in 1979.

After Cley Marshes the next acquisition was in Broadland in 1928. With money subscribed by a few friends the Trust was able to buy the 26 acres of Starch Grass, Martham, close to the coast near Winterton. Dr Long had made a study of bitterns and harriers that nested there and knew it well.

Next the trust bought Alderfen, a landlocked broad between Irstead and Neatishead. It was 1930 and farming was in the depth of depression, but the price of £2200 for seventy acres caused the auctioneer to exclaim, "I wish all of the land in Norfolk was water!" It was an ambitious development but a very important purchase - twenty acres of water surrounded by reedbeds, marsh and farmland that was undisturbed by water traffic. Alderfen was a sanctuary for bitterns and swallowtail butterflies and nourished a wealth of water lilies, reed mace and other aquatic plants.

Breckland, too, has reasons to thank Dr Long. Although his ashes are on Scolt Head a memorial to him stands beside Langmere on East Wretham Heath where, in the words of his old friend Billy Bishop, "he used to go every year, on the nearest Sunday to the 13th of March, to find the first wheatears".

Mass planting of pines by the Forestry Commission between 1922 and 1937 to redress war losses to the nation's reserves of timber sparked efforts to protect some of the original distinct, open landscape. In 1932 Dr Long hit upon the idea of the trust buying three cottages at Lakenheath together with their common rights over Lakenheath Warren, thereby securing the area.

Sadly, after his death in January 1939 the Second World War nullified his efforts at Lakenheath Warren which was lost to a new

**Russell Colman: First president of the Norfolk Naturalists' Trust, hailed in his obituary in the Eastern Daily Press as a great Norfolk man, "there being hardly an office of importance that he was not asked to fill". Before his death in 1946 he was to have served as Lord Lieutenant of Norfolk, Sheriff and then Mayor of Norwich (during the coronation year of King Edward VII), Chairman of the county council and High Sheriff of Norfolk, along with a host of other duties, not least his services to wildlife. Yachtsman, wildfowler, art collector, his friendship and partnership with Dr Sydney Long did so much to protect key sites in Norfolk – and showed the rest of the country what could be achieved.**

**From left, Charles Chestney (The Watcher), Russell Colman, W Dereham, Douglas Carruthers, Dr Sydney Long, E Mennell and Dr B G Sumpter at The Hut, Scolt Head on July 20th 1928.**

**Ted Ellis, the people's naturalist, who died in 1986. Long before environmental issues were popular his essays in the EDP vividly described the world of Norfolk's fens and waterways and emphasised the need to protect and conserve the area's richness.**

airfield. But another project of his late years did subsequently bear lasting fruit, namely the acquisition of Wretham Heath. But perhaps the greatest memorial to Dr Sydney Long is the Trust itself.

Today the Norfolk Wildlife Trust, as it is now known, remains the county's largest charity dealing with local wildlife. It is the oldest and biggest of the UK's wildlife trusts with around 17,500 members, 1000 volunteers and 38 reserves which together would cover an area the size of Norwich. Nine Norfolk broads are owned by the trust, along with five ancient woodlands and more than six miles of coastline.

More than 250,000 people and 200 schools visit these sites every year. What would probably please the good doctor more than anything else, though, is how the Trust is working with schoolchildren, landowners, other wildlife charities and local authorities to ensure his enthusiasm for reserving and restoring Norfolk's natural heritage is carried forward into the new millennium.

The year 1926 saw another, but then less obvious, milestone in the efforts to widen awareness of Norfolk's precious natural and environmental wealth. As members gathered for the meeting of the Norfolk and Norwich Naturalists' Society on January 26th they were introduced to a new face, a 16-year-old boy whose arms and pockets were laden with a hen pheasant, four live harvest mice and a sponge crab.

His name was Ted Ellis.

The teenager had been taken to join the society by Arthur Patterson, the well-known Breydon naturalist and writer who for three years had passed on his knowledge to his young companion. It was a remarkable friendship that was to remain strong until Patterson's death in 1935, and here lay the crucial helping hand for a career that was to blossom and make Ellis one of the best-known and best-loved naturalists of his generation.

Ted Ellis was born on Guernsey. When he left the island, aged ten, he was already a proven academic – having won a scholarship to Queen Elizabeth College – and committed naturalist. The family finally settled at Gorleston but the young boy missed the wilderness of the Channel Isle. Then he started to explore, roaming the local lanes and quizzing anyone with knowledge of nature, even the town ratcatcher. At the age of 12, in early 1922 he began a remarkable series of diaries – the Nature Notebooks – at first making simple jottings about the weather or where he had been, but soon vividly writing in remarkable detail.

The day in February 1923 when Ted made an excursion to meet Patterson proved so vital. The old naturalist, whose maxim was that "a true naturalist should always be ready to share his pleasures with others," quickly took to the young Ellis. As Pete Kelley writes in his detailed and wonderful biography (published by Jarrold's shortly after Ellis's death in 1986, under the name Eugene Stone) if communication was Patterson's gospel it was Ted's gift. Probably no-one influenced Ted Ellis more, and Patterson encouraged the teenager to meet and learn from many old 'characters' of Norfolk. It was also to prove a fascinating cultural study. The young naturalist was to meet wetland folk such as punt-gunners, wherrymen and farm workers who had a practical knowledge of nature - men such as Whiley the Gull-Slayer, who lived in a poor little place towards the South Denes.

*"I found him in a bad mood and received the impression that the persecution of gulls had done nothing to sweeten his outlook on the world or on people. It is on record that he made a bit on the side through his speciality, by shooting and selling any of the rarer species of gulls which happened to turn up in the neighbourhood.*

*"There was also Little John Thomas, whose wife kept a pork butcher's in the town. It became well-known to a few of his close acquaintances that he used to smuggle a good many gulls into the establishment to provide sausage meat, disguised with plenty of sage."*

At his home Ellis had a snailery, a vivarium and an aquarium. He had a lizard as a pet and cared for a black-headed gull, called Gulliver, which had been shot through the wing. He also, at about the time of his introduction to the Naturalists' Society, joined a nationwide investigation to discover whether the little owl, which had multiplied since its introduction in Britain in 1910, was a menace to partridge and pheasant chicks. The work involved collecting thousands of pellets that owls regurgitate. He studied these to show its diet to be mostly beetles and earwigs and so helped save the species from needless persecution.

Ellis was so nearly lost to Norfolk, but for a twist of fate. In 1926 he had written to the broadcaster/naturalist A Bonnet-Laird after hearing his BBC radio programme In the Open Air. He had included in his letter a vivid description of glow-worms on a fen which prompted an invitation to London where he was told that if he could learn typing and shorthand he could work for the corporation. He returned to Norfolk and studied hard, but when he wrote twice more to Bonnet-Laird there was no reply.

Patterson, meanwhile, had recommended Ellis for a short-term temporary job at Gerard Gurney's respected zoo and aviary at Keswick Hall, just south of Norwich. The keeper had left at short notice so, on Patterson's advice, the young Ellis was offered six months' work immediately. Puzzled by Bonnet-Laird's silence, he accepted and moved to Keswick Hall on October 4th 1926.

Only then did the BBC reply come urging him to take up the offer. The broadcaster had been ill and the letters had not been forwarded. Later Ted Ellis remarked that he "felt bound to honour my pledge" to Gerard Gurney, but he remembered the disappointment all his life - even speaking of it on his deathbed.

Ellis was to stay at Keswick for nine months. He learned a great deal, especially from Gerard Gurney who allowed him to study papers left by his ornithologist father J H Gurney who had, in his time, been Norfolk's leading authority on birds.

After returning to Gorleston he continued his rambles with Patterson, becoming the first secretary of the re-formed Great Yarmouth Naturalists' Society in 1927. Ellis also continued to harvest knowledge from local naturalists, including Dr Long who took him to Scolt Head. His many teachers included: Chester Doughty whose feather collection found a permanent home in Norwich Castle Museum; teacher H J Howard, who was keenly interested in slime moulds - mycetozoa - and encouraged Ellis to collect them; master plumber Philip E Rumbelow, a gifted self-taught naturalist and archaeologist who kept immaculate leather-bound nature books; Dr Hugh Ramage, who gave him demonstrations of the spectroscopic analysis of metallic elements in plant tissue; Alice Geldart, botanist and long-serving member of the Naturalists' Society; photographer Miss E L Turner; and Tom Petch, the authority on fungus-attacking insects. Crucially, too, he recorded the efforts of countless countrymen and wildfowlers to encourage respect for wildlife.

But it was Patterson who guided him most. Ellis later wrote of his mentor:

*"His sprightliness and sense of the comical*

**A 1962 poster is a reminder of the huge – and eventually successful – campaign to rid the county of its unwelcome "guest", the coypu.**

*ensured a welcome wherever we went. There was the salt of the sea in the mellow timbre of his voice, which echoed the dialectical blend special to his native town. He looked about like a Sir Thomas Browne, seeking new wonders and delving into mysteries with the eagerness of a child of the Renaissance.*

It was at this time that Patterson made a third attempt to write his memoirs - Wildfowlers and Poachers. The experience, he wrote, made him feel like *"a gentle curlew bidding kind goodnight"*. And it was Ellis who sat beside him, night after night, typing it, discussing it. The memoirs were published in 1929.

A year earlier Ellis had started writing articles in the Eastern Evening News and EDP. Then he took up another temporary job at the Tolhouse Museum in Yarmouth which proved another turning point. His work led to his appointment as natural history assistant at Norwich Castle Museum where, in a department of one, he was responsible for geology, zoology and botany, all natural history collections, and for answering any questions in these fields from the public.

Ellis made the job his own, was soon titled keeper of natural history and worked at the museum for 28 years.

In those early years many of the galleries within the castle, which had ceased to be a prison in 1894, were taken up by glass cases housing stuffed animals and birds, including the famous Gurney collection of birds of prey. Then came news from America of a new kind of display, three-dimensional landscaped vistas in which creatures which would most naturally occur together were arranged in realistic postures amid their native setting. Ellis was inspired and between 1931 and 1936 supervised the creation of Norfolk "dioramas" that were then regarded as the best in the world. He also set about an ambitious card-index record of every species of plant and animal known in Norfolk - where it had been seen, when, how often, and by whom.

The gallery of dioramas, the most conspicuous memorial to his work at the museum, was named The Norfolk Room, but in 1987 after his death it was fittingly renamed The Ted Ellis Norfolk Room.

He was to go on to become a celebrated Eastern Daily Press columnist of forty years standing and, from the Sixties, a popular radio and television broadcaster. From Wheatfen - two old marshmen's cottages and 150 acres of fen near Surlingham where he, wife Phyllis and their children moved in 1946 - Ellis vividly reported on the world of Norfolk's habitats and species, emphasising the need to protect and conserve the area's riches.

His impact on his adopted county was immense and soon after his death Phyllis and supporters established Wheatfen as a permanent nature reserve through the Ted Ellis Trust.

In his 1964 book In the Countryside he spoke of the need for constant vigilance in conserving the natural beauty of the region. *"I am very jealous for the pastoral peace of the East Anglian countryside,"* he wrote. *"If it is destroyed, where will town-dwellers and all the sick-of-suburbs people turn to find unspoilt country? Let us remain a breathing*

**November, and the late autumn sunshine tempts a visitor to sample the River Bure. In the background is Salhouse Broad.**

**Schoolmaster and naturalist Dick Bagnall-Oakeley with Holme reserve warden Peter Clarke at the opening of the Holme ringing laboratory in October 1969.**

*space for the cure of souls rejoicing in honest agriculture, forestry and the like and cherishing the serene beauty of our Broads and coast. I am sure we can still do this and survive."*

Among the many significant events of the Thirties, there were two which were to have a serious impact on the environment.

The first was the establishment in the wild of the coypu, the South American rodent that was brought to East Anglia to be bred for its pelt. The original population of 3000 expanded rapidly to an estimated 200,000 in the Fifties. The animals, which could weigh 20lb, undermined river banks and devastated crops, including sugar beet and cereals. Efforts to keep the numbers down had some success, but they expanded rapidly to populate most waterways, including Cley Marshes, and were even found in the heart of Norwich. In the Eighties it was decided to eradicate the coypu and after eight years of intensive trapping the campaign was declared a success in 1989.

The second event was the breaching of sea defences at Horsey on the night of February 12th 1938, causing massive salt water damage and serving as a portent of future flood facing homes and reserves around the coast and across Broadland. The inland sea created by the flooding covered 7500 acres, stretched four miles inland across precious reedbeds and encompassed Hickling and Martham broads as well as Horsey Mere and Heigham Sound.

Naturalists were stunned by the impact. Only about 120 acres of Horsey remained an island of green. Thousands of birds, plants and fish perished. In the transactions of the Naturalists' Trust J E Mosby recorded that after the water had subsided:

*"...the island was the one bright spot. Elsewhere in the marshes there was a strange and deathly silence. For weeks after their normal times of arrival not one single sedge warbler or grasshopper warbler was seen in the area where, in normal times, they are to be met with everywhere..."*

Some birds were returning by the autumn, but he feared the flood had proved disastrous for the freshwater plants such as the water violet and bladderwort.

Hickling keeper Jim Vincent was quoted in Country Life:

*"I have not the slightest evidence from the whole of the affected area that one single young mallard, shoveller, teal, coot, moorhen, water-rail, lapwing, redshank, snipe or great crested grebe has been reared, so complete has been the debacle."*

During the rest of the century the force of the sea was to be felt again and again - next in 1953 where defences were wrecked and human lives lost all around the coast from Lynn to Yarmouth. The sea surged through at Sea Palling, but this time the Horsey defences held.

Imagine the impact on Norfolk and the map of England if the Wash did not exist. The great expanse of shoals and channels carved out of the East coast – vital to Norfolk's identity and sense of remoteness – so nearly did not survive the century. It would have been the design of man, though, rather than the forces of nature which would have redrawn the coastline and married Hunstanton with Lincolnshire.

Renowned as the place where King John lost his treasure in the thirteenth century, and respected by all who earn a living among the ever-changing tidal water streams and sandbanks, the Wash continues to kindle the imagination of practical men as well as visionaries. Ever since Sir John Rennie proposed in 1839 to add a new county of 150,000 acres to the England of young Queen Victoria, the idea of reclaiming the Wash has been debated. But it was in the fast-track Sixties, when the explosion of population in the South-East raised concerns about the growing demand for water and building land, that respected national voices called for a barrage across the mouth of the estuary.

The Binnie Report of 1965 placed the whole issue firmly on the agenda. In a report for the Water Resources Board engineers Binnie and Partners concluded that a fresh water reservoir would yield 620 million gallons a day. Behind the new barrage 80,000 acres would be fresh water and 40,000 acres would be foreshore. The barrage and other works would cost £287 million but the project could not be completed before the early Eighties. Later top civil engineer Sir Owen Williams carried out a year-long independent geological and engineering survey and proposed in 1968 that 225 square miles of new land could be established, providing the perfect site for the world's largest airport and a new town.

**The Wash reservoir trial bank under construction in May 1975.**

Gatwick airport architect Dr Frank Hoar was advisor and it was envisaged that runways of at least four miles long would be built to cater for aircraft of the future. Sir Owen said that the Wash, accessible from both the north and south of England, was the sensible place for such development, with no conflict of residential or agricultural interests and no problem over ownership. Meanwhile an all-party "Wash Group" of twenty MPs was formed to further the scheme. The chairman was Derek Page, MP for the Lynn division and the members included Paul Hawkins (South West Norfolk) and Bert Hazell (North Norfolk). In 1969 a King's Lynn conference, organised by the town's Civic Society and sponsored by the Eastern Federation of Amenity Societies and the growth in Norfolk committee, unanimously agreed to lobby the government for a feasibility study to be made of the Wash barrage idea. Another even bolder plan had just been published, this time by top London architect Harry Teggin. His proposals combined a vast new urban area, Great Wash City, an international airport, large fresh water reservoirs, and port facilities able to take the world's largest shipping.

The whole project would cost £1250 million over thirty years (but Mr Teggin said he did not foresee it taking shape in his lifetime). Peterborough civil engineer Oliver Dawson was more optimistic. One of the most enthusiastic advocates of a reservoir, he suggested a Ministry of Construction be set up to do the job. Fred White, author of A Basin Full of Water, a book on the Wash barrage idea, did not agree with the Wash City idea but reiterated his concept of expanding Lynn to a city of some 750,000 inhabitants.

But it was on the issue of fresh water reservoirs that the Government finally agreed to a £2.5million feasibility study that would last five years. Trial embankments were built as a Lynn-based team looked at a scheme for four reservoirs covering about 100 square kilometres. In its report, published in 1976, the Central Water Planning Unit concluded that using the area for water storage was practical, but the water would cost at least one and a half times more than from a comparable inland reservoir. Predictions of population growth and future water demands had dropped.

Very importantly, though, the work was deemed invaluable should circumstances and demands change in the future, but that it was unlikely a decision to use the Wash in this way would have to be taken before the year 2000.

**Joyce Lambert, Norfolk-born botanist and past-president of the Norfolk and Norwich Naturalists' Society who, in 1953, dispelled the belief that the shallow lakes across the ancient wetland of the Broads were of natural origin. The results of her five-year research revealed: "On the evidence now available they (the Broads) are, beyond reasonable doubt, the flooded sites of former great peat pits, made in the natural fenland in medieval times."**

Norfolk's coastal defences were rebuilt and communities recovered, but the power of the spring tides, backed by a northerly gale, remains an annual lottery.

Every year the winter storms take their toll on the spectacular and rare striped cliffs at Hunstanton with their layer of white chalk overlaying the unusual red chalk with a base of ginger carstone. But further east the damage has been more dramatic.The soft cliffs east from Sheringham are formed from a mix of chalk blocks, clays and sands. They erode through the action of the sea and by water permeating from above, often creating huge slides.

As recently as 1996 Cley Marshes were flooded again when the shingle bank was breached. Waves lapped at the pathway leading to the nature centre dedicated to the memory of Dick Bagnall-Oakeley, the Greshams schoolmaster and naturalist who so loved the reserve. At that time the Norfolk Wildlife Trust, Suffolk Wildlife Trust, English Nature, the RSPB and the National Trust joined forces to press for defence planners to give greater recognition to the value of wildlife habitats, and to call for adequate funding to create new habitats safe from predicted sea-level rise.

Erosion - which in some places has been at the rate of three feet a year with clifftop homes falling victim to the relentless advance of the sea - remains a critical issue for the future of coastal homes and nature reserves as well as the greater wetland of the Broads.

The pressure on Norfolk's landscape has been relentless throughout the century, but after the Second World War - when the county lost a quarter of its remaining mature woodland - new trends in agriculture and leisure added to the rate of decline.There was also a new word in the English vocabulary - myxomatosis. The disease was introduced by mistake in 1953 after being used to control fast-breeding wild rabbits on a French estate and was to decimate the wild rabbit population in parts of East Anglia in several major outbreaks during the past forty years. It disease had a serious effect on some habitats like Breckland where, without the rabbits, the grassland began to turn to scrub, destroying the habitat of the stone curlew and other species.

More subtly, changing economic circumstances killed off many rural activities that created and conserved valuable habitats such as coppiced woodland, meadows and heaths. The coming years would see the removal of hedgerows and ponds, the seasonal drying up of small rivers and streams as aquifers were tapped for irrigation, the rapid sprawl of major towns and the serious decline in the quality of the Norfolk wetlands.

The once clear life-rich waters of the Broads and rivers became cloudy and the whole ecological system started to break down. Naturalists sounded alarm bells but it was many years before major action was taken to start to counter the use of nitrates on neighbouring land, the discharge of sewage and industrial waste into rivers, and the rapid growth in tourism traffic.

The over-enrichment of the waterways by nitrates and phosphates -- an issue with other Norfolk rivers too - fostered turbid algae that blocked the food chain and caused the decline of reedswamps that fringed the broads. This weakening of the natural barriers also led to a substantial increase in bank erosion by the wash from an ever-increasing fleet of holiday

**The Ouse Washes on the fen edge of Norfolk provide an environment of immense richness for thousands of birds.**

craft. In 1949, before the plight of the Broads was obvious, the National Parks and Access to the Countryside Act attempted to protect key areas across Britain deemed at risk. The Nature Conservancy government agency (now English Nature) was formed and it was armed with the power to designate parks and declare areas to be Sites of Special Scientific Interest.

Scolt Head was made the first of Norfolk's National Nature Reserves in 1954. It was also the county's first SSSI, but at that time the status only ensured that the conservation value of such sites was considered in the planning process. The Naturalists' Trust continued to acquire sites – Barton Broad had been taken over in 1945 – and key areas such as the Bure Marshes, the Ant Broads and Marshes and Hickling Broad were given National Nature Reserve status. The whole of the Broads had been proposed for national park status in 1947 but it was many years before it got national recognition.

What followed was a painfully slow reaction by governments both locally and nationally to the new crisis facing the wetland in the face of lauded advances in agriculture, industry and tourism. In a matter of decades an area once famed for its flora and fauna was reduced to mediocrity. While Fifties posters proclaimed the Norfolk Broads as a boating playground, naturalists and scientists continued their studies.

One of them was Norfolk-born botanist Dr Joyce Lambert, who in 1952, after several years of painstaking research, finally brought to an end the belief that some of the shallow lakes within the Broadland wetland were of natural origin.

While a research fellow at Newham College, Cambridge, she worked from 1947 with Dr Joe Jennings of Leicester University analysing the area by hand-boring for deposits of peats, clays and muds. Their 1500 borings revealed the astonishing fact that the mud and water-filled hollows had vertical sides and, for the most part, had almost flat bottoms; also that they contained steep-sided ridges and islands of solid peat. The only feasible explanation of such phenomena was that they represented the sites of former deep excavations for peat which had subsequently flooded.

The discovery was greeted with widespread

**Phillip Wayre: Pictured with some of his beloved otters, a species he helped bring back from the brink.**

incredulity when it hit the pages of the EDP in July 1953 as a result of her presidential address to the Naturalists' Society. Early support was offered by Ted Ellis - and formidable historical evidence was then produced by Dr Clifford Smith. He discovered deeds, leases, surveys and other documents which supported the idea of an important peat industry in Broadland during the twelfth, thirteenth and fourteenth centuries.

In the coming years naturalists and others continued to press for action over the decline of the wetland. In 1957, Len Ramuz of South Walsham founded the Broads Society, an organisation that would bring together lovers of the area and which, in time, would prove to be a powerful lobby for change. From its early days the society, which now has nearly 2000 members nationwide, encouraged those responsible to improve the care they took of the area. Today it works to widen knowledge of the key issues, to do all it can to safeguard the environment, to comment on the way the area is managed including planning proposals, and to preserve and where appropriate improve navigation.

But the Sixties were a time of despair for those who could see what was happening to the waterways. Tony Brown, now secretary of the Great Yarmouth Naturalists' Society and a council member of the Norfolk and Norwich Naturalists' Society, witnessed the decline. "I think a lot of people were keenly aware of the problems but they felt powerless to do anything. Single voices in the wilderness were struggling to be heard."

Elsewhere the picture was more positive.

In 1967 one of the country's largest nature reserves was declared at Holkham covering the beach, salt marsh, pinewoods and grazing marsh owned by the Earl of Leicester. Stretching between Scolt Head and Blakeney Point it is renowned for its beauty as well as its formations of noisy geese, other rare birds and rare species of plants. Managed by English Nature and the Holkham Estate it has also been popular with film makers, in 1999 starring at the end of the Oscar-winning Shakespeare in Love.

In 1968 North Norfolk's coast was declared an Area of Outstanding Natural Beauty - and the government gave landscape conservation more emphasis with the creation of the Countryside Commission. The body was to have a significant influence in the county, providing pressure and funds to tackle key issues. One example was the Amenity Tree Planting Scheme, funded by the commission and county council in the dramatic wake of Dutch elm disease.

The fate of the Broads finally captured the headlines in 1967 when Nature Conservancy published an alarming report about the state of the waterways. But it was not until after the Norfolk Naturalists' Trust (now the Norfolk Wildlife Trust) published its own study in 1976 that Norfolk and Suffolk county councils were made to act. During those intervening years, when holiday traffic was building to a peak and commercial shipping still worked the Yare and Wensum to Norwich, there was much debate - and in-fighting - between the bodies who had the power to change things. The county council, port and haven commissioners and rivers authority tried in vain to agree a solution that would not weaken their control. Bryan Read, now president of the Broads Society who was then chairman of the port and haven rivers committee, said it was a time of much soul-searching.

"I was concerned to see all the statutory authorities coming together and 'sinking' their differences for the sake of the Broads. It was vital the issue be resolved."

After the Naturalists' Trust report was published pressure was applied by all parties concerned for the Broads, including the Countryside Commission, urging the county authorities to provide proper management in order to halt and, if possible, reverse the decline.

Summing up the mood at that time the celebrated wildlife author, painter and broadcaster Sir Peter Scott, who founded the Wildfowl Trust refuge on the flooded Ouse Wash at Welney in South West Norfolk, wrote in support of the county's reserves:

*"Attitudes have greatly changed and nowadays large numbers of people have come to recognise the importance of the natural environment to themselves personally, as an enrichment of their own lives."*

Two years later the counties finally established the first Broads Authority, funded by and made up of representatives of eight local authorities and the Countryside Commission. Anglian Water and Great Yarmouth Port and Haven Commissioners were also represented.

Work was started for the first time in co-ordinating and involving everyone with a vested interest in the unique wetland, establishing links with the tourism business and launching conservation and restoration projects.

Important links were also established with science and a research and experimental management was started which led to the authority's first restoration project at Cockshoot Broad. Other early achievements included the building of information centres and the launch of the Broads Grazing Marsh Conservation Scheme which proved to be the forerunner of the national Environmentally Sensitive Areas scheme.

But change was still slow and hard to co-

**Balancing the demands of nature and man on the Broads has been the task of the Broads Authority, which started work on April 1st 1989, as reported in the EDP of that day.**

**Broads optimism as new authority moves in**

A NEW era for the Norfolk and Suffolk Broads dawns today as the network of fens and waterways becomes Britain's newest but unique national park.

From today the old Broads Authority is no more and the new statu-

ordinate. A review five years after the first authority was born showed that more could be achieved by one body with more teeth. It needed its own statutory powers and this was accomplished with the 1988 Norfolk and Suffolk Broads Act.

The Act placed a duty on the new authority - much like those of a national park - to conserve and enhance the natural beauty while promoting the enjoyment of the area by the public and protecting the interest of navigation. Special regard also had to be given to the needs of agriculture and the economic and social interests of those who lived and worked in the area.

The rivers and broads of east Norfolk and north Suffolk which were once one of the richest, most intricate and diverse freshwater systems in Europe today remain a pale shadow of their former selves. But the partnership is now in place - a strong (if fairly complicated) weave of wildlife and environmental organisations - offering real hope for the future. In its 1997 Broads Plan the new authority outlined its targets for large-scale restoration. And in his introduction the-then chairman Jonathan Peel spelled out the challenge for everyone to work in the *"... hope that the genius of the place will survive; that there will still be space, quiet, and creatures for those who wish to reflect and be inspired..."*

Dedicated to the memory of Ted Ellis, this vital - and very readable - document shows just how the twentieth century had an enormous effect on the vast wetland.

While the issue of the Broads was coming to a head in the Seventies an incredible conservation project was under way in Norfolk to save the otter.

When Philip and Jeanne Wayre set up the Otter Trust beside the Waveney at Earsham, near Bungay, in 1971 the species faced extinction. There were fewer than thirty in Norfolk, virtually none in Suffolk and fewer than 1000 in England as a whole. Although no-one had previously managed to breed otters successfully in captivity the couple released their first pair of otters into the wild in 1983, followed by a further ninety in the next 12 years. A survey in the middle of the decade put the nation's total population at 7350 and the couple's work went on breeding otters, identifying suitable release sites throughout East Anglia and the South-West and tracking and monitoring their animals in the wild. By 1995 it was clear that otter populations were expanding naturally and the mission was deemed complete.

It was not the couple's first wildlife achievement. Philip Wayre had come to Norfolk to learn to farm after a naval career during the war. A keen ornithologist, he was to become one of the country's leading maker of nature films and a naturalist with a world-wide reputation. He founded the Ornamental Pheasant Trust, and later converted his thirty-acre farm at Great Witchingham into the Norfolk Wildlife Park to spread awareness of species threatened with extinction, especially British mammals like the otter.

Today the forces ranged for conservation in Norfolk are impressive and growing in strength.

They need to be. So many problems and challenges remain as demands for more housing and better transport plus the by-products of our expanding society put an ever-increasing pressure on the environment. Just one example: early in 1999 the Environment Agency warned that the very existence of ancient rivers like the Wensum and Waveney - and of endangered species which rely on them, were under threat from poor management. A consultative document which also put the Bure, Yare, forty shallow Broadland lakes and the coastline from Happisburgh to Lowestoft at risk, called for action on a list of subjects that sums up the challenge for the new millennium.

The document called for: A study of "poorly understood" water systems to protect the internationally-important wetlands and rare species like the bittern and fen orchid; New methods to lessen the effect of swathes of new housing development which are causing "greater run-off" and increasing the risk of flooding; Greater control of discharges into the waters of the Broads area which "may not meet the expectations" of tourists; a review of

**The importance of the Wash as a centre for birdlife is underlined by this picture of hundreds of waders at Snettisham RSPB reserve.**

the way in which water is supplied to houses and businesses, in the light of a predicted rise in demand;The predicted rise in sea levels due to global warming to be taken into account when sizing up sea defence schemes; Better education and stricter penalties to crack down on people who pollute the rivers.

There remains a vast amount of work to do, all needing the public's understanding and cooperation. But, for all the legacies of passing century, there are important grounds for hope.

Over and above the county's 17 National Nature Reserves - more than ten per cent of the national total - there are thousands of acres under the care of the Royal Society for the Protection of Birds, English Nature, the National Trust, the Norfolk Wildlife Trust, the Broads Authority, The Wildfowl Trust, The Woodland Trust, responsible landowners and other groups.

The RSPB, which first started to manage areas of Norfolk in the early seventies, has among its sites the renowned north west Norfolk reserves at Titchwell near Scolt Head, home to bitterns, avocets and marsh harriers, and Snettisham on the Wash, the scene of spectacular mass migrations by thousands of wading birds. The society also works in partnership with the other organisations on key projects like Hickling Broad, and has a close association with the British Trust for Ornithology which, very significantly, has chosen to move its headquarters to Norfolk. Since it was founded in 1933 BTO members have monitored bird populations throughout the UK - impartial research supported with BTO scientists based at Thetford which has been key to many conservation measures.

English Nature, the government body responsible for nature conservation which under its old title played such an important role in protecting Norfolk sites since 1949, has

**The distemper virus outbreak in 1988 killed thousands of grey and common seals across the waters of Norfolk and indeed most of northern Europe. The Wash and Blakeney colonies suffered in particular with hundreds dying. Blakeney boatman Colin Bishop spoke at the time of his helplessness as seeing so many of the animals dead or dying – including 29 on just one day. "The agony," he said. "is that there is nothing we can do." By September Blakeney National Trust warden Joe Reed estimated the 700-strong colony was down to a mere 100.**

a dedicated county team based in Norwich. Its staff manage ten of the National Nature Reserves from Winterton Dunes in the east to the large Wash NNR in the west.

As the RSPB reserve on its shore proves, the whole Wash is one of Britain's most important winter feeding areas for waders and wildfowl outside the breeding season. The vast reserve area, leased by English Nature, sweeps north from the Nene lighthouse where Sir Peter Scott lived and, with a space for the shipping channel into Lynn port, sweeps north east across the tidal mudflats and sands towards Snettisham. The English Nature team also carry out the critical naming and monitoring of Sites of Special Scientific Interest (SSSI). Since Scolt Head became the first in 1954 a further 156 have been identified in Norfolk, ranging from vast landscapes to tiny sites such at Forncett Meadows which is just a few hectares. Some are managed reserves, but most are not and can be helped by grants from English Nature to encourage the landowners to manage the sites carefully.

For the National Trust, the first body to acquire a nature reserve in Norfolk (Blakeney Point), the century closes with it being responsible for more than 17,000 acres and huge stretches of coastline, rivers, ditches and hedges. As well as the famous common seals colony that draw the visitors to the Point, it cares for a vast array of species and landscapes on its coastal sites and estates at Horsey, Blickling, Felbrigg and Sheringham.

Then, as I summarised much earlier in this chapter, there has been the enormous achievement of the Norfolk Wildlife Trust.

In attempting to draw together in a few pages all this century's influences on Norfolk's nature and environment it is fitting to return to Dr Sydney Long. The good doctor, who set an example for the whole country, would have despaired on occasion during darkest moments of the last 100 years. But he would surely applaud (not forsaking the problems that remain) what has been a heartening fightback.

As David Dymond observed in 1985's The Norfolk Landscape: *"Rare and beautiful Norfolk, as John Sell Cotman called it in 1841, is undoubtedly less rare and beautiful than it was, but we have some grounds for hope... an increasing number of people care about the county, its buildings and its landscapes."*

# Chapter 3

# *Royal Norfolk*

The purchase of a country estate at Sandringham for Albert Edward, the Prince of Wales, in 1862 marked the start of a unique and enduring relationship between the Royal Family and Norfolk. Sandringham has a special significance because it is a privately-owned retreat where four generations of monarchs have chosen to relax away from the pomp and formality which dominates much of their lives. The estate, characterised by its glorious woodland, banks of rhododendron and extensive heathland, has played a central role in the life of the Royal Family - illustrated by the long-standing tradition that they spend each Christmas there.

In the early days Sandringham was the glittering centre of society but while entertaining guests from all over the world King Edward VII developed a very real affection for West Norfolk. His son, King George V, uttered the much-quoted words: "Dear old Sandringham, the place I love better than anywhere else in the world." The sentiment was shared by his son King George VI. *"I have always been happy here and I love the place,"* he wrote to his mother.

The estate has witnessed milestones in history and was the centre of world attention when both George V and George VI died there. George V made his first Christmas broadcast from his Norfolk home in 1932 and 25 years later the house was the setting for the Queen's first televised Christmas message. Ever since 1908 the gardens of Sandringham House have been open to the public in the summer months. In 1930 the museum created by George V was opened and in 1977, the year of her silver jubilee, the Queen decided to go into the stately homes business and opened the principal rooms of the house to the public.

The 21-year-old Prince moved into the house with his bride Princess Alexandra of Denmark and when the building became too cramped for their growing family it was demolished and replaced by a new house, significantly more impressive than its predecessor.

Prince Edward and Princess Alexandra were at the centre of fashionable society and their social life ranged from formal visits by heads of state to country weekend house parties at which neighbours from other Norfolk estates were among the guests. The pattern of weekends, which continued throughout the century, was dominated by pheasant and partridge shooting with members of the house party joining the guns for lunch. The Prince carried out public engagements in the area. He was also closely involved in the life of the 7000-acre estate - including the parishes of Wolferton, West Newton, Babingley and part of Appleton - which was gradually extended over the years.

The Prince was a racing enthusiast and established two stud farms on the estate - at Sandringham and Wolferton - in 1886. The most famous and successful of his horses, Persimmon, is remembered with a bronze statue outside Sandringham Stud. Prize-money from Persimmon's successes was ploughed into the estate. Prince Edward's interest in and affection for Sandringham never diminished - even when he ascended to the throne as Edward VII in 1901 and was forced to spend much less time in West Norfolk though Queen Alexandra was often there in his absence.

A small house built in the grounds was renamed York Cottage and given to Prince George, Duke of York, and his bride Princess

**ALISON CROOSE began her journalistic career with Northamptonshire Evening Telegraph at Kettering. She joined the EDP as a senior reporter at King's Lynn and subsequently became chief reporter and then news editor of its West Norfolk and Fens edition. During her 25 years with the EDP Alison became the Royal correspondent and reported on all the Royal Family's visits to Sandringham and the public engagements they carried out in the area. Alison is now a freelance journalist working from her home in West Norfolk and continues to contribute to the EDP. She is a board member of King's Lynn Festival and is the festival's publicity officer.**

THE KAISER IN NORFOLK

ARRIVAL AT WOLFERTON

BRILLIANT HOUSE PARTY AT SANDRINGHAM

STRINGENT PRECAUTIONS FOR PRIVACY

(FROM OUR SPECIAL CORRESPONDENT.)

KING'S MESSAGE TO HIS PEOPLES

CHRISTMAS DAY BROADCAST

"FROM MY HOME AND MY HEART"

LARGE FAMILY PARTY AT SANDRINGHAM

Reports from afar show that the King's broadcast message from Sandringham on Christmas Day was heard in Australia, New Zealand, South Africa, and Canada. Everywhere his Majesty's words created a deep impression.

A New York telegram says that, although the King's broadcast was not relayed to the United States, the principal New York papers yesterday carried a story from Sandringham on their front pages.

Christmas celebrations at Sandringham were carried out in the same homely way. On Sunday morning the whole of the Royal party attended service at Sandringham Church. A large crowd gathered at the entrance to the church to see the arrivals and departures.

THE KING'S MESSAGE

CHRISTMAS DAY BROADCAST

CHRISTMAS EVENTS AT SANDRINGHAM

ROYAL FAMILY AT CHURCH

DISTRIBUTION OF GIFTS

**Sandringham has seen many historic moments during the twentieth century. Two of them recorded in the EDP were the visit of Kaiser Wilhelm II in November 1902, and George V's first Christmas broadcast to the Empire in 1932.**

Mary, as their country home. Other changes initiated by Edward were to convert a bowling alley into a library, a nine-hole golf course was laid out and Queen Alexandra had an elaborate beach hut built at Snettisham. West Norfolk was known as the "King's Homeland" and the death of Edward VII at Buckingham Palace on May 1910 was felt keenly at Sandringham. The Duke of York continued to live at York Cottage after he came to the throne as George V. He and Queen Mary were very much at home having lived there for 17 years since their marriage.

The relatively modest house was enlarged twice to accommodate their family and though it was still too small the King found it a welcome change from a more formal palace existence. York Cottage remained his home for 16 more years as the late King had bequeathed Sandringham House to Queen Alexandra.

It was not until she died in 1925 that King George and Queen Mary moved to the Big House as it had become known. York Cottage was converted into the estate office and flats for employees. Six months after his accession George V carried out his first official visit to Lynn as monarch when he inspected a guard of honour of the Lynn detachment of the 5th Battalion of the Norfolk Regiment. He enjoyed the time he spent in the West Norfolk countryside. He was especially interested in the gardens at Sandringham and was a member of Norfolk and Norwich Naturalists' Trust.

The King took a special interest in the Sandringham Pigeon Lofts, a flock founded in 1886, and when he visited the Naval Centre at Lowestoft during the war he sent off a pigeon carrying a message for Sandringham. Pigeons from the Royal Lofts saw active service in the RAF in the Second World War. In 1940 one of George VI's pigeons brought back a message from an aircraft which made a forced landing and was awarded a special medal.

The King spent less time at Sandringham than he wished though he made his first Christmas Day broadcast to the Empire there in 1932. He died at his beloved Sandringham on January 20th 1936. For the second time between the wars Wolferton Station witnessed a royal funeral train – the first was in 1925 after the death of Queen Alexandra. The eyes of the world were again focused on the Royal estate when the body of George V was taken on a gun carriage drawn by six members of the Royal Horse Artillery from the Church of St Mary Magdalene near Sandringham House to Wolferton Station on its journey to London.

King Edward VIII and his brothers walked behind and the Queen and other members of the Royal household followed in closed carriages. Behind them, poignantly, walked Jock, the dead King's favourite pony. Villagers and estate workers followed and thousands lined the two-mile route.

George V's eldest son, the new King Edward, was much less enthusiastic about the estate. He preferred hunting to shooting and the number of game birds was reduced, cattle breeding was scaled down and the number of estate employees cut.

In contrast his brother Prince Albert Frederick Arthur George, who was born at York Cottage, was happiest in his native county. He was created Duke of York in 1920, married Elizabeth Bowes-Lyon in 1923 and was set to continue to enjoy life at Sandringham when his world was turned upside down by the abdication of his elder brother. King George VI was agonisingly shy, not physically robust and had a pronounced stammer when he had the huge weight of responsibility suddenly and unexpectedly thrust upon him. But he had a deep sense of duty and a modesty and essential decency which endeared him to a nation in disarray. He also had a wife with great charm and strength of character who helped him face up to the terrifying task ahead.

The King and Queen were perfectly attuned to the time and won the hearts of the nation so that King George VI was to become one of the most admired of British monarchs.

He was often called "the Norfolk Squire", having inherited his father's great love of the Royal estate and enjoyment of country pursuits, and he always turned to Sandringham for respite away from the

**Sandringham House: The cornerstone of the Royal Family's enduring affection for Norfolk.**

**Queen Mary leaves Norwich Castle Museum after paying an informal visit in August 1948 to see the exhibition Portraits in the Landscape Park.**

anxieties of kingship. The place where he was born and grew up remained a retreat from the cares of state – and undoubtedly Queen Elizabeth and their daughters Princess Elizabeth and Princess Margaret shared his affection for their Norfolk home.

Within weeks of his unexpected succession to the throne he and his family maintained the Royal Family's tradition and spent Christmas there. The war affected the Royal Family as it did every other family in the land. The "Big House" was closed down and six acres of lawn ploughed up as part of the "dig for victory" campaign. His father had bought adjoining land and increased the size of the estate to about 15,000 acres. While George V shared his own father's love of shooting he was even more interested in farming and concentrated on a stud of shire horses which won many prizes. George V also started what was to become a famous herd of Red Poll cattle and developed a flock of Southdown sheep which were exported all over the world. During his reign he built many cottages for estate and farm workers. So George VI inherited a fine sporting estate with valuable herds of pedigree stock.

He had spent much of his childhood at Sandringham where he learned to play football with village boys and explored the countryside with his elder brother, Edward. He became a keen all-round sportsman and a first-rate shot. George VI had a very practical outlook on farming matters and gave close personal attention to the running of his estate and the planning of work on his farms. This approach has been inherited by his daughter who shares with Prince Philip a great interest in the estate and both are closely involved in decisions affecting its development.

**George VI and Queen Elizabeth surrounding by a sea of well-wishers during their visit to the Royal Norfolk Show at Keswick on June 25th 1947.**

As one of the biggest estate owners in the county George VI identified himself with many of the county's farming institutions. In the early days of his reign he became patron of the Royal Norfolk Agricultural Association. In the association's centenary year in 1947, when the Royal Norfolk Show was held at Keswick Park near Norwich, he became its president. He achieved much through estate management, modernised properties, and provided electricity for the estate – except for a few isolated cottages – by 1948. Work pressed ahead with a big marsh reclamation scheme started at Wolferton before the war which became one of the most successful of its kind in the country. Similar projects were undertaken at Dersingham and Snettisham. During his reign the home farms were increased to about 1300 acres at Sandringham and the adjoining parishes of West Newton, Appleton and Flitcham plus about 1000 acres at Wolferton. He increased the whole estate to about 20,000 acres – its size at the end of the twentieth century.

Like his father and grandfather, George VI and his family regularly travelled to Sandringham by train, arriving at Wolferton station, where special royal waiting rooms had been built in 1898, and completing the journey by car. The little wayside station at Wolferton continued to feature prominently in the life of the nation, gaining considerable kudos from the association with Sandringham and the many special Royal trains which used it. The main Royal waiting rooms were on the down platform and incorporated a suite of retiring rooms complete with couches, easy chairs and oak panelling. The up side accommodation was almost as lavish.

This was no ordinary country station for Wolferton's population was just over 200 at its peak early in the century - but the station came to life when parties were held at Sandringham House, especially in the Edwardian era, and guests arrived with many servants and much luggage. The station was also used for entertaining during the shooting season. George VI frequently travelled between London and Sandringham by train and although his arrival and departure at the station were described at the time as "informal" the stationmaster, rector and the Chief Constable were usually there to greet him. On the drive to the house he would sometimes ask his chauffeur to stop if there was something he particularly wanted to see - such as in 1947 when he and the Queen saw the results of a fire which scarred 250 acres of forest and heathland.

The King sometimes took part in fire-fighting exercises involving Sandringham's own brigade. This involvement was typical of the very keen personal interest the King took in the people and activities on his Norfolk estate where he was a familiar figure among the tenants and workers.

When he opened the new village hall he presented to Flitcham he stayed to play a game of darts and he was a regular visitor to the cricket ground at Sandringham where he liked to watch the estate team in action. The King's interest was not confined to his estate and he undertook many engagements across the county. His first official visit to Norwich was as Duke of York in October 1925 when he presided at the centenary celebrations of Norwich Museum.

During that same visit in 1925 the Duke also opened the Bridewell as a museum of industry, the Stuart Hall, and the newly-restored Suckling House. The Duchess was unable to accompany him as she was unwell so, on her behalf, the Duke opened Samson and Hercules House as a YWCA centre.

King George VI, with Queen Elizabeth, drove from Sandringham to Norwich on October 29th 1938 for his first visit as monarch, to the capital of the his native county. The opening of the new City Hall was the highlight of a full programme of engagements carried out to the accompaniment of the cheering of tens of thousands of people. The crowds which gathered in the autumn sunshine in the market place outside the City Hall were unprecedented for their size and the warmth of the welcome.

One thousand children led the singing of the National Anthem and the King inspected military units and voluntary organisations and placed a wreath on the war memorial. After touring the new building the Royal visitors were entertained to lunch by the Lord Mayor and Mayoress, Mr and Mrs Charles Watling. In the afternoon the King received another big welcome when the crowd at the football match between Norwich City and Millwall sang For He's A Jolly Good Fellow.

Meanwhile the Queen visited Norfolk and Norwich Hospital to open the maternity wing built as a memorial to Captain Geoffrey Colman. She and the King met up at the Lads' Club and then went on to the Mutual Services Club at Pottergate. Wartime security meant the King's movements were very low key in the war years so that factory workers at Caleys, then being used by Siemens for battery making, looked up one day in October 1942 to find the King standing beside them.

The main purpose of his visit was to see the damage done by enemy air attacks and to meet Civil Defence workers. During his 25-mile tour of the battered city he went to Norfolk and Norfolk Hospital, the Cathedral and the Services' Club in St Andrew's Hall.

The Queen, Queen Mary and Princess Margaret attended a Thanksgiving for Victory concert by the London Philharmonic Orchestra in Norwich Cathedral in 1946.

After the war the King bought 3000 acres of agricultural land from the Houghton Estate which adjoins Sandringham, including most of the villages of Great Bircham and Bircham Tofts. He immediately gave Bircham Parish Council a playing field and a hut for use as a

PEACEFUL DEATH OF THE KING IN HIS SLEEP

THE PROCLAMATION OF THE ACCESSION OF QUEEN ELIZABETH II WAS SIGNED AT ST. JAMES'S PALACE LAST NIGHT BY 150 MEMBERS OF THE PRIVY COUNCIL. AN ANNOUNCEMENT FROM SANDRINGHAM AT 10.45 a.m. STATED: "THE KING, WHO RETIRED LAST NIGHT IN HIS USUAL HEALTH, PASSED PEACEFULLY AWAY IN HIS SLEEP AT SANDRINGHAM EARLY THIS MORNING."

It is understood that he was found by a manservant who went to call his Majesty at 7.30 a.m. King George VI died in the 57th year of his life and the 16th year of kingship.

Death came just over four months after his grave operation for lung resection, from which he seemed to have made a good recovery. His life ended where it began, at Sandringham, where King George V died.

In accordance with constitution, Princess Elizabeth became Queen immediately on the death of the King. This is the first time in British history a Sovereign has acceded to the Throne while abroad in the Commonwealth.

Peers and Members of Parliament last night began taking the Oath of Allegiance to the Queen. She is 25 years old, the same age as Queen Elizabeth I when she ascended the Throne in 1558.

ROYAL FAMILY AT SANDRINGHAM

The Queen Mother, Princess Margaret, Prince Charles, the new heir to the Throne, and his sister, Princess Anne, were all at Sandringham

**The death of George VI at Sandringham, as reported in the EDP of February 6th 1952.**

**Princess Elizabeth's first public engagement in Norfolk was to open the Norwich Festival of Britain fortnight in June 1951. Her visit was witnessed by thousands of city folk who crowded every vantage point and pavement to wish her well.**

cricket pavilion. He honoured his home county early in 1947 when he became Colonel-in-Chief of the Royal Norfolk Regiment.

The King and Queen were back in Norwich in June 1947 for the Royal Norfolk Agricultural Association's Centenary Show at Keswick Park. After a civic reception at City Hall they walked among cheering crowds in the Market Place and St Giles Street before driving to the show where they spent several hours.

News of the death of King George VI at Sandringham on February 6th 1952 was as much of a shock on the Royal estate in Norfolk as it was to the rest of the world. He seemed to have made a good recovery from a major lung operation and had looked cheerful a week earlier when he was at London Airport to see Princess Elizabeth and the Duke of Edinburgh leave for their Commonwealth tour. That was to be his last public appearance though the day before his death the King had been shooting hares on the Royal estate. He was a fine shot and was reported to be in good form and had planned another shoot the next day.

But he died at the age of 57 in his sleep at Sandringham where the Queen, Princess Margaret, Prince Charles and Princess Anne were spending their New Year holiday. His death was announced from Sandringham at 10.45am and a message was sent to Treetops

**The sudden death of George VI stunned Norfolk as it did the rest of the world. Tens of thousands of people lined the roads of the Royal Estate as the king's body was carried to Wolferton Station for the sad journey to London on February 11th 1952.**

Hotel in a Kenyan game park where Prince Philip broke the news to Princess Elizabeth.

Within minutes of the announcement the world's press, anxious for information, jammed telephone lines to newspaper offices at Lynn. Soon local reporters outside the gates of Sandringham were joined by others from national newspapers keen to glean what information they could.

All was quiet on the estate and many workers there did not hear the news until lunchtime. The first outward sign of what had happened was when the flag on Sandringham parish church was flown at half-mast.

As word spread businesses in the area draped their royal warrants in black and estate workers put on black arm bands. The King's body was moved to Sandringham church until it was taken to London.

There were unprecedented scenes when the coffin was taken from Sandringham to Wolferton Station when all the pomp and ceremony of a state occasion was enacted in the quiet countryside where the King was born and which he so loved. Grenadier guards marched at the head of the procession with the captain of the King's Troop of the Royal Horse Artillery riding behind.

Six glossy bay horses drew the gun carriage bearing the coffin covered with the Royal standard. Soldiers marched on either side. The Dukes of Gloucester and Edinburgh walked behind. The deeply-veiled Queen with her mother and sister drove by car. Behind them was a procession of country gentlemen in tall hats and long overcoats and lines and lines of estate workmen in their country clothes. Every yard of the two-mile route - more like a private drive than a public highway with its pines and rhododendrons - was thronged with people.

The many thousands stood hushed and still beneath the trees as the sombre procession passed by on it final journey from the King's rural homeland to its lying in state at Westminster Abbey before it was laid to rest beneath St George's Chapel, Windsor.

The Queen Mother has never been at Sandringham on the anniversary of the King's death - but she clearly shares his great affection for the estate. She makes no secret of her pleasure in being at Sandringham and she has remained central to many of the traditions, established during her very happy family life there with the King, which have been maintained over the years.

Christmas continues to be the great occasion at Sandringham. The Queen, Prince Philip and the Queen Mother spend about six weeks there during Christmas and New Year and are joined by well over a dozen other members of their immediate family for the main part of the holiday.

One of the Queen Mother's favourite weeks of the year is her week-long summer stay at Sandringham House at the end of July. It has always been a busy but happy visit when she frequently undertakes several public engagements in the area as well as attending two events especially close to her heart. The annual Sandringham Flower Show, established in 1866 by Sandringham Estate Cottage Horticultural Society, is held on the last Wednesday of July and the Queen Mother has maintained the Royal Family's long-established custom of touring the showground in Sandringham Park. As the twentieth century drew to a close no-one associated with the show could remember her missing the event. Her popularity has turned what was essentially a village show into a national event attracting crowds of some 16,000.

The other event which the Queen Mother has loyally supported is King's Lynn Festival of music and the arts of which she has been patron since it began in 1950. The festival was founded by Ruth, Lady Fermoy, a close friend and lady-in waiting to the Queen Mother, who was also maternal grandmother to Diana, Princess of Wales. Lady Fermoy, wife of a former MP and mayor of King's Lynn, helped maintain the Queen Mother's links with Lynn through their shared love of music and the arts and Lynn's rich history. Lynn Festival grew out of a celebration of the restoration of the fifteenth-century Guildhall of St George, reputed to be the largest and most complete surviving Medieval Guildhall in Britain where, it is said, Shakespeare once appeared. Lady Fermoy played a major part in ensuring the Guildhall was saved from demolition and the Queen Mother officially re-opened the building in 1950 and agreed to become the Festival's patron. The festival went from strength to strength with the Queen Mother a frequent member of the audience.

She attended talks and recitals and often arrived unannounced to see festival exhibitions. Such was her enthusiasm that she frequently drove into the town during the day and returned in the evening to attend a concert. Festival-goers were able to share the joy of a special present for the Queen Mother on her 85th birthday when world-famous cellist Mstislav Rostropovich gave a concert in her honour in a packed St Nicholas' Chapel. The Prince of Wales flew in specially for the event.

Norfolk has witnessed scenes unique in Britain when the Queen Mother, in her colourful outfits and trademark veiled hat, has taken an impromptu walk along town centre streets. Many times policemen's hearts have missed a beat as she has walked past her waiting limousine to go and explore a new conservation project she has just learned about. She has taken a close interest in the work of Lynn Preservation Trust, of which she is patron, and has seen most of the historic properties it has restored. Her unheralded visits may have caused nightmares for security officers but they have delighted trust members and passers-by who have found themselves face to smiling face with the Queen Mother.

The mutual affection shared by the Queen Mother and the people of West Norfolk is embodied in the honour bestowed on her in 1954 when she was given the honorary freedom of the borough. The historic occasion, on the 750th anniversary of Lynn being granted a borough charter, marked "the deep and loyal affection in which Her Majesty is held by the townspeople." She was the first woman to receive the town's highest honour as a token of Lynn's gratitude for the kindness and interest she had shown on so many occasions in the progress of the town.

The Queen Mother voiced publicly her feelings for Lynn and, particularly, her delight that she was thought of as a "neighbour". She said: "On a day many years ago when the King first brought me to Norfolk to show me his beloved Sandringham I fell in love with the place and its people, and this love has only grown with the years. King's Lynn, lying as it does so close to the home where I have spent so many happy days, has long held a special place in my heart.

"Its beauty and its long history, which speak to the passer-by at every corner, give an impression of continuity and steadfastness which I think must be found throughout most of Norfolk."

When the Queen Mother returned to Lynn Town Hall in 1979 for a special presentation to mark her 25 years as a freeman she revealed her affection for West Norfolk had deepened with the years. She said: "The passing of 25 years has only increased my affection for the county and I hope cemented the bond between this town and myself." On the fortieth anniversary of the freedom ceremony the Queen Mother could not disguise her delight at being back among so many familiar faces at the Town Hall when she told them: "I think you know how very close to my heart is this dear old town."

One example of her genuine concern for Lynn and its people took place in January 1978 when the Queen Mother opened new Regalia Rooms in the vaulted undercroft of the Town Hall. Just 24 hours after the Royal visit to the long-awaited showplace for the town's treasures – including the priceless King John Cup – floodwaters lapped three feet up the entrance door. A few days later the Queen Mother paid a surprise visit to see the flood damage. Fortunately the Regalia Rooms had been protected by sandbags and a flood board but nearby St Margaret's Church and homes in Nelson Street did not escape.

Like a good neighbour the Queen Mother brought a cheerful note to the clearing-up operation in homes which had been three feet under water. The incident typified the bond she has long enjoyed with the historic town in which she has such an enduring interest and was a further example of her spontaneous visits with which she has maintained her close links with the town and its architectural treasures.

The Queen Mother has visited the famous Lynn Mart, the charter fair which heralds the start of the showmen's year, she has opened new buildings at Lynn hospital, the College of West Anglia and Springwood High School to which she gives an annual prize. Her interest in people, which makes each person in a crowd seem as though they have been singled out for a special greeting, is never more evident than on the Sandringham estate.

She will call on friends, anxious to keep up to date with their news, and where better to chat over a cup of tea than at a Women's Institute meeting? The Queen Mother is president of Sandringham WI and tries not to miss their January meeting at which she is accompanied by the Queen who is also a member. Both obviously enjoy the informal get-together with others who live and work on the estate. The WI visit is another symbol of the link between the monarchy and Norfolk people which has been, and continues to be, fostered by generations of-the Royal Family.

George VI and Queen Elizabeth took Princess Elizabeth to Sandringham for the first time at Christmas 1926 when she was eight months old. Ever since her visits have been frequent and as children she and Princess Margaret

**The Queen Mother at the Sandringham Flower Show, the Norfolk event with which she is perhaps most closely associated, in July 1972.**

were able to grow up largely away from the public gaze. Prince Charles was born in November 1948 and was only five weeks old when he spent his first Christmas in West Norfolk.

And so the Christmas tradition continued but by 1963 there were 17 in the house party and four of them - the Queen, Princess Margaret, Princess Alexandra and the Duchess of Kent - were all expecting babies. It was decided to transfer the festivities to Windsor Castle in 1964, but the party always moved to Norfolk to see in the New Year. In 1989 extensive rewiring of the castle prompted the Royal Family to resume their established custom and once again they spent both Christmas and New Year at the Queen's country retreat. After the closure of the railway line between Lynn and Hunstanton in the late Sixties the Royal Family continued to use the railway between London and Lynn for some years until it became more convenient to travel by car or to fly into RAF Marham.

While the Royal Family preferred that their stays on the private estate should remain private there has always been a tacit agreement that certain outings could be treated as public appearances such as their arrivals and departures at the station and when they go to church. The gates of Sandringham Park are open on Sunday mornings and the Royal Family have always been pleased to see spectators and to have the opportunity to chat informally to them.

There was a telling demonstration of public affection for the Royal Family when they attended church on the first Sunday after Christmas in 1947. Although there was a ban on motoring for pleasure 5000 people arrived by bus, bicycle and on foot to greet the Royal party. There were especially large crowds to see the Royal Family during the Seventies. Nearly 10,000 from all over the Midlands and East Anglia streamed into the park in December 1973 despite calls for fuel economy and the threat of petrol rationing.

Sandringham House was closed from 1974 to 1976 while ninety of the original 360 rooms at the rear were demolished and the staff and service areas modernised so the house could be run more economically. The Queen abandoned plans to rebuild part of the house because of the high costs. There was a big welcome when, after a three-year break while the work was carried out, the Royal Family returned to the new-look Sandringham House for its New Year holiday in 1977.

A crowd of 10,000 witnessed their first public appearance at the start of a year which was to see radical changes on the Royal estate when the Queen decided to go into the stately homes business. The gardens have been open to the public during the summer months since the reign of Edward VII very early in the century.

Due to their popularity the length of opening times have increased over the years and Queen Elizabeth II has taken many positive steps to make the estate more accessible to visitors, at the same time making it more commercial. As the attractions at Sandringham have been developed so has its appeal to tourists and it has long been the destination for day trips for coach parties from all over the Midlands and East Anglia as well as for people holidaying in Norfolk.

For a long time facilities were fairly modest. There was a timber building selling teas, ice-cream and mementoes including tea towels which cost six shillings when they were first sold in 1967. The Queen's decision to open the doors of her private home to the public gaze in 1977 was seen as a major boost to Norfolk's tourism industry.

From May 3rd that year for just 30p - plus 30p admission to the grounds - people could have a fascinating insight into the main ground floor rooms used by the Royal Family.

The chance to dispel the mystique which surrounds the Royal Family proved a great magnet. A woman who queued for three hours to be the first to see inside the house headed 2000 on that first day and soon unlucky latecomers were being turned away.

Memorabilia reflecting the Royal Family's love of horses for recreation, dozens of gifts received on foreign tours and big game trophies, assembled by George V in the original museum, are included in displays which have wide appeal. The Sandringham estate holds the same appeal for the general public as it does the Royal Family and the Queen has been keen to share its pleasures with visitors. The development of the estate as a tourist attraction has evolved over the years. The opening of the doors of the house in 1977 was a milestone and since then the provision of facilities to cater for visitors has accelerated.

Despite the inevitable magnetism of the

**The Duchess of Kent and her family spent many happy years at Anmer Hall on the Royal Estate. She found time for many formal and informal visits to the county, including this one to the Norfolk and Norwich Hospital in September 1971. In an 1998 Radio Norfolk interview the Duchess spoke of her fondness for the county with its "big, big skies, beautiful views and astounding colours that cannot be seen anywhere else".**

Queen's private home to hordes of sightseers from all over the world the Royal estate is still characterised by its peacefulness. Although Sandringham Park has become the venue for major events attracting thousands of people, it is always possible to find a quiet spot on the estate's vast acres of woodland and heath. Each of the seasons has its own appeal – whether it is the magnificent trees in their autumnal colours, the winter frost and snow on the pines or the great banks of rhododendron bushes on a hot summer's day.

Wide stretches of springy turf create ideal picnic spots and paths which criss-cross the estate invite walkers to enjoy unrestricted access to the countryside. These characteristics of the estate remain untouched while subtle developments have been carried out to cater for visitors. A thirty-foot long cedarwood cafeteria, which in 1969 replaced a tea tent stall near the war memorial and car parks, was eventually unable to cope with the growing popularity of the estate.

By the early Nineties it was decided to build a substantial visitor centre which could also be used as a venue for social and charity events. The £750,000 timber-built complex with its air-conditioned self-service restaurant seating 200 has proved a huge success both in the facilities it offers and in the way it blends with its rustic setting. It also complements the extended gift shop nearby which is stocked with all sorts of Royal mementoes and a plant centre offers herbs, flowers and plants grown on the estate.

The Queen and Prince Philip took a keen interest in the project, designed by Lynn architect Desmond Waite. The centre was officially opened by the Queen in April 1994. It proved so popular its opening hours have continually been extended and it even serves coffee on Christmas Day to the crowd who watch the Royal Family attend morning service.

Year by year the number of days the house and grounds have been open has increased in response to public pressure and by 1993 the Queen was opening her Norfolk home seven days a week.

Previously Sandringham had been closed on Fridays and Saturdays which, it was felt, deterred many weekend visitors. This further boost for tourism in Norfolk was followed by extra events in the gardens including classical music concerts combined with firework displays, and open-air Shakespeare performances.

Sandringham Park has for many years provided the setting for a variety of large-scale events ranging from a world Scout jamboree to a national Caravan Club rally as well as the annual Sandringham Flower Show. In 1983 the national carriage driving trials were moved to West Norfolk and have become a fixture on the calendar.

Prince Philip has been a regular competitor and has often been seen out training his horse and pony teams during his stays on the estate. A number of other initiatives have actively encouraged people to use the estate.

Part has been developed as a 600-acre country park with a scenic drive, picnic sites and nature trails. For those who prefer a conducted tour there are rides on a trailer towed by a tractor whose driver identifies many of the rarities among the varied scenery.

Over the years there has been extensive woodland planting with a great variety of trees including some exotic species brought back by successive generations of the Royal Family from their travels abroad.

These areas provide the habitat for a wide variety of wildlife and part of the estate is designated an area of outstanding natural beauty within which is a site of special scientific interest.

Fitting in with this enhancement of natural history and encouragement of wildlife are two caravan and camping sites set unobtrusively amidst the woodland and scarcely visible from the road.

Efforts have been made to educate children about how a country estate is run and each year 4000 youngsters from all over Norfolk took part in a series of open days. Prince Philip initiated the visits which turned Sandringham into an outdoor classroom where 11- to 13-year-olds could see demonstrations of farming, gardening, forestry and gamekeeping and visit the kennels where the Royal Family's dogs are kept and trained.

Thousands of people make an annual pilgrimage to the Royal fruit farm for an exclusive "pick your own" gathering of apples. Apart from special selections of fruit reserved for the Royal household the entire crop is picked by the public.

The Queen has encouraged the sport of clay pigeon shooting by opening a school at Wolferton where members of the Royal Family were among the first to try out the facilities. Prince Philip has also visited the school several times to present prizes to winners of a special competition for young shooters. Many game shooting enthusiasts like to get their eye in with pre-season practice which provides a natural facility on what is a fine sporting estate maintained by the Royal Family for

**The Queen is given an enthusiastic welcome by the waiting crowds during a visit to Thetford in May 1993.**

generations. Game shooting is one of their main pursuits and the Queen often follows the guns and likes to see her retriever dogs in action. The estate regularly plays host to gundog trials which are likely to coincide with one of the Queen's visits.

At Sandringham the Queen can exchange tiaras and glittering evening gowns for a waterproof jacket, headscarf and rubber boots. She is a countrywoman at heart and can relax as she trudges across the fields or rides her horse far away from the formality which dominates so much of her life. The long season when Sandringham House is open – from Easter to October except for the July week when the Queen Mother stays there – does not preclude visits by the Queen and Prince Philip or other members of their family.

Isolated eight-bedroom Wood Farm at Wolferton, which looks across the fields to the Wash, has become a frequent and convenient retreat. One of the Queen's regular stays there is in the spring when she travels to Norfolk to see the season's new foals at the two royal studs. Much of her leisure time is devoted to horses about which she is very knowledgeable. She is an accomplished horsewoman who rides almost daily when she is in residence.

Aureole, Bustino and Shirley Heights are among the famous horses which have maintained the tradition of breeding the cream of British bloodstock at the royal studs where the Queen is a frequent caller. At Sandringham the Queen takes on a different role from that of the sovereign and becomes involved in the responsibilities of an estate owner.

Farmland accounts for 16,000 acres of the estate of which about two-thirds is farmed by tenants and 200 acres are devoted to the production of apples and soft fruit. Both the Queen and Prince Philip have been closely involved with decisions affecting the development of the estate and every month a report is sent to them wherever they may be.

Farming, forestry, the weather and game are not the only topics covered for the Queen's deep personal interest in Sandringham extends far beyond its efficiency and economic success. She has a particular concern for the 140 people who live and work on the estate so she receives news of employees too. The Queen is more reticent than her mother about calling at their homes but she stops and chats when she is out and about and is renowned for remembering the names of their dogs.

Her concern extends to perpetuating the community atmosphere in the eight villages on the estate such as encouraging the success of village clubs. The Queen has maintained the interest of her predecessors in the royal pigeon lofts which led to the rather unusual sight of a royal limousine pulling up at a modest semi-detached house at Kent Road, Gaywood.

For years Len Rush kept the Sandringham lofts in the back garden of his house where the Queen would see the pigeons and then sit and chat in front of a coal fire in his front room. Now the pigeon lofts are on the estate. Such informal visits are in great contrast to most of the Queen's public life. Her first public engagement in Norfolk was in June 1951 when, as Princess Elizabeth, she formally opened Norwich Festival of Britain fortnight.

Even then, as a 25-year-old, she spoke of her "great affection for Norfolk, born of many happy days amidst the peace of its countryside".

Her first official visit to the county as reigning monarch was on July 3rd 1957 when, accompanied by the Duke of Edinburgh, she opened a new operating suite at the Norfolk and Norwich Hospital. Thousands of cheering schoolchildren lined the royal route in the city and thousands more were waiting at the showground at Costessey where the Royal Show was being held. Her next visit was in May 1968 to open the new county hall at Martineau Lane and she then saw another example of contemporary architecture, the partially-completed University of East Anglia. At county hall the Queen again referred to the fact that Norfolk had "a special place in my affection, for my family and I are local residents for some part of each year".

When the Queen next returned to the city

**The Princess of Wales with Prince William at Sandringham on Christmas Day 1994.**

**The Prince of Wales meets ten-year-old Samantha Tungate during a visit to Larkman First and Middle Schools in Norwich in March 1998.**

in April 1975 it was to mark the culmination of 25 years of restoration fund-raising by the Friends of Norwich Cathedral where she attended a service of thanksgiving.

On a November day in 1976 the Queen opened Norfolk Naturalists Trust's conservation centre at Ranworth. She and the Duke took a three-mile river trip along the River Bure from Horning to the floating centre. The Royal couple were back in Norwich as part of the Queen's Silver Jubilee tour of East Anglia when 12,000 Norfolk school children gave her a rapturous welcome at Hewett School playing field. There was another very high profile visit to the city on April 4th 1996 when one of the most colourful and ancient events in the royal calendar was enacted in Norwich Cathedral. The cathedral's 900th anniversary celebrations were crowned when it was chosen as the setting for the Royal Maundy Service.

The Queen presented red purses of traditional Maundy money to seventy men and seventy women, all pensioners from around the county, who were chosen for their service to the community.

The county's RAF stations have received a number of royal visits over the years and RAF Marham enjoys a special relationship with the Queen who is the station's honorary air commodore. The Royal Family use Marham regularly when travelling to and from Sandringham and on alternate years the Queen makes a special visit there to spend several hours seeing how the base operates and meeting personnel and their families.

It is one of a few public engagements the Queen undertakes in West Norfolk during her New Year holiday. She has also been to the Sue Ryder Home at Snettisham, Dersingham Youth and Community Centre, the Queen Elizabeth Hospital at Lynn and on the fortieth anniversary of her accession she spent an hour with patients at a day hospice run by West Norfolk Home Hospice Support Group at Snettisham.

The Queen and Prince Philip arrived on the Royal Yacht Britannia in 1993 at the start of a visit to Yarmouth, the Queen's first visit to Thetford - where Prince Philip opened Kilverstone Mobility Centre - and Lynn.

Other visits by Prince Philip have ranged from seeing Yarmouth Technical High School when it opened in 1954 to visits to two of the county's best-known companies, Norwich Union and Lotus Cars in 1979.

All the Royal Family have carried out engagements in the county and two of the regular visitors have been the Duke and Duchess of Kent who lived at Anmer Hall on the Sandringham estate while their children were growing up. The family shopped at Lynn, the children entered the annual Hunstanton tennis tournament and the Duke and Duchess were regularly in the audience at Lynn Festival. The Duchess sang with the Bach Choir at a festival event. The Duchess made a number of official visits such as to Wells lifeboat in 1985 and she also supports the Norfolk and Norwich Festival.

Prince Charles and Princess Anne had their first experience of public life during stays in West Norfolk. Prince Charles read a lesson at a carol service at West Newton Church when he was 11 and Princess Anne's first official public engagement at the age of nine was to present the prizes at the annual party of Sandringham Sunday School. They also enjoyed informal outings in the area including shopping expeditions to Lynn. Once the Prince bought a water pistol and they both bought toys for their pet budgerigars. When they went with the Queen Mother to watch a meet of West Norfolk Foxhounds at Harpley Dams they threw snowballs at their grandmother.

When he was nine the Prince stayed with the Earl and Countess of Leicester at Holkham Hall to help him recuperate after having his tonsils and adenoids removed. Since then the Princess Royal has visited Norwich as Commandant-in-Chief of the St John Ambulance and has carried out engagements as president of the Save the Children Fund and president of the British Olympic Appeal. She officially opened Norwich Sports Village in 1988 and has also been to Kelling Hospital near Holt, the Equine Rehabilitation Centre at Larling, opened a sheltered housing scheme for the elderly at Aylsham, seen the Nancy Oldfield Trust at Barton Broad, the Clare School in Norwich and a community centre at Banham.

The Prince of Wales has undertaken a variety of official engagements in Norfolk including a trip on Caister lifeboat, a visit to Sheringham Park in 1988 soon after it was bought by the National Trust, and a tour of new building developments in North Norfolk including Letheringsett, Sharrington, Field Dalling, Binham and Walsingham. Prince Charles made several visits to see youngsters taking part in week-long Prince's Trust workshops at Caister. He made his first official visit to Fakenham to see Heath View, an Abbeyfield Society home in 1992 and the same year he joined in lessons at Glebe House School, Hunstanton. Five weeks after storms battered the North Norfolk coast the Prince toured new hides at Cley Marshes in March 1996 and spoke of his childhood memories of the reserve.

Prince Charles met up with Ruth, Lady Fermoy - close friend of his grandmother and maternal grandmother of the Princess of Wales - when he visited True's Yard fishermen's heritage centre at Lynn in 1993. The Prince

**The tragic death of Diana, Princess of Wales in 1997 once again brought home the closeness of Norfolk's royal home to the people of the county. Within hours dozens of floral tributes had appeared at the Norwich Gates; within days, hundreds.**

knew Lady Fermoy from his childhood and referred to her affectionately as "Granny Ruth". They shared a love of music and when Lady Fermoy started the Music in Country Churches charity in 1989 the Prince became its patron. The first concert was held at Salle near Reepham and the Prince has since attended others at Cawston, Walpole St Peter, West Walton and Dersingham. The Prince's choice of Norfolk-born Lady Diana Spencer as his bride inevitably caused great pride and excitement in the county. The Spencer family had close links with the Royal Family. Lady Diana's father, Earl Spencer, had been equerry to George VI and later to the Queen.

Lady Diana was born at Park House on July 1st 1961 and she and her two elder sisters and younger brother grew up as neighbours of the Royal children who used to ask to go for a swim in the heated pool at Park House.

Many West Norfolk people remember Lady Diana growing up at Park House and attending Silfield School at Lynn before going on to Riddlesworth Hall near Diss. She lived at Park House until she was 12 - one third of her life - until her father, then Viscount Althorpe, succeeded to the title and moved to the family home in Northamptonshire. There was an especially warm welcome when the former Lady Diana Spencer returned to Norfolk for her first public appearance in the county as the Princes of Wales and as a member of the Royal Family when they attended church during their Christmas and New Year holiday.

There was a noticeable increase in the size of the crowds at Sandringham when the Princess was there and when Prince William and Prince Harry were old enough to accompany her they were greeted with equal warmth and enthusiasm. The Princess always displayed her own unique relaxed style when she chatted with spectators and she used the informality of the occasion to coax the shy young princes in their first encounters with an admiring public.

In Norfolk, as everywhere else, the Princess's public appearances brought out the crowds such as when she opened the Splash centre at Sheringham. The Princess remained very sentimental about Park House and after it was given by the Queen to the Leonard Cheshire Foundation to be turned into a hotel for the disabled it was with some trepidation that she returned to her former home. But she soon overcame her apprehension when she witnessed the success of the project and she made several visit, often on Christmas Day. In her inimitable style she would kick off her boots in the hall and walk round in stockinged feet chatting to guests - and providing the highlight of their stay.

The tragic death of the Princess in August 1997 was felt very personally in Norfolk and the gates of her birthplace and the nearby Norwich Gates, the main entrance to Sandringham House, became a shrine with thousands of floral tributes.

The Royal estate continues to be a regular destination for the Prince of Wales who spends Christmas and New Year there with Prince William and Prince Harry. They also join their father during spring and autumn visits which last at least a week when Prince Charles combines work and relaxation. He entertains large house parties with members of foreign royal families, politicians and figures from the world of music and the arts among his guests giving him the opportunity to be briefed on current issues.

The last Royal wedding of the century was a fitting reminder of the Royal Family's links with Norfolk. When Prince Edward, newly created Earl of Wessex, married Sophie Rhys-Jones in the historic surroundings of St George's Chapel on June 19th 1999, it was the soon-to-retire Bishop of Norwich, the Rt Rev Peter Nott who conducted the service, assisted by the Rt Rev David Conner, Dean of Windsor - and former Bishop of Lynn. And so those Norfolk links had been underlined in the happiest manner.

## CHAPTER 4

# Norfolk Art and Culture

Any assessment of homespun culture in the twentieth century, especially work coated in the Norfolk vernacular, must be prefaced by what came - or did not come - earlier.

Just before a Victorian age dominated by pleasantly prettified village scenes bearing little or no relation to harsh rural life, a country parson compiled what is still regarded as the "bible" for local dialect lovers. The Rev Robert Forby (1759-1825) wrote A Vocabulary of East Anglia, published five years after his death and containing about 2000 words and phrases. He supplemented his own knowledge with notes from numerous correspondents in other parts of Norfolk and in Suffolk and Essex. His "Icenian Glossary" took shape while he was Rector of Fincham, and he clearly felt he was launching a final flourish for the local tongue.

Pointing to popular dialects in his introduction, Forby lamented: *"Will they not be overwhelmed and borne down by the general onset of the various plans and unwearied exertions for the education of us all?"*

The scholarly parson thus started a trend still going strong at the end of the nineteenth century, and persisting up to the present, even among those who cherish this vital aspect of local culture. Thankfully, every time the funeral is organised the corpse sits up and mocks the pall-bearers.

Harry Cozens-Hardy, who edited the first Broad Norfolk book published in 1893 from letters sent to the Eastern Daily Press, prophesied the dialect would die out within a generation under the influence of the Board Schools. Jonathan Mardle, delightful pseudonym of EDP essayist and leader writer Eric Fowler, was tempted to hold up "the end is nigh" placards when he edited and introduced another Broad Norfolk selection in 1949. In his volume of the same title in 1973 he suggested the dialect had lasted so long because of *"the unkind truth - true right down to the Twenties - of the saying that Norfolk is cut off to the north and east by the sea, and to the south and west by the London & North Eastern Railway."* Nevertheless, it was remarkable that the language of the North folk, the South folk and the East Saxons, whose ancestors settled 1500 years ago between the North Sea and the then undrained Fens, had survived until the Seventies with a different intonation and accent, a different turn of phrase, and to some extent a different vocabulary and grammar from those of any other part of Britain.

The "dew diffrunt" gospel still rules, surviving a considerable number of influences thrown up by unbridled development and a media explosion and chances are the preservation spirit will continue to make an impact deep into the next century. One of the main reasons behind that hope for survival could be the fact that newcomers will continue to be as interested as natives in the peculiar tongue of the province in which they have settled.

After Forby's priceless contribution to the local cause, another Norfolk parson made his distinctive mark by translating the Song of Solomon into Norfolk dialect. The Rev Edward Gillett (1819-1869) undertook the work in 1862 and it was printed with translations for 23 other counties at the expense of Prince Louis Bonaparte, in exile in Britain. Gillett, then the Vicar of Runham, admitted he was not acquainted with any suitable phonetic spelling with which to indicate the "Norfolk drant", but his rendering shows a relatively successful attempt at a reproduction of the dialect. His Song O' Sorlomun was reprinted in

**KEITH SKIPPER has been closely connected with the local media for almost forty years as writer, broadcaster and champion of the Norfolk cause. Still a regular contributor to the Eastern Daily Press, he has written nearly twenty books, all with a distinctive Norfolk flavour. He leads the Press Gang, a troupe of travelling entertainers preaching the local gospel, and is in regular demand at all kinds of functions to share his fund of dialect stories and love of the county. Born at Beeston, near Dereham, he attended the village school and Hamond's Grammar School at Swaffham before joining the old Norfolk News Company as a reporter in 1962. He now operates as a freelance from his Cromer home.**

**For many years the literary doyen of Norwich, Ralph Mottram (1883-1971) was born in the city of which he was to become Lord Mayor. He served in France from 1914 until 1919 and later published The Spanish Farm, his first novel. It won the Hawthornden Prize and featured a preface written by his champion, John Galsworthy. Its sequels, Sixty-Four! Ninety-Four! and The Crime at Vanderlynden's, were equally successful and in 1927 the three were published as The Spanish Farm Trilogy. In all, Mottram wrote more than sixty books, with many set locally. Our Mr Dormer was based on Gurney's Bank, later Barclays, where the author served for many years. He was awarded the honorary degree of Doctor of Letters by the UEA in 1966. On his death, old friend Eric Fowler said: "He recognised the defects as well as the virtues of the past and kept to the end of his life the Victorian faith in progress."**

1993 by the Larks Press, one of the county's best little publishing houses.

The most prolific dialect writer of them all was a Victorian editor of the EDP, blazing a trail destined to inspire so much humorous material ever after. James Spilling (1825-1897) was an intellectual who knew the value of a homely and jocular touch. Between 1870 and 1890 he wrote Sketches in dialect in Eastern Counties stories in the language of the people, possibly the most extended use of the vernacular that has been attempted. Giles's Trip to London, first and most successful of his humorous series, was singled out by London newspapers as "not only the best example of the Norfolk dialect ever given to the world, but also an admirable and spirited piece of farcical humour."

It was an immediate hit, going on to sell in its hundreds of thousands, and has recently been republished by Jarrolds, the Norwich family firm behind the original printing of Spilling's work. A rich mixture of affection and reverence prompted a telling forecast from a Norfolk News staff writer on Spilling's death in 1897: *"The fun in it (Giles's Trip) has no vein of cynicism or contemptuousness. James Spilling's bucolics are loveable ingenues with many homely virtues. They are a faithful type, and as such they will long survive in the public regard."*

During my research into Spilling's outstanding newspaper career for a new introduction for Giles's Trip to London, I discovered genuine concern for the plight of agricultural labourers – a strand destined to take on a darker and deeper significance in Norfolk writing at the turn of the century. In the Eastern Weekly Press, Spilling poured out leaders, special articles of rural interest and stories dealing with country life and the hardships of the labourers.

So, if Spilling inspired much of the comic dialect writing to follow, he must also be lauded for preparing the path to more serious dissertations when it became evident that for all its seductive images, the Norfolk countryside was falling apart in the closing years of the nineteenth century.

Enter the Norfolk School of Rural Realism brigade – a learned country parson, a Victorian romancer, a farmer's wife and a "drop-out" from London and the law.

Dr Augustus Jessopp (1824-1914) was headmaster of King Edward VI School in Norwich for twenty years before he became Rector of Scarning in 1879, looking after his country parish near Dereham for more than three decades. A number of historical works underlined an intense curiosity about everyday life in the past. Even so, Arcady For Better For Worse remains for many his most intriguing work, simply because it highlights his views on village life at a time when the gap between the haves and the have-nots was much wider than the Dereham bypass. His strictures on rural ignorance provoked an indignant response in the local press, including a lengthy "Defence of the Norfolk Labourer" with this curt suggestion: *"I would advise the author of this trash to hire a country shop and live right in the midst of these so-called ignorant people."* Such reaction was hardly surprising given memorable lines like these from Jessopp: *"Always shrewd, the Norfolk peasant is never tender. A wrong, real or imagined, rankles with him through a lifetime... refinement of feeling he is quite incapable of."* No change there, then, some newcomers might mutter today!

At least the learned cleric was reasonably close to those he felt obliged to chastise. All too regularly in more recent years Norfolk has had to put up with cheap and nasty jibes from smart metropolitans firing away from a safe distance. Remarkably, Jessopp did manage to gain the ear and then the confidence of surly and suspicious villagers, and they inspired his most powerful writing. For example, he struck up an unlikely liaison with "Loafing Ben", a burly ne'er-do-well who scraped a sort of living as a casual labourer. Jessopp called at the homestead:

*"His old parents were fading out of life, the vital spark in the mere ashes that remained gleaming every now and then, and twinkling, when a human dust was stirred by a basin of broth or a drop of some stimulant. They were feebly cowering over the shadow of a fire in*

*the miserable shanty, and as I sat with them and felt my way by speaking of 'such things as pass human understanding', I fancied I saw the semblance of faint emotion in one or the other. Somehow I found myself kneeling down upon the mud floor."*

Harrowing lines from the Scarning scholar, now enjoying a richly-deserved revival with the recent formation of an Arcadian Club to spotlight his life and work.The first meeting at Scarning in 1996 featured a collection towards paying for the restoration of the local graves of Augustus and his wife, Margaret.

Sir Henry Rider Haggard (1856-1925), born at West Bradenham, returned from colonial service in South Africa to become a gentleman-farmer on the Norfolk-Suffolk border. It remains a matter for some debate as to why one of the most successful novelists of the day should turn to farming when most of those who could were getting out. The drift from the land had become a stampede. Cheap corn from the prairies of Canada and the United States was flooding Europe. A run of wet summers had washed away harvests and hope. A million rural workers, half the workforce at the time, and their families emigrated to the cities. Rinderpest, sheep-liver rot and an outbreak of foot-and-mouth disease put black edges round a doom-laden picture.

To this scene of collapse, stagnation and abandonment rode the romancer of King Solomon's Mines and She. From the Boers and Transvaal to 365 acres at Bedingham and Ditchingham. Haggard used A Farmer's Year, his comprehensive diary of 1898, not just to record the degradation of English farming but also to make general recommendations; the government should give financial aid to agriculture, revise land taxes, alter ratings, take firmer measures against the adulteration of farm produce and devise cheaper transport to enable the farmer to sell his produce to market more effectively. A two-volume work, Rural England, published in 1902, reinforced calls for governments to cultivate salvation. Rudyard Kipling, a close friend and admirer, sent more praise from Sussex and there was enthusiastic support for Haggard from Thomas Hardy, from whose articles, The Dorsetshire Labourer, he had quoted.

Apostolic fervour did not wane, although it took far too long for Haggard's warnings and demands to rouse a profoundly conservative society. A fundamental belief in the superiority of village existence to that of the city remained at the heart of Haggard's creed, a creed followed with relish by a host of succeeding local writers, albeit without Haggard's international reputation.

Ronald Blythe, whose Akenfield stands as a memorable statement about living in an East Anglian village at the beginning of the second half of the twentieth century, described A Farmer's Year as "at once an important and authoritative compendium of farming practice, a private confessional, a history of turn-of-the-century Norfolk, and, in its way, an entertainment". Not bad for a diary put together by a purveyor of adventure fiction!

The other two members of the Norfolk School of Rural Realism to shine through countryside deprivation at the turn of the century have suffered sore neglect. Mary Mann (1848-1929) and James Blyth (1864-1933) were determined to show rural plight rather than rustic charm, and both employed the Norfolk dialect in ways it had not been used before. Rather than create a barrier between page and reader, it added extra power, poignancy and immediacy. It showed for the first time how dialect could be employed as a vehicle for radical enlightenment as well as for gentle amusement.

Born in Norwich, Mary Mann became a farmer's wife at Shropham, a rather isolated village used as the setting for The Fields of Dulditch, her most celebrated stories first published in 1902. They contained brutal accounts of the lives of labouring families at a time when grinding poverty was not only commonplace but also seemingly incurable. Her husband farmed 800 acres and assumed the role of caring squire. She helped teach reading at the village school, organised treats and was a frequent visitor at the labourers' homes. When her husband died in 1913, she took a home at Winterton and finally moved to Sheringham.

Adrian Bell, whose own books about his

**Sir Henry Rider Haggard: Farmer's diary.**

**Mary Mann: Sorely neglected.**

*The past is a foreign country: they do things differently there."* And so one of the most memorable first lines of any twentieth century novel begins L P Hartley's study of lost innocence, The Go-Between. His 1953 title is one of the very best of the many books set in Norfolk or written by Norfolk-based authors in the past 100 years.

In the same way Norfolk has attracted generations of painters with its combination of landscape, wide skies and - prosaically - its relative cheapness as a base, so writers have been attracted in their droves to the county. The Go-Between was not the only Norfolk-set book from Hartley (1895-1972), with lovers of Hunstanton finding a thinly-disguised version of the resort in the Eustace and Hilda trilogy.

It is interesting how often writers have set detective fiction in the county, seeing either an inherent brooding strangeness in the Norfolk landscape, or alternatively enjoying the dramatic juxtaposition of brutal events set against its natural beauty. Sylvia Harmon (1915-95), writing as S T Haymon, set her hero Det Insp Ben Jurney in many a county setting. C P Snow chose the peace and quiet of the Broads to set his murder mystery Death Under Sail (1932).

More recently P D James (1920- ) had her detective Adam Dalgleish come across evil in the idyllic surrounds of "Larksoken" in Devices and Desires. Ruth Rendell (1930- ), writing as Barbara Vine - a pseudonym she reserves for what often turn out as her darkest psychological studies - set her The Brimstone Wedding (1986) in the county.

Sir Arthur Conan Doyle's debt to North Norfolk's famous Black Shuck legend is mentioned elsewhere in this chapter, but the area also provided the setting for one of the most popular short stories of the canon, The Dancing Men. The "Ridling Thorpe Manor" of the story has been identified with Happisburgh.

**Happisburgh has been identified as the setting for a Sherlock Holmes story.**

Still on the subject of detection, Dorothy L Sayers (1893-1957) put her fenland years to use in setting The Nine Taylors (1934) against a Fens background. The Wimsey family seat at "Bredon Hall" is located at "Duke's Denver" which, if the clues in her books are followed, ought to be around Narborough.

P G Wodehouse stayed with the Le Strange family of Hunstanton Hall on many occasions and there are many Norfolk references in his works.

The brooding nature of the fenland western edge of Norfolk was brilliantly portrayed by Graham Swift (1949- ) in his award-winning Waterland (1983), a dark tale of sexual repression set against the backdrop of the "River Leem".

There was no disguising the setting Hopton-born author Henry Sutton (1963- ) chose for the setting of his 1995 novel. By calling it Gorleston he excited much local comment - and even threats of legal action. Hellesdon-born David Holbrook (1923- ) was on much less controversial ground with Getting It Wrong With Uncle Tom (1998), set in Glandford in 1936. The novel was notable for its splendid use of local dialect and colour.

Janet Mark (1943- ) won the Carnegie Medal for her children's novel Thunder and Lightnings (1976) set round "Polthorpe", based on Stalham, while Gissing was the location for another award-winning work, The Chymical Wedding (1989) which secured the Whitbread prize for author Lindsay Clarke (1939- ). Also worthy of note is Sylvia Townsend Warner (1893-1978) who set The Corner That Held Them (1954) in Oby during the fourteenth century

Thriller writer Jack Higgins' (1929- ) most famous work, The Eagle Has Landed, pondered a daring Nazi raid to kidnap Winston Churchill from a North Norfolk house.

And Dereham's proud links with Brian Aldiss (1925 - ), novelist and science fiction writer - noted elsewhere in this chapter - have also been celebrated with the naming of Aldiss Court after the family's former store.

experiences as a Suffolk farmer lit up heavy furrows in the early Thirties, wrote: *"The people of Dulditch are more real to me than Hardy's... although the record of rural penury is so shocking that it awes the writing to simplicity, it leaves an epic quality in the mind, a sort of noble rage which makes for life."*

D H Lawrence was another ardent admirer of Mary Mann's work, which included stark depiction of serious problems confronting farmers. Her first novel, The Parish of Hilby, includes an episode about a young farmer coping with a strike on his land, while Moonlight opens with the suicide of a bankrupt farmer. The Fields of Dulditch was reissued in 1976, while her Tales of Victorian Norfolk, selected by tireless champions Ted Goodwyn and John Baxter, were published in 1991. *"Norfolk's long indifference to Mary Mann is a disgrace,"* exclaimed the introduction, quoting Hugh Massingham's verdict when he reviewed her novel The Parish Nurse in 1905: *"Norfolk has in her a writer of whom it may well be proud, who should in time come into her kingdom."*

James Blyth is a much more complex and controversial figure. He wrote too much - he had 25 novels published between 1906 and 1909 - and tried his hand at many styles. But his best work has extraordinary power, his earliest volumes underlining a feeling and a flair for the local vernacular matched by few during the rest of the century. His rendering, not merely in humorous anecdotes but in serious, even tragic passages, is one of the hallmarks of his most outstanding contributions to Norfolk literature.

He was born Henry James Clabburn at Thorpe St Andrew, educated at Norwich School and Corpus Christi, Cambridge, and then articled to a firm of solicitors in Lincoln's Inn. Something happened which caused him to leave London - a doomed romance is the most popular theory - change his name and bury himself in a cottage on the edge of the marshes at Fritton on the south-east corner of Norfolk. He had to live by his pen. Juicy Joe, A Romance of the Norfolk Marshlands, was published in 1902.

It remains a powerful and original evocation of rural existence, not just for highlighting the extreme contrast between the metropolis and the sparsely-populated marshlands but for dealing with contemporary questions such as divorce laws and rights of women. Blyth spared no feeling in his introduction to Juicy Joe, making some attacks from trendy, attention-seeking "personalities" of more recent times appear like paeans of praise in comparison:

*"The habits, customs and morality have seen no change for centuries; Christianity is used solely as a cloak for vice. The more regular the church or chapel goer, the greater the hypocrite. Witches, wizards, ghosts and phantom animals are, if the tales of the marshes may be credited, as common as mushrooms. To throw any doubt upon the powers of the local witch is to incur the opprobrium and contempt of the whole neighbourhood. It is difficult to believe that such places exist in England in the twentieth century."*

A trifle melodramatic, perhaps, but Blyth knew there was little chance of those being so indicted reading all about it. Coarse, sensual, treacherous and drunken on a good day, according to him, they were unlikely to curl up with Blyth's first published novel after a lively session at the village inn. No such insurance for A N Wilson, a Fellow of the Royal Society of Literature, who launched a notorious attack in the Arts pages of the Sunday Telegraph in July 1991. He turned his talents to sizing up the week's television programmes, and out of disappointment in a play with a rural setting he contrived this savage summary: *"As well as being very flat, Norfolk is full of curmudgeonly human monsters. Tucked away in their bleak villages beneath the large threatening sky, they are still as belligerent as they were in the days of Queen Boadicea."*

Hail to thee, Blyth spirit, still going strong ninety years on! It is hardly surprising that Norfolk has betrayed regular pangs of a persecution complex during the past century. While geography bequeathed an isolation to shape character and largely protect it, the

**Best-selling author and a Methodist local preacher for more than sixty years, Cyril Jolly (1911-94) of Gressenhall was also a tireless champion of the Norfolk dialect. For many years he wrote dialect letters, published in a popular booklet called Jimma's Mathodist Latters. His best-known book – later filmed – is The Vengeance of Private Pooley, the true story of how two soldiers, one of them from Dereham, escaped the massacre of 97 of their comrades by the SS. Other work included the definitive biography of one of Britain's most famous lifeboatmen, Henry Blogg of Cromer, and The Spreading Flame, the story of Methodism in Norfolk. He also had a claim to fame as one of the most well-informed non-commissioned officers of the Second World War, holding a D-Day secret which in the wrong hands could have changed history – he knew full details of the RAF's invasion plans.**

**Arnold Wesker: Took Norfolk-set drama to the international stage.**

**Lilias Rider Haggard: I Walked By Night and The Rabbit Skin Cap are classic Norfolk works.**

world beyond, increasingly predatory and jealous of distinctiveness and individuality, has misunderstood and misrepresented to the point of absurdity. Bogus Norfolk voices on radio and television programmes are the most blatant example of this indifference to local pride, heritage and artistic accuracy. If programme makers take the trouble to make it clear they are in a specific place for a specific purpose, it must make sense to get the basics right.

That creed was accepted most memorably by playwright Arnold Wesker when he made genuine attempts to find out how Norfolk people talked for his play Roots, first staged at the Belgrade Theatre in Coventry on May 25th 1959, with Joan Plowright in the main role. *"This is a play about Norfolk people; it could be a play about any country people and the moral could certainly extend to the metropolis. But as it is about Norfolk people it is important that some attempt is made to find out how they talk,"* said Wesker, even including notes on pronunciation to help "furriners" get somewhere near the accent and intonation. A few years working in the county, and marriage to a Norfolk girl, obviously helped - but Wesker set a trend few have seen fit to follow.

Indeed, even he has admitted to embarrassment bordering on shame at some counterfeit coinage dispensed by casts of Roots on stage and television. No surprise to hear Wesker talk most fondly of a production at the Maddermarket Theatre in Norwich.

The difficulties of writing in dialect are obvious. There are no firm rules, and many native supporters have dubbed it "mission impossible", only to make stirring efforts to prove themselves wrong. Dick Bagnall-Oakeley (1908-1974) dialect expert, naturalist and teacher at Gresham's School in Holt, had serious misgivings about committing the local language to print. "Its accents and vowel sounds are too subtle, too varied and too rich for the alphabet which suffices for the rest of the English tongue." That didn't stop Dick writing down many of the tales he delivered with such gusto as a speaker in demand at all kinds of functions. He provided a warning for those who might not fully appreciate the art of understatement: "Just as their language, so also the people of Norfolk are tough, resilient and impenetrable. They guard to themselves the secrets of their language and of their humour. Yet humour there is in the Norfolk people, riotous and abundant. When you read Norfolk tales, remember they are tales about a highly-observant, subtle and recondite people. Therefore, always think twice before you laugh at a Norfolk tale - the laugh might be on you!"

Problems in setting down Norfolk speech have preoccupied many other leading figures lending it colourful and constant support. Russell Colman, Lord Lieutenant of the county and himself an impressive spinner of yarns, emphasised the difficulty in 1930 in his foreword to B Knyvet Wilson's Norfolk Tales and Memories: *"I have never experienced any difficulty in speaking Norfolk but, quite frankly, I do not know how to write it."* He was hinting strongly that this form of literature was more an art to be read aloud and listened to, intonation and accent being items for the ear rather than the eye.

Perhaps the most successful combination of the two, written and spoken entertainments, arrived just after the Second World War when a well-established rustic comedian dropped a few lines to the EDP. Sidney Grapes, alias The Boy John, wrote his first letter in January 1946, and kept up the habit until shortly before his death in 1958. The letters, written in the character of a Norfolk countryman who wrote as he spoke and spelled as he pleased, were eagerly awaited and remain the most oft-quoted examples of Norfolk's own tongue and sense of fun. It is not too fanciful to suggest these contributions have done as much as anything to keep Norfolk's precious sense of identity alive in an increasingly grey world. Certainly, they have inspired a whole generation of local entertainers to stay true to the traditional Norfolk credo - dare your listener to get there first and then milk the moment as you finish together in a gale of laughter.

Those weaned on the uncluttered delights of the Boy John Letters can hardly believe they

**Sidney Grapes: Much-loved Norfolk entertainer whose Boy John letters to the EDP retain a wide and loyal readership.**

**Norfolk fisherman and traditional singer, Sam Larner (1878-1965) was "discovered" when he was nearly eighty. With Harry Cox from Barton Turf, he represented the high point of East Anglian singing between the wars and immediately post-war. Born at Winterton, Sam first went to sea in 1892 and had eight years in sailing boats. In Singing the Fishing, a radio ballad by Charles Parker, Ewan MacColl and Peggy Seager, Sam relived those years, his vivid Norfolk speech beautifully integrated with the music. This venture brought him widespread fame, and he made two more equally successful recordings, Now is the Time for Fishing and Sam Larner, A Garland for Sam. He was a poet of the everyday. In his review of the recordings Tony Green wrote: "Not for him the nostalgia of the good old days, rather the ambivalent feelings of a man who knew the job backwards and felt pride in it, identified himself with it, but could never love it, for it was too hard and dangerous to love."**

are half a century old, especially when audiences of all ages fall under their spell at harvest supper, village concert or family reunion. Early epistles from Sidney Grapes, who lived all his life in the Broadland village of Potter Heigham, were full of post-war austerity, but a twinkling humour drawn from the very heart of the country shone through from the start. Collections of the letters have sold in their thousands. They are rooted in time and place but retain real charm and value because they are wholly unpretentious, gently amusing, generally accessible and admirably self-effacing.

Sidney, the archetypal Norfolk comedian at local concerts and dinners, knew his audience well, and he was able to transfer those prize instincts to his 12-year exercise destined to reach a far wider gathering.

An international expert in the dialect field has described The Boy John Letters as "work of not a little genius". Peter Trudgill, proud of his Norfolk roots, is Professor of English Linguistics at the University of Lausanne in Switzerland and his scrutiny of the close link between language and society is seen as a key weapon in the fight against a culturally standardised world. In a paper presented to a Helsinki conference a few years ago he said of the letters: *"Not only were the characterisations and vignettes of village life brilliant, and therefore enormously popular, but Sidney Grapes was also a superb writer of the local dialect, right down to subtleties such as Granfar speaking in a more conservative, traditional way than the other characters."*

While humour is a key component in Norfolk's battle to "dew diffrunt", the Professor warned that if dialects were to survive they must be used in as wide a range of contexts as possible. *"The Norfolk dialect is a vital means of helping preserve Norfolk values, culture, way of life. It is also important, more than many other dialects, since it is one of the last dialects in the south of England, and especially the south-east of England, to remain relatively distinctive and relatively widely spoken."* Can it survive? *"Yes, though, like all dialects, it will continue to change. It is most likely to survive if we can engender and preserve positive attitudes to all forms of Norfolk English – that is, not just traditional county speech but also the traditional and more recent vernaculars of Norwich and Yarmouth."*

Born in Norwich, with all of his 16 great-great-grandparents coming from the east of the county, Professor Trudgill thinks schools could do more to encourage the local dialect by fostering pride and interest and by countering snobbery and negative feelings.

That sort of academic interest and support, albeit from a fiercely-proud son of Norfolk, has lent significant weight to the campaign against directing Norfolk dialect towards the obituary columns. That campaign collected its biggest fillip in years when a special EDP survey sent out this uplifting message in May 1993: "There is a future for the Norfolk dialect!" An editorial headlined "Demise is Squit" began proudly: *"Twain-like, reports of the demise of the Norfolk dialect have been greatly exaggerated."* It said the survey showed a remarkable resilience confirming the dialect had a future which the National Curriculum Council should recognise. *"The council for good and obvious reasons wants to encourage spoken standard English. But dialect is a legitimate and honourable element of good speech, a vigorous and enhancing dimension that should be prized and encouraged. The enemy of good speech is not genuine dialect, but a rootless babble, or as we say with Norfolk succinctness, 'squit'."*

The survey, first serious attempt to measure the strength of the dialect for many years, asked readers to identify twenty dialect words, including "dodman" (snail), "harnser" (heron), "troshel" (threshold) and "dickey" (donkey). Nearly 500 adults and children proved that local vocabulary still figured in their speech. Although the over-sixties predictably came out on top with an average of 75 per cent, youngsters fared better than expected. A Thetford schoolgirl scored 17 out of twenty. A big crop of letters followed the survey and its results, most correspondents warming to the survival cause despite inevitable fears that it would continue to be diluted as the county became more

**Norfolk's churches, landscapes and wide skies have proved an inspiration for writers and artists for generations.**

cosmopolitan. At the outset of the twentieth century many old country people had a vocabulary of fewer than a thousand words which had changed little since the Middle Ages. Many words and expressions disappeared with the trades and pursuits that inspired them. The need to record remnants of a fast-disappearing rural culture was accepted and met long before the advent of the family video or the growth of the splendid local film archives at the University of East Anglia. George Ewart Evans (1911-1988) was the father of the oral history movement in this area and doyen of its development throughout the country. He spent his final years at Brooke, near Norwich, and his books on the old ways of farming and the rural conditions of the region, including The Horse in the Furrow, Ask the Fellows Who Cut The Hay, The Pattern Under The Plough and The Days That We Have Seen are an integral part of history libraries throughout this country and abroad. Born and educated among the miners of South Wales, he moved to Suffolk in 1948 and came to realise that the old villagers were the last link with a rural culture destroyed by mechanisation. He set about collecting details of their lives and their language, making full use of tape recordings.

In sharp contrast, the dog-eared and grimy pages of an old exercise book were transformed into one of the classics of countryside literature, first published in 1935 and still ensnaring readers with its simple directness. "*What is written here was born of an old man's loneliness as he sat in a little cottage perched high on a hill, overlooking the Waveney Valley, with no company but his dog. The life that he loved had passed him by. As he puts it 'Some said I had given up the game - but the game gave me up'.*" So begins the memorable preface by Lilias Rider Haggard (1893-1968) to I Walked By Night, the volume she fashioned from the notes of the self-styled King of the Norfolk Poachers, Frederick Rolfe.

**Colin Riches: Methodist minister who produced popular collections of Bible stories re-told in Norfolk dialect.**

A few years later she edited and shaped another outstanding work, The Rabbit Skin Cap, a tale of a Norfolk countryman's youth. This time George Baldry presented the willing Lilias with the raw material, again liberally spiced with dialect, and so she completed an impressive double. Youngest daughter of Sir Henry Rider Haggard, she inherited his writing talents and her books on Norfolk are among the best the county has inspired. Norfolk Life, Norfolk Notebook and Country Scrapbook are splendid selections of her articles for the EDP. The two books she prepared for publication from homespun notes are among the most original in local literature.

Another woman to earn tributes for her dialect writing was Ida Fenn (1899-1980), who dealt in the broad Norfolk of the Flegg villages around Yarmouth. For more than twenty years she contributed her Tales of a Countryman to the Yarmouth Mercury. She also wrote regular farming columns, many other articles for magazines and two novels set in Norfolk, but it will be for her yarns of the countryman, The Boy Jimma, that she will be best remembered. Recommending them when they were published in book form in 1973, Eric Fowler of the EDP said: *"She has lived the old Norfolk life - and the old Flegg life - and neither radio, TV nor 'foreign' settlers in our villages have changed the dialect she has spoken since childhood... Her characters are true to Norfolk in their nature as well as in their dialect."*

It is remarkable how much dialect writing has flourished in our local newspapers throughout the twentieth century. Arthur Patterson (1857-1935) was a self-taught naturalist who became an authority on Breydon Water, the estuary at Yarmouth which inspired much of his writing under the gloriously self-denigrating name of John Knowlittle. He produced 26 books as well as countless articles for all kinds of publications, but found time between 1893 and 1931 to contribute Melinda Twaddle's Notions, a weekly article in dialect, to the Yarmouth Mercury. Maurice Woods, a former London editor of the EDP, wrote Harbert's News from Dumpton in the local weekly papers for almost forty years - that's about 1900 episodes after agreeing to a trial run in 1951. Cyril Jolly's career as a Methodist local preacher for more than sixty years was punctuated by letters in the vernacular to the Methodist Recorder in London and the Dereham and Fakenham Times "just up the rood". He started the exercise in 1965, and Jimma's Mathodist Latters have more than a flavour of the Boy John about them. In more recent times, Michael Brindid of Hickling wrote regular dialect letters to the EDP and had two books of them published.

A widespread compulsion to transform items of temporary amusement into collections of permanent value became the cornerstone of that campaign to keep Norfolk dialect to the fore.

There was a twist in the Seventies tale when Methodist minister Colin Riches produced two books of Bible stories in the local dialect, Dew Yew Lissen Hare and Orl Bewtiful An' New, several of them originally featuring on Anglia Television late-night religious slot. Colin said one of his early influences was Bernard Miles telling Bible stories on the radio in his delightful Hertfordshire accent.

Former village headmaster John Kett, himself a lay reader, earned the title of doyen of local dialect poetry, delighting reflective readers and animated audiences for nearly half a century. Four volumes of Norfolk verse netted sales of well over 20,000. He pulled all strands together, from whimsical verses in dialect to more serious themes in his anthology, A Late Lark Singing, published in 1997.

The old adage about Norfolk entertainment being unfit for travel beyond the county boundary was mocked a few times, perhaps most effectively by The Singing Postman, Allan Smethurst, in the Sixties when he took his anthem Hev Yew Got A Loight, Boy? into the national popular music charts. A postman from Norfolk rubbing shoulders with The Beatles on television's Top of the Pops remains one of the most incongruous sights - and sounds - of the century!

Concert parties doing the local rounds put on a more formal footing the sort of banter and well-worn routines that used to be an automatic part of life at the village pub before fruit machines, satellite television, pool tables and eating areas took over. David "Muck Carter" Lambert, in rustic outfit to match his droll delivery, drew inevitable comparisons with Sidney Grapes as he elevated earthy humour to an art form for well over two decades. A shy, modest man, David gloried in the role of the countryman who wasn't such a fool as he looked. The audience would be laughing at him half way through a yarn but by the time he got to the punchline, they were laughing with him.

Sid Kipper, alias Chris Sugden, hailed from the fictitious parish of St Just-near-Trunch to blossom into the county's finest ambassador as a folk-singing megastar, engaging storyteller and writer of quality. Despite being resident in Yorkshire much of the time, he has lauded Norfolk on his extensive entertainment travels and most of his writing is based on the county. Sid's irreverent brand of humour and love of word play are admirably served by Prewd and Prejudice, the mock diary of a London lady who headed for the depths of rural Norfolk in 1904. St Just-near-Trunch was only half civilised. Plants grew unchecked, unruly birds woke her before dawn, there was not a milliner for miles and Harrods flatly refused to deliver. Despite these hardships, Miriam Prewd undertook a one-year, one-woman mission to bring refinement and manners to the village.

Sid Kipper, a regular at international folk festivals and in the recording studios, has added fresh dimensions to a proud cultural cause, capturing the true spirit of Norfolk, teaching it new tricks and then unleashing it to run riot across the land.

While dialect and humour combined to spearhead Norfolk's rejection of false images, and afford some protection against the slings and arrows of outrageous impersonation and misrepresentation, more "orthodox" methods of sustaining a county's pride and glory were operating alongside. Native scribes, literary newcomers, academic birds of passage, poetic refugees, homesick exiles - all used Norfolk as an inspiring backcloth.

The University of East Anglia was established on the edge of Norwich in 1962 and began to pull together strands of the region's cultural and artistic life. In 1970

**Allan Smethurst, The Singing Postman: Perhaps Norfolk's most unlikely cultural export. Some criticised him for reinforcing yokel stereotypes of Norfolk people, but Norwich-raised novelist and critic D J Taylor was more complimentary, saying in 1994 the singer reminded him of "a mostly roseate universe of following the combines over wheatfield at the fag-end of summer, watching the crab-boats set out, taking rattletrap trains into Norwich for the winter sales.**
**"The Singing Postman has gone now, along with the old Norwich cattle market and the Gaumont cinema. But I salute a man who seems as much a part of my childhood as Great Yarmouth funfair or the boats drawn up on the Sheringham shale."**

**A prolific writer who gloried in the true feel of Norfolk, Jane Hales (1904-95) lived all her years in the same seventeenth-century house on Norwich Road in Holt. Her final book reached the printers just before her death with the title Ninety Years in One House. Her books and countless articles for the EDP and other publications on Norfolk life, traditions and history entertained readers for more than half a century. She was welfare officer for the Norfolk branch of the Red Cross for thirty years, a period which included coping with the floods of 1953. She was made an MBE in 1982 for her work. "The moral in planning for floods," she once said, "is that there must be a local representative on the spot. And you have to remember that floods seem to come after dark, usually when the battery of your torch is running down!"**

Professor Malcolm Bradbury, along with celebrated literary figure Angus Wilson, a founder member of the University, pioneered the now world-famous post-graduate creative writing course, first of its kind in Britain. Its first student was Ian McEwan, soon followed by Kazuo Ishiguro. They and several others, including Rose Tremain, blossomed to give the Booker Prize competition a colourful name for being dominated by the "East Anglian literary mafia"! Norfolk references and backgrounds may have been thin on the ground in all this modern material, but the county's reputation as a base for encouraging talented writers was vigorously enhanced.

Certain landscapes beguile writers into pouring powers of description and unashamed affection into one specific part of an area renowned for beauty and variety. Arthur Ransome dipped his pen into Broadland before it became a packed holiday playground, and his charming adventure stories now reinforce that sense of loss felt most keenly by those who saw the encroaching tide of commercialism gather force. Ransome did sense big changes on the way, and his Coot Club provided a picture of pressures piling up on Broadland's fragile ecology, all seen through the eyes of childhood.

Michael Home (real name Christopher Bush) preserved lost landscapes and the lost communities that depended on them in his Breckland novels and memoirs. Vast Forestry Commission plantations and the setting up of the Stanford Battle Area hastened the end of a world he knew and drew so lovingly in books like God and the Rabbit and The Harvest Is Past.

Edward Storey has been influenced for over 50 years by the great distances, skies, fields, rivers and people of the Fens. He looks at history as well as geography: "There is a certain spirit about a place which makes it different from all other places, which gives it an identity and, in turn, draws from its local inhabitants a loyalty which is hard to define." Spirit of the Fens was his most penetrating study so far of this area, and in a foreword to the book, Graham Swift, author of the much-praised Waterland, said: *"I could indeed have wished for such a book as this beside me as I made my own independent and faltering investigations of the region. As these pages abundantly show, the Fens are, peculiarly, not just a landscape but a state of mind, a mood, a human as well as geographical condition."* Edward Storey was a founder-member of the Eastern Arts Association's Literature Panel and spent much time encouraging creative writing in the classroom.

Fresh voices rang out towards the end of the century to prove a little distance could lend much enchantment. D J Taylor, pursuing a career as storyteller and critic based in London, used his native Norwich liberally in work bold and inventive enough to defy his own printed claims that the novel was dead. The city played a pivotal role in Real Life (1992) in the same way it had fashioned so much of R H Mottram's writing in the first half of the century. Dereham-born Brian Aldiss, a past chairman of the Society of Authors, gave his knowledge of Norfolk life full rein in Remembrance Day (1993), which climaxed in an IRA bomb episode in a Yarmouth hotel. He was brave enough to test pronunciation qualities beyond the county boundaries by including Happisburgh in the story.

Childhood memories of north Norfolk spattered the pages of William Rivière's first novel, the lyrical Watercolour Sky (1990), and he found room for many more in Echoes of War, an epic tale of family unity and survival. The author grew up at Dilham Grange, and despite many years abroad, still clearly delights in his Norfolk connections: "In Norfolk the freezing wind which roared in the trees around Paston Church battered all the flint churches which stood parish after parish along that coast of muddy cliffs and salt marshes and shingle foreshores..."

John Timpson, who made the most enduring mark of his broadcasting years as co-presenter of the Radio Four early-morning programme Today, returned to Norfolk on retirement and immediately embarked on a hectic writing career. He used the county of the Fifties as the setting for his first novel Paper Trail, the story of a young reporter on the Toftham and Wettleford Journal – a carbon copy in some ways of the Timpson times as district man at Dereham for the EDP. More echoes in the sequel Sound Track, when our hero exchanged garden fetes and darts dinners for party conferences and Parliament as the BBC called.

Norfolk's ability to store secrets has made it a favourite hideout for shifty strangers and brazen beasts with murder and mayhem in mind, crime queens P D James and Ruth Rendell leading the way down more recent murky paths. The trend started very early in the twentieth century when Arthur Conan Doyle, creator of Sherlock Holmes, visited Cromer for a golfing holiday and left with the plot for The Hound of the Baskervilles. Black Shuck, giant dog with eyes burning like coals, had been let off the leash again.

More human foibles dogged another pipe-smoking sleuth, Chief Inspector George Gently, in more than forty cases put his way by Brundall writer Alan Hunter since 1955.

Sadly, some prolific writers appear to be largely forgotten. Doreen Wallace (1897-1989) is one such example. She had 48 novels to her name and Sir John Betjeman enthused: "Her books are all her own, and I like them very much." She gained national recognition in a forty-year battle to abolish the "iniquitous tithe tax". A landowner and farmer at Wortham, near Diss, she joined forces with Dick Bagnall-Oakeley in 1951 to produce Norfolk in the County Books series.

One of Norfolk's most celebrated "guests" of the twentieth century was Tarka the Otter author Henry Williamson, who invested his entire capital in a run-down farm at Stiffkey just before the Second World War. He had scarcely any idea about agriculture, and his adventures were recounted in The Story of a Norfolk Farm, first published in 1941 and dedicated *"to all who have worked and suffered for the land and the peoples of Great Britain"*. Eventually Williamson became disenchanted with local people who spread rumours about him being in league with Germany, and he returned to Devon to write 17 more books. A collections of Williamson's contributions to the EDP between 1941 and 1944, Green Fields and Pavements, was first published in 1995 to celebrate the centenary of his birth.

**Eric Fowler (1909-81) was one of the most authoritative essayists to work for the EDP. For 35 years his Wednesday morning articles, under the pseudonym of Jonathan Mardle, delighted a wide readership. He was an authority on Norfolk dialect, speaking and writing it with native resource and humour. Born in Norwich, he joined the EDP straight from school in 1925. After war service, he soon began writing editorials and the Mardle column, one of the most distinguished expressions of English regional journalism. Made an MBE in 1968 for services to journalism, he retired in 1974, an occasion marked by a unique "function of honour" in the City Hall.**

Norfolk has also played host to several outstanding poets, including George Barker (1913-1991) who settled at Itteringham, and George MacBeth (1932-1992), who sought rural seclusion at Oby, near Yarmouth, and later in a gaunt Victorian Gothic manor close to King's Lynn. Kevin Crossley-Holland, poet, Anglo-Saxon scholar and children's writer, rediscovered his spiritual heartland around Burnham Overy Staithe, while one of his contemporaries Alan Brownjohn, drew much from the "raw silence of reeds and waters" as he explored from bases at Sedgeford and Stanhoe.

Like Henry Rider Haggard musing at the dawn of the twentieth century, countless inspired and inspiring characters have sized up Norfolk, its mysteries, its past:. *"How many dead hands have tilled that fallow, mown that pasture? And the land itself? Scarcely changed I believe."* There speaks the independence of spirit and the air of permanence about a place

**Sir Alfred Munnings (1878-1959) grew up at Mendham Mill on the Waveney and, despite the loss of an eye, entered the twentieth century as one of the great hopes of British art. Influenced by Impressionism in early years, he became the best British painter of horses since George Stubbs. But he could be wayward and occasionally wild – once raging because the painter Laura Knight, his guest at the Maid's Head Hotel in Norwich, had enjoyed a bath at his expense. To this day the Royal Academy is embarrassed that he used his Forties presidency as a platform for attacking modern art. He is a bigger and better painter than his prejudices – if not his huge prices – might suggest.**

where you have to arrive rather than just pass through.

In 1900 Norfolk was a popular destination and inspiration for painters. They were drawn by some of the wild scenes and subjects, and the same light and atmosphere, which had enthused Cotman, Crome and their Norwich School followers almost a century before.

Bitterns boomed across Broadland, nightjar wings whipcracked over the Brecks, and corncrakes rasped in a patchwork of small, unkempt fields hemmed by hedges, woods and ponds. Coastal subjects ranged from buffeted seas and bustling docks to swathes of tourist beaches between King's Lynn and Lowestoft. And, at the heart of the region, castle and cathedral-centred Norwich remained a place of ancient wonder, still extending barely a mile beyond its medieval walls.

These vast and varied vistas comprised an accessible wilderness. Belle coastal steamers from London connected with wherries, yachts and, ultimately, cruisers; a network of rural railways (adorned with some superb posters) survived until the Beeching axe of the Sixties. Drivers of carts and then cars could long feel they had country roads all to themselves. While Norfolk had the remote air of Northumberland, it was reached fairly easily. Plus, the county - actually dogged by severe agricultural recession - was delightfully cheap.

Although Norfolk would breed its own artists, most arrived as visitors. A pattern emerged of summer sketching tours and winter painting stints in London studios. Local lad Alfred Munnings (1878-1959) spent warm Edwardian months in a horse-drawn caravan wandering the Ringland Hills, before returning to his base at Swainsthorpe, near Norwich, when autumn advanced. And, late in 1909, a rather more Bohemian trek from Epsom

**Sir Alfred Munnings, *Sunny June*, 1901, oil on canvas, 76.5cm x 128cm.**

**IAN COLLINS, EDP London correspondent, was born in Norwich of a long line of Broadland boat-builders. He has written several books, including A Broad Canvas: Art in East Anglia Since 1880 (Black Dog Books, £25), curated exhibitions and co-produced arts documentaries for Anglia Television.**

**Arnesby Brown, *View of Norwich*, 1934-5, oil on canvas, 61.6cm x 111cm.**

ended with a final limp from Norwich to Sea Palling, before illness and exhaustion finished the enterprise. Augustus John and his lover, Dorelia McNeill, then fled home to Chelsea with a horde of howling children.

Norfolk's teeming birdlife, especially the October influx of wildfowl, obsessed Frank Southgate (1872-1916), a Hunstanton postmaster's son who haunted the saltmarshes as far as Blakeney. He went armed with weapons – once killing 203 wading birds with a single blast from a punt gun – and sketching materials. Having dug himself into the Norfolk mud on so many wintry nights, ready to take aim at dawn, he died in the mire of the First World War. Southgate's legacy of lyrical watercolours was praised by fellow artist Peter Scott – himself a convert to conservation while living in a disused lighthouse on the Wash – for pioneering an impressionist technique in bird painting. Surviving the Great War, Hainford's John Cyril Harrison (1898-1985) and Hickling's Roland Green (1890-1972) added to the gallery of fine and feathery portraits. But Broadland was alive each summer with amateur and professional artists. Among the best was Stephen John Batchelder (1849-1932), a tireless recorder of Norfolk wherries – the juggernauts of the pre-M11 era. Most of all, however, this watery world is now associated with the three most prized Norfolk landscape painters of the twentieth century: Alfred Munnings, John Alfred Arnesby Brown and Edward Seago.

Born at Mendham on the Waveney, Munnings was, like Constable, a miller's son. Having studied at the Norwich School of Art – then, as now, a crucial focus for creativity in the county – he moved from commercial (literally chocolate box) art to an inspired and innovative Impressionism. His brilliant oil landscapes of East Anglian scenes in the early years of the century, in which horses appeared more heroic than humans, were the best things he ever did. Later, his talent deadened in Constable's Dedham and fame turned to notoriety. In 1949, when a bombastic president of the Royal Academy, he blurted out where he wanted to boot Picasso. His major works may now fetch more than £1 million at auction, but his critical reputation has never recovered.

To Arnesby Brown (1866-1955) the ox was king of beasts, but over the years even majestic cattle were erased from his sublime scenes. From his eyrie at Haddiscoe he surveyed a panoramic marshland stretching virtually unbroken from Acle to Beccles. At first he could watch dozens of windpump sails turning, yet slowly the scene stilled (after his death there would be a great and ultimately successful battle to save the glorious Halvergate Marshes from the plough). All that moved were banks of cloud billowing across a sky comprising two-thirds of the picture. He caught this ocean of space in which, time and again, the outline of Haddiscoe church loomed like a stranded galleon. Ironically, his only pupil was Campbell Mellon (1876-1955), who specialised in crowded beach scenes at Yarmouth and Gorleston.

Edward Seago (1910-74) was the son of a Norwich coal merchant, who took to painting views from his window when a child bedridden with a heart complaint. Early infirmity can aid an artist: Welsh-born watercolourist Arthur Davies, ruled unfit for active service in the First World War, charted Norfolk scenes over seventy years and died as the Castle Museum was staging a display to mark his 95th birthday! But Seago reacted against youthful confinement by running off to the circus, producing two illustrated books about his life with Bevin's Travelling Show. In later decades he still wandered widely, often sailing on his sea-going ketch Capricorn, in search of fresh landscapes to paint in oil and watercolour. But he was always inspired by the "cool greens and greys" of Norfolk and the scenes around his home, at The Dutch House, Ludham, whose breezy, bracing atmosphere he captured so well.

**Norwich-born Edward Seago (1910-74) was the century's most celebrated painter of Norfolk marshes, broads and beaches. From 1929 his London exhibitions drew a warm response which at times amounted to frenzy; his oils and watercolours continue to command high prices in the salerooms. Although critics complained that his early style never developed, he searched the world – sailing to Africa, Asia and Antarctica – for fresh subjects. He was a firm favourite of the Royal Family and a frequent visitor to Sandringham.**

Norfolk made early impressions on some of Britain's finest twentieth-century artists. A 1912 visit to Mundesley convinced Paul Nash of the value of landscape painting; between 1925 and 1936 the tubercular Mark Gertler had three spells in the local sanatorium, now a drug and alcohol rehabilitation centre. Henry Moore spent student summers in the Twenties

**Colin Self, *Postwick Grove – evening*, July 1982, mixed media, 78.8cm x 55cm.**

collecting fossils along the north Norfolk coast and carving stone blocks in the yard of Wighton village school, where his sister was headmistress. In 1925 he wrote that, but for a lack of money, he would stay on and wed *"one of those richly-formed, big-limbed, fresh-faced, full-blooded country wenches... I've seen about here"*. These were the models for an array of reclining figures. He also took a seminal holiday at Happisburgh, in 1931, with artists Barbara Hepworth, Ben Nicholson and Ivon Hitchens. And throughout a long career John Piper liked to depict the halls and towers of Norfolk in ghostly and glistening colours - hitting a peak with the Fenland churches of Walsoken, West Walton, Walpole St Peter (thought by John Betjeman to be the most beautiful in England), the Wiggenhalls, Tilneys and Terringtons.

Apart from legendary hardships of the weather - and with electricity reaching rural Norfolk only from the Fifties - certain artistic visitors have met with a frosty welcome. Just as the Scottish painter and architect Charles Rennie Mackintosh had been held as a suspected spy in Walberswick in 1915, so the pacifist artist Claughton Pellew-Harvey (1890-1966) was arrested at Gunton station, near Cromer, during the Second World War. He had received a letter written in German and was detained until his British status could be established.

Otherwise, noted painters have worked quietly in rural retreats - among them, in latter decades, abstractionist Roger Ackling, seaside satirist Brian Lewis, portraitist Ivy Smith (whose double likeness of the Attenborough brothers is in the National Portrait Gallery), former Kitchen Sink Group painter Derrick Greaves and erstwhile London Group member Michael Andrews (1928-95), who was born in Norwich and ended in the Norfolk countryside working on huge studies of deer stalking in the Scottish Highlands and of Ayers Rock in Australia.

In the last three decades two artists in particular have expanded the way we look at our county. Born near Rackheath in 1941, Pop Art's Colin Self turned from images of Swinging London and a menacing Cold War world to work in Thorpe as a one-man art school. In collage, watercolour, oil, pen, pencil and charcoal, photography, prints,

**The Sainsbury Centre, University of East Anglia, the construction and endowment of which has added enormously to the artistic life of the county.**

sculpture and ceramics, he has evoked revelatory rural images – markets and car boot sales, desolate railway tracks and near-prairie landscapes. Meanwhile Mary Newcomb (born 1922), the poetic painter of south Norfolk and the Waveney Valley, has produced quirky, deceptively-naive studies of the universe around us, from microscopic insects to the night sky. These quiet works speak volumes about our place in nature.

Art in Norfolk has benefited from two key institutional developments during the century. Building on the 1946 Russell Colman bequest of Norwich School masterpieces, the Castle Museum has steadily enhanced its art collection – all of which can be viewed, at least on request, when the revamped museum opens late in 2000. And the Norman Foster-designed Sainsbury Centre, housing treasures collected by Robert and Lisa Sainsbury which span time and culture, has created a superb gallery and helped the University of East Anglia to establish a distinguished history of art department.

But art depends most of all on individual expression. Across the region known and unknown artists are now working to put us into the picture for the next millennium.

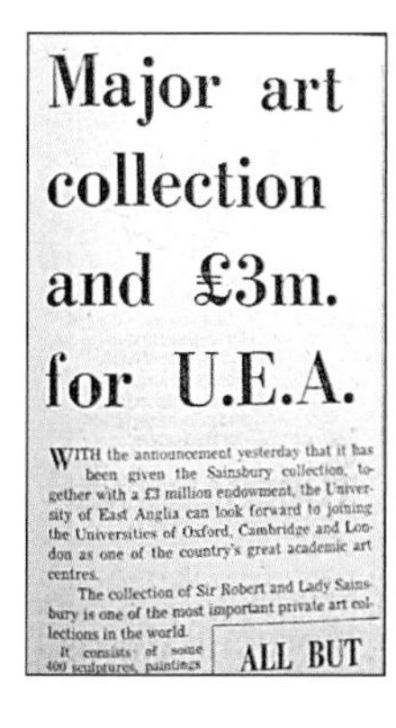

Major art collection and £3m. for U.E.A.

WITH the announcement yesterday that it has been given the Sainsbury collection, together with a £3 million endowment, the University of East Anglia can look forward to joining the Universities of Oxford, Cambridge and London as one of the country's great academic art centres.

The collection of Sir Robert and Lady Sainsbury is one of the most important private art collections in the world.

It consists of some 400 sculptures, paintings

ALL BUT

**How the EDP reported the story on November 26th 1973**

# Chapter 5

# *Faith*

**DENNIS TOMLINSON was born in Berkshire. After training as a reporter on the Maidenhead Advertiser and working on farming magazines in London, he came to Norwich in 1968 as news editor of Farming World. When that paper closed, he moved to the Evening News as a sub-editor, subsequently becoming ECN's training officer, retiring in 1993. He has been an accredited Methodist local preacher since 1958 and writes the Cross Talk column of church news in the Evening News. In 1998 he wrote and published A Village at War – a 1939-45 history of White Waltham, his home village.**

**TREVOR HEATON**

It is an axiom of every generation to look back with fondness to a Golden Age – which usually ends in the first few years of the teller's childhood. Our vision of the Church, and in particular the Church of England, is no different.

The vision of a rural idyll portrayed in every television adaptation of an Agatha Christie novel or some other drama set in the Twenties and Thirties usually has a well-attended Matins led by the local Squire and with every village having its own vicar living in a well-supplied vicarage.

But the truth was often very different. The merging of benefices is held up as something born of the last few years. In fact as early as 1914 it was not unusual for parishes to be merged on the death or retirement of the incumbent, although it is also true to say that in 1900 most parishes had their own vicar or rector and many a curate as well. At the start of the century, most people attending church went to their parish church if they were Anglicans or a chapel close to home if they were Nonconformists. Today people attend church less frequently and there has been a growing trend of people travelling by car to a church which offers their favoured style of worship.

Part of the county falls into the Diocese of Ely, but the great majority is in the Norwich diocese. Today there are more than 280 priests serving the Diocese of Norwich's 580 parishes – all but 22 of which are in Norfolk. The priests are supported in their ministry by an equal number of lay readers – men and women who are licensed to preach, take services and help with other parochial duties.

As part of his pioneering strategy for the diocese, the Bishop of Norwich from 1985-99, the Rt Rev Peter Nott, faithfully promoted the idea of restoring weekly worship to every community, much of which could be led by lay people. In 1995-96 he made a pilgrimage throughout the diocese and recorded in his diary afterwards: *"I received enormous encouragement through what I saw, experienced and sensed. We have been moving forward quietly and steadily. God is, and has been, at work among us."*

In the latter half of the century, a great deal of effort was put into maintaining the fabric of the churches, helped by grants from English Heritage, Norfolk Churches Trust and local fund-raising. The spark for this activity was the introduction in 1955 by the Church Assembly of legislation making five-yearly inspections of all church buildings compulsory, the dreaded "quinquennial". Initially and inevitably, a huge backlog of repair work was discovered. Some churches have been declared redundant and in Norwich other uses have been found for deconsecrated buildings – such as an antiques centre at St Michael-at-Plea, an arts centre in St Swithin's and a night shelter for the homeless in St Martin-at-Oak.

Norwich still treasures the largest collection of medieval churches in any city in Europe. Indeed Sir John Betjeman, that celebrator of the best of English life, remarked to the EDP in 1970 that its churches were "as important to Norwich as the canals are to Venice. They have got to be kept". And the most magnificent of them all, the city's Norman cathedral was in dire straits financially after the Second World War with a backlog of repairs to the cathedral and the freehold properties which provided much of its income. Collections at services in 1949 failed to pay the cathedral's heating bill of £540.

But by the next year, a number of windfall gifts had been received and influential laymen

**Norwich Cathedral, an enduring symbol Christian faith, which celebrated its 900th anniversary during the century.**

in city and county launched an appeal for £20,000 to pay for repairs to the fabric, a figure later raised to £35,000. The Friends of Norwich Cathedral took on the role of being financially responsible for the fabric.

The cathedral launched an appeal for £10 million in March 1999. It is aiming to conserve the thirteenth-century cloister – the largest monastic cloister in the country; to build a new building on the site of the hostry (the guesthouse of the Benedictine priory that served the cathedral until the Reformation) which will provide seminar rooms and exhibition areas; to upgrade the library and provide better refreshment facilities for the 600,000 visitors who come to the cathedral each year. Ten thousand of the visitors come in organised school parties.

Two other religious centres in the county have drawn increasing numbers of visitors this century. The Anglican Shrine at Walsingham, re-established by the Rev Alfred Hope Patten, who became Vicar of Walsingham in 1921, shares in the 250,000 people who come to the village annually to offer their devotion to Mary, the Mother of Jesus. The Holy House of Nazareth and part of the shrine church were built in 1931 and the church was completed in 1938.

In Norwich, the Julian Shrine, containing the reconstructed cell where the fourteenth-century mystic, Mother Julian, lived attracts many thousands of visitors a year. The present cell was built in 1952 during the post-war reconstruction of the bombed St Julian's Church.

One of the biggest changes of the century has been in the relations between the churches. But a chapter in Joan Bain's The Two Farms (Robert Hale, 1989) shows that church and chapel could live happily together provided the rector understood his people and was diplomat as well as priest. She writes of her home village, Trunch, in the Twenties: *"Two chapels as well as a large parish church in a village with a population of fewer than 400 souls created rivalry and occasional backbiting, yet gave a lot of people a chance to organise religious activity or serve their own church in a way that might not have been open to them had they remained in the Church of England.*

*"Although church and chapel had their own distinctive ways of worship, there was always a certain amount of give and take between them. When a Methodist farmer married a Church of England girl, they solved their denominational problems by attending chapel in the morning and church at Evensong."* The rector was still looked up to as the top man in the parish and was expected to lead in village affairs as well as those of the church.

Nationally, the Church of England faced a crisis in 1927 over the proposal to introduce a new Prayer Book to replace the 1662 Book of Common Prayer. The report of the debate in the House of Commons occupied six columns of the EDP. The new book failed to win the necessary Parliamentary approval and when the Measure was reintroduced into the Commons in June 1928, it was again rejected. However, the bishops gave approval for the new book to be used and many parts of it were in common use until 1980 when the Alternative Service Book was introduced.

Occasionally, the county has found itself, often unwillingly, the focus of a nation's interest. In 1932, for example, Norfolk found itself in the national headlines over the bizarre case of the dismissed Rector of Stiffkey, the Rev Harold Davidson, the so-called "Prostitutes' Padre". Davidson spent all his week in London ministering to girls who were likely to become prostitutes or had already succumbed. A consistory court at Church House, Westminster, found him guilty of immoral conduct. Davidson spent the next few years mostly in a barrel on Blackpool's Golden Mile, still claiming he was innocent. In 1937 he went into a cage with a lion at Skegness and was fatally mauled. Years later there were still people in Stiffkey who spoke well of him.

A pastoral difficulty arose within Norwich Diocese in 1995 when some parishioners living in Threxton, Bodney, Little Cressingham, Oxborough and Didlington decided to no longer accept the authority of the Bishop of Norwich. This arose following the withdrawal

**A spectacular view of the enthronement ceremony for the 69th Bishop of Norwich, the Rt Rev Maurice Wood, on October 14th 1971.**

Norfolk has more medieval churches than the rest of England put together, in fact it is said to have more medieval churches per acre than anywhere else in the world.

Those simple, and astonishing, facts have left each subsequent generation with an ever-increasing burden of maintenance. Taken with a general decline in churchgoing, the picture should be bleak.

And yet communities have rallied time and again to restore and preserve their community churches.

English Heritage (and its earlier incarnations) has given millions of pounds in grant aid this century, and since 1976 the Norfolk Churches Trust has performed a sterling service in helping to keep buildings in use, raising a seven-figure sum.

Its doughty and determined founder, Lady Harrod, once told the EDP: "We want to make sure that no parish has to close its church through lack of money. When a church goes, the place loses much more than just a building. It also loses its history and its roots - and indeed its soul."

**Communities and fund-raising bodies have worked together to try and prevent churches ending up sharing the fate of others such as the ruinous St James', Bawsey, seen here during a September 1974 Harvest Festival.**

The Society for the Protection of Ancient Buildings claimed in 1992 that Norfolk's problems were probably the most acute in the region. The claims were disputed by the Bishop of Norwich, the Rt Rev Peter Nott, who told the EDP: "The churches of Norfolk are in a better state than they have been for 400 years."

But conscious, no doubt, of the awesome legacy of buildings in his care Bishop Peter prompted a parliamentary debate in 1995 to (unsuccessfully) persuade the Government to lower the rate of VAT. "The Government giveth and the Government taketh away," he observed. "Blessed be the name of the Government that giveth just a little more than it taketh away." But at the opposite end of the scale from the House of Lords there have been many inspiring stories of how communities or even individuals have turned the tide.

One of the most inspiring stories of the century must be that of St Mary the Virgin at Houghton-on-the-Hill, a decayed village near Swaffham. Retired engineer Bob Davey fell in love with the ivy-clad building on a chance visit in 1992. The church, abandoned in 1937, had never been deconsecrated, a fact which made it a centre for pagan activities. Mr Davey rescued it from the clutches of the Satanists and set about restoring the building.

Major restoration funded by a number of organisations led to a sensational discovery when the remains of Romanesque wall paintings were uncovered, said to be the most important to be discovered in twenty years.

That find, of international importance, would appear to finally secure the future of this lovely little church. "The greatest pleasure is to see the people coming back," said Mr Davey. "I am just privileged that I could play a small part in it."

of the licence of the then priest-in-charge, the Rev Kit Chalcraft, after the announcement of his third marriage, following two divorces, and his failure to keep a promise to reside in the parsonage house. Although the lawful priest-in-charge is the Rev Graham Drake, the breakaway group remain loyal to the Rev Chalcraft.

Of deep significance for the Church was the proposal to ordain women to the priesthood which finally happened in 1994. Twenty women were ordained in Norwich Diocese and today they serve as vicars or rectors in charge of parishes and some as hospital or prison chaplains. The integration of this new form of ministry has gone relatively smoothly and even though a small minority of male clergy do not accept the validity of women's orders, they still continue to minister in their parishes.

A move in the other direction is for men to be admitted as members of the Mothers' Union. Only a few have joined in Norfolk but the organisation is strong, with more than 2000 members in 105 branches. The first branch in the diocese was at Redenhall in 1889, formed by Mrs Sancroft and Miss Pelham. Members meet regularly and study and reflect on family life. They raise money for the organisation overseas, provide needy families with caravan holidays, run parenting courses and monitor media programmes.

Despite the failure of the scheme to unite the Anglican and Methodist Churches nationally in 1969, churches of all denominations have continued to work together locally. There are 15 Local Ecumenical Partnerships. Some, such as Bowthorpe, near Norwich, and Thorpe Marriott, resulted in the building of a new church to serve all denominations. On his pilgrimage, the Bishop of Norwich was amazed at the extent of joint church activity. He wrote in his diary: *"There is warm fellowship, shared worship and study and engagement in the local community. Locally parishioners are often streets ahead of the church at national level."*

Roman Catholics entered the twentieth century with a partly-built St John's Church on an elevated site in Norwich. It would later become the cathedral of the Diocese of East Anglia. The first architect of St John's was George Gilbert Scott, who died in 1899. His brother, J Oldrid Scott, then took over. (Giles Gilbert Scott, son of George Gilbert, was architect of Liverpool Anglican Cathedral.)

The foundation stone of the new church, built on the site of the former city gaol, was laid on July 17th 1884. According to the author of A Great Gothic Fane, *"Much caution was needed to render the foundations secure, for the neighbourhood was more or less honeycombed with disused old quarries of chalk and flint. There is one such, in fact, only a few yards from the western boundary."*

There was a reminder of this when the back end of an Eastern Counties double-decker bus fell into a hole in Earlham Road, just outside the cathedral on March 3rd 1988. Fortunately the foundations of the cathedral go down 25-thirty feet and are on solid chalk.

On August 29rd 1894, the nave was opened for worship and services ceased to be held at the Willow Lane Chapel. The completed church was opened on December 8rd 1910.

**Aubrey Aitken, who was Bishop of Lynn from 1973-80 – he is seen here taking part in the traditional celebrations to mark the opening of its annual Mart – was born at North Walsham in 1911. He was ordained deacon in 1934 on Tyneside. His father, Canon Aubrey Aitken, had been Vicar of Yarmouth from 1920-41 and his grandfather Canon and Vice-Dean of Norwich Cathedral. He became Rector of Kessingland in 1940, and was Vicar of Sprowston from 1943-53. He then became Vicar of St Margaret's, Lynn, and in 1961 Archdeacon of Norwich. Twelve years later he became Bishop and Archdeacon of Lynn, retiring from the Archdeaconry in 1980. He had suffered a serious setback in 1962 after a major throat operation seriously affected his voice. He was President of the Royal Norfolk Agricultural Association in 1976. He had played rugby and cricket for Norwich in his younger days. A lifelong supporter of Norwich City, he became an honorary life vice-president of the club. Bishop Aubrey preached his last sermon three weeks before he died in 1985.**

**The Rt Rev Alan Clark was named as the first Bishop of the Roman Catholic Diocese of East Anglia when it was created in 1976. He was involved in the movement for church unity from 1969 when he was appointed joint chairman of the Anglican/Roman Catholic International Commission. He played a leading role in the ecumenical movement and was the first Roman Catholic bishop to address the General Synod of the Church of England. He was ordained to the priesthood at Bromley in Kent in 1945 and was for ten years from 1954 Vice-rector of the English College in Rome. He was consecrated Auxiliary Bishop of Northampton in 1969 and in 1970 became President of the Ecumenical Commission for England and Wales. His forty years in the priesthood was marked with a concelebrated Mass in St John's Cathedral in Norwich in February 1985. He retired in 1985 but continued to live close to the diocesan offices in Poringland.**

The Bishop of Northampton, the Rt Rev F W Keating, preached the sermon.

St John's was built at the sole expense of the 15th Duke of Norfolk, Henry Fitzalan Howard, as a thankoffering after his marriage to Lady Flora Hastings in 1877. She died ten years later and the Duke remarried in 1904. The Duke and Duchess were present at the opening which was attended by the Lord Mayor of Norwich, Mr (Later Sir) Eustace Gurney. Later, 250 people were entertained to lunch in the Thatched Assembly Room.

In 1913, there were 11 Roman Catholic parish churches in Norfolk, six convents and eight stations (places) where Mass was said. The four assistant priests at St John's served Stoke Holy Cross; East Harling, where Mass was said every Thursday in a room at the Women's Inebriates Home; Diss; Aylsham and Wymondham.

Wymondham was one of the places visited by the motor chapel in 1911. As a result, services were held in a little chapel at Town Green. Of the congregation of forty, only a quarter were Catholics.The idea of a travelling mission, or mobile church, continued until 1975. The last travelling missioner for the Diocese of Northampton was Father Robert McCormick who, in 1999, was parish priest at Diss. Father Robert made quarterly visits to say Mass at sites in Northamptonshire, Norfolk, Suffolk, and Cambridgeshire, plus Bedfordshire, Buckinghamshire and Huntingdonshire. He used pubs, cinemas, village halls and, as ecumenism progressed, Anglican churches. In the summer, he used a mobile chapel holding up to 25 people.

The 1913 records mention Wroxham, which had a chapel adjoining Wroxham Hall, dedicated to St Michael and St Helena. It had been built by the late squire, Edward Southwell Trafford. *"It is a much appreciated boon to the hundreds of visitors who spend their summer holidays on the winding River Bure and the enchanting Broads,"* A Great Gothic Fane records.

The Catholic League, a men's organisation formed in 1904, was active in Norwich and through organising the Catholic vote, secured representation on the city council and increased membership of the Board of Guardians.

The Third National Catholic Congress opened in Norwich on August 2nd 1912. Cardinal Bourne arrived for the occasion at Thorpe Station with the Duke of Norfolk. The inaugural evening meeting was held in St Andrew's Hall with a welcome from the Lord Mayor, Mr Henry J Copeman. During the congress, more than 500 people made a pilgrimage to St Walstan's Well at Bawburgh, most of them travelling in horse-drawn brakes.

Early in the century, there were 3000 Catholics in the city parish of St John's. In 1997, the number was estimated at 5000 with 5200 in the parish of St George's which stretches to the North Norfolk coast. Weekly Mass attendances in 1997 were 970 and 918 respectively.

The number of Catholics in the county has been swelled by the arrival of a number of Italian families in Norwich, before and after the turn of the century. There was further growth when people from Eastern Europe, especially from Poland, Lithuania and the Ukraine, came to Norfolk during and after the Second World War. In 1999 a regular Polish Mass was still being held at St George's, Sprowston Road, Norwich, and at Brandon. London overspill population moving to Thetford and King's Lynn post-war, a percentage of whom were Catholics, brought a further increase.

But the largest number of Catholics who come to Norfolk are the pilgrims who visit the National Shrine of Our Lady at Little Walsingham. Its origins go back to 1061 when Richeldis, the Saxon Lady of the Manor, had a vision in which she was taken to the home of Joseph and Mary in Nazareth. She believed that she was being asked to build a copy of that house. She did this and Walsingham became a centre for pilgrimages and prayer. Augustine canons and Franciscan friars, who had come to look after the visitors, built an abbey and a friary. For 500 years Walsingham was known as "England's Nazareth", but after the dissolution of the monasteries by Henry VIII in 1536, the shrine was disused.

In 1897, Charlotte Boyd undertook the

restoration of the fourteenth-century Slipper Chapel and this led to it being named the National Shrine of Our Lady in 1934. Catholic pilgrims began to visit once again and in 1998 a celebration of 100 years of modern pilgrimage was held, led by the Archbishop of Westminster, Cardinal Basil Hume, and the Bishop of East Anglia, the Rt Rev Peter Smith.

The shrine, together with the Anglican shrine elsewhere in the village, attracts 250,000 visitors a year, a large proportion of whom are pilgrims. The tiny Slipper Chapel could no longer accommodate the numbers. In 1981 a new Chapel of Reconciliation was built nearby. It holds 500 people but its front wall can be removed so that Mass can be served to outdoor congregations. The Roman Catholic National Pilgrimage in September brings more than 2000 pilgrims, the New Dawn Conference in August about 4000 and the pilgrimage for Tamils up to 4000.

In addition to the cathedral, there are now 23 Catholic churches, well spread throughout the county, many of them built in this century. At Attleborough, the Methodist Church is used for Sunday Mass, an indication of the much-improved relations between churches today. The Catholic population in the county is an estimated 29,000; weekly Mass attendances average nearly 7000.

Largest of the parish churches is St George's, Norwich, built in 1964. The biggest change to come to Catholic worship this century was the decision of the Second Vatican Council in the Sixties to allow Mass to be said in local languages (the vernacular, as it is referred to) rather than Latin. Some people still ask for Latin, rather than English, to be used at funerals.

The parish priest at Downham Market, Father Oswald Baker, who objected to the reform, was dismissed by the Church in 1975 for continuing to say the Mass in Latin. He later established a chapel in Bexwell Road, Downham Market, and continued the Latin service there. In 1995, film star and devout Roman Catholic Mel Gibson, who was in Ireland for the shooting of the film Braveheart, attended a Mass at the chapel. In 1999, a Latin Mass was still being said twice a month at The Old Priory, Horsham St Faith, by a visiting priest from Wimbledon.

The other major change in this area was the creation of the new Diocese of East Anglia in 1976 with the Rt Rev Alan Clark as its first bishop. The diocese consists of Norfolk, Suffolk and Cambridgeshire, which were formerly part of the Diocese of Northampton. Bishop Clark was succeeded by the Right Rev Peter Smith in 1994.

As in other churches, lay people are taking increasing responsibility. In 1967, married men

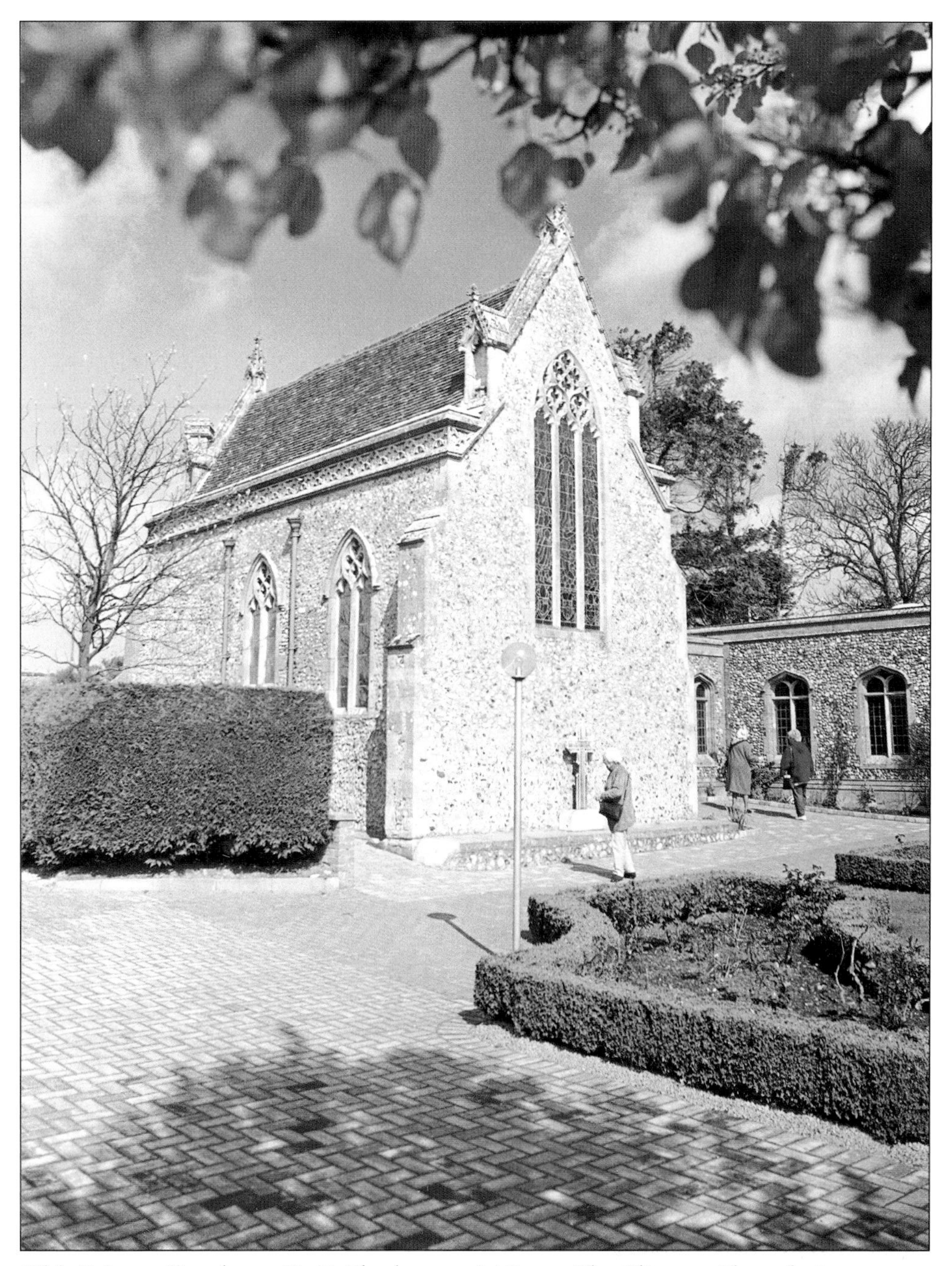

**The Slipper Chapel at Houghton St Giles, once again a centre for pilgrimage.**

**Sydney Cozens-Hardy was born at Letheringsett Hall in 1850. He began work as a solicitor in Surrey Street, Norwich, in 1873. He became a member of Princes Street Congregational Church in 1874, was a deacon for 64 years and one of the treasurers for 45 years.**
**He did Sunday School work, first as a teacher, then as a secretary and later one of the superintendents, at the Carrow Sunday School for more than fifty years. The Sunday School was undenominational and was held at the day school built for the children of Colman's employees. The Sunday School was open to any children. He retired from it in 1919.**
**He was a director of Laurence, Scott and Co from 1899-1938 and Sheriff of Norwich in 1900-1. He married Jessie Beaumont from Wilmslow, Cheshire, in 1882. They had four children – Basil, Cecilia Jessie, Margaret Joyce and Sydney Noel. Mr Cozens-Hardy died in 1942, aged 91.**

of at least 35 and single men of at least 25 years of age were allowed to become deacons and perform most of the tasks of a parish priest except celebrate Mass and hear confessions. Older men are able to be part-time deacons and continue with their secular job. Eucharistic ministers (lay men and women) assist with the distribution of Communion at Mass and are also able to take Communion to the sick.

Since the turn of the century, when Catholics were not allowed to worship with other Christians, they are now able to join in many activities with other Christians but not take part in a joint service of Holy Communion.

The United Reformed Church was formed in October 1972 as a union of most of the Congregational Churches in England and Wales and the Presbyterian Church of England. The Churches of Christ joined in 1981.The Norwich District of the URC, which includes the Lowestoft area, has 1209 members and 27 churches, some of which are linked with other denominations.

From these figures it is hard to realise that at the beginning of the century there were as many Free Churchmen as active Anglicans in England. Membership of Free Churches, predominantly Methodist, Baptist and Congregational, reached a peak of 5000 in Norwich in 1910. This represented 6.5 per cent of the population over 15 years old. Total attendance at Sunday Schools was 16,000 under-15s – 44 per cent of the city's children.

The Congregationalists had 1800 members in seven churches in the city and nearly 2500 Sunday School children. Predominant among the churches was Princes Street.Writing in the Journal of the United Reformed Church History Society in May 1995, Barry M Doyle notes that J J Colman and his family transferred from St Mary's Baptist Church, Duke Street, in 1870. This *"made Princes Street the place to go and did much to cement the tight-knit and highly middle-class community which gathered there in the Edwardian period,"* he says. Mr Doyle suggests that some prominent individuals attended Princes Street because it was socially, politically and even economically expedient to do so. Perhaps this was particularly true for the leaders of the church.

The other major city Congregational churches early in the century were Chapel-in-the-Field, built in 1858 and seating 850; Magdalen Road, opened 1903 and seating 800; and Old Meeting in Colegate. Mr Doyle describes Chapel-in-the-Field members as comfortable – solid citizens, not social leaders. An exception was Henry J Copeman, "head of a regional wholesale company, co-director of the Eastern Daily Press and Liberal member of the city council for forty years".

A centenary history of Chapel-in-the-Field in 1958 records that the envelope system for offerings was introduced in 1900 "to steady finance which was a matter of continuous concern". (Under this system, still used by churches, dated envelopes are issued to members to ensure that they contribute both when they are at church and when they are absent.) Individual Communion cups, in place of a chalice, were introduced in 1902. Thetford Congregational Church adopted them three years later.

In 1915, lighting restrictions caused Chapel-in-the-Field to switch evening service to 3.30pm for three months "until all windows were dealt with." The First World War hit congregations: 252 men joined up from Princes Street and 40 were killed. From Chapel-in-the Field, 179 joined up.

Princes Street membership was 561 at the end of the war and had gone up to 637 in 1929. In that year, the church appointed a female visitor and elected two women as deacons – Miss Ethel Colman and Mrs Southwell.

Chapel-in-the-Field closed in 1966 when the church united with Jessopp Road Congregational Church, now part of the URC.

Shipdham Congregational Church did its bit in the First World War, fund-raising for war relief funds and the Red Cross. It also held an egg service from which 410 eggs were sent for wounded soldiers in hospital. In 1946, 100 German prisoners-of-war took part in Shipdham's harvest festival. The sermon was translated into German for them by their pastor, the Rev Heinrich Hoffman, a Baptist. In 1977 Shipdham signed a sharing agreement with the Methodist Church.

Dereham has the historic Cowper Congregational Church, opened in 1874. It stands on the site of the house where the hymn-writer and poet, William Cowper (1731-1800) spent his final days. The church maintains two services on Sundays with a morning congregation of forty to fifty and twenty-plus in the evening. The church is part of an Evangelical Fellowship of Congregational Churches - one of two groups which chose not to come into the URC. In Norfolk, nine other Congregational churches voted to stay out - Hemsby, North Walsham, Old Meeting (Norwich), Long Stratton (all now in the Congregational Federation); Briston, Guestwick, Oulton (near Aylsham), Hingham and Yaxham (all in the Evangelical Fellowship). Wells initially joined the URC but then withdrew. Guestwick and Oulton have both since closed.

Nationally, nearly 600 Congregational churches did not join the URC. It would have meant surrendering their independent status and handing over their property to a central body. The Norfolk non-joiners set up the Norfolk Association of Congregational Churches in January 1972; this is now the Norfolk Area Congregational Federation.

The city's sole Presbyterian Church, Trinity, next door to the Roman Catholic Cathedral, joined the URC. Its present building is the successor to the Presbyterian Church in Theatre Street, destroyed in the 1942 blitz. The new church, opened in 1956, is on the site of the former Unthank Road Baptist Church. Ipswich Road URC, dating from 1952 and one of the many mission churches founded by Princes Street, also joined.

Princes Street, hoping to ease the financial burden of its large buildings with a 1989 scheme to turn its lecture hall block into commercial offices, was unable to find tenants when the conversion of the central hall and 32 siderooms was completed. Old Meeting, built in 1693, hosted a civic service for 46 direct descendants of the Pilgrim Fathers from America in 1896. Now the church holds only one service a month but still draws visitors - more than 600 in 1998.

**This roundel, representing six world faiths, was installed above the pulpit of the Octagon Unitarian Chapel in Colegate, Norwich, in 1999. It was crafted in glass and ironwork by Steven Pask, a friend of the Octagon and a member of the Norfolk Unitarians. The centrepiece is the flaming chalice of Unitarianism, signifying the movement's openness to other faiths. At the top is the Cross, symbol of Christianity; next (clockwise) is the Crescent Moon and Star of Islam; then the Sanskri word Om for Hinduism, followed by the Star of David for Judaism, the Yin and Yang of Taoism and then the Wheel of Buddhism.**

Almost every parish in Norfolk had at least one Nonconformist chapel by the close of the nineteenth century. The majority of these chapels were Methodist - sometimes more than one in the same village. The reason for this was that Methodism split into several branches during the nineteenth century and each built its own chapels.

It was not until 1932, when the three main branches of Methodism - Wesleyan, Primitive Methodist and United Methodist - came together that overlapping began to be tackled. The union celebration took place in the Royal Albert Hall on September 20th 1932, with the Duke and Duchess of York (the future George VI and his consort, the present Queen Mother) among the 10,000 present. The ceremony was broadcast on radio and thousands of people in churches and homes heard it.

Holt had its own representatives at the Albert Hall and, like many other places, held special services in its three Methodist chapels on October 2nd. There was a united service at Albert Road in the morning and another at Norwich Road in the evening. The next day there was a united women's gathering at Cley Road, followed by a union tea and a thanksgiving service.

The newly-united denomination began to

**Since 1968 the Rev Jack Burton has been driving a bus in the Norwich area. He is an ordained Methodist minister but chose to earn his living in this way so that he could function as a worker-priest. Norwich-born Jack attended Thorpe Hamlet and City of Norwich Schools. He began training for the ministry in 1959 at Handsworth College, Birmingham. He served as a minister in Glasgow and at Littleport, Cambridgeshire, but came back to Norwich in 1968. Jack was Sheriff of the city in 1988-89 and in 1993 received an honorary MA from UEA. In 1978 he took responsibility for the redundant St Clement's Church in Colegate, Norwich. He has written four books, including The Gap, published in 1991, which looks at the gap between Christians and those who do not attend church.**

work together. (In Norfolk only the twenty or so Wesleyan Reform Union chapels had not joined the new church.) But it was another two generations before the old labels had died out and chapels were called churches. Closure of overlapping and redundant chapels happened slowly but during the second half of the century, numbers more than halved. New buildings replaced old in some places - notably the new St Peter's Park Lane, Norwich, which opened on September 3rd 1939 - the day the Second World War started.

In the Norwich area in 1940, there were four circuits with a total of 41 chapels. Elsewhere in the county there were a further 19 circuits with 428 chapels. By 1998 there was just one Norwich circuit with 23 churches. The other 14 circuits in the county had just 163 churches.

Of the 23 churches in the Norwich circuit, eight have been built since 1950 and another two are Local Ecumenical Partnerships, where several denominations work and worship together. White Woman Lane, Old Catton, has no building of its own and has met for more than twenty years for Sunday worship in the Middle School.

Circuits, groups of churches with one or more ministers, have always been central to Methodist organisation. Two-thirds of Methodist services are taken by local preachers (men and women) - the equivalent of lay preachers in other denominations. They are so named to distinguish them from the travelling preachers who eventually became Methodism's ministers.

In 1929, East Dereham Circuit had 26 chapels and two ministers. Local preachers took up to 20 services in 13 weeks - often preaching twice in the same chapel on the same day, and being entertained to lunch or tea by a member of the congregation.

Women have been ordained as ministers since 1974 and four were serving in Norfolk circuits in 1999. In addition, the Rev Rosemary Wakelin, a retired minister, was serving as Methodist chaplain to Norwich Prison and partnering an Anglican, Canon Ivan Bailey, in organising the religious input to Radio Norfolk.

The Primitive Methodists had strong links with the Labour Party and resolutions from their quarterly meetings reflected current thinking on social issues such as resistance to football pools, the opening of cinemas on Sunday and proposals to establish a greyhound track in Norwich.

The East Dereham Circuit opposed the Prayer Book Measure of 1928 and *"... in the interests of Protestantism and Nonconformity requests all our members and adherents to use their influence in defeating the Measure, and thus save England from Roman Catholicism."* (The Prayer Book Measure was the proposal for a new Prayer Book for the Anglican Church, which Parliament turned down.)

But attitudes to other churches changed and during the Second World War Anglicans worshipped in the ex-Primitive Methodist Chapel at Bawdeswell until their damaged parish church could be rebuilt. In 1999, a history of nineteenth-century Methodism in Walsingham was on sale at the Roman Catholic National Shrine.

Outdoor worship, in the form of camp meetings, was still practised by Primitive Methodists in the Thirties. Roy Craske's Methodism in Sheringham - a Brief History, records the Sunday School meeting at 9.30am and ministers, teachers and scholars marching in procession to the top of Gun Street. A short service was held and a meeting on Beeston Common announced for the afternoon. To this people came from the villages, marching in procession to the common, singing and holding short services on the way. On the common, several speakers used a farm wagon as their pulpit.

As populations moved, Methodists built new churches, especially in urban areas and larger villages. The new church at Spixworth opened in January 1999 - just two weeks before Coltishall closed.

At Yarmouth in 1938, the large church on the corner of King Street and Regent Road was given up and a Central Hall established in the redundant Congregational Church on the corner of King Street and Deneside. Fifty years later the Central Hall site was redeveloped for what was to become Christchurch

Methodist/United Reformed Church, embracing Methodists and the congregations of the former Middlegate and Cobholm United Reformed Churches.

Methodists had high hopes of unity nationally with the Church of England during the Sixties but failure of the scheme did not hinder co-operation between local churches. Norwich Cathedral was used for two services during the 1981 Methodist Conference in Norwich. In 1988 more than 1000 Methodists from all over the county gathered in the cathedral to celebrate the 250th anniversary of the conversion of John Wesley, the founder of Methodism. They were there again in 1993 for a farewell service to the Rev Dr Richard Jones, retiring chairman of the East Anglia District of the Methodist Church.

Membership of Baptist churches in the Norfolk Association of Baptist Churches, which includes Lowestoft, was 3284 in 1901. By 1998 this had dropped to just under 2000 in 31 churches. Lay preachers, of whom there were 120 between the wars, are now down to 25. As with the other Free Churches, Baptists were strong supporters of the Liberal Party and spoke out on political issues. In 1901 the Norfolk Association deplored the British policy in the Boer War of farm burning and imprisonment of women and children in concentrated (sic) camps in South Africa.

Liberals opposed the 1902 Balfour Education Act which allowed money from the rates to be given towards the maintenance costs of Anglican and Roman Catholic schools. The opposition was led by Sir George White, a Baptist and Liberal MP for North Norfolk. Many Nonconformists refused to pay the education rate. In Norwich in 1904, two Baptist ministers and thirty of their members were summonsed and had goods sold to defray the cost of the unpaid rate.

**Christchurch, Yarmouth, created from the merger of Methodists and United Reformed Church congregations.**

**Charles Jewson, prominent businessman and local historian, had a long association with St Mary's Baptist Church, Duke Street, Norwich. He was secretary of the church for 25 years and served as president of the Norfolk Association of Baptist Churches. Mr Jewson was born in Norwich, trained as a chartered accountant and joined the family firm of timber merchants, Jewson and Sons, in 1934. He was the third member of his family to become Lord Mayor of Norwich. He served in 1965-66 and was the first Lord Mayor from outside the corporation to serve as a non-political nominee of the whole city council. His great-uncle, Richard, was Lord Mayor in 1917-18 and his father, Percy, in 1934-35. He wrote The Baptists of Norfolk, published in 1957. His wife Joyce, was the daughter of a distinguished minister of St Mary's, Dr Gilbert Laws. Mr Jewson died in 1981, aged 71. Charles Jewson Court, the flats built by the Baptist Housing Association at Mile Cross, Norwich, are named after him.**

Baptists were active in social work. In December 1904, 759 Norwich men who had applied for relief work which the Lord Mayor was trying to organise marched behind a band to St Mary's Baptist Church, Duke Street. They received parcels for their families after the service. In January 1905, 150 Yarmouth unemployed received tickets for one shilling (5p) for grocery or coals at Park Chapel, Yarmouth. In the same year, Park Chapel appointed a deaconess, Sister Edith Pearce, to work among the sick and poor. St Mary's appointed Nurse Mary Guyton and in 1907, the 927 people who attended her surgery paid one penny per visit.

The First World War saw men joining the forces – by spring 1915, thirty had gone from Dereham Road, Norwich, 80 from Park Chapel, Yarmouth, and 31 from Diss. Stalham Baptist Chapel opened its schoolroom as a writing-room for soldiers and provided a buffet. Bacton arranged a morning service for soldiers in the area. In the Second World War, many Baptist churches provided hospitality for the forces.

Sheringham (1930) was the first Baptist Church built after the First World War. Today it has 132 members and holds services in Sheringham High School in the peak summer season to accommodate the many visitors. Mile Cross, Norwich, was built in 1937 as a Sunday School, staffed with teachers from St Mary's, Duke Street. It remained under St Mary's wing until becoming a church in its own right in 1987. Witard Road, on the Heartsease estate, Norwich, opened as the J H Shakespeare Memorial Church in 1960. The Rev J H Shakespeare was minister of St Mary's from 1883-98 and his son, Sir Geoffrey Shakespeare, was Liberal MP for Norwich (1929-45).

Since the Second World War, churches which have come up to date with music and have good leadership, have made good progress. Examples include Wymondham, Lowestoft, Hunstanton (joint Baptist-URC), Witard Road and Dereham Road, Norwich, and Fakenham. The social witness continues, with two houses for homeless young men and women run by Baptists at Lynn; a cafe for children and young people at Stalham; a drop-in centre at Lowestoft; a monthly tea club for people living alone at Foulsham; and luncheon clubs at St Mary's and Dereham Road.

The Salvation Army has always been one of the most visible of the churches with its bands, uniforms, open-air meetings and constant fund-raising for the needs of other people. It continues to fulfil its pledge that "Wherever there is need, there is the Salvation Army."

In 1999 there were 16 centres in Norfolk – all but one formed in the last twenty years of the nineteenth century, often against fierce opposition such as stone-throwing and physical attacks. The twentieth-century corps is Mile Cross, Norwich, formed in 1937.

The Salvation Army's evangelism was styled "aggressive" by Cyril Jolly, in the EDP (October 26th 1967). Writing of the Sheringham corps, he said: *"The Army went for the worst and some notable conversions took place. Men notorious for wickedness became stalwarts of the cause. Some were won by drunk raids; the band marched through the streets as the public-houses closed and the men worse for drink often followed to the hall, where a late service was held."*

The Sheringham Corps, founded in 1888 by a group of fishermen who went to Grimsby, met Salvationists and came back and held services in a net loft over Calley Emery's boat-building shed on Lifeboat Plain. The first band was formed in 1890 under Bandmaster Harry Grice. A new hall was opened in 1896 and extended in 1985 by taking in the old Co-op bakehouse. On Armistice night 1918, Sheringham Salvationists led a march through the town, with the band lit by heavy carbide lights. In the Second World War and after, Salvationists serving locally in the Army and RAF attended meetings and played in the band.

The band also entertained German prisoners-of-war at Matlaske. For many years the annual Harvest of the Sea – a thanksgiving for the harvest and the safety of the fishermen – was organised by Henry (Downtide) West, coxswain of Sheringham lifeboat from 1951-62. The meeting was conducted by Scottish

**Repairing and refurbishing Norfolk's rich heritage of churches is a constant process, with much of the work going on out of the public eye, such as this re-gilding work for Norwich Cathedral spire finial, pictured in April 1975.**

fishermen who had come to Yarmouth for the herring fishing. The Sheringham hall was decorated with fishing nets and crab pots with the names of all the local boats hung above the pulpit. The service was televised in 1955. Sheringham band has made many broadcasts and travelled extensively in the UK. Its bandmaster and deputy bandmaster for many years, Brian Pegg, was on the lifeboat for nearly forty years – 26 years as mechanic and six as coxswain. In 1989 he was awarded the BEM for services to the RNLI.

Other corps in the county offered hospitality to troops in the Second World War, both Dereham and Fakenham opening canteens. In the Thirties, Fakenham several times held a Christmas dinner for poor people. In 1934, Captain W V Russell, Fakenham corps commanding officer, organised the local fund to support dependants of the victims of the Gresford colliery disaster.

Fakenham also took part in the annual Hospital Sunday service which was the culmination of fund-raising events for the Norfolk and Norwich Hospital. Post-war, Fakenham musicians visited the Ukrainians at a prisoner-of-war camp on the edge of the town; some of the Ukrainians came to their services.

General William Booth, founder of the Salvation Army, made 16 visits to Norwich. The "Army's" first meetings were held in the Old Skating Rink in Bethel Street; the present citadel in St Giles Street was opened nearby in 1892. The former Catholic chapel (now the Maddermarket) was leased for young people's work from 1900-22.

The work then moved to a refurbished boot and shoe factory in Pottergate. In 1950 the Sunday School transferred to new premises in Wellington Lane in 1950. The final move for the young people was to the refurbished Mortimer's Hotel which was previously closely associated with actors who performed at the Hippodrome Theatre. This building houses the Norwich Citadel Community Centre and was opened on November 6th 1974, by the Duchess of Kent. The cost of buying and renovating the premises was £84,000. A further extension of the premises took place in 1994 with the acquisition of the Conservative Club and resulted in the Catherine's Coffee Lounge being opened in the former bar, and a new day centre.

City Salvationist were honoured in 1997 when Harry W Watson became the first Salvation Army member to be elected Lord Mayor of Norwich. His wife, Jackie, became Lady Mayoress.

Thousands queue to hear evangelist

GRAHAM PACKS CARROW ROAD

Evangelist Billy Graham attracted 62,000 people to Carrow Road in just four days in June 1984.

The Nineties were designated the Decade of Evangelism. The period saw a big growth in the training of lay people - more than 1000 attended courses in Norwich Diocese in 1995. Alpha, a course in basic Christianity, proved increasingly popular as a means of introducing non-Christians to the faith.

St Margaret's parish in Lowestoft appointed a Church Army captain evangelist as a minister to the unchurched. He set up a Saturday service in the church hall, but worship remained mainly a Sunday activity with new hymns in contemporary style widely used. Norfolk has had two hymn-writers whose work is known nationally and beyond. One, the Right Rev Timothy Dudley-Smith, was Bishop of Thetford from 1980-91. The other, the Rev Dr Fred Pratt Green, took up hymn-writing after retiring from the Methodist ministry and moving to Norwich in 1969.

Outside the main denominations, many other churches have formed during the century. By the Nineties there were eight Assembly of God (Pentecostal) churches in the county and up to a hundred churches meeting in schools or halls with no link to any denomination. The 350 Quakers (Society of Friends) in the county maintain their tradition of silent worship at ten meeting houses.

There are strong independent evangelical churches, like Surrey Chapel in Norwich, founded in 1845 by the Rev Robert Govett who had left the Church of England. Its chapel, between Surrey Street and Ber Street, was demolished when the congregation moved to Botolph Street in 1985. Mount Zion Family Life Centre, a Pentecostal Church, opened a new building, seating 850, in Norwich in 1996.

One of the most ambitious independent evangelical projects was at the former maternity hospital at Drayton Hall, which was converted in the Nineties to become the national base for Christian organisation Proclaimers International. The hall was fully refurbished and extended, grounds restored and staff housing provided in a major refurbishment programme. A church was started by the organisation in the mid-Nineties. A 650-seat auditorium was recently opened at a cost of more than £500,000. Proclaimers International is involved in conferences and evangelism and has bases in a number of other countries.

The Orthodox Church, the Christadelphians, the Church of Jesus Christ of Latter Day Saints (the Mormons) and the Jehovah's Witnesses all have their churches. The Orthodox Jews have their synagogue in Norwich and the only other Jewish community in Norfolk, the Progressive Jewish

Community, meets monthly in the city.

To this rich tapestry has been added in the final quarter of the century the Buddhists, with a worship centre in Norwich and a retreat centre at Surlingham. The first Muslims to come to Norfolk in any numbers were seamen visiting the ports. The resident population in 1999 was 2000-plus. This had been boosted by the arrival of Bangladeshis in the city after the Second World War. They now number around 600. There is a population of about 300 Egyptian teachers who come to UEA for three months. There are also about 200 undergraduate and post-graduate students plus another 100 British Muslim citizens. UEA provides a meeting-place for Friday prayers for students and local people.

As the new millennium dawns, there has never been a wider choice of alternatives, both for Christians and those following other faiths, for people wishing to find a path to greater spirituality.

Norfolk's unique position as a repository of so rich a medieval legacy of churches has often been seen as a burden by tiny communities struggling with yet another repair bill. Yet it is astonishing how many have greeted the news of such a bill with a sigh - and then immediately followed by a simple determination to roll up their sleeves and get on with the job of saving the village church for the next generation.

As Charles Roberts and D P Mortlock have observed: *"A church is not just a building... it is, much more importantly, a mirror of the community it has served for centuries and a microcosm of the history of England itself.*

*"Also, in a wonderful, indefinable way, it is a living thing, an ageless symbol of continuity, the links of its chain formed through the years by the countless good souls who have worshipped here, loved the place, and at last been buried here."*

In many rural communities much beset with a decline in facilities such as schools, pubs, shops and post offices the church has, *de facto*, resumed its original role as the village's only community building. The very act of raising money through community efforts to preserve and beautify the church for those to follow is helping to bring that community together. In an era when most people no longer work in the villages they live in, this need to link together for a common cause has never been more important.

The baton of Norfolk's churches had passed through perhaps 25 or 26 generations by the beginning of the twentieth century. It has now passed through three or four more. Occasionally the hand that has reached to grasp it has had to struggle to hold on. Sometimes a generation has stumbled in its share of the race. But it is a source of inspiration to all of Norfolk - believers and non-believers alike - that the baton has been dropped so few times.

## Chapter 6

# The First World War

**STEVE SNELLING is a feature writer on the Eastern Daily Press with a particular interest in military history. Educated at the City of Norwich School, he joined Eastern Counties Newspapers in 1974 and has worked in a variety of roles, including sports editor and features editor of the Evening News and editor of the EDP's What's On supplement. He is the author of four books of local and military history: Images of Norwich (1994), VCs of Gallipoli (1995), Over Here: The Americans in Norfolk in World War II (1996) and VCs of Passchendaele (1998). He is currently writing a biographical study of the Naval VCs of the First World War.**

The last holidaymakers had long since departed. Boarding houses had become billets and the grey waters of the North Sea were sewn with mines. Yet for many of Yarmouth's citizens life went on as normal. Fishermen still plied their hazardous trade, vaudeville comedians still trod the boards at the Hippodrome where Griff "the original joking juggler" was topping the bill and the biting wind, that age-old adversary and arbiter of maritime life, still held bitter sway along the exposed East Anglian coastline.

It was the ninetieth day of a war that, despite the presence of a naval air station on the South Denes and an obsolete shore battery, seemed far away. A few miles out to sea, the daily patrol consisting of a couple of destroyers and an antiquated fishery protection gunboat was passing uneventfully as it had done since war was declared. Inside the narrow harbour, the remainder of the Yarmouth Patrol stood by the quay. Moored alongside them were three submarines, waiting for the equinoctial gales to blow themselves out before embarking on their missions. The largest of them, the E10, was bound for the icy waters of the Baltic. The others, the smaller and older D3 and D5, were on an hour's notice to make for their patrol area off Terschelling. So rough were the sea conditions and so cramped the quarters aboard the D-class boats, the commander of one sought and was granted permission to spend the night with friends in Norwich. Lt Cdr Godfrey Herbert, a vastly experienced if rather unlucky submariner, left his able deputy, Lt Donald Brodie, in command and set off inland with the assurance that he could be back within an hour.

The evening passed off quietly, but shortly after 7am on November 3rd 1914, Herbert was rudely awakened by a maid hammering at his door. "Wanted on the telephone, sir... says it's very urgent!" Scrambling downstairs in his pyjamas, Herbert picked up the telephone. It was Brodie in a state of considerable excitement. "For goodness sake, sir, hurry back at once," he shouted. "We're off to sea. German fleet is dropping shells all around us!"

In fact, this was something of an exaggeration, albeit an understandable one in the circumstances. An enemy squadron, consisting of the battle-cruisers Seydiltz, Moltke and the Von der Tann, the cruiser Blucher and three light-cruisers, had indeed stolen through dawn's autumn mists to the evident surprise of the Yarmouth Patrol and the resort's unsuspecting population. But the bombardment, which most ashore initially took to be British ships engaged in gunnery practice, was short-lived and largely inaccurate. A few heavy shells churned the sea off the North Beach, but the closest any came to land was one which burst within a few hundred yards of the town's seaside scenic railway. The action, however, was not without incident.

Among the first to detect the Germans' unheralded arrival were the crews of numerous steam drifters, riding at their nets, near the Cross Sands Light Vessel. The Boy Daniel was reportedly only a "warship's length" away from the rearmost enemy cruiser when the shooting war began. Her skipper, Robert Green, later remarked: "The concussion was so great that the wheelhouse windows were shattered." His shock was shared on land as soon as the truth dawned. "Many women were sadly upset by the sound of the firing and ran into the streets only partially dressed in great alarm," commented one eyewitness.

For others fear gave way to grimly compelling fascination. As the thunder of the guns rolled across the sea, many lined the seafront in the hope of catching a glimpse of the raiders. With the aid of binoculars, one man saw lights flickering through the mist, an estimated ten miles off Corton. "Then suddenly the leading one fired, and I could distinctly see the flash and hear the roar. My house shook a great deal..." Another observed: "The first sound came from the northward... Suddenly flash! flash! flash! Then after a perceptible interval the sound. Then again, flash! flash! flash!" The firing shook houses and rattled windows as far away as Mundesley and Stalham.

Yet it might have been far worse but for the gallant intervention of the gunboat Halcyon and the destroyers Lively and Leopard. Challenging the superior enemy force, they not only deflected it from its course but also miraculously survived their brief encounter with only trifling damage and a handful of casualties. Some time around 7.45am, the destroyers and submarines lying in the river at Yarmouth were seen hurrying out. But an eyewitness recorded: *"Before they had proceeded far, with three or four heavy crashes of big guns, the whole thing ended..."* Well, not quite.

Herbert only just made it back to D5 in time. According to one account, the submarine's motors were already running when its commander leapt aboard. Running on the surface the D5 made for the Corton Gap and a sea freckled with drifters, their crews pointing the way to the last sighting of the enemy ships. One skipper shouted a warning about floating mines in the vicinity. Not long after, around 10.10am, the sound of an explosion carried across the water. In less than a minute, the D5, her hull ruptured by a mine, had disappeared, leaving Herbert and about a dozen crewmen thrashing about in the icy sea.

Herbert later recorded: *"Most were obviously beginning to feel the strain of keeping afloat. It was too much for them; first one and then another would throw up his hands and go down. For some minutes I held on to one of the stokers, who was close to me, urging him to keep his head; but he got heavier and heavier till, seeing that we should both go under, I had to release my hold of him. The cold water, and the heavy clothing worn by a submarine crew, were the cause of this early fatigue. But to have been shipmates with these men for a whole 12 months; to have known them all so intimately; and now to see them perish, was terribly grim..."*

By the time a steam drifter reached them, there were only five survivors, including Herbert and one other officer. The twenty members of the D5's crew who died represented the heaviest loss of life in the entire engagement. What became known as the "raid on Gorleston" was dismissed by the Official Naval Historian as "an operation of no military significance whatever". But the true importance of this minor skirmish lay elsewhere, in the minds of a citizenry for whom the war once so distant had become frighteningly real. To many the hapless encounter off Yarmouth marked the realisation of a new kind of warfare in which the civilian population was no longer inviolate.

More than anything, the raid had exposed the shortcomings in the country's defences and the vulnerability of towns such as Yarmouth. *"To put it finely,"* observed one local journal, *"it is not exactly comforting to know that enemy battleships and cruisers can go prowling about the North Sea, within easy range of the East Coast, without let or hindrance."* As events would soon prove, however, that vulnerability was not restricted to seaward attack.

A war greater in scale and suffering than any previously experienced, fought with weapons more destructive than ever wielded before and waged by nations that would be transformed forever, took many in Norfolk by surprise. If the country's politicians were distracted by a crisis over Home Rule for Ireland, the thoughts of many local people were concentrated on such perennial issues as the quality of the harvest and the outcome of the summer sport festivals being played out on the cricket field at Lakenham and the

ANGLO-GERMAN WAR BEGINS.

BRITISH MINE LAYER SUNK.

ULTIMATUM ON BELGIAN NEUTRALITY

AN UNSATISFACTORY REPLY.

BRITISH DECLARATION OF WAR.

KING'S MESSAGE TO THE NAVY.

CHEERING CROWDS IN LONDON.

GOVERNMENT TAKE CONTROL OF THE RAILWAYS.

**August 5th 1914: The EDP reports the start of the First World War.**

**Harry Cator (1894-1966) and his bride-to-be, Rose Morriss, shortly before the outbreak of war. Cator, who was born at Drayton, enlisted in Kitchener's New Army in September 1914, and went on to become one of Norfolk's most highly-decorated soldiers. Awarded the Military Medal for saving lives on the Somme, he won the Victoria Cross at Arras on April 9th 1917 for a single-handed attack on a German trench which led to the capture of 100 prisoners and five machine-guns. The French added the Croix de Guerre to his honours. During the Second World War, he served in the Home Guard and as a prison camp commandant. He was dismissive of his many honours. "Real soldiers curse all war and all warmakers," he once said. "I have seen men driven mad in the trenches. They gave me a decoration. In that hell a soldier may easily do one thing as another..."**

waterways of the Broads. Few doubted the justice of the country's cause and fewer still understood the realities of the war to come. On August 4th 1914, the day Asquith's ultimatum to Germany ran out, the Eastern Daily Press assured its readers: *"whatever the part we are to take in the lamentable war into which Europe is now driven, we shall go in with clean hands".*

But unlike other parts of the country, the announcement that Britain was at war induced little rejoicing, only the cancellation of a few church fetes "due to the international situation", the postponement of the Norwich Festival and an outbreak of panic-buying which prompted one observer to note: *"The assumption appears to be that all within a week or two we may expect to see a bivouac of foreign jabbering troops at the corners of our sweet suburban roads."*

Contrary to popular myth, there was no immediate rush to enlist in Norfolk. Reservists, naval and army, quickly found themselves back in uniform. The county regiment's three under-strength Territorial units, which included one battalion of cyclists, were mobilised. And the regulars who helped make up the country's highly-trained but pitifully small professional army marched away to the horrors of Mons, Le Cateau and the long retreat to the Marne. But for many men eligible for military service there were other priorities which served to keep recruitment figures low in Norfolk. The EDP touched on one when it reported on August 29th: *"During the past few weeks harvest operations in the rural districts have held back a good many men..."* Others were constrained by concern over their families and jobs at the end of the war.

Some companies, Steward and Patteson Brewery among them, offered any workers who enlisted their jobs back at the end of their service. A few firms pledged to take care of the dependents of those who volunteered. Such initiatives combined with peer pressure, rampant anti-German propaganda and tub-thumping appeals to patriotism to open the floodgates. On the day Ian Malcolm MP brought what he called Lord Kitchener's "travelling recruiting bureau" to Norwich, via similar meetings at Thetford, Watton, Wymondham and Hethersett, Cromer FC announced it was abandoning football "for the present" and urged players and supporters to enlist. In a letter to the EDP, a club official added: *"One earnestly prays that as many as possible of the friends of Cromer football will follow the example of 'Theo', 'Roshy' and Gardner and the two Jeffreys, not forgetting our old friends Herbert Palmer, Ralph Ling and many others who have already responded to the call of King and Country."*

Hundreds answered Malcolm's appeal at a packed St Andrew's Hall. The following day recruiting offices at Britannia Barracks and Blackfriars Hall were besieged as more than 1000 signed up. According to one account, whole detachments of "intending recruits" hurried up Mousehold Heath towards the barracks "as if the fate of the Empire depended upon their being enrolled before the day was out..." One of those heading for Mousehold, W H Barrett, later wrote: *"The barracks gates stood wide open and a milling crowd swarmed all over the place, some having been there for days sleeping under the trees. It was two days before we could register our arrival, for ordinary methods of running the depot had broken down, and though a skeleton staff were doing their best, they were swamped by the flood of recruits."*

In the space of less than a fortnight there were sufficient men to form two Kitchener battalions, the 8th and 9th Norfolks, to add to the already established 7th battalion. Included among the ranks of the 8th battalion were a Company of Norwich businessmen who had answered a letter published in the EDP. Signed by A E Winter, K J Little, F W Mase and G C Thompson, it urged anyone interested in joining up to meet at the foot of Gas Hill before marching *en bloc* to enlist. In the best traditions of British amateurism, they were told to report the following Saturday with their oldest clothes, shaving equipment, a toothbrush, brush and comb! The headlong rush was mirrored by a rash of weddings.

Among the young couples tying the knot were Harry Cator, a twenty-year-old former porter on the Midland and Great Northern

Joint Railway, and his cousin, Rose Morriss, who travelled to the church on a bus. *"We shouldn't have been married so soon,"* she wrote to a relative, *"only he felt he ought to go and he wanted me to be his wife before he went. We had it very quiet..."* The marriage took place in Yarmouth on September 2nd 1914. The next day Harry enlisted and was posted to the 7th East Surreys. September witnessed many such separations as thousands of volunteers, most of them without uniforms or rifles, left Norfolk bound for vast tented encampments to begin training for war. Travelling in the opposite direction that autumn were thousands of cavalrymen, yeomanry units of the 2nd Mounted Division hastily despatched to this corner of East Anglia in the wake of the naval encounter of November 3rd. They included the men of the Middlesex Yeomanry who left Reading for what they thought was a war zone only to find themselves disembarking at Cromer.

The unit quickly established its HQ in Mundesley's Grand Hotel and the men were scattered in billets around Bacton and Paston. By December, Norfolk was crawling with troops engaged in feverish activity. Sheringham golf course was gashed with trenches, reserve lines were dug between Briston and Hunworth and gun positions sited around the coast from Weybourne to Mundesley. The thinking was clear enough, as L-Cpl S F Hatton, one of the Middlesex Yeomen, related: *"A German invasion was expected before Christmas, and it was rumoured that the north-eastern Norfolk coast was the enemy's chosen landing-place. Hearsay had it that from Holkham Bay to Happisburgh were many places where German transports and battleships could come close into the shore... and, honestly, the folk in Cromer, and like towns, were really very 'windy'.*

*"My own troop was billeted in the quaint old cliff village of Trimingham, and here training during the day was very strenuous indeed. At nights we formed a series of cavalry patrols all round the coast... I shall long*

**Crowds cheer as Lynn's Naval Reservists march down King Street in late 1914. Many of these men were to be lost in the brief but bloody U-boat attack on the Aboukir, Hogue and Cressy in an action notorious as the first time a submarine had fired on vessels that had stopped to pick up survivors.**

**August 1914, and the centre of Norwich is transformed into an armed camp as soldiers enjoy a final haircut before leaving for France as part of the British Expeditionary Force.**

*remember those winter night rides like smugglers along the windy cliffs, with the wind singing, whining rhythmic songs among the trees and telegraph wires; the biting cold and the rapid movement making the blood to tingle attune with the merry rattle of hoofs through the silent countryside. There was a large house with a flat cement roof standing right out by itself on the cliff, a mile from the village, known as Trimingham House. It was rumoured that signals had been seen from this house to ships at sea, and the owner, a German, was promptly interned. The spy was supposed to be rife in Norfolk at this time. Any bearded elderly entomologist riding around with a box in search of specimens became an obvious object of suspicion..."*

For some it was no laughing matter. Ruby Marson, a teacher at Tattersett School, near Fakenham, was convinced that the bright lights she saw in the sky on numerous occasions that autumn and winter were German signals. She even wondered if there was a connection between the lights and an electricity mast installed two years earlier at Barmer Hall by strangers. "The people of Syderstone said, 'They are three dirty German spies' to me when I asked who the strange men were I passed on the common. There's many a true word spoken in jest."

So seriously did the military take the rumours of a Christmas invasion that the Middlesex Yeomen found themselves manning their shore defences on a nightly basis throughout the festive week. In fact, while British and German troops were serenading each other with carols and playing football in No-Man's-Land, L-Cpl Hatton and his pals were shivering in their clifftop trenches. It had been a bitterly cold night, and he recorded: *"the rime was on our hair and moustaches as we scrambled out to wish each other 'happy morn'."* There was, of course, no landing. But the Germans did put in an appearance the following month, although they came not by sea but by air in a pioneering mission that would usher in a disturbing new era in warfare while provoking another outbreak of spy mania.

History records the German Zeppelin raid on Norfolk carried out on the night of January 19-20th 1915, to be the first-ever air assault on mainland Britain. It earned for the unfortunate towns of Yarmouth and King's Lynn a grim notoriety and destroyed forever the notion that the country's major towns and cities were safe from attack. Yet the epoch-making sortie was riddled with misjudgements on both sides. It was like a story straight from the pages of H G Wells, a bewildering sequence of startling events which ranged from farce to tragedy and resulted in four civilian deaths and thousands of pounds worth of damage.

Norfolk had never been the Zeppelins' intended target. Their orders were to bomb port installations in the Humber estuary. But a combination of foul weather and poor navigation carried them off course. Of the three airships which took off from their bases at Fuhlsbuttel and Nordholz, only two crossed the British coast and the closest any of them came to their planned destination was passing over Hunstanton. L3, commanded by Kapitanleutnant Hans Fritz, was spotted by an astonished member of the Norfolk Volunteers, the equivalent of the Second World War's Home Guard, as he left band practice at Happisburgh. It was shortly after 8pm. Further to the north, the L4 made its landfall near Bacton, although the airship's aristocratic commander Kapitanleutnant Magnus Count von Platen-Hallermund, was convinced he was south-east of Grimsby.

The two raiders set off in different directions, Fritz to the south and Platen-Hallermund to the west. Little went according to plan. *"Meandering about mist-veiled Norfolk, uncertain of their navigation and freezing cold in their open cars, they dropped their bombs indiscriminately wherever they saw a large cluster of lights,"* wrote the historian Kenneth Poolman.

The L3's wayward course took her over Horsey Mere, Hickling Broad, narrowly missing Martham church tower, before approaching Yarmouth. In all, 11 missiles rained down, ten on Yarmouth of which the most destructive was the fourth. The explosion caused by a bomb, probably weighing little more than 100lb, tore through the yards and cottages around St Peter's Plain, killing 72-year-old spinster Martha Mary Taylor and 53-year-old shoemaker Sam Smith. They were the first people to die in England as a result of bombs dropped from the air.

**As the British army mobilised for its first continental conflict since the Crimean war, there were echoes of the past as cavalrymen of the 12th Lancers trotted out of their Norwich barracks and headed into Thorpe railway station on the first leg of their journey to France and the horrors of modern warfare.**

It was a miracle the death toll was not higher. An eyewitness recorded: *"Not a single building in the district escaped damage. Several were completely wrecked, and almost every window in every house within a radius of 200yds were broken... The experience of the inhabitants was terrible... The west wall of St Peter's church was practically peeled in many places... There was a profusion of debris on the Plain, roofs as well as house fronts having been demolished."*

The bombing had lasted little more than ten minutes, and worse was to follow more than sixty miles to the west. From the dropping of his first bomb, an incendiary, on Windham Street, Sheringham, Platen-Hallermund had spread mayhem, alarm and a few bombs across a swathe of north-west Norfolk. He arrived over Lynn at 10.50pm, by way of Holme, Hunstanton, Heacham and Snettisham. Taking the town to be Grimsby, he disgorged eight bombs in the space of 15 minutes, and once again it was a single missile which proved devastating. It fell among the thickly-populated terraces around Bentinck Street and cost the lives of a 14-year-old delivery boy, Percy Goate, and 26-year-old Alice Gazley, whose husband had been killed in action only a few months earlier. The two victims came from neighbouring houses, the worst affected of more than 100 that were damaged.

**Martha Taylor (1842-1915) was one of the first two victims of aerial bombardment in the country's history. The spinster, who lived at No 1 Drake's Buildings, St Peter's Plain, Yarmouth, died in the explosion that also killed Sam Smith. According to evidence given at their inquest by her sister, who lived next door, Martha had left her home shortly before 8pm to go to the grocer's shop in Victoria Road. Her shattered body was found in St Peter's Plain. Consideration was given at her inquest to delivering a verdict of "wilful murder against some persons unknown", but eventually the jury settled for the historic declaration that she had died as a result of "the explosion of a bomb dropped by hostile aircraft..."**

One resident living nearby recorded: *"We had just gone to bed. We got the boy and the girl downstairs and we heard the report. There was a terrific sound when the two houses collapsed. They found the boy Goate about midnight, and Mrs Gazley on Wednesday morning. I think she heard the report and ran to the door, and the house collapsed and fell on her. We heard Mr Goate shrieking under the ruins. The boy Goate was more smothered to death than anything else... The curious thing is that we did not get a scratch on ourselves... The most heart-rending thing was the people in the street who were shrieking..."*

Shock and horror soon gave way to hysteria. Even as the crews of the L3 and L4 were being feted in Germany, a blustering British press was painting them as "barbarians" and "baby-killers". Unaware of just how far off course the Zeppelins actually were, some newspapers accused the Germans of deliberately targeting the Royal residence at Sandringham. Others repeated extraordinary tales of spies and a chain of lights that led Platen-Hallermund to his fatal rendezvous over Lynn. One report ran: *"A close inquiry makes it abundantly clear the murderers were guided in their stealthy flight... over the peaceful towns and villages of the Norfolk coast by a pilot who knew the ground beneath him most intimately."* This was, of course, the same pilot who thought he was over the Humber! Yet far-fetched as the stories were they found a prominent advocate in Lynn MP Holcombe Ingleby who insisted it was "certain that two or more cars were assisting the Zeppelin in its raid on West Norfolk". Citing graphic descriptions of cars variously carrying "a fiery light", "a green light" and occupants with "strangely muffled headgear", he even went so far as to claim that one vehicle had even led the airship away from Lynn as far as the western suburbs of Norwich.

It was almost three months before any Zeppelins returned to the East Coast. Once again, they were aiming for the Humber, but on this occasion the heaviest attack fell on Henham Park, where one bomb burst within fifty yards of the hall itself. That same night incendiaries fell near Southwold and a timber yard was set ablaze in Lowestoft. Overall, the damage was slight, even by the standards of the first raid, but together these operations, little more than aerial experiments, helped pave the way towards much deeper penetrations culminating in audacious attacks on London itself. The airship operations served also to concentrate minds on how to counter the threat.

Primitive anti-aircraft defences were, in time, provided by mobile Royal Naval Air Service units, and parties of the 2/4th Norfolks, moved to Lowestoft in January to bolster the coastal defences, were trained in the art of operating a 12-pounder shore battery specially adapted for high-angle fire. The Navy's motley collection of fighters and seaplanes based at Yarmouth's South Denes air station were largely ineffective. Even when they found the Zeppelins, which was rare enough, they lacked both the climbing power and the armament to tackle them. For the time being at least the airship held the ascendancy of the skies.

On land there were other changes afoot. While the 2/4th Norfolks were settling into their new role not far from where their comrades of the 1/6th (Cyclist) Battalion were patrolling the coast, the Yeomanry were at last preparing to see real action. At midnight on April 11th, the Middlesex Yeomanry were given "a splendid send-off" by the people of Mundesley. L-Cpl Hatton recorded: *"They loaded us with provisions and smokes galore as we moved off for the big adventure..."*

A little more than three months later and some 100 miles further south, those scenes were repeated as the 1/4th Norfolks entrained at Watford on the first leg of their journey into war. In a letter to his wife in Attleborough, Sgt John Dye proudly related: *"Never shall we forget it. It was a magnificent send-off and without boasting I may honestly say the 1/4th Norfolks had once more kept up their reputation and made themselves much liked by the people generally. It was a sight to see them carrying the men's kit-bags... all the way to the Station and when we arrived there and*

**Another rubicon in the conduct of war was crossed in January 1915 when Zeppelins carried out the first air raids over British soil. Yarmouth and King's Lynn received the brunt. The main picture shows damage to a house in Albert Street. Elsewhere, two children pose with an unexploded bomb from one of the airships on a later raid.**

**Harry Daniels (1884-1953) was Norfolk's first soldier-hero of the war. Born in Wymondham, he had run away from a boys' home in Norwich to join the army in 1903. After peace-time service in India, his unit returned to Europe following the outbreak of war. At Neuve Chapelle, in March 1915, he won a Victoria Cross for a near-suicidal attempt to cut a gap in the enemy wire. Badly wounded, he was given a hero's homecoming in Norwich. Accorded a civic reception, he was feted wherever he went. Later commissioned, he returned to the front and was reported killed in action. But Harry was not dead. Although wounded again, he survived the war, earned a second gallantry award and went on to represent Britain as a member of the boxing team at the 1920 Olympic Games in Antwerp. After spells as a recruiting officer, he retired from the army to run a string of hotels before taking up the post of manager of the Leeds Grand Opera House and Theatre. "Dan VC", as he was popularly known, died of a heart attack as he prepared to attend the Queen's Coronation in 1953.**

*the public were not admitted the sight came to a climax; some were singing, some were crying and hanging round the chaps' necks and the officers and NCOs had all we could do to get them apart. They had, up to now, marched hand-in-hand or arm-in-arm and any other way that lovers have till suddenly they find they are not allowed to go any further. It was a sudden stop, but it had to be done..."*

They were bound, like the Yeomanry, for a narrow neck of land few had ever heard of and fewer still could pronounce. It was called Gallipoli.

The campaign waged on that arid, sun-baked peninsula was the first in a succession of tragedies that would befall Norfolk's citizen soldiers and bring home to their families the fearful realities of modern warfare. The distinguished writer Ralph Mottram, a volunteer himself who served with the 9th Norfolks on the Western Front, was undoubtedly correct when, years later, he declared: *"What no 'war histories' ever say is that no civilian soldier 'fights' with grenade, bayonet, machine-gun or cannon except for short, desperate moments. For the remaining hours of the day and night, he has to move or sleep, be fed and clothed, cared for in wounds or sickness and buried if he dies. Such jobs by turns eighty per cent at least of them did, for years, mostly out of bullet range."*

Yet it was the fortunes or misfortunes of the remaining twenty per cent during all too many "short, desperate moments" which left an indelible impression on a whole generation. Or at least those fortunate enough to survive. It was a war in which the weaponry of mass destruction had far outstripped military thinking. As the warring armies found themselves bogged down in France and Belgium, the tactics of despair took over and the slaughter all but beggared belief. Ironically, the Gallipoli campaign, boldly conceived and audaciously mounted, had been designed to break the deadlock by dealing Germany's ally a swift and decisive blow. But by the time the men of the 1/4th and 1/5th Norfolks arrived in August, it too had resolved itself into a bloody slogging match. And within days the carnage had engulfed them. The confused battle fought on August 12th 1915 was one of those "short, desperate moments" to which Mottram referred. It was a disastrous affair characterised by muddle and incompetence made famous by the apparent disappearance of around 170 men of the 1/5th Norfolks, including their commanding officer and a part of the Sandringham Company led by the King's Agent, Captain Frank Beck. *"They... were lost to sight or sound,"* reported Sir Ian Hamilton, the British commander. *"Not one of them ever came back."* Although inaccurate, the losses sustained during the late afternoon advance towards the ridge of Tekke Tepe were heavy indeed. The 1/5th casualty list ran to more than 300 men. Many of the dead were too far forward to be recovered. Consequently, they could only be reported "missing, believed killed", thus compounding the agony of their relatives. To these were added a number of men from the 1/4th Norfolks whose dead included Sgt John Dye.

For most of the inexperienced Norfolks, the action represented the most brutal initiation to war. The chaos was summed up more than half a century later by Stan Burtenshaw, one of the last survivors of the old 1/5th: *"Men were going down, hit, and bushes were catching fire,"* he recalled. *"In the smoke, we all got split up. We didn't seem to know what was happening or where we were going... It was only some days after the attack that I heard that the Colonel and his headquarters company had all been chopped up..."*

Fred Frostick, a 21-year-old member of the 1/5th, left a graphic account of his experiences: *"We moved off in groups of platoons under enemy artillery gunfire, then a long single line when we came into rifle and machine-gun fire. I kept to my platoon sergeant (Ben Yunnes from Aylsham). We ran forward several yards over rough land, then drop (sic) down to rest. A sniper soon had... most of our officers leading us. As I ran, my sun helmet dropped lower on my head. The 'mushroom' for ventilation on the top... hit the top of my head making me think it was a bullet.*

*"I was expecting one as I could hear them whistling pass (sic). What was left of my*

**The stained glass window in Swardeston parish church pays glorious tribute to the Norfolk nurse who achieved a kind of martyrdom. Edith Cavell (1865-1915) was helping run a training school for nurses in Brussels when war broke out. As the Germans advanced, the school became a Red Cross Hospital, treating the wounded of both sides. But by the end of the year, with Brussels and much of Belgium occupied by the Germans, the vicar's daughter from Norfolk had become increasingly involved in a clandestine 'escape line' designed to assist Allied soldiers reach freedom. Arrested in August 1915, Cavell openly admitted to assisting Belgians of military age to go to the front as well as guiding British and French fugitives to neutral Holland. The penalty under German military law was death, and she was duly shot by firing squad on October 12th 1915, despite frantic diplomatic efforts to have the sentence commuted to a term of imprisonment. Although legally justified, it was a propaganda disaster for the Germans. In Britain, her death prompted a rush of men to enlist and, in a war of so many horrors, her death served as a powerful symbol of self-sacrifice. When her body was brought back to Norwich in May 1919, to be buried on Life's Green, beside the Cathedral, the nation mourned a woman whose tragic fate had come to represent 'an essential indictment of militarism...'**

*platoon, ten or a dozen of us, we stopped for a rest by the side of a small wood or clump of trees. I didn't hear or see my lot move off again. When I looked they were gone. I waited there for a while then decided to go back. I saw two 5th Norfolks' men. One was Bob Self from Swafield. The rest of my platoon which went on were never seen or heard of again..."*

Thus did the big adventure turn into a nightmare to recur with grim regularity again and again. For almost every one of the Norfolk battalions there were catastrophes every bit as costly. The 2nd was decimated at Ctesiphon before passing into barbarous captivity at Kut. The 4th together with the reconstructed 5th Battalion were all but annihilated in another misguided frontal assault on Turkish positions at Gaza. The 7th, Kitchener volunteers, suffered 433 casualties in a single day near Loos. The 8th achieved one of the few complete successes on the first day of the Somme offensive, but at a cost of 345 men, killed, wounded and missing. To these were added a further 293 casualties sustained in an attack on Delville Wood three weeks later. The 9th, which had been blooded at Loos, fared little better. In the space of a little over a month, in two separate actions fought amid the shell-churned desolation of the Somme battlefield the battalion raised in Norwich two years earlier suffered a staggering total of 696 casualties. And so the attrition went on.

By the autumn of 1916 many of the volunteer units formed in that surge of patriotism had been bled white; communities and families torn apart. George and Robert Bailey, of Thursford, had enlisted together in the 8th Norfolks and died together on the first day of the "big push". A third brother serving with them had the painful task of writing home, reporting their deaths. Nineteen days later, Pte Ernest Bailey was dead too.

The gains for so much sacrifice were pitifully small. In four and a half months of bitter fighting, the British army had advanced six miles at a cost of 400,000 casualties. It worked out at 75 yards a day. The furthest point reached was a wretched charnel house called Mild Trench which fell to the men of the 9th Norfolks on October 18th.

One of their officers, Terence Cubitt, a 21-year-old soldier-poet and former pupil of Paston School, penned the following:

*The rain came down in torrents, and the mud was thick as paste,*
*As we waited for the dawn in Rainbow Trench;*
*It was mud and blood and shelling, and cries of wounded men;*
*The air was thick with sulphur and flesh-decaying stench.*

*Nights were dark in mid-October, you couldn't see your pal,*
*But you'd hear him gulp and slither in the mud;*
*He wouldn't move again, for they'd got him in the brain,*
*And you'd hear the sickly gurgling of his blood.*

*As an officer you'd laugh at all the horrors*
*(You are paid to smile and treat it as a joke),*
*But it's hard to keep 'em cheery, when you're frightened, wet and weary,*
*And you wonder (when it's over) how you spoke.*

*It's raining more than ever, when the time for action comes,*
*And the autumn dawn comes creeping from the west;*
*Your knees are sore with knocking, and your heart is in your mouth,*
*But the least a man can do is, try his best...*

The Somme marked the beginning and the end for so many of Kitchener's army. As well as losing thousands of volunteers, it had lost its innocence. George Cleveland, one of the 8th Norfolks who went over the top on July 1st 1916 and survived the war, wrote home: *"It was all a horrible nightmare... I've imagined similar battles, but never did I realise how awful it was."*

One of those fortunate enough to survive the struggle on the Somme was Harry Cator. His unit had helped rescue no fewer than 250 wounded from No-Man's-Land after the first day's debacle. He had brought in 36 alone, a remarkable feat which earned him a Military Medal, to which he would later add a Victoria Cross and Croix de Guerre. A few months earlier, his young wife, had written a short letter to a relative in the United States in which she reviewed the tumultuous events of the war: the Zeppelin raids, the loss of the Lusitania and Harry's passage into the trenches. *"Oh! It seems,"* she wrote, *"as if our world has been all turned upside down..."*

There were many who would have shared those sentiments, particularly in the coastal towns of Yarmouth and Lowestoft, for whom the war had become an everyday reality. Already assailed from the air, they found themselves increasingly threatened by raiders from beneath the sea. From the spring of 1915 onwards, German submarines of the Flanders Flotilla, based on the Belgian coast, began taking a heavy toll of the fishing fleets with damaging repercussions for local economies. By summer the losses had risen sharply; almost twenty Lowestoft vessels lost in June, the same in July and almost thirty in August. The pattern of destruction was simple and effective. U-boats would enter the fishing grounds, ordering the crews of the drifters and smacks into their small boats before sending parties aboard to sink the abandoned vessels with time bombs.

Ober-leutnant zur See Steinbruck, commander of the UB-10 operating out of Zeebrugge, reported one such encounter:

*"July 29th to August 2nd, towards Yarmouth. On 30th sunk eight English fishing cutters, Coriander, Fitzgerald, Quest, Achieve, Strive, Prospector... by means of explosive charges... The crews consisted of four or five men. With one exception they were all co-operative; they offered us fish and provisions, were in every respect ready to assist and even in one case drew our attention to a heavy and rapidly approaching cloud of smoke... One of the fishermen had already been sunk earlier in the same week by the UB-12..."*

The loss of the Coriander (LT 153) was particularly poignant. Ten months earlier, this Lowestoft smack, together with the JGC, had achieved a measure of fame by rescuing hundreds of survivors from the ill-starred armoured cruisers Aboukir, Hogue and Cressy, all sunk within the space of 75 minutes by a single U-boat off the Dutch coast. The little Coriander, with a crew of five, had picked up more than 150 men, some of them elderly Norfolk reservists called up at the start of the war. Her skipper, Tom Phillips, a doughty fisherman in his early forties, was decorated and his crew rewarded by a grateful Admiralty.

In the aftermath of his boat's demise, however, Phillips together with other Lowestoft fishing skippers was anxious to fight back. After listening to their pleas for guns to be fitted, the Admiralty relented. In the summer of 1915, four smacks were secretly armed with hidden three-pounders. They were among the first of a clandestine fleet of "special service" vessels, more famously known as Q-ships, designed to combat the U-boat menace. Over the following years, these boats and their volunteer crews, bolstered by a handful of naval gunners, took part in one of the most hazardous campaigns of the war with the object of luring unsuspecting submarines to their doom.

There would be many notable and heroic encounters, none more so than the clash which cost the life of Skipper Tom Crisp in August 1917. His legs smashed by a shell during the smack Nelson's unequal struggle with a better-armed U-boat, he fought to the finish. One of his last orders was to send off a message by pigeon. It read: *"Nelson being attacked by submarine. Skipper killed. Send assistance at once."*

His final order, read out by Lloyd George to the House of Commons, was given to his son as the Nelson sank beneath them: *"Throw the confidential books overboard and throw me after them."* In other fights, it was the smacks which triumphed. Over the course of the struggle, the fishermen claimed the destruction of around ten U-boats. Many had been seen to be holed, but post-war research showed only one submarine to have fallen victim to an armed smack.

This was the UB-4, lost on August 15th 1915, after an encounter with the 93-ton Inverlyon

**Lowestoft fisherman Tom Crisp (1876-1917) was awarded a posthumous Victoria Cross following his armed smack's encounter with a German submarine near the Jim Howe Shoal. Born in Burgh St Peter, he served in the Merchant Navy before taking up fishing from Lowestoft. He became skipper of the George Borrow (LT956) in 1902 and sailed her until she was sunk by a U-boat 15 miles ENE of Cromer on August 11th 1915. He then volunteered for "special service" aboard the small fleet of disguised smacks. His services earned him a Distinguished Service Cross as well as the VC he did not live to receive. His crew, who included his son as second hand, all survived his final action, being rescued after two days adrift in an open boat. The crew of another smack sunk in the engagement were less fortunate. They were last seen with their hands in the air, standing on the casing of the German submarine.**

(LT 687), whose crew included Tom Phillips. The success had been achieved on his first anti-submarine patrol and he very nearly repeated it on his next sortie, putting a shot through the U-boat's conning tower and forcing her to dive.

Although ultimately unsuccessful, the second clash highlighted the nature of the fighting and the bitterness engendered by a form of combat the Germans considered contrary to the rules of war. In opening fire on the submarine, the gun's blast had blown the smack's white ensign overboard. While attempting to recover it, a periscope was spotted roughly 1100 yards away. Phillips recorded: *"We tried several shots at it... but could not hit it, and when he was about forty or sixty yards from us he launched a torpedo straight for our quarter. I saw it coming quite plainly and jambed (sic) my tiller hard to starboard and by so doing it just cleared us."*

Later in port, Phillips met the skipper of a smack sunk by the same submarine he had damaged and he was able to fill in more of the story: *"They ordered him on board the submarine whilst they sent his crew to sink their ship in their own boat by dynamite cartridge, and in the meantime showing him the patched conning tower, and asking him if he knew the names of any of the crew of the trawler Inverlyon... The skipper replied he did not, and the submarine skipper told him if he did not give the required information he would shoot him; but he would not divulge anything and eventually he was cast adrift in his boat... The reason why the submarine skipper was furious was because we had not got the white ensign up..."*

Tom Phillips' luck ran out the following spring, when on April 25th 1916, he found himself in the path of a flotilla of German destroyers and he, together with the crew of his new command, was taken prisoner. The enemy ships were part of a larger force, which included four battle-cruisers, four light-cruisers and another destroyer flotilla, returning after carrying out a bombardment of Lowestoft. The deliberate attack, designed to lure a portion of the British fleet against superior opposition, was carried out with ruthless efficiency. Around 4.10am, the first ranging shots fell just short of the beach. Within minutes, shells were bursting in the town itself. *"Slates, tiles, masonry and bits of metal - shrapnel and the rest - were flying in all directions,"* wrote one observer. The bombardment, which could be heard as far away as Norwich, continued for almost twenty minutes in which time four people were killed, three of them in one house on Sandringham Street, 12 injured and around 200 houses variously damaged. Some of the shells screamed over the town to land near Somerleyton and Carlton Colville, sparking near panic. Canon Reginald Bignold, Rector of Carlton Colville and Rural Dean of Lothingland, recorded: *"The people poured out of Lowestoft. On the Long Road, between here and Kirkley, they were so thick I had to get off my bicycle and walk. It was a very piteous sight - men, women and children all rushing along - some of them went beyond Bungay. It was most merciful that none of them was killed, as shells fell on both sides of the road, Some twenty high explosive shells fell on this Parish but did no harm here. My curate had a very narrow escape as a huge fragment fell within ten feet of him. In Lowestoft, though, some forty houses were demolished, much other damage was done though none of any military importance..."*

The intervention of a British naval force spared the town further destruction and almost certainly prevented similar havoc being wrought in Yarmouth, where some shells fell without adding to the toll of casualties.

Among those woken by the "ear-splitting sound" of the bombardment was Rosa Bull, who had spent much of the night listening to the "dreaded hum" of prowling Zeppelins. *"Just after dawn came the terrible thunder of the guns,"* she wrote, *"any moment dreading one would drop on us. Fortunately, they never got the correct range. The Empire Cinema on Marine Parade was slightly damaged and it later had a brass plate fitted on the building commemorating this event..."*

Although the raid had failed to achieve its purpose, morale had been shaken along with

**Injured men pose for the camera with nurses at a tented extension of Norwich War Hospital. Initial arrangements to cope with the wounded were haphazard. The Norfolk and Norwich Hospital swiftly announced that 150 beds were to be made available. Individuals, meanwhile, offered their services. One woman from Rougham provided calico and flannel to make garments for the Ambulance Brigade and the Soldiers and Sailors Family Association. As the war progressed, some of the county's great homes were opened up as hospitals.**

the local population's faith in the Navy's ability to protect them. So much so, that the Admiralty took the unusual step of writing to the mayors of both Yarmouth and Lowestoft assuring them that measures would be taken to prevent any further attacks. As a direct consequence of the raid, the heavily-armed monitor HMS Havelock and the gunboat HMS Glowworm were dispatched to Lowestoft, miles of trenches dug, a battery of six 4.7-inch field guns posted at Pakefield and a single 4.7-inch gun sited on Gorleston cliffs.

The ships' stay was a brief one, designed to calm strained nerves. The guns were also cosmetic, being of little value against shipping. But the threat of invasion, whether real or imagined, persisted throughout the war. Defence lines were established and plans to evacuate local communities remained in force well into 1918. From 1917 onwards, the rudimentary coastal defences were further strengthened by the construction of a line of circular pill-boxes, modelled on the German fortifications built in France and Flanders, which studded the countryside from Weybourne through North Walsham to Sea Palling. Among the more novel additions was an armoured train, boasting two 12-pdrs and a couple of machine-guns, which chugged up and down the Mundesley branch line from its base at North Walsham. Officially styled No 2 Armoured Train, it was manned by a small detachment of the 2/4th Norfolks.

One of them, Pte F G Cobb, later recalled:

"A captain of the Royal Artillery and RA gunners had charge of the guns, and Lt Turnbull, a son of the general manager of the Great Western Railway, was in charge of train movements. The engine driver was a sergeant and the fireman a private in the Royal Engineers and both were enlisted railwaymen.

"When the train travelled at full speed we were jolted up and down like yo-yos as we sat facing each other on wooden forms in the

**As the war dragged on, increasing efforts were made to bolster morale and raise money. Tanks, real and fake, were enlisted as fund-raising tools on tours around the country to help promote the sale of War Bonds. This one was photographed on Yarmouth's Hall Quay and has been given a special port number, YH777, to mark the occasion. After the war one of the tanks was kept for many years on display in St James' Park, King's Lynn.**

heavy steel-plated wagon, but it was most enjoyable when we cruised slowly along the North Norfolk coast and down the picturesque stretch from Cromer to Yarmouth Beach station, where the railway flanked deserted beaches for miles and miles."

The lumbering train was subsequently withdrawn at the end of the war without ever having fired a shot in anger. The same, however, could not be said about the anti-aircraft batteries established around Bacton. For while invasion remained no more than a worrying possibility, the threat presented by airships marauding over Norfolk was all too real. After the initial shock of their first forays, the visit of the Zeppelin raiders became so frequent as to become almost commonplace.

Anthony Hamond, then no more than a child, later recorded: *"Zeppelins used to be great sport. Armed with a hurricane lamp, if you please, my grandmother's old maid, Alice Brown, used to take me out on to the lawn at Twyford Hall to shake our fists at the Zeppelins as they went over, and to shout, 'Go home, go home, you wicked, wicked men'."*

For the most part, the scattered communities of Norfolk were not the airships' intended targets. They merely happened to lie beneath their flightpaths as they headed for London and the industrial centres of the Midlands. Most of the bombs that did actually fall on Norfolk were the result of misjudgement rather than design. So it was on September 8th 1915 that the L14, having aborted its mission to the capital because of engine trouble, bombed Dereham and left, by way of a bizarre calling card, a bunch of German newspapers and a cap which fluttered down into a field near Scarning tied to a parachute. A little more than a month later, the L11, also bound for London, straddled Coltishall railway station and her commander returned to Germany convinced he had struck his intended target – Woolwich Arsenal!

Air defences were improving, although they never entirely shook off a certain air of eccentricity. R S McNaught, a member of the 49th Provisional Battalion (nicknamed the Old Grocers') who were guarding the north Norfolk coast during the winter of 1915-16, recalled how a colony of pheasants became the country's "top secret" early warning system: *"These were kept behind the dunes because they had wonderful hearing and became restless and vocal when they heard aircraft engines a long way off, and this was the signal for a telephone message to Norwich and other places that a possible Zeppelin raid was signalled... The tiny garrison of pheasant-minders had the cushiest job of World War One... and when battling on the Somme in days ahead I wondered how they were enduring their share of war's privations."*

But try as they might they could not train birds to attack airships. For that they relied on the courage and skill of a small band of intrepid aviators allied to ever more sophisticated weaponry. Early tactics had ranged from the sublime to the ridiculous; from ramming the enemy airship in a suicidal charge to tearing it apart with a lethal grapnel hook! By June 1916, however, the first stocks of incendiary ammunition were supplied which, together with improved aircraft and a better co-ordinated system of air defence, had swift results. Over the next six months, six Zeppelins were destroyed during raids on Britain, the last to fall being the L21 which was shot down into the sea off Lowestoft by aircraft from Yarmouth. It was their first success after months of frustration. Credit for the L21's destruction was given to Flt Sub Lt Edward Pulling, although it is now widely accepted that the decisive attack was made by Flt Lt Egbert Cadbury, heir to a family fortune and a commercial empire founded on cocoa and chocolate who would become arguably the greatest Zepp fighter of the war.

Years later, Cadbury remembered the attack on L21: *"We were warned that the Zeppelin had dropped bombs in the Midlands and was making its way to the coast and I, with two other pilots, immediately got into the air to wait for it. I saw the Zeppelin approaching the coast and immediately chased after it. It was flying at about 5000ft when I first saw it and it immediately climbed to 8000ft and I went after it. I approached from the stern about 300ft below and fired four drums of explosive ammunition into its stern which immediately started to light.*

*"At the same time one of the other pilots was flying over the top of the Zeppelin and to his horror he saw a man in the machine-gun pit run to the side and leap overboard. Having seen the Zeppelin circle down to the sea in a blazing mass - most horrible sight - I went back to Yarmouth and landed. I could not say I felt very elated or pleased at this, somehow I was overawed at the spectacle of this Zeppelin and all the people aboard going down into the sea... I didn't feel any satisfaction about it at all and didn't want to discuss the matter..."*

Watching L21's fiery death throes from Lowestoft pier, the port's senior naval officer, Commodore A Ellison estimated that it took barely a minute from the moment the airship ignited to when she struck the water where *"she engulfed and entirely sank, leaving a large area of oil-covered water..."*

The aerial victories of the autumn of 1916 marked a turning point. For the rest of the war, the balance of power would remain with the fighter defence as was most graphically demonstrated by the shooting down of the L48 over Theberton the following summer and the destruction of the L70 off the north Norfolk coast a year later. The disaster which overtook the L70 and the commander of the German Zeppelin fleet, in August 1918, signalled the end of the enemy airship campaign. The last raid of the war had been halted by a Yarmouth-based aircraft, crewed by Cadbury and Capt Robert Leckie, thus ensuring that the town which suffered first at the hands of the Zeppelin had seized the final victory.

In the space of four years, Norfolk's naval air station had grown out of all recognition. From six aircraft, with five officers and a small party of men to operate them, the South Denes establishment eventually rose to eighty-odd machines, more than 100 officers and around 800 men. And such expansion was not confined to Yarmouth. In February 1916 the Royal Navy opened an airship base in South Norfolk, thus launching the legend of the Pulham "Pigs". In contrast to the German rigid designs most of the airships flying out of Pulham were coastal "Blimps" employed on long, occasionally dangerous, anti-submarine patrols over the southern North Sea. All over the county, military aviation was spreading its wings and laying the foundations for a lasting legacy. As well as satellite landing grounds at Bacton, Burgh Castle, Holt, Mattishall and Sedgeford, Home Defence squadrons were based at Harling Road, Hingham, Marham and Snarehill, near Thetford. Training stations were created to meet the growing demands for new pilots. They included Mousehold, an airfield established on the city's former cavalry drill ground, and Narborough, which covered 908 acres making it the biggest of all Britain's First World War aerodromes. During the course of the war, these airstrips played host to some of the country's most notable aviators, the aces James McCudden, Albert Ball and Billy Barker, the post-war trailblazer Alan Cobham and the future writer W E Johns, who based his hero Biggles' early flying days on his own experiences at Narborough.

The development of aviation had an impact also on the local economy, stimulating industrial growth for two Norwich companies, one new and the other long-established. Car manufacturers Mann Egerton were awarded their first contract in mid-1915

**Egbert Cadbury (1893-1967) quit his studies as a Cambridge undergraduate to join the Royal Navy as an able seaman in 1914. The following spring he transferred to the Royal Naval Air Service and was promptly posted to Yarmouth, where he remained for the rest of the war, becoming the most celebrated and successful of the Norfolk station's anti-Zeppelin fighter force. His exploits earned him a Distinguished Service Cross and a Distinguished Flying Cross. During his time in Yarmouth, he met and married Mary Phillips, daughter of the vicar of Gorleston. Bertie Cadbury, who returned to his family's chocolate empire, was knighted in 1957. Some years later, his eldest son, Peter, who was born in Yarmouth in the midst of a Zeppelin raid, bought the former Cromer lifeboat H F Bailey III and presented it to the town for permanent display as a tribute to the men who had rescued so many of his father's friends during the First World War.**

to build Short 184 seaplanes for the Admiralty. Over the next three years, the company, operating from a specially-built workshop on Aylsham Road, was to construct hundreds of aircraft of different designs, including Spads and DH9s, some of which were employed at Yarmouth. Boulton & Paul completed its first aircraft, a FE2b, in October 1915. It was the first of 550 of this model to leave the firm's Riverside works. Boulton & Paul went to produce more Sopwith Camels than any other aircraft manufacturer, and by 1917 both companies were actively involved in developing their own designs with flight tests at Mousehold. It was a dangerous business and accidents were frequent. Captain Richard Lee, late of the 6th Norfolks and a flight commander in the Royal Flying Corps, was killed while service testing a new design at Mousehold on June 23rd 1917. The son of the rector of Woodton, he was one of two brothers to die in the war, neither of them to enemy action.

Mann Egerton, which continued to build military vehicles, produced two shipboard fighters, while Boulton & Paul unveiled the Bobolink, a fighter designed to replace the Camel, the P6 and twin-engined P7 Bourges. None of these aircraft made any significant impact on the war effort, but for Boulton & Paul, at least, they opened the door on new post-war markets.

Demand for war production created a boom for other manufacturers too. Burrell's of Thetford moved into the armaments business, building tanks, one of the conflict's outstanding military innovations and Savage's of Lynn turned to constructing aircraft wings. Norwich, however, was the hub of the county's war effort. From Caley's "Marching Chocolate" to producing the boots with which hundreds of thousands of soldiers marched into action, the city bustled with activity. As well as its newly-developed aircraft manufacturing concerns, there were munitions components factories, established under Government licence, and engineering plants, such as Laurence Scott, making electrical equipment. The war transformed Norwich from a cathedral city with its businesses centred on agricultural markets to a large-scale industrial centre.

There were jobs in abundance and manpower shortages meant that many of them were taken by women, thus fuelling a social revolution that spilled over into almost every walk of life. The changes wrought were immense. There were restrictions on fuel consumption and what newspapers could record. Rationing, forced on the Government by Germany's unrestricted U-boat campaign, altered people's eating habits and tighter controls were matched by far wider State intervention. Nowhere was this more evident than in agriculture where haphazard planning and inefficient farming methods coupled with a poor harvest had finally forced the Government to establish a Food Production Department. From 1917 onwards, farm inspectors were given draconian powers to dispossess where necessary, to enforce more efficient cultivation methods and to foster the production of new crops. Acute shortages of skilled labour, meanwhile, forced an army bled white by a war of attrition to reluctantly release desperately needed frontline soldiers. In November 1917, for example, five ploughmen serving with the 8th Norfolks were sent home to work the land.

The improved production which followed owed more than a little to the increasing mechanisation of agriculture. Tractors began to reach Norfolk, initially ferried across the Atlantic and then built under licence by local firms. By the last summer of the war, the EDP was filled with advertisements for tractors. One such, for the Moline one-man tractor, declared: *"Runs entirely on Paraffin. One machine in Norfolk in 1917 ploughed 400 acres. Repairs nil."* The reality, however, was rather different. The breakdown rate was prodigious. This, coupled with a shortage of skilled mechanics, led many farms to resist wholesale change, despite substantial Government incentives.

Even so, there were those who recognised the first stirrings of a rural revolution. According to George Ewart Evans, that distinguished chronicler of country life, *"the First World*

**The EDP recorded this poignant return of the Norfolk and Norwich Ypres Association to the trenches in June 1974.**

**"After four years service in the Great War his end was peace". So reads the poignant inscription on the headstone marking the last resting place of Ernest Bean, a 24-year-old second lieutenant in the Norfolk Regiment who succumbed on November 11th 1918, as the nation celebrated an end to the conflict. He was buried in Norwich cemetery, less than two miles from his mother's home in Wodehouse Street. The circumstances of his death are unclear, although it is probable he either died of wounds or fell victim to the influenza pandemic which claimed more lives than the war itself.**

*War was a definite watershed in the transmission of the traditional lore. For it saw the beginning of mechanisation, and the erosion of the domination of the horse."*

A war which had generated political, social and technological revolutions ended just in time to prevent one more pioneering military operation. For almost five months, the men of 166 Squadron, Britain's first experimental night bomber unit, based at Bircham Newton had been preparing to mount the first long-range attacks on Berlin. By November 1918, two new Handley Page V/1500s were ready. Originally scheduled for November 9th, poor weather forced a 48-hr postponement. On the morning of November 11th the crews were standing by ready to go, but just as they received the final briefing word came through that an armistice had been signed.

War weariness had long since set in, but it did not prevent one last hurrah. In Norwich, the streets were awash with rejoicing people. Thousands of children, off school due to the influenza epidemic sweeping the world, swelled the crowds and as a Union Flag fluttered from the Guildhall the bells of St Peter Mancroft *"sent up a paean, all the more delightful because of its rarity..."* On the coast, ship's sirens joined the cacophony of celebration as airmen from Yarmouth's South Denes air station indulged in low-flying joy-rides. As fireworks "fizzled and banged" in the sky over Lynn, one observer appears to have caught the mood of the time. *"Over all the celebrations, whether devotional or demonstrative,"* he wrote, *"was the emotional relief that the appalling terror of a long drawn out nightmare had vanished."*

And after the joy had subsided, there was, eventually, the realisation that nothing would ever be quite the same again. The vast unreturning army that now populated Kipling's "silent cities" ensured that much. Hardly a family had not been touched in some way by one of the war's myriad tragedies. In Norfolk, the sacrifice amounted to a little less than 12,000, a staggeringly high figure which, based on the 1911 census, worked out at one man killed or missing from every nine aged between 18 and 41. The highest number of deaths suffered by a single parish was 171 in St Barnabas, Norwich.

According to Sir Henry Rider Haggard's reckoning, the county's losses were proportionally higher than anywhere else in the country, being one in 42 of the population as compared with a national average of one in every 57. *"Such,"* he wrote, *"is the sheaf which Norfolk gave to swell the harvest of the war."* And to this dreadful tally were to be added the many thousands crippled or maimed in body or mind by the conflict.

For many of those who survived, the suffering did not end with the war. The promise of a "Land fit for heroes" was a hollow one, a mirage of hope that lingered like a festering sore to fuel resentment during the post-war depression. Socialism fed off the discontent and transparent injustice. The war also served to hasten the growing exodus from a countryside in which the fabric of life was irrevocably changed. Faced with static rents, high taxation and the lure of soaring land values, many landowners sold up. In the first spring of peace, it was estimated that half a million acres were on the market.

*"In a movement which rivalled the effects of the dissolution of the monasteries or the Civil War, many of the great estates were broken up, and the purchasers were largely the tenants themselves,"* wrote historian Nicholas Mansfield. *"The large country houses were often retained by the gentry, but the role of the big house started to decline from 1918... The centuries-old triad of squire, tenant farmer and labourer began to decay..."*

Most damaging of all, however, were the vengeful peace terms. In the immediate aftermath of war, there was little room for reconciliation. The EDP, in its first peacetime leader article, encapsulated the nation's unforgiving mood. *"Germany has before her a hard lot of her own making,"* it declared, *"and must be prepared to endure it for many a long day to come..."* Thus were the seeds sown for a second and more destructive conflict. The war to end all war had achieved little beyond ensuring there would be another one within twenty years.

## CHAPTER 7

# *The Land*

**MICHAEL POLLITT joined the Eastern Daily Press as agricultural editor in 1984. The eldest son of a Yorkshire dales farmer, he spent his formative years helping on the family's 98-acre dairy farm. An agricultural journalist in Yorkshire, Oxfordshire and now Norfolk, he promoted the world's first human ploughing championship near Norwich in 1997. He is also a former president of the Norfolk Farm Machinery Club.**

For almost forty years until shortly before the Second World War, agriculture and horticulture struggled for survival. The longest recession in the modern history of agriculture caused real hardship for farmers and farmworkers, which rippled through the economy of the countryside. In a predominantly rural county such as Norfolk, the impact of years of low wages and lack of profitability had a devastating impact on the social structure and the economic fabric.

Seven decades of recession discouraged investment, new thinking and ideas, which could have improved the industry's outlook. The result was reliance on tried-and-trusted methods involving horse and hand labour, coupled with low wages, productivity and appalling housing conditions for most people living in England's green and pleasant land. Many farmers felt trapped in a vicious circle, unable to change their cropping and still too reliant on fattening bullocks in yards.

But the second half of the century brought about the third agricultural revolution. A combination of mechanical genius, built on the back of great inventors such as Harry Ferguson with his little Grey Fergie tractor, dramatic improvement in yields achieved by plant breeders at Cambridge, and an effective and cheap range of crop protection products, made it possible to grow and harvest four or even eight ears of corn where one had grown a generation earlier.

In the livestock industry, the world owed a debt to scientists such as Norfolk farmer's son John Hammond, later knighted, for his contribution to developing artificial insemination (AI) of cattle. His work at Cambridge led to the creation of the Beccles AI Centre by far-sighted farmers including Ivor Bond, of Ellough, and Charles Cargill, of Benacre, Beccles. Instead of using village or scrub bulls, which tended to spread disease, it became possible to breed higher-yielding cows, and transform the dairy industry. The implication of this technology, which has since spread to the sheep and pig industry and even into the human population, has been incalculable.

A sustained policy of investment in agriculture by governments, launched in austere post-war Britain by the Agriculture Act 1947, put food production at the top of the political agenda. While food was rationed for the duration of the war, there was immense will to boost the agricultural and horticultural industries as rations were cut even further in the grim late Forties.

Meat was rationed for almost 15 years until it was decontrolled on July 3rd 1954. For most of the war, the meat ration was 1/2d (6p) a week per head. It was twice reduced to the lowest rate of 10d (4p) a week in March 1949 and again in spring 1951. Even bread, which contained barley in the national loaf, was rationed after the end of the war from July 1946 to January 1948. The cheese ration was introduced at an ounce a week in May 1941 although it did fluctuate, peaking at eight ounces in July 1942, but was usually about two ounces a week. It was de-rationed on May 8th 1954 after 13 years of control. Given this background, it is understandable that all sides backed more production of home-grown food. The drive to drain, remove hedges and plough permanent grassland was funded by substantial grant aid and free advice from the Ministry of Agriculture's technical specialists.

The science and research budget was considerable as the Agricultural Research Council funded plant breeding and encouraged for three decades the development of new and improved chemicals to protect crops. This policy ran for almost fifty years until the early Eighties when Whitehall turned off the funding tap. The investment yielded an impressive return when costed in balance of payment terms.

One could speculate whether the concern about the new "green" sciences such as genetically-modified organisms would be as great if it had been funded by taxpayers rather than the private sector and industry. For example, in 1966 the farmer-owned independent research centre, Norfolk Agricultural Station had average wheat yields of under forty cwt an acre (two tonnes) while barley ranged from thirty to 35 cwt (1.75 tonnes) at Morley, near Wymondham. Three decades later, the same land produced twice as much wheat averaging 72 cwt (3.63 tonnes) and barley 61 cwt or 3.15 tonnes in 1998.

Cereal yields peaked in 1984 when Britain's grain farmers produced more than 26 million tonnes. Then, winning export markets became ever more vital. By the mid-Eighties, Britain was exporting hundreds of millions of pounds of grain, lamb, beef and even pig and poultry. Agriculture was making a significant contribution to the balance of payments and East Anglia's broad acres were recognised as the country's breadbasket. New techniques of breeding and rearing poultry, not least turkeys pioneered by Bernard and Joyce Matthews, made table fowl and eggs affordable and not a seasonal luxury. At the 1948 Diss Christmas turkey sale, few birds were forward when 20,000 were common before the war. A "good average gobbler" made £7.50 while turkey hens averaged £5.50 – an expensive luxury.

It was a different story two decades earlier. The impact of unfettered free trade for agricultural commodities in the early Thirties and later the prospect of looming war forced politicians to take notice. The voice of Norfolk's large estate owners, largely ignored for decades, coupled with the virile Norfolk National Farmers' Union, and powerful Labour MPs, supported by the county's farmworkers, set the scene for decades of investment.

Whitehall officials and many MPs remembered that Britain was almost starved to submission by the loss of four million tonnes of shipping in the Great War in 1916. It was then that the first steps to exercise control over food production were taken in 1917.

Farms went to rack and ruin in the Twenties and Thirties and when it was at its worst, large areas of the county became virtually derelict, notably across Breckland. Such was the rural poverty, which was a feature of the countryside for several decades, that Norfolk was a centre of radical politics, driven by the ambitions of farm and land workers to secure higher wages. In the Twenties, for example, the average farmworker was paid 1s (5p) a week less than in other counties. It was this sort of anger that led to the 1923 great farmworkers' strike, recalled Arthur Amis, of Trunch, who was just 14 when it started. It was a time of much bitterness when farmers wanted to cut wages from 25s (£1.25) for a 48-hour week.

Employers and workers had equal reason for feeling betrayed when, without warning, the Government acted. In June 1922, it announced that the Agriculture Act 1920 would be scrapped. Whether by coincidence or irony, the Corn Production (Repeal) Act was given its second reading on July 4th – the 75th anniversary of the repeal of the Corn Laws. Wheat prices on Norwich corn market fell from 92s (£4.60) a quarter in June to 41s (£2.05) by December 1922. The price of this key commodity, wheat, dropped like a stone. Farmers had enjoyed a guaranteed price for corn, vital for a county such as Norfolk, which had around forty per cent of the land in cereals employing large numbers of workers.

The ending of the guaranteed price for corn, which set prices for four years ahead, infuriated the farming community. Farmworkers were equally angered by the decision to scrap the Agricultural Wages Board, the other half of the corn price guarantee. Their former leader George Edwards, newly-elected Labour MP for South Norfolk in 1920, told the Commons that abolition of the wages board was the *"basest betrayal that any Government ever committed*

**The widespread introduction of tractors meant the end of the horse teams – a heart-breaking decision on many farms.**

*on any class... a violation of the pledged word of the Government."*

Wages had risen to the heady heights of 46s (£2.30) a week in the early Twenties. When corn prices slumped, wages were cut to 42s and then to 25s (£1.25) within just two years. At a time without social security, except for a tiny old age pension, there was a feeling of desperation in the countryside. It was shared by many farmers, who were losing money and facing bankruptcy. In 1923, an estimated 10,000 workers came out on strike, except staff looking after farm animals, although accurate information was difficult to obtain. Both sides were quick to use the EDP for their own ends as claims of intimidation and strike-breaking gangs were reported. Many reported incidents, as it later turned out, were not true.

It was a measure of the crisis that eventually a deputation, six from each side, went to 10 Downing Street on March 16th to press Bonar Law to intervene. After a lengthy discussion, the weak and ineffectual Prime Minister refused to act: *"I think that, like every other industry, agriculture must become self-supporting."* Talks were deadlocked. The sides were divided over one shilling, 5p. Proposals for a three-month truce by the workers came to nothing and even intervention by the Bishop of Norwich failed. The strike was finally settled on April 21st and the workers accepted 25s for fifty hours and a promise of no-victimisation, which was not always honoured.

The actions of Government, not for the first time, and withdrawal of the corn price guarantee, were to haunt relations between farmers and Whitehall for decades. Agriculture had struggled through recession, which had hit the industry from around the mid-1870s, and disease had struck sheep flocks and cattle herds. There was little willingness or even ability for farmers to look for alternative solutions. Survival was the only option. On large arable farms especially in the western half of the county, there seemed to be few realistic alternatives.

The first tenant farmer MP, Sewell Read,

FARM WAGES CRISIS.

N.F.U. TO MEET MEN TO-MORROW

SEVERAL HUNDRED MEN ALREADY OUT.

JOINT DEPUTATION TO PREMIER TO-DAY.

Important developments in the farm wages crisis occurred yesterday, when it was announced that the Executive Committee of the Norfolk branch of the N.F.U. will at noon to-morrow meet at Norwich the Emergency Committee of the National Union of Agricultural workers.

**How the EDP reported the attempts on March 16th 1923 to end the bitter farmworkers' strike.**

**George Edwards was born at Marsham in 1850. One of his earliest memories was being taken with his mother, brothers and sisters to the workhouse when his father was imprisoned for 14 days for carrying five turnips home from a field. He had no schooling and began work, scaring crows, at the age of six. Although he was illiterate, he became a local Primitive Methodist preacher, his wife having taught him to read. At the age of 56, he became general secretary of the National Union of Agricultural Workers and was the first Labour member of Norfolk County Council. He was appointed a magistrate in 1914, elected to Parliament as Labour member for South Norfolk in 1920 and was knighted by George V in 1930. He died in 1933. Annual memorial services to Sir George were still being held in the Nineties at his memorial (above) in Fakenham cemetery.**

who farmed 700 acres near Dereham, told the Commons of the industry's plight in 1894. As a result, the first of many Royal Commissions was established to examine the problem. By the turn of the century, the county's sheep flock had fallen dramatically and there were 1000 fewer farmers than forty years earlier. One in twenty farmers had gone bankrupt. While rents fell by almost thirty per cent on many estates in two decades, it was not enough. And, it was to get worse for the next generation.

Landlords, particularly on many great estates, faced higher taxation and severe decline in rents. However, tenants and most of the county was farmed on long and fairly restrictive leases, were struggling. By 1914, about ninety per cent of the county's one million acres was farmed by tenants.

There were occasional periods of better fortunes, especially from the later stages of the Great War when domestic food production was encouraged. From 1917, farmers were given a guarantee of price support. By 1919, it had revived confidence, which later led to the most comprehensive change in the modern history of Norfolk farming.

Grain prices, the key to prosperity, had improved and reached £21 per ton by June 1921. As a result of promised firm support for cereals, many seriously-indebted estate owners took the opportunity to sell. Land worth between £13 and £15 an acre before 1914, rose to £21 an acre in 1918, almost £25 in 1919 and even £28 an acre by early 1920. Retired grain merchant Alec Douet, who wrote a definitive account of Norfolk's Agriculture 1914 to 1972, Breaking New Ground, for his PhD at the UEA - upon which much of this chapter has been based - estimated that the proportion of Norfolk owner-occupiers almost trebled within four years by 1921. The yeoman tenant had become owner of almost forty per cent of the county by buying around 250,000 acres. It was a remarkable countryside revolution. But then, prices collapsed.

While farmers were buying, Norfolk County Council also responded to political pressure and encouragement by pioneers of smallholdings. Richard Winfrey formed Norfolk Small Holders' Association, which bought a 132-acre farm near Swaffham in 1900 and established 32 holdings, each between one and 15 acres. Others followed at Downham Market (190 acres) and also 97 acres at Whissonsett.

This drive to improve the lot of the rural working man had its appeal. Winfrey pushed the county council to acquire land and the first smallholdings' estate was bought at auction in May 1903 - the 92 acres cost £4100. The 30 holdings, between two and four acres, were a success and also generated a tidy rent. In 1907, the county bought another 75 acres at Outwell for £4750. It was pioneering because by 1907, only 800 acres nationally had been bought for smallholdings. Encouraged by Government, the county council, always reluctant to spend ratepayers' funds, had bought or leased 13,000 acres by 1913 for 1400 men to settle. It had become one of the county's largest landowners with a tenth of the national acreage of smallholdings.

On the whole, the county council bought wisely when it expanded its acreage again in the twenty years from 1919 to a total of 32,000 acres by the outbreak of the Second World War. Some early purchases were expensive, 279 acres of good skirt land at West Walton cost almost £90 acre. It acquired 5000 acres in East Norfolk including the 3000-acre Burlingham estate although these purchases were not always too popular with farmers. They wanted the land and resented the rival's deeper pockets. The rush to acquire land was not matched by the administrative skills needed to manage this large and complex estate, which was much criticised by many at county hall, the farming community and Whitehall. However, the steep fall in land values - amounting to a loss of almost £40 an acre across the estate by 1925 - were also an increasing anxiety for the banking community. Many tenants were badly under-capitalised.

Norfolk County Council was the first to introduce a system of yearly inspections and appraisals to encourage the performance of each tenant and identify potential opportunities. This measure, introduced to encourage better cost and management control, produced other benefits for the rest of the farming community. These early moves to encourage better agricultural education were to lead to far-reaching changes at a time when on-farm national advisory services did not appear for another quarter of a century.

One of the major headaches facing farming was the reluctance of many to change their traditional ways. Of course, some pioneers did look at alternatives or using the buzzword of the late Eighties to diversify. For example, the urban population of Norwich, Great Yarmouth and King's Lynn rose by almost forty per cent in the three decades to 1901. This fuelled the demand for milk and cow numbers rose by more than one third but many traditional Norfolk farmers were very reluctant to be "tied to a cow's tail".

Some farmers did look ahead and experiment with new breeds and methods such as the black and white cow, the Friesian. When the first herd book of the newly-formed British Friesian Herd Book was published in 1912, it listed 14 members from Norfolk. A pioneer was Mrs ME Case, of Stanfield, near Dereham, who had started what became a very large pedigree herd in 1892. Friesians were first exhibited at the Royal Show, Norwich, at the Crown Point estate, in 1911. It was during that show week that her Friesian herd, one of the earliest and largest to be dispersed, saw 132 animals average more than £17 per head. Four of her animals went on to win first prizes at Royal Shows.

Three years later, Friesians were shown for the first time at the Royal Norfolk Show, which was granted the royal prefix in 1907. There were other pioneers including the Ryburgh herd, established in 1905 by Arthur Savory, later dispersed in 1968, where his family still farm near Fakenham.

Two bulls imported three days before the outbreak of war on August 4th 1914 came to Norfolk. Richard Buxton established the Petygards herd at Swaffham in 1911 with animals from Lord Rayleigh's Terling sale in Essex. He paid £241 for one bull, later sold for £2000 and became Royal Show champion in 1919. A great enthusiast, Capt Buxton, was the first Norfolk breeder to be elected president of the British Friesian Cattle Society. When he died on Boxing Day 1972, aged 85, there were 250 pedigree Friesian herds in Norfolk.

Another Dutch bull went to the Norton herd of Herbert Murton and Edward Long, of Norton Hall, Fakenham. They dispersed their herd in 1918 for an average £171 for 64 head or £31 more than the national average for the breed in that year. It was good timing because by 1930, the average breed price had slumped to £30 per head. While the Norfolk yeoman was a reluctant dairy farmer, the lead in this field was being taken by a new generation of progressive producers. They came down, lock, stock and barrel and brought a new breed with them.

The influence of this new generation of tenant farmers from Scotland was considerable over the decades. While some switched from their native Ayrshire cattle and eventually developed other enterprises, the impact over

**The Royal Norfolk Show – granted the 'royal' prefix in 1907 – continues to be the showpiece agricultural event in the county, despite the ups and downs of local farming.**

**Dr Frank Rayns, who died in 1976 aged 81, was director of the Norfolk Agricultural Station at Sprowston for 35 years during a revolutionary period for Norfolk farming. Dr Rayns, who came to the station from the Midlands in 1924, changed the balance sheets on many a Norfolk farm by showing how livestock could be fattened more cheaply, and also popularised the growing of sugar beet, recognising in it a crop of the future. On his retirement in 1960 he told his audience: "Your farming is good and progressive; it will stand comparison with the arable farming anywhere in the world. Whether I realise it or not I have just become one of you: I have ended up by being a Norfolk farmer and I cannot think of anything better." The EDP compared his importance to the eighteenth-century pioneer Thomas William Coke.**

the generations of farming families including Alston, Cargill, Paterson, Ritchie, and Gilmour has been considerable. While milk production has declined in overall importance and especially in the final decade of this century, it does remain significant. The success of the Norfolk Holstein Club's Spring Fling 1999, which attracted one of the largest entries of black and white cattle to the Norfolk showground, was appropriate to mark the club's golden jubilee.

In the early years of the century, dairying became a popular alternative cash cow for many farmers and a new generation of tenants and smallholders. Although milk prices fell by forty per cent between 1921 and 1930, it provided a steady income. A bullock yard, which had bled many farmers dry, could be converted into a small dairy for ten or a dozen cows. It was not easy and many farmers failed. However, with the right permanent pasture, it was possible to at least keep head above water. For some farmers, a retail milk round could reap a handsome dividend. The trend towards larger herds was also noticeable. For example, Charles Wharton at Thrigby, near Acle, started with a dozen cows in 1930. Nine years later, he was milking 100 and one of the county's leading dairy farmers, James Alston at Uphall more than tripled his milking herd from seventy in 1924 to 240 in 1931.

The impact of this new generation of farmers, the thrifty Scots, also changed attitudes although there was much hostility in some circles. Many were quick to look for other solutions including winter feeding of kale and later sugar beet tops, which would eke out fodder supplies given the difficulty of growing grass in the late summer months. While cows were unfashionable and felt by many traditional Norfolk farmers to be "ungentlemanly", according to historian Dr Douet's research, there were pedigree breeders prepared to stick by their cattle. There were famous Shorthorn herds such as Sir Edward Mann's Thelveton, TRC Blofeld's Hoveton and the Stokeleycross herd of RW Kidner. They faced an unequal challenge from the Friesian. By 1932, an estimated one-third of the county's herds were Friesian and the top herds were producing an average of 1125 gallons per year. The county's traditional breed, the Red Poll, had its favourites with Lord Hastings having sixty adorn his park at Melton Constable. Davis Brown, of Marham, whose father had been a founder member of the breed society in 1856, stuck by the old cattle but it was a losing battle.

One of the biggest handicaps faced by dairy farming was the appalling quality of milk. Research at the Institute of Dairying at Reading in the Twenties found that almost two-third of cows tested were infected by tuberculosis. Although efforts were made to encourage higher health standards, little was achieved for several years. It was the action of Norfolk County Council in 1927 through the agricultural education sub-committee that progress was achieved. Around the same time, the Norfolk Agricultural Station recruited the great dairy champion, Robert Boutflour, to highlight the extent of the problem. The clean milk campaign was soon backed by bodies including the Royal Norfolk Agricultural Association, Norwich City Council and the Norfolk Milk Recording Society. One of the earlier winners of a new annual competition in 1938, the Milkers Mardle, was Arthur Amis, of Trunch.

One of Norfolk's great agricultural innovators and champions, John Colman Mann, of the Norfolk Agricultural Station, which was established in 1908 by a group of progressive farmers and landowners, campaigned hard to improve dairy hygiene. He had seen at first hand the terrible effect of tubercular infection on young children and determined to prompt the industry into action. The key to survival in the Thirties was making a profit and investments in better buildings, clean dairies and sterilising equipment, were an added drain on the business. This attitude did not change until higher payments were introduced for cleaner grades of milk from 1933.

In those days, farmers relied on hand labour although the first milking machine had been in use in Norfolk from 1914. Most farmers did not favour this new technology. It was in 1915 another innovation arrived when a group of

Norfolk farmers formed a Milk Recording Society, which had become the fourth largest in the country by 1926. For the first time, farmers knew about their costs and yields. By 1934, Norfolk's average of 820 gallons was the highest of any milk recording society in England - and 15 per cent above the national level. On the price front, all was not well. From 18p a gallon in 1919, the price was cut to almost 4p per gallon in two years. Although it subsequently improved, prices slumped even further from 1929 and by 1931 had reached less than 2p (4d) per gallon.

The extent of the financial crisis in agriculture could not be over-stated. By 1932, the eastern counties of Norfolk, Suffolk and Essex were said to be in "chronic indebtedness" and most farmers were living on bank overdrafts. In a private note, it was claimed that in the depression Barclays owned half Norfolk. By December 1932, total debts owed by Norfolk farmers rose to £3.5 million or roughly £3.50 for every acre in the county or 35 per cent of tenants' capital. Bankers estimated that almost 13 per cent of borrowing was considered doubtful. In central Norfolk, on roughly 400,000 acres, farmers were reckoned to have made a loss of £1.40 an acre in 1931 by economists at the University of Cambridge. The following year losses were a third worse and were an average £2.10 an acre. It was little wonder that farmers were desperate and cash crops the only solution.

As the situation became even more chaotic, especially for farmers in Norfolk, long distant from the main London market, leading Norfolk producer, James Alston took the helm of the newly-formed East Anglian Milk and Dairies Organisation Committee in July 1932. As the 1931 Agricultural Marketing Act encouraged farmers to exercise greater control over the sale of produce and further legislation would protect commodities with a marketing board, farmers took control. In September 1933, the Milk Marketing Board was formed, backed by 96 per cent of producers.

Charles Wharton maintained that this single decision saved Norfolk's farming because prices rose gradually, farmers had confidence that the monthly milk cheque would arrive. In April 1938, the country's largest depot and creamery at Harford Bridges began to turn surplus milk into butter and skimmed milk powder. Sixty years later, the dairy cow has almost became an endangered species in Norfolk as herd numbers fell below 200 or one per cent of the total in England and Wales. By 1997, the sale of two herds at Cantley, when 600 cows went under the hammer in one day, was a sign. However, in the same year, the introduction of two robot milking machines at Ditchingham showed some had confidence about the future.

The dairy industry in Norfolk also lost a much larger percentage of its prime cattle than almost any other region of Britain. Although there were relatively few herds compared with the West of England, significantly more cattle were lost to BSE or "mad cow" disease. A total of almost 4750 confirmed cases were identified in 460 beef and dairy herds since figures were compiled by the Ministry of Agriculture in the 13 years from November 1986. Quite why Norfolk had such

**Bernard Matthews CBE, pictured outside his headquarters at Great Witchingham Hall, is the best-known face connected with Norfolk farming – and a multi-millionaire. Famously beginning his poultry empire in the early Fifties with a pound's worth of turkey eggs, he built his company to be worth almost £170 million by mid-1999. He has changed the nation's eating habits by making turkey a year-round non-luxury item. His face – and Norfolk accent – became nationally known after the 'bootiful' advertising campaign which increased the sales of some of his products twenty-fold.**

a significant number of cases has never been satisfactorily explained.

Many farmers took advantage of an opportunity to capitalise by selling milk quota or to retire and liquidate a valuable asset of pedigree dairy cows. A combination of tougher environmental rules and regulations and the need for massive investment in new milking parlours certainly discouraged many producers.The traffic was not all one-way. The Colman family's Crown Point estate on the outskirts of Norwich decided to invest in milk and put up a new dairy unit in 1998.

In the first two decades, livestock were an essential part of most traditional arable farms because many farmers kept bullocks, winter finished in yards, to produce quantities of farmyard manure. It became a long-term research project at Norfolk Agricultural Station and in 1911, the results of the first trials were reported to members. A batch of ten yarded bullocks were fed a low-cake diet diet and 12 others a high-cake diet. The 77 tonnes of manure at ten tonnes an acre would have grown almost eight acres of roots, producing an additional 44cwt of mangels.

In hindsight, this determination to keep cattle to produce manure probably did more to impoverish many Norfolk farmers. Some thirty years later the station's research team headed by Dr Frank Rayns came to the conclusion that switching to artificial fertiliser was probably a lot more effective and less damaging to the bank balance.

For decades, sheep flocks were vital to the prosperity of arable farming. Ewe flocks had been an integral part of arable farming for more than a century – the influence of Thomas Edward Coke on the Holkham estate. At the height of sheep popularity in 1870, there were an estimated 750,000 sheep grazing the county – almost one to every acre. After the war, the sheep population had declined by more than half a million and in 1920, the number of ewes had fallen to 98,000. Sheep enjoyed a modest recovery in popularity because by 1939, there were just 200,000. Numbers slumped during the war to a mere 67,000 by 1945. Many farmers gave up sheep as too much trouble, partly because of the competing demand for labour for flocks on arable farms. In addition, the flock had to stand the cost of wages for a shepherd, paid about a fifth above minimum rates, and the need for fodder crops to get ewes into good condition. In 1931, the Norfolk Agricultural Station, now Morley Research Centre, started trials to evaluate the importance of sheep to the arable farmer. Were sheep vital to arable farming? In the early results of a twenty-year trial, the evidence did suggest a benefit for arable crops because of the value of the manure. However, the best results could be achieved by using modest amounts of bagged fertiliser. Norfolk could be farmed, it was proved conclusively, without sheep and cattle.

Some made sheep pay by using an alternative approach – feeding sugar beet tops and producing lambs for butchers wanting smaller, leaner joints. Two Midland graziers, William Parker and Richard Proctor, who became tenants on the Fountaine estate at Narborough, adapted the Norfolk four-course rotation from 1925 and built up a formidable farming enterprise.

The drive to mechanise was surprisingly slow in Norfolk for several reasons. The first was the capital cost of tractors, which were often unreliable.There was a distinct shortage of skilled mechanics, spares and expertise. Secondly, the early machines were heavy and in wet conditions became stuck on badly-drained land. Although a Ministry of Agriculture committee in 1919 thought that farmers would build on wartime experience to use more labour-saving machinery, it did not happen.Tractor sales slumped.The reason as the committee itself concluded: *"Tractors were regarded with unreasonable hostility and prejudice."*

As farm incomes plunged, there were few who could afford to invest in tractors. However, when the first diesel tractors arrived from Marshall of Gainsborough in 1931, the revolution had started. Gradually, farmers began to appreciate the advantage of the new horse power. A farmer turned contractor and agricultural engineer Ben Burgess, who started the family business in 1931, was another

**Sheep, once in such vast numbers that there was the equivalent of one for every Norfolk acre, became less popular. In this evocative 1975 picture shepherd Andrew Wilson cares for a frail lamb born at Park Farm, Stow Bardolph.**

**Ben Burgess MBE (1902- ), who remains one of the county's leading farmers and agricultural engineers, is a member of the famous Burgess family which has been engaged in agricultural engineering since 1700. He left his studies at Cambridge to take over the Howe farms – which employed sixty men – in 1922 on the death of his father. "It was a bit of a tall order for a boy of 19, but I knew my responsibilities," he said later. He sold the first full diesel tractor in Norfolk on September 12th 1931 in a field just south of the Poringland Dove public house, laying the foundations for his famous tractor distribution business. The great efforts to produce more food after the Second World War led to a sharp increase in the use of tractors on local farms. He was president of the Royal Norfolk Show in 1971 and was made an MBE in 1986. A life-long interest in Horatio Nelson led to his donation of around 550 items collected over fifty years to a trust which aims to set up a permanent museum to the Norfolk hero in the county.**

pioneer of tractors. A Field Marshall with a four-furrow Ransome Multitrac plough could do the work of many horses. He was also a leading figure in establishing the Norfolk Farm Machinery Club in 1946, which sought to to promote the use of labour-saving tackle and tractors.

On many farms when the horses went down the road at the weekend, instruction on driving the new-fangled tractors was rudimentary. It was also a heart-breaking decision on many farms because the workers often cared more for their horses than their nearest and dearest. Broadland farmer Ivan Cooke recalled an incident on a neighbouring farm in those early days when a farmworker was put on a tractor. When he did not return at midday, the farmer found him driving around and around a field. He had not been told how to stop the tractor!

Once Ben Burgess was teaching his father to drive a tractor. When the tractor approached the headland, Mr Burgess senior called "whoa". The tractor continued and the instruction was repeated with greater volume and more urgency. "Obviously, it can't hear," said the driver.

There were other very significant advantages by switching to mechanical power because about a quarter of a typical farm was needed to grow fodder crops to feed horses. Replacing horses brought land into productive use for cash crops. On the farms of Proctor and Parker at Narford, the director of Norfolk Agricultural Station Dr Rayns estimated that land to feed the 250 horses could have yielded £8 an acre - £2000 - when planted in cash crops. Horses, not least for sentimental reasons, kept their place. They were cheap. Dr Douet's comprehensive study estimated that a horse cost about £22 in 1931 and over a 14-year working life, the depreciation was £1.50 a year. Tractors, which cost £150 with a working life of seven years, depreciated at an average £22 a year. In 1929, the cost of a working horse was calculated at 7d (3p) an hour compared with 2/2d (11p) an hour for a Fordson.

The new workhorses were slowly winning friends particularly on the heavy soils of South Norfolk, which needed mole drainage. A small mole plough, set at 18ins deep and three-yard spacing, could drain ten acres in a day. Tractor power had other advantages. It could be used for deep ploughing, which van Rossum, the pioneer of the modern beet sugar industry introduced from his native Holland. At Narford, Proctor and Naylor went deep ploughing to "everyone's horror", which had the great benefit of breaking the plough pan and enabling crops to tap deeper sources of moisture. For generations, light lands had been ploughed at less than six inches deep in order to preserve the fertility of top soil.

Other novel techniques were adopted, albeit slowly, and often to a sceptical audience. The introduction of pneumatic tyres, first demonstrated nationally on a Marshall Model M at Shotesham in 1935 by Ben Burgess, was another example. A trial three years earlier with the free provision of Dunlop land tyres and wheels to the Norfolk Agricultural Station "justified every claim the inventors had made".

For the first four decades, the horse-drawn binder used to reap almost all of cereal crops in 1900, brought in the harvest. Teams of three horses, working alternate shifts, cutting ten acres a day with a binder, were replaced by tractors on some farms. However, most of the county's grain was actually thrashed by seventy contractors with some 180 threshing drums although some of the largest farmers had their own threshing tackle. Of 308 sets in Norfolk, 97 were on farms of more than 500 acres.

It was a very labour intensive and expensive because a team of 11 workers, often working for sixty days a year, was needed to thresh the corn, according to Alfred Lewis, who farmed 1600 acres in West Norfolk. Once again, some progressive farmers looked ahead. One of the first to acquire a combined harvester in 1931, William Newcombe Baker, farmed 1000 acres at Sedgeford. Six years later, there were only 23 combines working and many had nightmares with these machines.

The experience of Parker and Proctor, then growing 3000 acres of cereals, served as an example to many. They bought two Clayton

and Shuttleworth combines but replaced them after two years because the old binders were faster. Some had slightly better experiences, George Milligen, who farms at East Ruston, bought a Claas combine in 1935, and was probably one of the "smallest combine users in the country" with just 180 acres.

There were other innovators including the remarkable experiment at Bluestone Farm, which attracted national interest. In 1930, two brothers, Eric and John Alley, from Worcestershire, took a lease of the 1130-acre farm at South Creake on the Townshend estate. The land was in a filthy condition, covered in twitch and docks, and had become derelict two years earlier when 32 men and forty horses had been employed. The decision to farm with just four regular workers and four tractors - two caterpillars, a four-wheel drive Massey Harris, and an experimental tractor, which weighed 6.5 tons and powered by a 70hp engine, cost £1200 against £155 for a smaller Fordson.

This mechanised farming scandalised the farming community. The crawlers could plough an acre an hour compared with an acre a day with two horses, and used a four-furrow plough. Their Massey Harris drill was the largest in Europe and could sow eight acres an hour. The operation was costed and even at the depth of the recession with wheat at £4.50 a ton, they made a profit. Others including neighbours tried farming without stock and failed. One of the reasons for the hostility to stockless farming was obvious. It was based on the continuous wheat-growing experiment at Rothamsted - wheat, wheat, fallow followed by ploughed-in mustard - then unknown in West Norfolk. Critics were concerned that it would deplete the land.

**Increased mechanisation revolutionised the way cereals were harvested over the century. By 1946 there were 300 combine harvesters working in the county, drastically reducing the man-power needed to bring in the crop.**

The other more financial objection was the implications for most farming businesses. It would mean scrapping equipment with a useful working life. Within a dozen years, the combine harvester showed the way forward because of the problems obtaining labour during the war. William Cave, of Terrington St Clement, said that a combine and four men could do in a day the work of 54 men and 18 horses. By 1946, there were more than 300 combines working in the county. Numbers doubled again by 1950, re-doubled by 1954.

By the end of the war, there had been great change on the land. The number of regular workers was unchanged at around 20,000 while the arable acreage had increased by 12 per cent, thirty per cent of rough grazing had been reclaimed, milking cow numbers were up by a tenth and 15 per cent more cattle were kept on farms.

The extent of the rural dereliction problem was enormous. During the depth of the depression thousands of acres of arable land was left to bracken, weeds and rabbits. In South Norfolk, hedges were left untrimmed and just grew. Peter West, whose family have farmed at Brome, near Eye, since 1820, said that hedges were left to become dozens of yards wide. On his family's farm, it was estimated that around ten acres of land were lost to scrub and production every year through the Thirties.

It was a common story and hardly surprising that on the even lighter land of the Brecks, the Forestry Commission, founded in 1919, was a ready buyer of land. It offered £6 an acre and was swamped. It bought the 5000-acre Downham Hall estate for £3.20 an acre and paid 70s or £3.50 an acre for the 6200-acre Lynford Hall estate. In all, a total of 78,000 acres was acquired by the Commission.

Others decided to have a go. On a neighbouring spread of Breckland, John Mann at Manor Farm, Bridgham, inherited a 750-acre farm, which was saddled by the cost of a mortgage of 15s an acre. His many friends suggested that he disclaim his inheritance because it was a typical sour Breckland farm with field names such as Starve Crow, Labour-in-Vain and Sourdale. It is a measure of the calibre of Mann, surely one of the greats of Norfolk agriculture and later, incidentally a benefactor to Morley Research Centre, that he persevered. Rejecting the stifling Norfolk four-course rotation, he concentrated on sugar beet and became one of the biggest growers of the area. In 1931 and 1932, it was the only crop making a profit and one-third of the farm was down to alternative crops including blackcurrants, sprouts and asparagus as further cash crops.

Other good farmers identified an opportunity to expand. For example, Major James Keith, a dairy farmer from Aberdeenshire rented the Wicken at Castle Acre in 1920 – some 1200 acres of the best land on the Holkham estate. Within a few years, he had acquired or leased a 10,000 acre estate including 600 acres at Weasenham Manor bought for £16 an acre in 1933. He even reclaimed 1500 acres of common including the rabbit-infested Massingham Common hired at 1s (5p) an acre.

A few miles down the road, another pair of entrepreneurs, Billy Parker, who started as an errand boy in a pork butcher's shop in Leicester, and his partner cattle dealer Richard Proctor, were prepared to put alternative cropping into practice. When prices slumped in the Thirties, they decided to grow carrots – 900 acres plus 2000 acres of lucerne on the blowing soils at Narford and South Acre. Drying lucerne for animal feed was profitable and it employed about seventy men. By 1946, Billy Parker was the largest farmer in England with 32,000 acres in Norfolk, Lincolnshire and the Midlands.

Other farmers were ruthless including Leonard Mason, of Fincham Hall, who took on land that no-one else would touch. He might hire a farm at 5s an acre, sack the men, lay it down to grass and keep a flock of sheep. At one time, it was reckoned he farmed more than any one man in Norfolk and could have ridden from Downham Market to Fakenham without leaving his own land. Henry Thompson was another great farmer, who acquired extensive land in the fens and was involved in the formation of the Wissington beet sugar factory. He later bought two farms

**A £46 million redevelopment in the early Nineties transformed the Wissington beet sugar factory into Europe's largest sugar processing plant. The expansion – which sadly meant the closure of the Saddlebow plant at King's Lynn – increased its factory capacity by almost half and involved £4.6 million being spent on two major road projects and a new bridge.**

at Brancaster and Burnham Deepdale for £12 an acre and built an enterprise running to some 10,000 acres.

While some farmers were able to survive, the overall condition of the land was appalling and the task of reversing the decline from the outbreak of war was to be the responsibility of the County War Agricultural Executive Committees, the so-called War Ags. A high-quality team, headed by Sir Henry Upcher, of the Sheringham estate, included some of the county's best farming brains, Dr Rayns as chief executive, the secretary James Christie (later the second NFU county secretary from 1948) and leading farmers including James Alston, of Uphall, CR Birkbeck, one of the county's leading land agents, FC Newling, of Terrington St Clement, TRC Blofeld, of Hoveton, farmworkers' leader Edwin Gooch, and the Dowager Lady Suffield, of the Women's Land Army and the Norfolk Federation of WIs.

Farms were graded A, B or C and only half of the county's farms were regarded as "satisfactory", while a further 3500 were poor or graded B. Another 1300 farms were singled out as worse or in need of fundamental changes. The challenge to farmers was simple: plough, plough and plough. Many landowners set a great example and King George VI described as a "willing plougher" brought 3500 acres into arable cultivation at Sandringham. Parks at Blickling, Elmham, Barningham, Westwick, Gunton, Raynham, Beeston and Felbrigg were among those

**Lord Hastings (1882-1956), the 21st baron and head of the ancient Norfolk Astley family, was an outstanding servant to Norfolk agriculture during the century. He was one of the founders, in 1908, of the Norfolk Agricultural Station, and remained a leading light in its development until his death. In 1951 he was president of the Royal Norfolk Agricultural Association and was the recognised spokesman for Norfolk farming in the House of Lords. Sadly, after the Second World War he was forced to sell Melton Constable Hall, the seat of the family since 1235, due to the increased burden of taxation. He accepted the office of High Steward of Norwich Cathedral in 1949 and successfully led efforts to save its spire.**

ploughed for the first time since their creation. Fakenham lost its racecourse and sports grounds and parks were ploughed.

However, farmers faced a big cost in ploughing although a £2 per acre grant enabled 24,000 new acres to be ploughed between May and September 1939. It was not enough. One of the biggest headaches was the lack of drainage - outfalls were choked, rivers were blocked, ditches clogged by mud and clay. Drainage was given top priority. The Wissey was dredged by the Great Ouse River Catchment Board from Holme Hale to Wash bringing 1000 acres into arable cultivation. Once rivers were drained, water meadows at Stoke Ferry and Oxborough were transformed into 600 acres of productive corn land. By 1945, one-sixth of the county's agricultural land or some 161,000 acres had been drained.

There was a huge problem with land down to almost impenetrable scrub, especially in South Norfolk. There were some great success stories. For example, the 500-acre Massingham Heath was covered by bracken, strong gorse and thousands of self-sown thorn bushes. Four steam engines, four caterpillar tractor, 11 wheeled tractors, ten ploughs and all the cultivating equipment plus a workforce of forty descended on the heath on March 1st 1940. Within two months, it had been reclaimed.

Huge areas of the fens were also derelict. The committee, keen to flex its muscles, decided to tackle 12,000 acres of peat fenland at Methwold, Feltwell and Hockwold in 1940. Undrained, covered by scrub, deficient in almost every mineral, it was so valueless that owners were reluctant to admit ownership in case they were asked to pay drainage rates. There were no roads, boundaries or inhabitants. A district officer, John Young, who later was a distinguished farmer at Ringstead, went armed with a map to survey the wilderness. He was arrested by the King's Own Yorkshire Light Infantry as a spy!

Around 6000 acres was to be reclaimed at Feltwell. It had not been farmed since 1915 when the river banks burst and covered the land to a depth of six feet. It was so wet that the land was not even negotiable on horseback. Within a year, 1500 acres was in production but there were other major problems. It was formidable and very expensive task when 18 miles of concrete roads had been laid at cost of £125,000 to service the 4000-acre block of land. It was later sold to Weasenham Farms for £4 an acre, as Dr Douet's detailed history records.

Henry Brun, of Weasenham Farm, who directed the reclamation project, said that there were five main problems - the five Ws - weeds, wireworm, wind, water and workers. The weed population was ten times greater per sq yard than upland soils and the fen had a wireworm infestation of an incredible ten tons per acre. Without chemical control, in the first season wireworms ate half the 400-acre potato crop. Ironically, the hard graft to reclaim derelict land was offset by requisition of more than 51,000 acres of land for airfields. In Norfolk, there were 37 built, each taking 500 acres. Then, a large chunk of Breckland was needed for troop training and the War Office wanted 30,000 acres. Eventually, 17,000 acres around Stanford was taken and 750 people were evicted from homes and farms never to return. The War Ag was not informed of the decision until June 1942 and the military rejected requests to allow crops to be harvested. James Christie, MP for South Norfolk, pressed the Agriculture Minister Robert Hudson and questions were asked in the Commons. The army was forced to give way, allowing two weeks in August and two in October to harvest crops. In 13 days, a task force of sixty three-ton lorries, 14 tractors, ten combines, three binders, 300 soldiers and a contingent from Repton School harvested 2793 acres of corn, ten tons of blackcurrants and even a crop of clover seed. The beet was lifted in October.

Sugar beet, still regarded as the cornerstone crop of Norfolk farming, had a very hesitant start. More than a third of the national acreage is grown on Norfolk's farms and processed at beet sugar factories at Wissington, near Downham Market, and Cantley. The crop was introduced by a Dutch industrialist, JP van Rossum around 1911. He proposed building

**Despite the introduction of tractors and other mechanical aids, the changeover from horse-power was still not complete by the Sixties. At Rookery Farm, Walcot, in 1964 – when this photograph was taken – three horses were kept "and there is still plenty of work for them," said foreman Fred Farrow. Pictured is seven-year-old Peggy carting sugar beet, which is being unloaded by Mr A Andrews.**

the country's first modern beet sugar factory on the banks of the Yare ready to process beet from 1912. Unfortunately, the terrible floods in August that year wrecked the half-built factory, which had second-hand machinery imported from his native Holland. The Norfolk Agricultural Station, which was established in 1908 at Station Farm, Little Snoring, was keen to look at new ideas. The station, which was provided with the 132-acre farm, rent-free by Lord Hastings for eight years, drilled a trial crop of sugar beet in a narrow strip of one rod (30 sq yards).

The reluctance of farmers to grow sugar beet was hardly surprising. It did not pay until subsidies were offered almost a decade later. Furthermore, it required 210 hours of hand labour an acre. Cantley's early years were nothing short of disastrous. The acreage fell from 4085 acres in 1913 to 2334 acres the following year and then the factory was closed in 1915. After the war, the factory re-opened in 1919 but did not attract enough growers. Fortunately for Cantley's investors, a Nottinghamshire factory at Kelham went bankrupt and beet was diverted to Norfolk. It saved the factory.

In 1924, the Labour Government heeded the pleas of farmers and introduced a five-year subsidy of 44s (£2.20) a tonne. It encouraged farmers to grow beet and 7000 acres were grown for the 1924 campaign. New factories were opened at Wissington and Bury St Edmunds in 1925 and Lynn in 1927, since closed in 1994. The acreage doubled in 1924, doubled again the following year and reached 50,000 acres in 1927. More than seven decades later, the county's farmers produced almost one-third of a record production of sugar of almost 1.476 million tonnes from 135,000 acres. It is worth noting two facts about the UK sugar industry. During the Second World War, the beet industry produced every ton of sugar needed to feed the nation. Before 1914, Britain relied on Germany's huge beet sugar industry for an estimated four-fifths of national consumption.

While the crop could be grown, it was hardly profitable because of the costs of weed control. In a typical season, one worker would hoe 55 miles of rows with a seven-inch hoe, singling (taking out beet plants to leave a single root) in late May and then scoring (weeding between the beet plants) in July. Weeds between rows would be removed by horse, later tractor hoes. Once the crop was ready to harvest, it had to be lifted by hand. It was back-breaking work and during each campaign some 300,000 roots were lifted and topped, and then loaded for carting to road or rail head. Farmers were extremely reluctant to grow this new crop. It was expensive, weed control was a major problem and the yields were relatively low. Even Norfolk Agricultural Station, which carried out trials with beet crops as early as 1910, concluded that the crop was not economic.

Weed control was a horrendous problem and the development of selective herbicides, led by people including Dr Rayns, was the technical breakthorough of the war years. Early weed control involved use of very crude and nasty chemicals, dilute sulphuric acid sprayed from a wooden tumbrel using a hand-pumped lance. It was effective on man, beast and probably weeds in that order.

The first field trials of two compounds, which would revolutionise the world's modern agriculture, were carried out in conditions of absolute secrecy at Thompson. In December 1942, a select band including the Ministry of Agriculture's chief scientist; Lord Melchett, chairman of ICI, which has discovered one of the products, and Dr Rayns, agreed to hold the first trials in Norfolk. Behind barbed wire, in conditions of strict secrecy (details were not published until 1945) on the ninety-acre farm, crops of wheat, barley, potatoes and sugar beet were treated. Within six weeks, one product had killed every weed. It transformed yield potential and even a "sniff of a tin" was enough to kill some troublesome weeds, said one farmer involved in the wider trials. MCPA, the first translocated hormone weedkiller, was available in limited quantities from 1946 as "Corn Land Cleaner".

After the war, the drive to produce more food continued. With rationing of staple products not ended until 1954, farmers were very much the nation's favourites. There were other pests such as the rabbit. One rabbit could graze an acre of early-sown winter wheat and thirty rabbits could eat as much as one bullock, said one Norfolk farmer. The introduction of myxomatosis, which reached Norfolk by spring 1954, controlled a major problem. The entire county gained and in Breckland, land which would not be let, was bringing an annual rent of £6 an acre by 1961.

Rents, or the level of rents, as ever generated much heat and dispute, and certainly after the war when tenants were guaranteed security of tenure. Landlords also found it very difficult to raise rents. On the whole, rents had slipped behind the productive capacity of land. Lord Hastings, who looked at old rent rolls found in 1955 that rents were 1s an acre, 5p, less an acre than those paid to an ancestor in 1868.

There were other innovations. For the first time, intensive vegetable growing became widespread, helped by access to irrigation. Characters such as Arthur Rickwood, the Carrot King, who farmed 4000 acres in Norfolk and adjoining counties, were successful. Other vegetable crops such as onions - Norfolk produced three-quarters of the national crop on the fens - and celery also become more popular. In other parts of the county, other niche crops were grown and developed such as frozen peas. Colman's of Norwich encouraged growing of white and brown mustard and other farmers on the Breckland soils looked for asparagus as a potential source of income.

Potatoes became more important as the increased acreage shifted to East Norfolk with more than a tenth of the national crop grown in the county. While root crops have underwritten many farm businesses, there has always been reliance on top and soft fruit. Apples and soft fruit such as blackcurrants and strawberries, were important on farms.

One of the biggest changes seen by many farmers was the disappearance of livestock markets. As the drift from livestock continued and the virtual disappearance of sheep from the county, dozens of markets were lost. Where almost every town had a livestock market, centres such as Stalham, Acle, Lynn, went. It is once of the most obvious features of the modern agricultural landscape that there are just two markets left in Norfolk in the final year of the century, Norwich and Aylsham.

The combination of new machinery ideas, plant varieties and the launch of mono-germ (single plant) sugar beet, agricultural education, coupled with five decades of capital grants for farming, fuelled the agricultural industry's prosperity. While many contend that agriculture had got out of control in a relentless drive for productivity, it produced major consumer benefits. For the first time, ample supplies of food were available from UK farming and another generation avoided starvation which haunted many European countries in the late Forties.

Farmers also achieved significant import savings and lowered the price of food at the farmgate. For the five decades from the Fifties, farmgate prices rose at a much slower rate than consumer prices. Food such as turkeys, chicken and eggs became affordable and everyday products for a new generation, which now spends less than 11 per cent of household expenditure on food.

The growth of advisory services through the Ministry of Agriculture, which had exercised total control over food production for so many years, was also matched by a determination to improve agricultural education. The drive of such characters as James Alston, who was instrumental in pressing for a Norfolk College of Agriculture, and other influential men such as Ben Burgess, who backed the launch of the Norfolk Farm Machinery Club, were part of the industry's tremendous self-confidence. Other organisations such as Norfolk Agricultural Station and including the Royal Norfolk Agricultural Association, which promoted new ideas and achievements, and work of the dozens of young farmers' clubs, helped to encourage higher standards. The nature and quality of food has improved out of all recognition – milk produced by Britain's farms is the cleanest in Europe and is free from terrible diseases such as tuberculosis and brucellosis. The livestock industry, with the exception of cattle because of the BSE crisis, has become a major exporter of lamb and pork, when the pound is competitive, and hundreds of millions of pounds of farm machinery and tractors are exported around the world.

Of course, the improved productivity has come at a cost, many would argue, to the environment. However, the story of farming in Norfolk this century owes more to the willingness or inability of politicians to intervene. When food production was the national priority for more than five decades, the agricultural industry responded with enthusiasm and style. Farmers ripped out more hedges, dykes, ditches and ploughed permanent pasture than ever seemed possible. Since, the political priority changed from around the middle of the Eighties, Norfolk again became a pioneer in developing more sensitive land management techniques. The success of the environmentally sensitive areas project, which lanced the boil of the conflict over the Halvergate marshes, has shown the way ahead.

The biggest impact has surely been on the land. Where once everything had to be carried on or off the farm on someone's back, machinery has taken the terrible strain out of farming. No longer does a modern generation have to wear a broad belt, carry 18-stone sacks of wheat or 16-stone sacks of barley on their back, and anticipate an early death partly caused by exhaustion and fatigue.

No one would want to turn the clock back to the early years of the century.

**Mechanisation has transformed the efficiency of Norfolk farming and meant the disappearance of thousands of jobs over the century.**

## CHAPTER 8

# *Entertainment and the Media*

**COLIN CHINERY**

**CHARLES ROBERTS, writing on Norfolk entertainment, is well known in Norfolk not only in his roles as journalist and writer, but also as speaker, author, lecturer and actor. In 1997 he left the EDP after 28 years as its literary and arts editor to go freelance. He still contributes regularly to the EDP and its magazines; also to other magazines, books and European Union and internet publications. He has a string of stage and radio scripts to his credit, and lectures regularly on Norfolk's medieval churches. He is an Honorary MA of the UEA, and a Fellow of the Royal Society of Arts.**

**DAVID WAKEFIELD entered journalism with the Sharman Group of newspapers in his home town of Peterborough, and subsequently worked at the Huntingdon and March offices before joining Eastern Counties Newspapers' Great Yarmouth office in 1963. He was thus ideally placed to cover the seaside entertainment scene in its golden days.**

*To ride upon upon the broad back of a gilded ostrich... to smell the odour of smoke and steam and sulphur, of fresh-made rock and kerosene and the mingling of supper stew... to hear the showman's cry of 'Roll up, roll up! Five shies for tuppence'... was to attain the very zenith of youthful ecstasy..."*

So half a century ago one man's memory took him back almost another 50 years to that most enduring of entertainments, the fairground, at a time when steam power reigned. Dominating all were the mighty showmen's traction engines which not only hauled the fair from town to town, but also produced the power for roundabouts, sideshows, shooting galleries, swings and stalls and switchbacks, for wonderfully raucous fairground organs – and for thousands of bulbs which illuminated the nighttime scene in a fantastical way which people had never seen before.

Let us focus in on one year in particular. It is 1920, the place is King's Lynn, the occasion the great annual mart – opening on St Valentine's Day now as it has done for four and a half centuries – and among the huge crowd a teenage boy is gazing wonderstruck at the enormous, simmering steam engines, as they gently rock and hiss, generating the electricity for all around them.

The lad so entranced in Lynn's Tuesday Market Place nigh on eighty years ago was George Cushing, who in years to come would buy a whole collection of those engines, when time had passed them by and nobody wanted them any more; quite apart from a posse of fairground organs and a very special roundabout. From that came the establishment of The Thursford Collection, near Fakenham, where youngsters today can gaze – perhaps in equal awe – at the very same machines which George admired all those years ago, Edward VII and Victory, Alexandra and Medina. And happily George, hale, hearty and keen in memory, is still around (spring 1999), a sprightly presence in the museum, and as enduring as his beloved traction engines.

Leaning against a 7ft wheel of the twenty-ton Edward VII, he recalled a decade ago those events of 1920: "I remember country people standing round this engine, six and seven deep. All they'd ever seen was a threshing machine on the land round their villages. What they were seeing and hearing was terrific for them. They'd be going home to oil lamps. But on the fairground it was all electricity, almost magical. Normally the only music they heard was the organ in the church or a concertina or fiddle in the pub. And here were these great, colourful, fairground organs. It was out of this world."

It was the Thetford firm of Charles Burrell which built those great engines and altered the landscape of the travelling fairs. But it was Lynn's Frederick Savage who mastered steam to bring a glorious, colourful new aspect to England's fairgrounds – because apart from making steam-powered agricultural machines, he made merry-go-rounds, which up to then had been hand-cranked or pulled by horses.

He not only speeded them up and mechanised them. He made them superb to look at, a blaze of gold and gilt, colour and opulence, and so obviously made to be enjoyed that even today, no-one can resist them. The proof can be seen daily through the season at The Thursford Collection, where one of Savage's most magnificent gondola creations (a very posh roundabout) is as

**King's Lynn Mart has a unique place in the showmen's calendar as the first fair of the year. Its traditional opening on St Valentine's Day is marked by civic ceremony at which East Anglian mayors, councillors and civic officers attend – and then enjoy the rides. This shows one of those civic openings from around 1909.**

dazzling as the day it was produced, though its original steam has given way to electricity.

Look across the years of the twentieth century, and perhaps four things have most consistently provided entertainment for the public at large - fairgrounds, the cinema (whose origins were in the fairground), the theatre and pubs!

All four may have changed enormously through those decades. But the spirit and appeal with which they held the public imagination in the opening years of the twentieth century are still enduringly with us in 1999 and into the millennium.

Television, as instant entertainment, may be universal. But all those who prophesied darkly that it would see off into the history books "all the fun of the fair", the lure of the silver screen and live theatre and the alcoholic pull of pubs, have been proved resoundingly wrong. All have changed with their times. Fairs are smaller in number, but are constantly seeking new attractions in addition to the well-tried and traditional.

Cinemas went through a low phase, but have soared back triumphantly. Theatres are fewer in number but surviving strongly. And though there are certainly fewer pubs than there used to be (Norwich could famously claim at the beginning of the century that it had one for every day of the year), they remain as resilient as ever, with the accent far more now on food and entertainment than on the drinks which are the stock of their trade.

But to return to fairs. A hundred and fifty years ago there were annual stock and pleasure fairs in about seventy parishes in Norfolk, and many of them survived into the twentieth century. The majority traced their sources to medieval Royal Charters - a valuable privilege for which, at their onset, large sums had been paid to the Sovereign by the Church, by members of the nobility or by individual towns.

Trade was at the forefront - but entertainment was only a short neck behind. The changing business scene, improved transport and general progress gradually lessened the trade element and merged into the travelling pleasure fairs whose successors we recognise today.

The travelling year nationwide begins here

in Norfolk with the Lynn Mart, which has already been mentioned. Held on the broad expanse of the Tuesday Market Place, it opens, regardless of the weather, on February 14th. Although it takes its present date from a Charter granted by Henry VIII, its history goes back to the thirteenth century.

At Lynn grand tradition holds sway, for it continues to mirror the involvement in fairs from medieval times of the Church and local government. There is a splendid opening ceremony in which local worthies and clerics, in their full finery, come to give it their blessing - literally. The Mayor's Chaplain blesses the event - and his Worship samples the rides, a relic of his duty to see that all is safe.

After Lynn the showmen in former days would make their way to the Winnold Fair at Downham Market, which survived until 1941. Its beginnings were believed to go back as far as the time of William the Conqueror, and its business was horses - and a great deal of fun on the side. Many fairs disappeared following the Abolition of Fairs Act in 1871 - but a goodly number in Norfolk kept going for a long time after that.

There was the Rogue Fair at Attleborough, dating from 1226; fairs at Walsingham (1227), Hempton Green, Harpley, West Dereham, Loddon, Southrepps, Stoke Ferry, Burnham Market, Docking, Bridgham, Sheringham, Swaffham (1253), Grimston (1200), Lyng (1295) and Dereham. As late as 1932, Ingham Fair, held on Trinity Monday, was reported as being "as important as ever, with several hundred head of cattle on offer".

A happy survivor is the Aldborough Fair, near Aylsham, which falls on or near June 21st/22nd. Of very ancient foundation, it continues as it has through the centuries to attract people from villages from all around for a pleasurable day out, when the village green is awash with activity and the pubs full to overflowing.

Contemporary accounts describe it as *"the one big holiday of the year when all North Norfolk met together"*. Well into this century, there were "steam horses, boxing booths, singing, country dancing and step dancing in clogs and music was provided by violins from Norwich". It was on the fairground that the bioscope, the forerunner of the modern cinema, began around 1900 - and it was a sensation. The projector initially was cranked by hand, and the films were simplicity itself. The home-made sound effects (rushing trains, head on collisions, mighty storms!) were as elementary as could be. But the crowds loved them, and flocked in to see the new wonder of moving figures. However it was the extravagant razzamatazz outside which encouraged them to come in.

On the platform in front of the entrance would be the show's owner, or a "barker" paid to do the job, elegantly dressed, enticing the crowd to come in and view "the new wonder of the age - The Cinematograph". As if all that wasn't enough, he would be backed up by clowns, a big bass drum - and "Paraders". These last were troupes of shapely dancing girls, plumed, sequinned and booted to catch susceptible eyes.

Charles Thurston travelled up and down East Anglia with his shows in the years before the Great War. He was there at Lynn at the beginning of the season. Later he would set up in Norwich next to Agricultural Hall (Anglia Television's headquarters today).

Film subjects then were simplicity itself - such as the Proclamation of the King (Edward VII) from Norwich Market Place in 1901; or employees from Colman's and Sexton's (mustard and shoe factories respectively) leaving for dinner. The cameras were at Queen Victoria's funeral in 1901, and that very night just three cities in England screened the event - Manchester, London... and Norwich.

As technology improved, albeit slowly, cinema established itself in static buildings, mostly converted from other uses, but many soon built for the purpose. By the Thirties it had completely deserted the fairground. Just how the lure of the silver screen took hold can be grasped in this extract from the late Clifford Temple: *"For evening entertainment, Norwich was well catered for, there being nearly twenty establishments to go to... Charlie Chaplin was the favourite film star during the Great War, with Tom Mix and W S*

GILBERT'S CIRCUS, NORWICH.

The BIO-TABLEAUX
from the London Hippodrome will illustrate the
**Queen's Funeral**
VIEWS SPECIALLY TAKEN on
SATURDAY
in LONDON (HYDE PARK), also at PORTSMOUTH and COWES.

These Films will be Exhibited in the leading London Places of Amusement this Evening.

ALL VIEWS CLEAR AND STEADY.

APOLLO, the Ideal Athlete.

**End of an era: Gilbert's Circus advertises its film of the funeral of Queen Victoria in the EDP in January 1901. "All views clear and steady," it promised.**

**The opulent interior of the Majestic Cinema at King's Lynn took picture-houses in the west of the county to new heights of luxury.**

*Hart the best-known cowboys. Elmo Lincoln featured as the first Tarzan, while Mary Pickford always brought good attendances, as did little Shirley Temple later. When the talkies came to Norwich they caused something of a sensation, the first starring Al Jolson in The Singing Fool."*

Norfolk's larger centres such as Yarmouth and Lynn also built up flourishing cinema business. What is surprising is that so many small towns and villages had their own picture houses.

By March 1901 the Theatre Royal in Lynn saw the moving pictures as a threat to its live entertainment. So they booked Mr Joseph Poole with his cinematograph, with yet more patriotic footage of events in the Boer War. In his pamphlet, The Cinema in Lynn, Stephen Worfolk tells of the first purpose-built cinema in the town, The Electric Theatre in Broad Street, which opened on September 23rd 1911. It was a great success, as was its *"quick witted and very versatile pianist, playing mood-setting music throughout a film she may not have seen before"*.

In 1928 Lynn cinema was taken into new heights with the opening of a bigger and more opulent establishment, the Majestic, whose opening attraction, the epic Ben Hur, pulled in a capacity audience of 1275. In keeping with the religious character of the story, the Choir of All Saints' Church sang hymns and sacred pieces during the intervals!

But "talkies" were still to come – and that happened in July 1929 when the St James Theatre screened Lucky Boy, starring George Jessel, "the Original jazz singer".

For one local character, Ben Culey, there was still room for cinema development, and he had the money to make it happen. Stephen Worfolk describes him with a nice touch of humour: *"Mr Culey, a Lynn man of many interests, had owned fishing smacks and was a farmer; a colourful personality... he was readily identified by his powerful build, vividly distressed suits and ancient trilby hat. His habit of smoking good cigars in his pipe, in which they stood like chimneys, gave him an air of imminent combustion."*

His Pilot Cinema opened in November 1938 with Snow White and the Seven Dwarfs as main feature. It seated 797 – but with a contro-

**The Theatre De Luxe in Norwich was just one of a plethora of cinemas which opened in the county as the film boom got under way in earnest in the early years of the twentieth century.**

versial element. At the rear of the balcony were double seats, an irresistible lure for courting couples. But adult Lynn was not amused, and parents would give their daughters and their "young men" positive instructions on where they should sit.

But by the Fifties television had taken hold and increasingly people were staying at home to be entertained, so rivalry between cinemas for audiences grew intense. In Lynn the Majestic converted to Cinemascope in 1955, beating down the opposition. Soon only the Majestic and The Pilot were left. Two decades later the Majestic made another bold move, when it turned its ballroom into a small cinema seating only 180. The Pilot closed its doors on March 27th 1983, following a screening of Gandhi.

So the Majestic was left as the only surviving full-time cinema in the town. This year (1999) it is back in the news. It was about to be demolished to make way for a multiplex cinema, destroying a handsome Twenties building, its splendid foyer and extravagant scarlet and gold auditorium; as well as features salvaged from the old Empire Theatre in London's Leicester Square, which was demolished as the Majestic was being built.

Then in stepped Chris Smith, Secretary of State for Culture, Media and Sport, and gave it immediate Grade II listing and protection. The developers' reaction was that, if they could not touch the building, the multiplex scheme was likely to falter.

In Norwich the cinema scene through the last 99 years has been even more varied and changing than in Lynn, with a multiplicity of picture houses arriving and disappearing through the decades. Right at the very beginning of the century, the first cinema in the city, according to movie man David Elgood, was a little place on Bank Plain. It opened in 1903, without any specific name, and for just five years it showed early films, offered piano entertainment - and when films weren't showing went into another kind of entertainment entirely... such as "The Funniest Face" competitions and Joyride, a machine which threw off its riders. In the same year the Hippodrome was built, otherwise The Grand Opera House, opened in style on St Giles Hill. Its operatic pretensions were brief. It also showed early bioscope films, became a noted old-time music hall, a full-time cinema for a spell in the Thirties and finally reverted to live variety theatre. We shall meet the Hippodrome again - and mourn its loss in 1960 at the hands of civic vandalism. Up in St Stephen's they were queuing to get into Victoria Hall, where a couple of pennies would buy a bare wooden seat. It was supposed to seat 400, but tales are told of 600-odd being squeezed in at times.

The full cast list of Norwich cinemas is a formidable one. Here are the survivors - and some whose character, even after they are long gone, makes them remembered in local picture-going annals. The city's first building designed for showing films was the Theatre de Luxe (pronounce it - de'loo!) in St Andrew's Street, which was demolished in 1957 after 47 years of sterling service. For it was a great favourite and, because of all the westerns it showed, known to its habitues as The Ranch

Norfolk has proved a considerable lure for film- and programme-makers searching for perfect settings for their productions. Stars of the calibre of Meryl Streep, Jane Fonda, Gwyneth Paltrow, Al Pacino, Donald Sutherland, Julie Christie and Alan Bates have all filmed in the county.

Productions filmed or partly filmed in the county include One of Our Aircraft is Missing (1941), The Dam Busters (1954), Operation Crossbow (1965), The Go Between (1971), Out of Africa (1985) and Eyes Wide Shut (1999)

In 1985 Goldcrest took over Lynn's historic core for weeks for the filming of ill-fated epic Revolution (pictured above), transforming the ancient riverside streets of the town into eighteenth-century New York – and providing a bonanza for local suppliers and extras.

Television producers have also beaten a path to the county for series including Dad's Army, Sherlock Holmes and the 1998 production of Vanity Fair, (Nathaniel Parker and Natasha Little pictured right), filmed at Rainthorpe Hall at Flordon, Barningham Hall near Holt and Thelverton Hall near Diss. 1999 saw perhaps what is destined to be the most famous Norfolk-shot scene of the century when Oscar winner Gwyneth Paltrow walked on Holkham beach in the closing minutes of Shakespeare in Love.

MEETINGS, ENTERTAINMENTS, &c.

NEW
Theatre Royal
NORWICH.
Proprietor .......... JACK GLADWIN

TO-NIGHT at 7.45 p.m.

PRINCE LITTLER
Presents
ERIK CHARELL'S
White Horse Inn
FROM THE LONDON COLISEUM.
COMPANY OF 100.

All Bookable Seats are Sold for To-night's Performance, but Unreserved Seats at 1/6 Pit and 1/- Balcony can be obtained at the doors opening at 7 p.m.

**The opening night of the re-built Norwich Theatre Royal, as advertised in the EDP on September 30th 1935**

House. Within almost the same time span was The Picture House/Gaumont in Haymarket, built in 1911 and demolished in 1959. In 1931 it became the first in Norwich to install a cinema organ. Its site is now occupied by Top Shop.

Only 15 years of life were allotted to the Thatched Theatre in All Saints Green, but it was fondly remembered for many years after it closed its doors in 1930. Among picture houses it was really rather posh, the building having begun life as The Thatched Assembly Rooms, with a top restaurant and elegant ballroom. While the best films were screened, a fine string orchestra played and afternoon teas were served.

Still open is The Regent, though now it is under the ABC banner. Having opened in 1923, this is the longest-running cinema in Norwich. Last of the silent era movie houses in Norwich when it was built, it was also with 1800 seats the biggest cinema in the city. The Odeon opened in Botolph Street in 1938. The Lord Mayor, Charles Watling, idealistically intoned: "May this new Odeon begin a successful career of amusement, instruction and inspiration, that will broaden men's minds, widen their vision and lift their souls above the cares of daily life." And that, assuredly, is what in an ideal world the best entertainment is all about. The place had 33 years to live up to those high ideals, before it was knocked down in favour of a new Odeon in Anglia Square, which is still open and has three screens.

Then there was the Noverre, at the Assembly House in Theatre Street. It closed just before Christmas 1992, after years of falling ticket sales.

Finally, within the city bounds, to one of the great success stories of recent years, Cinema City, whose recent generous Lottery grant means that it can move ahead to even greater achievements. Built within the historic Stuart Hall and Suckling House (they date back to the fourteenth century) one might call Cinema City a "cinema theatre", for this is the place to see those films which still did not make it on to the main circuit.

As the twentieth century ended, the multi-screen cinema revolution which had swept across the country in the last decade arrived in Norwich with the construction of an eight-screen venture occupying part of Castle Mall, and a rival 14-screen site planned for the redeveloped Riverside area.

Turning back the clock again to the beginning of this century, out in the county there was a remarkable surge in small picture houses, often family-created and -run establishments, or backed by the cash of local entrepreneurs. North Walsham's Picturedrome, built in 1912, was a case in point, though in the years just before and during the Great War its success was due to the enthusiasm and flair of a London couple named Coates, who ran the place, produced the publicity material, looked after the gas engine and dynamo which generated electricity (North Walsham had no mains supply at that time), manned the box office and operated the projectors.

The Picturedrome closed down in 1931, chased off by the new Regal, which ran until 1977. Even little Mattishall, near Dereham, had its "flicks", called the Electric. It operated for eleven years up to 1927, but there is nothing left of it today to mark its site. Just after the First World War, Attleborough turned its town hall into a picture theatre, which ran until 1959, leaving many memories behind – such as the hard Thirties, when inmates of Wayland Workhouse were route marched two miles into the town – and charitably given free cinema tickets; and during the Second World War, when the Attleborough movies attracted droves of GIs from bases in the locality.

Stalham had a small picture house for just eight years in the Fifties and Sixties. Gorleston had three early cinemas, two of which had gone by 1930. The third, the Coliseum, survived until 1970 when it went out with the ironically-named film, Monte Carlo or Bust. A fourth establishment was the Palace, opened in 1939 – the last to be launched in the county before the Second World War – which went under in 1964.

Wymondham's Picture House opened during the Great War and lasted until the Second. The Town's celebrated Regal opened in 1937, and had some characterful people fighting to keep it going through the years - but it finally succumbed in 1993. Before the Second World War, Aylsham had two short-lived establishments. A third, the County, served its town and surrounding villages for 23 years, until in 1960 it joined the long list of disappearances.

Downham Market had its own cinemas too. They've long since gone, but have left behind rich seams of anecdote, lovingly collected by Stephen Peart. Downham's Electric, for example, had problems maintaining the gas pressure to its dynamo. The gas was fed from a large bag, from which the pressure frequently fell. So a fat boy was employed to watch the bag and to deposit his weight upon it at the right moments to keep the gas flow going strong.

But even this net of small town cinemas left smaller sprats space to pass through and find a viable working opportunity in those hard and jobless Thirties. Dick Joice, later an Anglia television presenter became keenly interested in photography and then in cine-photograph as a young fellow. Then he and Ernest Swain of Hunstanton ("He was THE film man around here then") went into partnership, each bought a 16mm projector (so that a film could be kept running without having to stop to change reels) and formed Norfolk Mobile Cinemas. Travelling with an old farm pick-up or an ancient Ford Prefect ("As long as you could get two projectors in the back . . .") they took film shows on a regular weekly basis to village halls and the like in Massingham, Grimston, Docking, Bilney and the Burnhams.

In north-west Norfolk another weekly film man was Bert Wells, who for a time in the early Twenties ran a little 200-seater in Hunstanton called The Mikado. Then he decided to take films to village halls on a regular schedule taking in Docking, Snettisham, Dersingham, Heacham and Hunstanton.

That fascinating snapshot of Fifties Norfolk, Norwich and Its Region, published in 1961 lamented: *"The trend in local entertainment services is that which is common in other parts of the country, namely the decline in the cinema in the face of competition from television, and of the growing popularity of car and motor cycle owning, which diverts cash from the box office. Since the end of the war, six cinemas have closed in Norwich..."*

At least, as the century draws to its close, the picture within Norfolk in entertainment generally and across the whole face of the arts, is immensely better than that so darkly painted in 1961. A year earlier the Hippodrome had already gone, a treasure of an Edwardian building, all gilt and plush within, which the city allowed to be pulled out like a bad tooth and replaced in due course by a multi-storey car park. But it had enjoyed its glory days in the late Thirties and in the war years, when it and its neighbour a couple of hundred yards away, the Theatre Royal, provided entertainment vital at such a time - and frequently of West End quality, for the top stars who had been bombed out of London came to play to the provinces. Both buildings too were in perfect order to greet their patrons.

In June 1934 a fire destroyed the old Theatre Royal. Gallantly, despite the grim depression, its owner Jack Gladwin determined to rebuild, and did so in just 15 months, reopening his fine new building, with all comforts and mod cons of the era, on September 30th 1935, with Prince Littler's production of White Horse Inn. Two years later to the month, the Hippodrome re-opened, specifically for variety theatre, after a £20,000 refit, no mean sum at the time.

On the opening night, as the EDP reported, *"enthusiasm was unbounded . . . The programme was one of the best ever presented in the city, not a seat was vacant, and the hundreds who were unable to gain admission watched with many others the arrival of the more fortunate."* A couple of weeks later came *"those clever young artists Hughie Green and his Gang, who have made themselves so well known and popular in wireless broadcasts."* Close on their heels came a double treat for Norwich. At the Hippodrome was the celebrated comedienne Nellie Wallace - matched at the Royal by the equally famous, and funny, Elsie and Doris Waters. Fame in another medium came to the

**Jack Gladwin, who rebuilt the fire-ravaged Norwich Theatre Royal in just 15 months. He later wrote: "In the disastrous fire... many of the irreplaceable relics of its former glory were lost but I like to think that there is an atmosphere about the old theatre that is indestructible."**

Royal in November 1937, when Sybil Thorndike starred in Yes, My Darling Daughter, "an exhilarating, enjoyable piece of entertainment". The Hippodrome countered with popular "pull" in the shape of Carroll Levis' BBC Discoveries, followed by Max Miller, beguiling his audiences "in his coat of many colours", and fresh from a Royal Variety performance. But it was the Royal which bagged the "First Visit to Norwich & Exclusive Engagement of Stanley Holloway, the Famous Star of Stage, Screen and Radio."

When war was declared on September 3rd, both theatres closed - but in a few months were up and running again.

But with Meet the Girls, City Hall and its Watch Committee clearly decided that the Hippodrome was trying too hard to entertain the populace. The truth was, the Lord Chamberlain's authority was being flouted. Unauthorised lines and questionable jokes were creeping in. The theatre and its offending performers were hauled before the Magistrates' Court. A former manager of the Hippodrome noted: "Being a cathedral city they [The Authorities] are very strict, but just lately they have got worse than ever, and I think they are the strictest in the country. They will not tolerate any 'blue' gags or vulgarity of any kind whatever... Three weeks ago they sent a shorthand writer to take down the whole of the dialogue of the show." One would have loved to have been a fly on the wall when the notes were read back to the City Fathers. One Hylda Baker had included a sketch about ARPs in the offending show. The Lord Chamberlain promptly banned it - and Miss Baker was fined £1.

Through the war years both theatres pulled out the stops to keep their patrons happy. Tom Walls played in farce. Emlyn Williams and Angela Baddeley appeared in his own play, The Light of Heart. Tommy Handley and ITMA, young Tommy "You Lucky People" Trinder, Elsie and Doris Waters kept the people laughing. So did Ralph Lynn in Rookery Nook; and Jack Hulbert and Cicely Courtneidge in The Hulbert Follies. And musicals, too, were hugely popular. Only once was this wartime calendar interrupted. The first German "reprisal" air raids hit Norwich on April 27th 1942, just before midnight. Both theatres escaped unscathed. Two nights later the bombers were back and this time the Hippodrome was struck, though the auditorium was untouched. Unhappily stage manager Les Pitchford and his wife were in the theatre, and were killed. So were variety artists Mr and Mrs Buddy Petersen, who presented Buddy the Performing Seal. They had bedded down in the dressing rooms to be on hand to look after Buddy. Miraculously the seal was unharmed, and was quickly found a home in a private zoo.

With the end of the war, both theatres fell on increasingly hard times. For the Hippodrome it was the end, for in 1960, as already noted, this beautiful building was wantonly destroyed. The Theatre Royal became a cinema, but though its future looked grim, regeneration lay ahead.

In 1967 Essoldo bought the Theatre Royal for £50,000, unsuccessfully attempted to turn it into a bingo hall - and announced that they would not be seeking a renewal of the stage licence. As a live theatre, the place seemed doomed. Determined to keep theatre alive in Norwich, the City Council then bought the building from Essoldo - for £90,000. The initial efforts to establish it as a civic theatre were less than successful. It was at this juncture that Laurence Hill, who had moved to Norfolk to retire from the pressures of London theatre administration, arrived on the scene. He was persuaded to become administrator of the Royal.

Despite the building's general air of decay he worked wonders, booking excellent product to bring in audiences. It was enough for the city, with help from the Arts Council, to undertake a major restoration, both backstage and front-of-house. The re-born theatre enjoyed steady growth under Laurence Hill's guidance, until ill-health brought his premature retirement.

Into the administrator's role stepped a young, cocky, genial Irishman named Dick Condon. He was a brilliant publicist and impresario, with huge energy and resolve, who became a greatly-loved personality among theatre-goers. He had a vision of the theatre as a vital force in the community, from the start set out his stall of objectives - and ten years later had achieved every one of them. Under his inspirational leadership the Theatre Royal went from strength to strength.

Such heavy use of the building took its toll until, in 1987, the Trust chairman announced that a major facelift was now necessary. A £2.7 million appeal was launched. With only £1.6 million raised, the theatre closed at the end of March 1990 and major works began. Disagreements over management of the project soon became evident and Dick Condon, at odds with the Trust, resigned as administrator. At the end of May work ground to a halt, beginning a period of bitter recrimination which resulted in the departure of the Trust's chairman.

The theatre was to be closed for nearly two and a half years, a victim of what Condon termed "the Trust without trust", and what many saw as a combination of lack of leadership, delegation without control and Trust members failing until it was too late to understand the true situation. In due course, Norfolk County Council's leadership pushed through a plan for the theatre's salvation, under a newly-appointed Trust.

Just as at the end of the Sixties, and again in the Seventies, the right men had been there when most wanted, so in 1991 (the year Dick Condon died in Ireland) the Royal was again fortunate, this time with an immensely experienced actor, producer, administrator and impresario, Peter Wilson, appointed to the helm. By the time the theatre re-opened at the end of 1992 he had established himself locally, earned respect and trust - and put together a programme which wholly met his declared aim: "A balanced programme with something for everyone." His vision of touring for East Anglia was "nothing but the best, and with a European aspect". Each and every season since then, that balance has been excitingly maintained, with his "European aspect" reaching its greatest peak thus far with a presentation of the mighty Wagner Ring Cycle by the Norwegian State Opera Company - a 101 per cent sell-out (ie, standing room taken too), attracting an international audience, and in the process bringing about £500,000 into the local economy. The Theatre Royal seems well set for the millennium - and when the time comes for another facelift, one hopes that past lessons will have been learned well in advance.

**Dick Condon: Much-loved Irish theatre manager who transformed the fortunes of the Norwich Theatre Royal and the Cromer Pier Theatre.**

In December 1995, with a royal gala and high hopes all round, the new Norwich Playhouse opened, spurred on by the drive and considerable personal generosity of local business couple, Jane and Henry Burke, and in large measure paid for by local individuals and companies. Its objective was to give the city a small-scale play theatre with a core repertory company.

But after only 18 months of life the Playhouse closed its doors, the money having run out. Soon afterwards the spectre loomed of the building being bought by a major brewery and turned into a theme pub, deeply upsetting all those who had worked for and contributed to the Playhouse's creation.

Fortunately a rescue package was brought together, under which a new, small board was

**Norfolk amateur talent has produced many memorable moments in the county's entertainment venues over the years. In this March 1975 picture some of the boys' chorus of the Yarmouth Operatic and Drama Society get into the Oliver! mood.**

able to pay off the theatre's debts and to re-open it in 1998 as a space for hire, whether for theatrical, artistic or business purposes.

Through the decades, serenely untouched by the ups and downs of its professional peers, the Maddermarket Theatre in Norwich has continued to occupy a very special niche in the affections of city and county playgoers, with its blend of professional direction and amateur actors. This continues a tradition laid down by its founder, the legendary Nugent Monck, who founded the company in its present setting (a former Roman Catholic Chapel) in 1921. Norwich also has the Sewell Barn Theatre, an intimate 100-seater space housed in the barn in which, by repute, Anna Sewell's brother stabled the horse upon which Anna based her immortal Black Beauty. Across the whole of Norfolk, amateur dramatic societies are legion; and if many of them rarely look beyond their parish boundaries for inspiration and artistic growth, they do serve a valuable dual purpose in being, of themselves, a tremendous social catalyst within their membership; and a source of entertainment and still wider social contact for their audiences.

Out on the North Norfolk coast, the neighbouring towns of Sheringham and Cromer have a definite place in the county's theatrical story. For a long period, within a very cramped space, Sheringham Little Theatre maintained a much-praised professional summer rep attracting holiday-makers and locals alike – in winter reverting to being the town's own centre of entertainment. In the last few years a full-scale renovation and yet more space has allowed it to flourish still more and to enhance its already established role.

At Cromer the pier, its Pavilion Theatre and not least the celebrated Seaside Special variety show presented there throughout each summer, have become an institution. In the last century the pier provided a discreet promenade for Victorian gentlefolk. And at the end of the century entertainment arrived with the construction of a small bandstand. In 1901, following severe storm damage, the pier was repaired and much improved and visitors were promised that "Here, while the season lasts, strains of charming music will be constantly heard." Four years later the bandstand was extended into a pavilion, where for many years concert parties played, featuring such artistic luminaries as The Perfect Scamps and Mademoiselle Vivienne, The Perfect Contortionist.

By the mid-Fifties the pier was in pretty poor shape and local ratepayers were grumbling about its cost and by February 1976 the council was told: "With most hotels providing colour television in their comfortable lounges, the public are not persuaded that a visit to a concert party at the end of the pier is itself an attraction."

But district councillors, to their credit, did not waver. They would, they declared, develop the Pavilion Theatre to a higher level and win back public support. At which point Richard Condon (Management) Ltd – otherwise that brilliant, breezy and charismatic showman who had worked such wonders at the Theatre Royal in Norwich – offered "a first-class programme of theatre entertainment during the summer of 1978". And so it happened, and continues still, with astonishing box office success, in the mildly old-fashioned yet ageless end-of-the-pier style which Condon re-created.

A little further along the coast, a dream which for a few short years became a fact was not so lucky. Wells Arts Centre, though it died ten years ago, deserves a place in the county's entertainment story. It was a courageous venture to turn part of a decaying complex of old granaries into a theatre and arts centre.

Music-making across the county burgeons through a network of amateur operatic societies, choirs and orchestras from Cromer and Sheringham to Diss; and Yarmouth via Norwich and Dereham to Downham and Lynn. Norwich alone has three orchestras, technically amateur since they are not paid, but largely made up of enthusiasts whose profession is music, and in venerable years led by the Philharmonic Society, which dates back to 1839. The Academy of St Thomas, founded 1973, which from the start has been committed to baroque music and early classical music. Then there is the Mozart orchestra (only "Mozart" is given a capital letter, laying the accent on The Divine M. rather than on the players), founded in 1962, and at first a predominantly classical orchestra.

Among Norfolk choirs, perhaps the best known and cherished during its 31-year life was the Broadland Singers, founded and directed throughout that time by Angela Dugdale until her retirement in 1989. Through that period the choir undertook thousands of concerts in this corner of England, all presented free of charge and thus raising considerable sums of money for charity.

In professional music making, Norfolk has long been blessed by two outstanding Festivals, the Norfolk & Norwich and the King's Lynn, with the N&N, in addition to its ten-day October festival, bringing in top orchestras and other attractions periodically through the year, as well as promoting mini-festivals of early music; and adventurous visual arts events.

Back in 1951 the important and splendid restoration was completed of the ancient St George's Guildhall in Lynn and the Queen Mother came along to open it officially. To mark this event a one-off festival of music and the arts had been conceived by Ruth, Lady Fermoy. It featured such as Shura Cherkassy, Peter Ustinov, Peggy Ashcroft, Joan Cross, Peter Pears, Benjamin Britten, Leon Goossens, Sir Osbert Sitwell, Gerald Moore and the never-to-be-forgotten Kathleen Ferrier. Such was its success that it became an annual event; and St George's became The Fermoy Arts Centre. And since that first festival, the Queen Mother has remained a firm supporter.

In late 1987 troubled times came. The Arts Centre was fairly heavily in debt and the Festival notably declining in popularity. An EDP leader put it bluntly: *"At the heart of the Fermoy's problem lies not 'elitism' but esotericism, the presentation of artistic and cultural forms that appeal to a minority of a minority."*

**Ruth, Lady Fermoy, who died in 1993 aged 84, began her close association with the county in 1931 when she married Lord Fermoy, MP for King's Lynn. As a concert pianist and founder of the Lynn Festival, she brought world-famous names such as Yehudi Menuhin to the Norfolk town. A lady-in-waiting and close friend to the Queen Mother, her links with the Royal Family were strengthened when her grand-daughter Lady Diana Spencer married the Prince of Wales in 1981. Paying tribute to Lady Fermoy, Sir Timothy Colman, Lord Lieutenant of Norfolk, said: "Her inspiration and leadership has done more to widen the opportunity and enjoyment of the arts in the region than any other I can recall."**

**Jack Jay was the man who put Yarmouth firmly on the British entertainment map. A showbiz veteran at seven – he was billed as "England's Jackie Coogan" – he became the country's youngest cinema manager at 16. His father, Ben, arrived in Yarmouth in 1937 to begin the Jay entertainments empire in the resort. Jack was the person who spotted the opportunity to bring big-name acts to the town. He also had a flair for spotting future stars, which led to early breaks for then-unknowns such as Norman Wisdom and Max Bygraves. He was made a Companion of the Grand Order of Water Rats in the mid-Seventies. The impresario died in 1995 aged 80. His family, notably his son Peter, continues to build on the proud Jay entertainment legacy.**

Many seaside resorts will claim to have witnessed a "golden era" of entertainment; but while it never quite matched its great rival Blackpool either for the splendour of its facilities, the length of its season or its illuminations, Yarmouth, particularly in the late Fifties, the Sixties and Seventies, provided a feast of summer stars the like of which will not be seen again.

In common with many famous watering places, Yarmouth had had traditional holiday entertainment for much of the century; one of only two indoor circus arenas in the country, opened at the turn of the century, survives to this day. But it was the coming of the television age that changed everything. Famous names who were, after all, first and foremost stars of the variety theatre and music hall, found that doing "summer season" was a good way of putting their talents before a huge family audience.

These post-war years also saw the golden age of the family holiday. Yarmouth, much like Blackpool, benefited from the traditional "works holiday" weeks and fortnights - particularly from the North, Midlands and Scotland. They came from the industrial areas, and many were miners to whom the bracing East Coast air was Manna from heaven after spending the rest of the year underground. These folk brought money a-plenty and needed to be entertained. Yarmouth could supply it. In its heyday it had not only the permanent circus but two pier shows plus four theatres (some also doubling as cinemas in the day-time) plus the smaller "bread and butter" shows - no star names, but thoroughly professional in the way they were staged.

The season would begin at the late spring bank holiday and continue right through to the end of the school holidays. The shows would start up in early June and not end until midway through September. Most of them did two houses a night, six nights a week, with the stars then going off to perform the very lucrative Sunday one-night shows.

The big names rolled in. A resort which had already hosted big radio stars such as Charlie Chester, Frankie Howerd and George Formby in the Fifties now received the giants of television - Morecambe and Wise, Mike and Bernie Winters, Harry Secombe, Danny La Rue, Des O'Connor, Bruce Forsyth and Harry Worth; and later, Little and Large, Mike Yarwood and Cannon and Ball. The early Sixties also ushered in the pop revolution, and some of the big names of the time also became family favourites (not so the Beatles and the Rolling Stones, although both played one-night gigs at Yarmouth's 1500-seater ABC Theatre - formerly the Regal, subsequently the Cannon, and now no more, its former shell occupying part of the Market Gates shopping precinct). Famed pop promoter Larry Parnes forged a close link with the resort, and brought in big pop names such as Tommy Steele, Billy Fury and Gerry and the Pacemakers.

With this influx of star names came a greater awareness of how to make better use of existing facilities. On Yarmouth's seafront stands The Winter Gardens, a huge, greenhouse-styled protected building which looks picturesque but is of limited practical use. The Sixties answer? A German oompah-styled biergarten show, complete with yodellers, Tyrolean band and waitresses in dirndls. The holiday crowds loved it. Likewise the old open-air Marina, scene of many a concert party, eventually became a white elephant. It is now the site of the modern leisure complex that bears its name.

Sheer economic reality finally overtook the golden era and, just as television had sparked it all, so television began to kill it off. Fewer big stars were willing to spend a summer by the seaside, and they could now earn far more from a television series than from a season by the seaside. Although there were a few exceptions - Michael Barrymore and Jim Davidson remained staunch supporters of the summer season longer

than most – the seasons shortened and the names lost their gloss. Yarmouth also suffered from the competition provided by the package holiday: The socio-economic state of the nation was another factor, with much of the traditional market area changing dramatically. The miners' strike of the Eighties meant that many Northern and Midland families could no longer afford holidays; many of them had been coming for years.

Families do still come, although in decreasing numbers. Another revolution – the self-catering holiday – has taken over, and they are drawn to the holiday camps that have sprung up around Yarmouth, where in-house entertainment is part of the package. It is all highly polished – but it will never match the era when a day on the beach could be followed by an evening with some of the country's most popular entertainers.

**Yarmouth was a magnet for the stars – and the crowds – for many years in the Fifties, Sixties and Seventies. The picture above was taken at the Windmill Theatre during the 1963 summer season. (Left) Mrs Doreen Wise helps her husband Ernie get ready for his next show with Eric Morecambe at the ABC Theatre on July 14th 1967.**

An unseemly row erupted between Centre and Borough Council. Fortunately all was settled in due course and the festival was able to "re-draw" itself and to reclaim its true place at the heart of Lynn's musical year.

Since 1985 Festival Too, a separate venture funded by local businesses and well-wishers, has raised hundreds of thousands of pounds to stage free open-air shows in the marvellous surroundings of the Tuesday Market Place, at times attracting crowds of 15,000-plus.

The draughty and unloved Lynn Corn Exchange (only 16 years after its construction in 1854 Walter Rye was describing it as *"perhaps the most hideous and heavy erection in the county"*) was imaginatively converted into a state-of-the-art concert venue at a cost of £4.1 million in 1996. Lynn and West Norfolk Borough Council's leap of faith had been spectacularly vindicated, as it had a few years earlier with the opening of the £6 million Lynnsport sports centre. Both venues demonstrated the town's determination to compete with other regional centres such as Norwich, Peterborough and Cambridge to provide first-class leisure and entertainment facilities.

Among English festivals, the Norfolk & Norwich is one of the most venerable, for it dates back to the reign of George IV. The first Norfolk & Norwich Triennial Festival was held for three days in September 1824 in St Andrew's Hall in Norwich. It remained a three-yearly event until the great decision was reached in 1989 that it should become annual. During its long and distinguished history it has brought the finest orchestras and artists to Norwich and continuously recognised as one of its functions the commissioning of new musical works. The list of those works, right up to the present, has been an immensely impressive one.

But only in the last quarter century has the Festival positively aimed, and with heartening success, to widen its appeal to a broader audience. Since the October event "went annual", that broadening process has accelerated, and with exciting results both in the range of programme content and in the increased selling of tickets.

The 1991 festival, by which the annual pattern had already taken firm root, was an optimistic indicator of what was to follow. It placed a strong stress on children and the family, with a string of events aimed at young people – and all eagerly taken up. A festival officer said at the time: "We have wanted to make people realise that the festival is for everyone – and that it is fun." Each year that philosophy has been increasingly strengthened, and the choice of events widened still further.

In the brilliant summer of 1959 as Alec Issigonis was introducing Britain to his Morris Mini, and two monkeys called Able and Baker soared into space aboard a US Jupiter rocket, a lattice steel structure was making its 1000ft ascent alongside the A140 at Mendelsham in Suffolk.

Then the tallest construction of its kind in Britain, the Mendelsham television transmitter went up three years after the 500ft mast at Tacolneston in South Norfolk. But by October 1959 the duo were in competition, Tacolneston transmitting the BBC's first televised Norwich-based regional news programme, followed three weeks later by Anglia Television, making its debut via Mendelsham. Prime Minister Harold Macmillan was telling the British people they had never had it so good, and for Norfolk, television and regional broadcasting came with a late and sudden acceleration.

Only twelve years earlier the BBC had dismissed "for the foreseeable future" the possibility of a distinctly regional radio programming for Norfolk and Suffolk. While Norwich and other local towns were venues for Workers' Playtime, Children's Hour, and edge of the world visitations from Birmingham, Norfolk it seemed was to remain a remote dependency of the BBC Midland Region. East Anglia had been switched to the Midlands from the London region at the end of the war to take advantage of the Sutton Coldfield transmitter. What it wanted of course was neither London nor Birmingham, but a separate and distinctive voice. In April 1946 the BBC held a Norwich "Exhibition Week" which included a concert by the BBC Symphony Orchestra conducted by Sir Adrian Boult, and Godfrey Baseley, subsequently creator of The Archers talking to Mr L A Jewell, chairman of the Earlham Poultry and Rabbit Club. When during a song recital at the Castle Museum the newsreader Frank Phillips introduced Come My Own One, the audience's response might have been unusually heartfelt.

Norfolk and East Anglian disaffection with its "non-status" was long-standing, in November 1937 a BBC mandarin publicly acknowledging before a critical Norwich public meeting the region's poor radio reception and indifferent coverage. Two years later the BBC was seeking International Broadcasting Union backing for a new station at Norwich, but all that was to emerge in the privations of war was a low-powered transmitter at Caley's chocolate factory.

The first sign that the BBC was taking its Midland Region outer dependency seriously was the opening of the Postwick transmitter in 1949, and by the mid-Fifties East Anglia was slowly acquiring a more distinct identity. In 1955, David Bryson, a talks producer of studious appearance, and a mountaineer, (he had written and produced the main sound broadcast on the 1953 ascent of Everest) was appointed the BBC's first East Anglian representative, with an office in All Saints Green. If the title carried overtones of head office tentativeness, Bryson's arrival was more than symbolic. Earlier that year in a small wood at Tacolneston near Wymondham, a 30 by 12ft wooden temporary station had been built, and on the first of February via a 230ft provisional mast, began transmitting across a 15-mile radius. The next year saw a more powerful 500ft mast, while in Norwich Bryson and his staff moved down the street to the elegant eighteenth-century house that has ever since been the BBC's regional headquarters.

Jean Goodman, who made the first radio broadcast from All Saints Green recalls that the BBC hierarchy thought Norfolk was so extraordinary, so far back in time "that things happened here which happened nowhere else, which of course was true". Less impressed, one senior and exasperated figure rang up from London complaining that he was fed up with all the made-up stories coming out of Norwich.

**For more than thirty years Tony Scase was the pre-eminent news reporter on BBC East and Anglia. Born at Downham Market, the former EDP journalist turned freelance in 1960, and right up to his death in 1994 aged 56, his news sense and prodigious industry made him a celebrated figure among his newspaper, radio and television colleagues. "He was a damned good journalist and a very, very nice man, a really nice fellow," recalled Doug Salmon. "You could always rely on him entirely. In many ways he was unsophisticated, but he never went wrong. If you join any big organisation the best thing your mother can buy you is a knife-proof back shield, but you never had anything like that with Tony. He was as straight as a die."**

By the end of 1956, the nation in turmoil over the Suez invasion, Tacolneston was carrying VHF programmes, and nine years after the BBC had discounted it East Anglian regional broadcasting had arrived. From the start, BBC Norwich acquired in those swan song years of radio's Golden Age, a wonderfully close and distinctive East Anglian character, having acquired contributors such as naturalist Ted Ellis, R H Mottram, the Norfolk humorist Sidney Grapes, the EDP

**Anglia's decision in 1987 to pension off its much-loved Silver Knight emblem caused something of a stir. The knight, which dates from the last century, was considered out of place in the changing world of television. Anglia chief executive David McCall explained: "It is impossible to adapt it to the sophisticated demands of modern screen technology." In its place came the now-familiar colourful logo.**

essayist Eric Fowler, F R Buckley, an American who had settled in Lynn where, with his 'Monty' beret, he became a familiar figure, Dick Bagnall-Oakeley, and Ted Chamberlin, head of a Norwich press agency and editor of The Norfolk Magazine.

"We were all good chums," recalled Malcolm Freegard, who came to BBC Norwich from Birmingham in 1960. "It depended to quite a large extent on the unusual, but to me delightful, personality of David Bryson, a somewhat tactless but extremely civilised man with a wonderful humour, who went round Norwich and the region gathering up suitable people."

Like Bagnall-Oakeley, Freegard had been a master at Gresham's. A wartime Wellington bomber pilot stationed at Marham, and twice shot down, he joined the BBC in 1955 as a Midland Region talks producer, and arrived at All Saints Green from the London Television Centre as THE Television Producer for East Anglia. When he told the legendary Grace Wyndham Goldie he was moving to Norwich, the formidable BBC dame told him if he wished to work "in a place like that I've completely lost all interest in you". Wacko! thought Freegard. "That suits me fine."

There was a compelling amiability and local self-sufficiency in these early years that set East Anglian radio and television apart. The gifted amateur was prized, and the early television newsreaders were initially part-timers, Geoff Harvey for example taught at the CNS, Ian Emmerson was the director of the Maddermarket Theatre, while John Crowest and John Bacon (later an Anglia newsreader) ran their own Norwich businesses. Hugh Barrett, an excellent presenter, was a writer and Suffolk land agent. When in the early Seventies the regional news programmes were re-designed, to become in effect mini-clones of the new Nationwide, something distinctive was stripped irrevocably from BBC East Anglia.

Independent or "commercial" television, had opened in London and the south east in late 1955, followed shortly by Birmingham and much of the Midlands. It was an innovation long resisted not only by the BBC and certain newspapers, but by many who feared its popularist programming and style would have trivialising cultural consequences. Such apprehensions proved largely baseless, but for nearly four years Norfolk had been a stranger to Wagon Train and Emergency Ward 10, its Sunday Nights unvisited by the variety acts from the London Palladium.

All this changed from October 27th when Anglia Television was opened by Sir Ivone Kirkpatrick, former diplomat and chairman of the Independent Television Authority. Kirkpatrick had been met at Norwich Station by the stationmaster, togged out in frock coat and top hat. As well as having an insight into the day's significance, had he some understanding of the men and women who made up Anglia's upper deck? For despite independent television's egalitarian image, Anglia was powered by significant local inputs of top drawer and old money. Its chairman was Lord Townshend of Raynham, Aubrey (later Lord) Buxton, executive director was a colleague, as was Sir Robert Bignold, chairman of Norwich Union. For anyone apprehensive about the possibly pervasive influence of quiz shows and crime dramas, the Cambridge high table representation of Dr Glyn Daniel, chairman of BBC's Animal, Vegetable, Mineral (fellow of St John's) and Dr Audrey Richards, vice-principal of Newnham, would have been reassuring.

Farming programmes, a core speciality for England's premier agricultural region, had the imprimatur of another board member, Sir Peter Greenwell, a leading Suffolk farmer and industrialist, as well of course as Lord Townshend himself. Anglia moreover, had settled itself in to the former Agricultural Hall. Farming Diary an early in-house production, was introduced – following unsuccessful approaches to the then pre-eminent A G Street and Ralph Whiteman – by a neighbour of Lord Townshend, Dick Joice. Townshend had told him that with his farming background and exposure to public speaking, he had better have a go. "I think you could get away with it." This jovial but immensely shrewd Norfolk man was to become the most memorable figure produced by East Anglian television. Along with Aubrey Buxton – whose Survival programmes were to achieve international recognition – the chubby, avuncular Joice was that rare being, a natural broadcaster. "Dick was a real Norfolk man," says Douglas Salmon, an early Anglia, and later of BBC East producer. "He understood Norfolk people and yet he was in a curious way, sophisticated. He was a godsend to them."

Joice's involvement had begun the previous summer when in a chance encounter in Raynham park, Lord Townshend told him that along with a group of associates he was bidding for the new independent franchise for East Anglia. A few weeks later, as Dick Joice recounts in his autobiography Full Circle, Townshend arrived with two visitors, John Woolf, joint head of Romulus and Remus Films, and Laurence Scott, chairman of Manchester Guardian Newspapers. The conversation turned to the kind of television likely to be favoured by East Anglians. *"I remember remarking that as I didn't have a television set, indeed had hardly seen any television at all, I was probably not the chap to talk to. Lord Townshend said that he didn't have a set either, although his butler did and occasionally he watched his."*

Undeterred, his guests asked Joice to meet some associates in a plush London hotel. Joice arrived dressed in twills, sports jacket and brogues, and carrying a blackboard and easel proceeded to give a farming presentation "very similar to the talks I had given to the Bawdeswell and Helhoughton schools". Much impressed, a guest told Lord Townshend that anyone who could hold an audience of that calibre for an hour deserved to get on. Dick Joice was to do precisely that. From Farming Diary he became anchor man for the news and feature magazine About Anglia which grew from a short twice-weekly to an extended five-nightly. But his most enduring success was Bygones, a mixture of short and documentary length films and studio features celebrating – just in time – our rural heritage. The programme ran from 1969 to 1988 and is still the subject of popular revivals.

Douglas Salmon recalls the early mix at Anglia, of "professionals from outside and local amateurs, country gents really. All the typists were terribly well-spoken." One of the first locally-produced programmes to go out (October 29th) was The Midday Show, with Susan Hampshire as resident singer, Roger Gale, Jean Goodman, and Norman Hackforth, who had been Noel Coward's pianist, as well as the famous 'basement' voice in the popular radio quiz Twenty Questions. Other soon to be familiar faces were Newman Sanders, for years an anchorman news reader (the regional news service has always been an Anglia forte), Drew Russell, and Michael Hunt, the handlebar moustachioed meteorologist, a pioneer in forecasting as entertaining education, and almost certainly Britain's first weatherman 'personality'.

Not long after its debut, Anglia held a party for those who had had appeared in the first week's programming, among them Dawn Adams, a leading actress of the time. A call was put through to her London flat, but on checking her diary, she told her Anglia caller that regretfully she was shooting at Elstree that day. The caller understood. There was a pause. "By the way," inquired the voice from Anglia, "who owns the shooting at Elstree?"

If this is revealing of an agrarian innocence or patrician 'other worldliness', Adams' early involvement was a consequence of Anglia's unusually strong attachment to drama. As well as Woolf, the board also included Donald Albery, a prominent member of the London theatrical family, while John Jacobs and John Rosenberg were to be two outstanding heads of drama. Dawn Adams' abortive invitation arose from her appearance in Anglia's second play, Sweet Poison which, when it was networked in December 1959, reached fourth in the Top Ten behind Wagon Train, The Army Game and Take Your Pick. In fact by 1961 nine of Anglia's 12 plays in the Play of the Week series had entered the Top Five, an extraordinary achievement, and one which when viewed from the vale of contemporary television culture, is not without poignancy. This was the year that a Survival production, SOS Rhino became the first natural history programme to make the Top Ten. For long after, Survival was to pick up prestigious

**In a poll for the region's most identifiable and popular television personality, Helen McDermott would win on a landslide. The Home Counties-born former nightclub singer joined Anglia twenty years ago and has been presenting About Anglia since 1988. Her first professional appearance was at the age of 12 in a London Festival Ballet production of The Nutcracker. But at 5ft one and a half inches she was thought too small for a career, and when 17 moved to the Northern club circuit as a singer. She recalls an "horrendous week" at Middlesbrough. "They didn't clap once. They just sat there." She was lucky; in the same week the comedian Jimmy Cricket was shouted down and pelted. McDermott joined Anglia from Westward Television, Plymouth, since when her bubbly, approachable personality, and un-tele lack of affectation, has made her the First Lady of the region's screens.**

**Tales of the Unexpected brought considerable acclaim – and overseas sales – for Anglia. It also provided an opportunity for many famous names to be filmed on home turf, such as this scene on a Norfolk farm location with Sir John Gielgud, Lord Miles and Godfrey James.**

television awards - many of them international - as a matter of routine, its US sales record even winning a Queen's Award for Industry. Anglia's drama output likewise, Dame of Sark with Celia Johnson, one of three of its productions to reach the Top Ten in the mid-Seventies.

Romper Room with the delightful Miss Rosalyn in charge from inception to nine months before the closing of its door in early 1977, was ITV's first pre-school series. This was the decade when Sale of the Century, a quiz programme with incomparably the best prizes, became for a moment the most popular programme on British television.

Anglia may have had its failures - the relatively well-received rural soap Weavers Green was axed in 1966 following networking difficulties - but from 1979 through to the mid-Eighties it achieved a national ascendancy with hugely-successful adaptations of works by two major authors. The first was Roald Dahl's Tales of the Unexpected - the first of which knocked Match of the Day off its accustomed number one spot - and from 1984 the serialisation of P D James' outstanding crime novels featuring the cerebral police detective Adam Dalgliesh. The Chief, a police drama of the early Nineties, was another success.

While BBC East had neither the resources nor the scale of programming responsibilities of Anglia, national recognition came the way of its news documentaries, including Royal Television Society awards for the 1990 portrait of the Cambridge scientist Stephen Hawking. Two years earlier Ruth's Story, an investigation into the Church of Scientology produced by Dick Meadows, won the RTS's regional current affairs programme of the year.

Rather like Elgar's famous lines, the bounds of the television region have been set wider still and wider. In the first years Anglia programmes were transmitted solely through Mendelsham, a primary reception area extending from the North Norfolk coast into North Essex which gave Anglia an intimate East Anglian character. When first Sandy Heath in Bedfordshire and then Belmont in Lincolnshire were added, this regional cohesion was diffused, as was to happen when BBC East likewise went down to Luton and the Thames estuary. But Belmont's inclusion took the Anglia signal to Lynn and parts of North and West Norfolk for the first time, while bringing via the commentaries of the late John Campkin and Match of the Week the exotic pleasures of watching Hull City. But when in 1974 Belmont was switched to Yorkshire Television, Norwich was once again lost to these western parts of the county, a deeply-resented anomaly which continues to this day.

Anglia, like other successful ITV companies, had always had its contract renewed on its record. But the qualitative approach was changed by the 1990 Broadcasting Act which in effect caused the franchises to be sold off to the highest bidder in a "sealed envelope" auction that took no account of the merit of the existing holder. In early 1991 Anglia bid for the ten-year East of England Channel 3 franchise, to run from January 1st 1993. It faced two challengers, Three East and Richard Branson/David Frost's East of England Television. Both would have closed down the Norwich operation and switched it to Cambridge. The previous year, BBC East confirmed it would be staying in Norwich, having also entertained a Cambridge switch.

By October Anglia had won, the Branson/Frost having failed the "quality test", and Three East under-bidding Anglia's £17.8 million winning hand by nearly £4 million. Since the final ten-year period was secure on evidence of continuing good performance, Anglia had effectively won a twenty-year franchise.

But within the industry Anglia's assertion that it would retain its independence were viewed with scepticism. The tide, like the rules, was flowing in favour of ever-bigger companies. Either Anglia would acquire or be acquired. In the event it was the latter. In March 1994, its 36-year reign as a sovereign East Anglian company came to an end with the £292 million take-over by MAI, the financial services and media group headed by Labour peer Lord Hollick, which had a 61 per cent stake in the south of England broadcaster Meridian.

When Terry Wogan brought BBC Radio Norfolk on air on September 11th 1980, it was among the first of a second wave of local stations launched against a proliferation of 'pop, news and adverts' independent stations.

Norfolk had been without county-based local radio of any brand - parts of the West were covered by the independent Radio Hereward of Peterborough - though both the BBC and Independent Broadcasting Authority had laid vigorous claim to its airwaves. When in October 1978 the Government announced the next list of stations, it was the BBC which had been awarded the Norfolk slot. A disappointed IBA said it would be back, as indeed it was six years later.

While most of the early BBC local stations had been in the larger cities - the first in Leicester in 1967 - BBC Radio Norfolk became the first to serve a substantial county. As John Mountford, a seasoned East Anglian regional radio broadcaster, opened the microphones at 5.55p.m. that September evening, he ushered in the station's distinctive and intimate style, popularised by what were to become familiar names including Rob Bonnet, Keith Skipper, David Clayton, Peter Glanville (programme controller), Wally Webb, Olly Day, and Roy Waller. But the beginning of local radio was also the end of regional, the early-morning Roundabout East Anglia with an audience of up to 100,000 having been axed earlier that spring, followed by the Radio 4 VHF news in September.

With a full-time staff of only 22, Radio Norfolk's "new wave" remit also included tight budgeting. The overriding challenge has been to get "Norfolkness" and mainstream local radio in the right proportions. Unlike many counties, Norfolk's disposition does not fit into a mono-cultural national template, an idiosyncrasy that was to cause irritation among the local radio's national controllers. When Keith Skipper, the Voice of Norfolk for 15 years, and a broadcaster with an exceptionally large personal following, left abruptly in 1995 following a disagreement

*New radio station is born*

**A rooftop trumpet fanfare heralded the arrival of Norfolk's new neighbour yesterday evening.**

As the echo of the bandsmen's trumpets died away and a cluster of balloons took to the air, producer John Mountford welcomed the county to BBC Radio Norfolk.

The launch of Radio Norfolk, the first new BBC local radio station launched since the early 'seventies, and the first purpose-built for stereo broadcasting, was shown live on BBC's "Look East" television programme.

**Radio Norfolk arrives on the local broadcasting scene on September 10th 1980, as reported in the EDP the next day.**

with the station management, many concluded that "Norfolkness" had suffered a reversal. The balancing act goes on, but the style of BBC Radio Norfolk remains one of the most indigenous of any local station, to the satisfaction of one of the consistently highest listening figures in its field.

Norfolk's attachment to local broadcasting can also be seen in the high audiences of the independent local station, Radio Broadland. Primed by a half million pound investment, Broadland opened on October 1st 1984 in the former Norvic shoe factory in Norwich's Colegate. Thereafter listeners became familiar with a second new breed of presenters, including Rob Chandler, Chrissie Jackson, and Broadland's news chief, the late Julian Smith. The formula included extensive pop music and a local news service which has never sought to compete with its rival's deeply Norfolk flavour.

For ten years Broadland's listening figures have put it consistently in the top five of the national table of independent stations. Broadland's profitability and business performance has been another winning factor. In January 1990 it took over Radio Orwell and the Bury-based Saxon Radio in a £5.2 million deal. A further expansion took its parent company East Anglian Radio into Colchester. Five years later it expanded its range, launching Classic Gold Amber Radio ("Great Music - Golden Memories") a Sixties and Seventies music programme targeted at Norfolk's 36-60 age groups. Then in 1996 EAR was itself taken over - at a figure of £23.4 million - by the Wiltshire-based local radio giant GWR. Meanwhile new independent stations were opening, the Lynn-based KLFM in 1992, Beach, serving Lowestoft and Yarmouth in 1996, and the 24-hour dance music station Vibe the following year. All these stations are drawing sizeable audiences.

If Norfolk is now spoilt for radio, it will be hoped that its choice will always include local and word-driven excellence. That choice will be revolutionised by the imminent emergence of digital radio. "When radio goes digital there will be a proliferation of stations," says the EDP's radio critic Stuart Lake. "You can anticipate say Radio Stokesby or Radio Holme Hale, and there is a danger that talent will be spread too thinly."

The Eastern Daily Press is the country's biggest-selling regional morning newspaper. Yet long before assuming this title - in April 1995 - it had long been outselling every national rival including the mass tabloids, a phenomenon unique to Norfolk.

Is it a conceit to suggest this says something about Norfolk and much about the EDP? A newspaper in modern marketing-speak is "a product", but to its reader and its creators it is much more, establishing between buyer and seller a relationship unique in commercial life. And this bond is unusually strong in Norfolk and in the circulation areas beyond its borders, a part of England which retains a powerful sense of its distinctive character and identity.

The EDP has been favoured with the extraordinary goodwill and even affection of its readers. This was shown to effect for example in 1957 when the EDP became the first paper to be scrutinised over the air by the BBC Midland Region Critics ( Francis Williams, editor of the Daily Herald and Bernard Hollowood, editor of Punch). It emerged with golden tributes minus a few technical points. *"I, for one,"* wrote Frederick Hopper of Taverham, *"have been crouched for the last few days ready to spring on any critic who dared to say anything derogatory about our paper."* Such tenacious and touching fidelity remains a feature of Norfolk life.

"Our Paper" entered the twentieth century in 1902 at 57 London Street, Norwich, then the last word in newspaper offices (it had been published since October 1870, first as the Eastern Counties Daily Press, changing to its familiar title a few months later).

There under five editors, it was to remain for the next 57 years. By far the longest tenure was the forty-year editorship of Archie Cozens-Hardy (1897-1937), Norfolk and Fleet Street background, bachelor, workaholic, wholly ignorant of the workings of the motor car and mildly distrustful of the telephone.

Cozens-Hardy was succeeded by Tom

Copeman, a member of one of the founding families. He was busy with a modernisation of the EDP when war broke out, reducing it from six to four thin, grey pages. But the war so increased circulation that by 1946, the emaciated, rationed sheets had twice the circulation of the fat pre-war papers. Thereafter Copeman's reforms proceeded as fast as newsprint rationing would allow. His most striking - indeed revolutionary - innovation was in June 1940. With Hitler's forces at the Channel Coast, Copeman brought news to the front page, hitherto reserved for auctioneers' notices of agricultural sales. Simultaneously he was improving design, enlarging the photographic staff, nursing the quality of a distinguished leader page, and appointing a small but gifted London and Westminster editorial staff.

By 1949 with the London Street offices straining at its walls, Copeman, together with chairman Sir Basil Mayhew and a new and enterprising general manager from Dundee, W M Young, began planning a reconstruction, in effect swinging it to a different axis, and creating in 1959 offices in Redwell Street.

By then Tom Copeman had retired and been succeeded as editor-in-chief by Stanley Bagshaw, son of a former EDP chief reporter. A gifted linguist and great traveller, Bagshaw was a chief who had the capacity to inspire unswerving loyalty and deep affection. An internationalist with a passionate belief in freedom and democracy and an intense pride in his craft and its purpose, Bagshaw famously marked the visit of the Soviet leaders Bulganin and Kruschev to Norfolk in April 1956, by writing an "Open Letter" leader in Russian, with an English translation by its side. His death from leukaemia in March 1964 at the age of fifty, left an abiding legend.

Three years earlier, shortly before the Norfolk News Company became Eastern Counties Newspapers, the EDP's circulation had topped 58,000, easily the highest in its history. Circulation had reached reached 95,000 in late 1981.

By then the newspaper industry was hurrying through the greatest technological revolution in its history. In 1968, a year before ECN moved from Redwell Street to its present site in Rouen Road, emerged computer-assisted typesetting. In the EDP's centenary year, 1970, 'Prospect House' the new headquarters, was officially opened by Princess Alexandra. Five years later began the the phasing-out of hot metal typesetting, that traditional craft whose clattering urgency provided the sound background to innumerable "Front Page" type movies. Then in 1986 came the completion of direct input, the moving of a journalists' story or picture to the print centre via a computerised system.

Since 1995 the Eastern Daily Press has been printed at the £23 million Print Centre on a five-acre site at the Thorpe Business Park. Two years later the EDP was named Daily Newspaper of the Year (BT London and Northern Home Counties Press Awards), one of many industry and professional accolades won in recent years by the paper and members of its staff. The Newspaper of the Year title came between by far the most radical change in the EDP's history, and its most ambitious and successful innovation, the launch in September 1997 of the Saturday Magazine. The change - long debated - was the switch in page size from broadsheet to tabloid. For the publishers, the change carried the all-too-obvious risk of unsettling loyal readers. Indeed some feared that their EDP might succumb to 'tabloid values' but in the event confidence held firm, suspicions were allayed and the circulation was sustained to such effect that the EDP has become the top-selling regional morning.

By the end of the first year in a new century, the EDP will be 130 years old. And through all the changes is a consistent set of convictions, chief of which are integrity, independence of mind, a belief in excellence, and an attachment to its community whose life, opinions and values it reflects and with which it identifies.

**Peter Roberts, Editor of the Eastern Daily Press from 1964 to 1977 was a journalists' journalist. A spirited Welshman and an East Anglian patriot, he was a man of wide-ranging abilities and gifts, not the least of which was a robust integrity together with an unswayable loyalty to his colleagues and to the paper he loved. Roberts came to Norfolk after wartime RAF service, and was variously EDP sports editor, news editor, and from 1956 to 1964, editor of the Evening News. Such was his grasp of issues and disciplines that he never asked his editorial staff to do anything he could not do perfectly well himself. During his editorship the EDP circulation rose from 64,000 to 91,000. When he died in 1991, aged 79, Colin Chinery wrote, "Peter Roberts was a great editor, a lively, gifted companion, and a good man to have beside you when your trench was under fire."**

## CHAPTER 9

# *Industry and Commerce*

**MALCOLM PERKINS, who joined Eastern Counties Newspapers in 1966, had two spells with the company which included a period as industrial editor for both daily publications. Born in Leicester, he started his career in that city with the Evening Mail. He also worked on newspapers in Gloucester, Nottingham and Burton on Trent. After returning to ECN in 1992 he worked from the Diss office, and retired from the company in the spring of 1999.**

**HARRY DAY has worked on the EDP Business Desk as a writer/sub-editor for the last ten years. His interest in the offshore industry began while working at the paper's Lowestoft office reporting on the town's significant gas. On moving to the EDP's Norwich headquarters he took over covering the whole of Norfolk and Waveney offshore industry.**

**TREVOR HEATON**

*The people are skilful, intelligent and conscientious workers, their employers shrewd and ingenious, and it is to these qualities of character that Norfolk and North East Suffolk owe their remarkable variety of industries.*

From the Eastern Daily Press, 1958

A glance at the map sums up Norfolk's main problems in becoming a big player in the industrial game. Only two major trunk roads - neither of them fully dualled - and almost a hundred miles from the nearest large urban centres of Leicester or London. With no huge mineral resources (until the Southern North Sea finds of the Sixties) and no large centres of population on hand to generate demand, the county had to rely on its own ingenuity to create wealth.

Yet it is remarkable just how much of a variety of industries the county has provided over the years. The proximity of a rich agricultural base helped with the development of industries such as brewing and canning. The North Sea oil and gas boom from the Sixties created its own mini-industrial bonanza for Great Yarmouth, but for the rest the county has had to draw upon its own resources: a hard-working labour force plus that priceless commodity, business acumen.

That 1958 report went on to cite shoe and clothing manufacture, confectionery, food processing, canning and quick-freezing, brewing, ship and boat building, printing, insurance, motor body building, brush making, and the manufacture of agricultural fertilisers and sprays.

An impressive array of businesses - and although an end of century list would show many changes, notably the rise of the service and financial sectors, that variety is still very much in evidence.

The need to plan for Norfolk's continuing prosperity was being recognised even as the Second World War was reaching its decisive phase. For example, The 1945 City of Norwich Plan, that remarkable document of frankness and vision, recognised the urgent need to widen the industrial base.

*"No one with the true welfare of the city at heart wishes to see it become an 'industrial town', as that term is usually understood,"* it reported. *"But that in order that it may flourish and that full employment may be found for its many skilled workers, it is essential that the present industries should be retained and that, if possible, some new industries of the lighter type should be attracted by good conditions of transport, housing and general amenity."*

The success of a small town such as Thetford in the Fifties in attracting large inward investment through the London Overspill scheme was an example of this philosophy in action. The town had seen its flagship heavy industry - the famous steam engine firm Burrell's - collapse a generation before. As we have seen earlier in this book, a determined local council succeeded in turning round the town's fortunes within a handful of years.

The Thetford experience was a superb demonstration of how a single-minded local authority could create the conditions for new businesses to move in and flourish. Its overspill example was imitated with success by King's Lynn early in the next decade. Not all East Anglian towns wanting overspill managed to secure a deal - Hunstanton was one such

**Diversification and business acumen has been the key to maintaining Norfolk's prosperity over the century.**

place which tried and failed. London largesse would help a few places in the region, but for the rest it was up to local councils to plan for growth.

In late 1957 the Norfolk County Council planning committee became involved in the need for industrial expansion. The scheme soon paid off handsomely. Roughly one million feet of industrial floorspace was added every year between then and 1975 in the county, excluding Norwich and Yarmouth, with an average of 1000 new jobs created annually. After 1974, the county council took over the strategic planning for the whole of Norfolk and raised its jobs target to 3500 per year.

By the late Fifties the county had, in that most familiar phrase of the era "never had it so good" for industry. The EDP in 1958 referred to *"the remarkable industrial development which has taken place since the war"*, going so far as to call it the county's "industrial revolution". It identified the factors involved in this change as the growth of motor transport, that aforementioned business shrewdness and hard work, electricity supplies, post-war regeneration and the mechanisation of agriculture.

At the time county planning officer Richard Maxwell identified two pressing reasons for attracting new jobs: the imminent arrival on the jobs market of the "bulge" generation of baby boomers, and the young men who would otherwise have gone for the newly-abolished National Service. He highlighted the following advantages for the county: good, relatively-cheap industrial sites (the release of de-commissioned air bases helped in this), a loyal and hard-working local labour force, and an efficient local building industry. By 1960 the county had only 1.8 per cent unemployment; in other words, as near to full employment as was just about possible.

In the mid-Seventies, EDP industrial editor Ken Holmes summed up the area's ideal new business as either one which complemented agriculture - dealing with produce or processing - or a small concern employing about fifty people, in, say, electronics, precision engineering or chemicals. Such a strategy has the merit of not over-stretching local resources and making an area as recession-proof as possible by providing the widest spread of industry.

The Sixties' clarion cry was "Export or Die". But it was a lesson Norfolk had learned long ago in the Middle Ages through the cloth and wool industry, Yarmouth with its herring trade, and the position of Lynn at the mouth of the vast Great Ouse river network. Day-to-day dealings with Europe were not a matter of political dogma, but a question of history and hard-headed business. In 1975 Common Market commissioner George Thomson was pointing out the region's bulge into the North Sea made it a perfectly-designed springboard for trade with Belgium, Holland, Germany and Denmark, and, as we will see in the rest of this chapter, dozens of firms have grasped that opportunity. The position of ports at Lynn, Yarmouth, Lowestoft and Sutton Bridge, plus the development of Harwich and Felixstowe, provided vital export outlets.

And the importance of small firms should not be overlooked. In 1956 the Norfolk Rural Industries Committee, in the first comprehensive survey of its kind, found there were 2545 firms with twenty workers or fewer, covering forty different trades. They employed around 10,000 in Norfolk's smaller towns and large villages, helping to cushion their perceived dangerous over-dependence on agriculture.

Thetford, once just one of those small country towns, changed out of all recognition in just a couple of decades. The population level which had remained unchanged for the best part of a thousand years was set to quadruple in the next 25 as new firms were drawn to this corner of the county. The new firms were mainly in the area of light engineering but also included well known names such as Thermos, Jeyes and Conrans. Some of the early industrial arrivals found themselves in financial difficulties and were forced into liquidation. But subsequent years have seen a number of major concerns establishing manufacturing and processing plants.

Long before most of the present industrial

firms at Thetford were even in business the town had achieved an international reputation thanks to one name - that of Burrell. The steam locomotive became a highly successful power source used for driving threshing and other farm equipment. The development of the self-moving road engine which could negotiate turns, hills and most surfaces proved a major turning point in the success story and they were used for towing funfair equipment from site to site.

At the turn of the century, Burrell steam engines were being sold all over the world and were even put to use in the Boer War and Great War. The company had a work force of 400 to 500 but its days were numbered by the time the recession of the Twenties. That, and competition from the petrol engine marked the end. By 1930 the company had closed.

Other Norfolk market towns may not have matched the Thetford experience, but they have also provided the foundation and infrastructure for a wide range of industrial activities which developed in the county. Changes in society during the inter-war period saw small town trades such as the tanner, farming implement maker, miller, seed merchant, tailor and shoemaker virtually gone by 1930.

Agriculture was going through a difficult period during the Thirties and redundant farm workers provided a pool of cheap non-union labour for industries attracted to the area. Examples were brushmaking at Wymondham, printing at Fakenham, coffee grinding in Thetford, engineering in Cromer and Diss and engineering and cabinet making at Dereham.

Obvious industrial links with the farming community have been the growth of canning plants for fruit and vegetables at North Walsham while in the Waveney Valley at Harleston the processing and freezing of poultry was evident.

Dereham, with a railway junction and population of more than 5000, was the largest market town in the early part of the century and became a focus for change in later years. Crane's, which began as a wheelwright and wagon building concern, later built gun wheels for use in the First World War leading to the growth of its trailer industry after hostilities ended. By the outbreak of the Second World War industry and agriculture were both recovering from the depression.

**EcoTech at Swaffham, the centre of an innovative development of 'green' companies.**

A decade after the war and until the Seventies, Norfolk's market towns had been fairly successful in attracting industrialists and this period saw the development of industrial estates. Dereham attracted few newcomers whereas Crane's who arrived before the war expanded and have continued to do so ever since. Now trading as General Trailers their specialised heavy road trailers are sold worldwide. Other well-established businesses include Hobbies and furniture makers Jentique.

Swaffham, once the home of Brocks Fireworks nowadays houses mainly small-scale businesses with leisure firm Kitfix Hobbies being one household name. But development of the EcoTech centre and its associated "green" industrial park offers exciting prospects. Nearby at Gooderstone, W H Knights and Son provide a valuable food processing and packaging facility serving the supermarkets.

Diss, on the main London-Norwich line

**William Gaymer (1842-1936) was the real founder of the cider business which once employed 400 people at Attleborough. Though he followed the farming activities of his father and grandfather, he became much more interested in cider as a commercial proposition. He developed the sale of cider from Banham and introduced the first hydraulic press in 1870. A national distribution was built up and an export business developed until 1896 a new factory was built at Attleborough to cope with expansion. Mr Gaymer once said he attributed the success of the business to hard work and never took a holiday until he was in his eighties – and that consisted of a motor tour of England to enable him to renew acquaintance with old customers. He was not fond of talking about himself, but when once pressed for the secret of his success said it was due to "hard work, concentration, having a good article and getting the confidence of the public and loyalty of my staff".**

attracted a number of new industries and the number of jobs there increased considerably between 1961 and 1971. A notable arrival was Alma Components from Holloway in 1960, now known as Hamlin Electronics. Neighbouring Harleston's largest factory is Dowdeswells, standing on a seven-acre site, manufacturing agricultural equipment and employing around 100 people.At the northern end of the town Harleston Foods processes poultry.

Attleborough is an expanding market town with four industrial estates. Among its biggest employers is Hamilton Acorn, which makes paintbrushes, and food processors Grampian Food and Banham Poultry. Between Attleborough and Norwich lies Wymondham with a population of more than 11,000 and a fast-growing community.The town has a large industrial estate containing a variety of manufacturing and service businesses, many of them hi-tech concerns.

One of the best-known firms in South Norfolk, Blooms of Bressingham, was established in 1946 by plantsman Alan Bloom and soon won a world-wide reputation for innovation in plant varieties. The firm, which built up to be one of Europe's biggest nurseries fell on troubled times in the early Nineties and began to look for redundancies among its 300 or so staff. The firm was taken over by Jersey-based mail order specialist Flying Flowers in 1996, but the parent company sold Blooms to a management buy-in team for £1.7 million in March 1999. With a television-fuelled interest in gardening in the late Nineties, the company is well-placed to exploit its highly-regarded brand name in the new century.

At North Walsham, Eastern Coast Plastics is a significant employer with manufacturing capacity while just out of town on the edge of the town food processing interests are evident. But 1999 brought the announcement of the closure of General Trailers' plant in the town, although some of the jobs were transferred to its Dereham operation.

Picturesque Holt is home to Sanders Coaches, one of Norfolk's bigger operators, and Structure Flex, fabricators in plastic materials. Fakenham is one Norfolk town which moved quickly to cash in on the regeneration initiative, making use of European Union money to attract industry. This has helped the town to recover ground lost in 1982 by the closure of Cox and Wyman printers, the town's largest employer, which at its peak had 600 staff. The achievements have been encouraging with the arrival in 1999 of J W Automarine, manufacturers of specialist equipment for the marine industry. McVitie's Prepared Foods are among the better-known businesses through their production of the Linda McCartney range, while Fakenham Laundry is a long-established family business servicing industry. Gilchris Confectionery with its chocolate products and FMC, makers of agricultural machinery are two other major names in the town.

The post-war years saw Downham Market have ups and downs on the industrial front. In 1962 ironmongers Bussens and Parkin celebrated fifty years in business in the town but eleven years later its ironmongery and builders merchants operations were closed down. During the early Eighties fears were expressed for the industrial future of the town but by the end of the decade Williams Refrigeration, a major employer announced expansion plans.

One of the earliest-established industries to take advantage of the county's agricultural riches was brewing. Norwich could claim to have as many as seven sizeable producers while Yarmouth, Lynn and some smaller towns also had medium-sized operations. Though trade was generally with the immediate locality, several firms did sent their products further afield with Lacons of Yarmouth exporting more than 30,000 barrels of beer annually as far afield as London, Newcastle-upon-Tyne and Plymouth.

However the second half of the nineteenth century saw a rapid move towards increased production in fewer but larger breweries. The picture changed during the First World War when there was a national trend towards lower levels of beer consumption. Taxation increased, and there were restrictions on the

**The century's greatest commercial project was the building of Castle Mall, one of the boldest, and most controversial, plans ever contemplated in Norfolk.**

**Faced with pressure for out-of-town malls in Norwich, and regional competition from centres such as Peterborough and Cambridge, the decision was taken to support developer Estates and General's application for a £35 million "fantasy world" of shopping in 1983.**

**However the fantasy nearly turned to nightmare with a decade of delays, setbacks and financial ups and downs. The cost of the project – albeit now considerably amended – eventually reached £145 million.**

**But when it opened on September 23rd 1993 Norwich had not only succeeded in hosting a brilliant planning and construction achievement but also restoring the city's place as the region's number one shopping centre.**

**That day of triumph was a long, long way off in the early Eighties when the project slipped behind schedule as developers sought to lure in those key tenants who would trigger a stampede of smaller retailers. The House of Fraser was wooed, unsuccessfully. A final agreement between the developers, fellow backers Friends Provident, and Norwich City Council was not signed until 1988, five years after the project was first mooted.**

**After so much delay many predicted it would never happen. But it did, and the statistics of the project were simply mind-boggling.**

**It was described as Europe's biggest construction project; it led to the country's largest archaeological dig; 800,000 tons of rubble and earth were removed; 180,000 tons of concrete were used; a four and a half acre park was created on top with 132 trees and 32,000 shrubs and plants; more than 1000 parking spaces were provided.**

**And the mall continues to develop, with an eight-screen cinema under construction in 1999.**

**The project continues to represent an outstanding vote of confidence in the city's future.**

raw materials and also shorter licensing hours.

At Steward and Patteson's Pockthorpe brewery in Norwich both quality and quantity suffered as elsewhere. However, the war did not prove as a disruptive force in Norfolk as it had to the large brewers in the country's industrial heartlands. This was largely thanks to the comparative prosperity enjoyed by agriculture enjoying Government support and import-controls at this time. Nevertheless wartime restrictions put pressure on supplies. And with the large number of small rural pubs being run by Steward and Patteson, Bullards, Morgan and Youngs Crawshay, life became difficult for those on small margins of profitability.

Though the Second World War produced similar conditions to those experienced during the earlier conflict, the outcome was different and the four breweries based in Norwich prospered. Churchill's government did not attempt to limit consumption as Lloyd George had done, since the strength of beer and the level of drunkenness had both fallen. As a result beer production actually increased during this period and beer drinking was seen as important factor in maintaining civilian morale and industrial output.

**John Loynes (1843-1939) was a man who pioneered the boat hire business on the Norfolk Broads starting late in the nineteenth century. A native of Woodton in south Norfolk, he later trained as a carpenter and set up his own boat building business at Elm Hill in Norwich in 1878. He hired out yachts to a growing clientele and eventually switched the business to Wroxham. This was after finding many visitors left vessels there and Loynes was left to collect them as best he could. Hiring activities starts with "day sailing" enabling the traveller to reach overnight accommodation. But later craft were equipped with canvas covers, cooking and sleeping facilities – and sailing instructions. The business prospered, helped no doubt by visits Loynes made to town and cities throughout England to promote the Broads as a holiday area. The development of the railways meant that for the first time the Broads were within the reach of thousands of day trippers and holidaymakers.**

In East Anglia, like the rest of Britain, the end of the war was followed by rationing and austerity and gloomy conditions for the brewing industry. There followed in this region mergers and takeovers with smaller operations being taken over by their bigger competitors. Lacons of Yarmouth were taken over in 1957 by Whitbread while in Norwich Youngs Crawshay merged with Bullards in 1958. In 1961 Steward and Patteson and Bullards each bought a half share in the Norwich-based Morgans Brewery.

But the time had come for Steward and Patteson to find itself on the receiving end. This came in November 1963 from the giant Watney Mann which in one swallow wanted to digest Bullards too. Both bids were successful and now Watneys controlled East Anglian brewing. By the end of the decade Watney Mann decided to close Bullards Brewery in Westwick Street and Steward and Patteson's Pockthorpe Brewery in Barrack Street, concentrating operations on the King Street site where brewing had been carried on for 700 years.

But another merger was not far away, this time Watney Mann being taken over by Grand Metropolitan. From the mid-Seventies, Norwich Brewery operated as an independent regional company, and beers produced at King Street were also given names which revived historic connections. Only a decade later, in 1985, the brewery closed.

The last twenty years of the twentieth century have seen the brewing industry going full circle with numerous small-scale operations being set up, to supply not only local outlets by meeting demand from further afield as well. This has been largely due to changes in demand from the drinking public influenced in part by the Campaign for Real Ale, surely one of the most influential consumer groups of the century. The most notable of those small brewers has been Woodforde's of Woodbastwick, which has secured national acclaim for the quality of its beers.

Though household brewing names such as Bass, Whitbread and Scottish and Newcastle remain the big-name players, East Anglian breweries Greene King and Adnams continue to hold their market share. In 1925 the number of breweries in Norfolk was down to just a dozen with more closures to follow. Nowadays there are well over a dozen in the region and numbers appear to be growing. The number of maltings in the county has fallen mainly because of developments in machinery making the production of larger quantities of malt more rapid on fewer sites.

The story of Gaymers, Norfolk cider producers for more than 200 years, was of a family business started by a Banham farmer trying his hand at a little diversification. It proved a small-town success story, when production was switched to Attleborough, before eventually becoming a victim of Nineties' big business.

Cider making has been a Norfolk village industry for centuries. A 1941 EDP advertisement for apple crush by Routs of Banham even proclaimed Banham the home of Norfolk cider *"for seven centuries"*. The real founder of the business was the second William Gaymer. From a one-man business he built up an enterprise which employed nearly 400 men, a concern with considerable London staff, a contract with the House of Commons, a Royal Warrant and an export trade which connected Attleborough with almost every part of the world. He took sole control of the business in 1884 on the death of his father and made improvements to the operation, moving the business to Attleborough.

In December 1940, a German raider destroyed more than half the premises. This included the original building completed in 1896 and contained part of the bottling department reducing its bottling capacity by at least one third. The business rebuilt a new factory fronting the main road.

However, other far-reaching changes were just around the corner. In May 1961 the old-established business was the subject of a successful £152,000 takeover bid by Showerings, makers of Babycham. It marked the end of the firm's Norfolk independence though a Gaymer continued the family line as managing director.

But more changes were to follow.

**Boatbuilder Bernard Denny works on a Broads cruiser at South River Marine, St Olaves, an example of a skilled trade which makes a significant contribution to the economy of the county.**

Showerings merged with Allied Lyons and in 1992 the Gaymer Group was sold for £140 million in a management buy-out.The deal was not a great success and Matthew Clark, Britain's third-largest cider maker bought the business for £109 million in 1994.The days of Gaymer's cider were numbered. By October Matthew Clark announced the phased shutdown of the Attleborough plant.

Norfolk's holiday industry may have undergone some far-reaching changes since its birth early in the last century but today it is earning the county in the region of £1.1 billion and supporting and estimated 39,000 jobs.

The final 25 years of the nineteenth century saw the rapid growth of resorts all around the Norfolk coast and by the end of the First World War they had reached their height. The early years of this century also saw the holiday industry providing considerable employment, particularly valuable in places such as Yarmouth where the fishing industry was in some decline. The drawback, of course, was the seasonal nature of this fast-growing type of commerce.

A sample survey carried out by the British Travel and Holidays Association in 1955 showed that about two per cent of Britain's population had a holiday in Norfolk, representing one million people. Recent years have seen more and more visitors heading inland to sample the delights of Norfolk's villages and market towns as well as Norwich itself – thanks largely to sophisticated marketing by the tourist industry. And not just aimed at British visitors either: by 1997, overseas tourists were spending £68 million in the county compared with only £38 million just eight years earlier.

At the peak of the season, Norfolk's population is swollen by a third, thanks to the influx of visitors. However the last thirty years has seen the home holiday industry having to increasingly compete with the attractions of package trips abroad offering the guarantee – almost – of dry, hot, sunny weather.

Norfolk's greatest holiday asset remains the Broads, which as well as boat hiring also boasts boat building as a significant industrial activity. In 1945 there were fewer than 500 boats for hire, very few equipped with a motor. Now there are well over 2000, most of them large launches.

It is estimated that the rivers and Broads are seen by more than a million visitors every year. A consequence of this growth in Broads holidays has also been the extensive development of some centres, notably Wroxham-Hoveton and Horning to cater for the needs of holiday makers. Attempting to maintain a balance between the interests of the holiday makers with the valuable revenue they bring to the county and protecting the environment of the area is the Broads Authority. In 1997 it published the Broads Plan setting out its role and responsibilities. This document estimates the one million visitors in a year spend the equivalent of 5.4 million visitor days in the Broads and about 200,000 people annually spend their holiday on cruisers hired for a week or more.

One of the biggest players in the Broads tourism business is Hoseasons, which began arranging boating holidays from its Oulton Broad base in 1945 and now provides more than a million boating and self-catering breaks every year. Chairman James Hoseason, celebrating fifty years at the helm of the company in 2000, has seen it grow to become one of Britain's best-known leisure names.

In recent years the Broads hire boat industry has suffered cutbacks caused by the recession and a switch in people's holiday patterns. The Broads Authority believed this was the result of booking agents spreading their interests to areas outside the Broads. Thus the area has become less well-known and less well-promoted. Hire bookings have declined and many boatyards have gone out of business. Some boatyards have been sold off for redevelopment, very often with housing. Originally the trend was encouraged by the planners in the belief that having fewer hire boats would be of benefit to the Broads and during the property boom of the late Eighties a riverside plot was seen as a very attractive investment.

The hire fleet has declined from 2633 boats in 1980 to 1481 in 1995 and is still falling, not good news for an industry which makes a vital contribution to the local economy. Today the Broads may be a playground but a century ago they were used extensively by commercial wherry traffic. Steam wherries were built in the second half of the century and the birth of the internal combustion engine in the twentieth century saw a number fitted to wherries.

A few continued to trade under sail into the Thirties and motorised wherries were still operating into the Fifties, though road competition began to prove too much. The banks of the rivers and Broads were once home to scores of boatyards. The industry underwent many upheavals as new developments emerged. Those who diversified tended to thrive, while many of the smaller wherry builders declined and closed down.

The arrival of the internal combustion engine prompted many yards to start producing wooden motor craft. The years after the Second World War saw a major growth in boatbuilding and new yards began to appear in places such as Stalham, Loddon, Beccles and Acle. The boatyards remain a significant employer and the boatbuilding industry has an estimated turnover of more than £15 million.

The rise and fall of Norwich's footwear industry is something that lingers in the memory of many, even at the turn of a new century. Forty years ago there were nearly thirty shoe factories in Norwich, but by the late Nineties just three of any significance remained. Unhappily the demise of Norwich's once staple industry has parallels wherever the boot and shoe industry is found in this country, with a growing flow of cheap foreign imports the main factor.

Shoemaking was carried on in the city back in medieval times but it was the decline of spinning and weaving which saw it develop as a large-scale industry. The manufacture of ladies' and children's high-class footwear was the foundation on which the city's manufacturers built a worldwide reputation. Norwich had been very much a pioneer, with technical education taking in the theory and practice of shoemaking first provided in Norwich over a century ago, one of the first centres to do so outside its factories.

By 1910 Norwich's shoe industry was in good health, with factories working full time most of the year following a period of steady growth and a workforce numbering in the region of 10,000. Firms were enlarging their premises and the introduction of electrical power saw a switch from steam and gas engines to drive equipment. The export trade was growing fast and represented a large proportion of Norwich's shoe output.

But the First World War was to change these good times. The withdrawal of labour as operatives signed up and changed into uniform together with a shortage of leather both had serious repercussions. The Government introduced "war-time shoes" but the reduction in exports due to hostilities meant a loss of output which could not be restored immediately by factories turning to the needs of the home market.

Though footwear manufacturers came through the war with all their factories and plant intact, there was one major setback which was probably not apparent until the hostilities had ceased. The lost four years had brought a virtual halt to the development of the trade. It meant Norwich, like the rest of the British shoe industry, had lost several years of progress. That was not the case across the Atlantic where the American shoe industry, it was claimed, had gained a twenty-year lead in technical efficiency.

On the other hand changes in women's fashions introduced a new factor to footwear manufacture in Norwich. As they changed to shorter skirts, the demand grew for shoes rather than boots. It marked the arrival of the fashion shoe, something manufacturers in Norwich quickly warmed to. The popularity of dancing also helped boost demand for the fine quality shoe the city's factories could produce in large quantities. With the possible exception of London, no other centre manufacturing shoes could produce these elegant styles, giving Norwich a virtual monopoly. Increasingly the city companies found themselves unable to compete against the centres that specialised in lower- and medium-priced footwear. So it turned to what it did best – manufacturing ladies' high-grade shoes.

By the mid-Thirties the boot and shoe industry in Norwich had become the city's staple industry. In 1935 there were 26 shoe manufacturers employing 12,000 people making six million pairs of ladies' and children's shoes every year. But six years of war saw the industry facing many problems

**Start-rite of Norwich – one firm which has escaped the fate of most of the shoe industry by exploiting market demand for its top-quality children's footwear.**

**Colin Chapman (1928-1982) founder of Lotus, was an engineer and designer of rare genius and negotiator of great skill, who in his lifetime shared in controversy too. He had studied engineering at London University and his first Lotus car was built in 1948, based on the Thirties Austin Seven saloon. He drove it successfully in competition. Later and improved Lotus models followed and in 1952 the Lotus Engineering Company was formed. The Mark VI was designed as the first Lotus road car and orders poured in. Colin Chapman's innovative ideas were to have a worldwide impact on automotive engineering. Without Chapman's drive and dedication, Team Lotus may never have existed and in three decades it is unlikely any man gave more to the world of international motor racing.**

over materials and labour availability, not to mention disruption through air raids on the city. Peacetime brought a determination to succeed and the immediate post-war years were a period of rebuilding and planning a new shoe industry. About thirty firms were in business and upwards of 10,000 workers were employed by them.

The oldest firm was James Southall and Co founded in 1792 by James Smith. Prior to 1914 it had exported worldwide and had originally worked from a factory standing on the site of the present City Hall, moving to the edge of Norwich in 1907. Today it is better known as Start-rite and famous for the production of children's shoes. Other notable firms of the immediate post-war period were Bally's Shoe Factories (Norwich), formed from a pre-war amalgamation of P Haldinstein and Sons (founded in 1799) with Bally's of Switzerland; the Norvic Shoe Company, then Norwich's premier producer, founded in 1846 as Howlett and White; Sexton Son and Everard, founded in 1886 by Henry Sexton and his three sons, all of whom had worked for Howlett and White; and Edwards and Holmes, whose factory had been totally destroyed in 1942, but was building up a thriving export trade.

However the Fifties showed the first signs of contraction, a trend that was to continue throughout the next three decades. A survival factor was production of high-quality shoes and strong brand names. Start-rite, the largest of the shoe firms, expanded by taking over other Norwich companies. The first acquisition was the Ward Shoe Company in 1957, followed four years later by Bowhill and Hubbard. Start-rite chairman David White had repeatedly sounded warnings from the Sixties that the industry must act to beat increasing stagnation in exports.

By the end of 1971 the numbers employed had shrunk to 5800, as imports continued to rise. Decline worsened in the mid-Seventies with Pell Footwear in Mile Cross Lane closing in 1975. The following year Trimfoot announced its closure too. In 1976 alone, 600 workers lost their jobs, including those at Sexton's which ceased trading and those at one of two K Shoes works. Worse was to follow in 1981, which saw Norvic, the second largest in the county succumb, closing with the loss of 400 more jobs. K Shoes and CWS continued to decline and by 1983 there were just 2200 footwear union members employed in five factories. Shorten and Arms called in the receiver in 1984, although some of the 77 jobs were saved by a management buyout. The CWS closed in 1987.

The century's end sees Norwich with just three city shoe producers remaining in business. Start-rite has maintained its pre-eminent position thanks to a policy of concentrating on children's shoes at the top end of the market and a growing export trade. Expansion of the company's retailing arm, Domani, had helped sales. The Florida Group's concentration on wider fitting shoes, popular among older and better-off women, has proved a successful formula. In 1987 it took over Edwards and Holmes.

The third city survivor is Bally who in 1990 took the decision to close its Lowestoft factory and concentrate operations in Norwich. Elsewhere Rombah Wallace, manufacturers of medium- and high-priced men's and women's fashion continues to thrive at Hingham.

Arrival of the Lotus Group at Hethel just a few miles south of Norwich brought not only a new industry to Norfolk, but also a new dynamism being played on a world stage. Its inspiration and founder Colin Chapman was a supreme innovator, an attribute he coupled with a brilliant mind on engineering matters.

The success of early models led to the creation of Lotus Engineering Company in 1952 and seven years later it occupied a purpose-built factory in Hertfordshire. The move to Norfolk came in 1966 following an exhaustive search for the right location. Construction of the £750,000 factory was quickly under way and the first Norfolk-built Lotus car emerged on November 28th 1966. The Elan sports car and a new rear-engined Europa were announced by the company and by the spring of 1967 the company workforce was operating at full stretch.

Lotus, which went public in 1968,

**Celebrating the first anniversary of the Lotus Elise at Ketteringham Hall, the company's ancestral home, in September 1996.**

continued to make the headlines for a variety of reasons. Success on the race track was accompanied by achievements in technology. A Lotus Esprit also featured in James Bond films.

But four years later Lotus, the racing sport and the motor industry was left devastated by the death of Chapman from a heart attack. Nevertheless a production milestone was reached in 1984 when the Hethel factory recorded completion of its 30,000th Lotus road car. But change was on the horizon and four years after Chapman's death General Motors acquired Lotus. The early Nineties saw Lotus going through a difficult trading period, blamed on a slump in the United States and in 1993 Romano Artioli owner of the Italian sports car maker Bugatti became owner of Lotus for a period. But in October 1996 majority ownership passed to the Malaysian Proton car company.

Today two divisions operate within Group Lotus. One is Lotus Cars, the prestigious performance sports car manufacturer and the other Lotus Engineering. The latter is a leading engineering consultancy working for many of the world's major automotive manufacturers.

As elsewhere in Norfolk, the arrival of the railways at King's Lynn were to create an industrial revolution in a town which hitherto had been first and foremost a seaport. Three names to figure prominently in the town's emerging industrial sector during the nineteenth century were engineers Frederick Savage, Alfred Dodman and Thomas Cooper. However as the need for coal-fired steam-driven engines declined so did the prosperity of Savage's and Dodman's, and both closed in the Seventies.

The third engineer was Thomas Cooper, a prolific inventor, who gained his reputation for traction engines and later steam diggers. It was his continual inventiveness which was to eventually produce the Cooper roller bearing. It was a product on which a company, trading as Cooper Roller Bearings, was to be launched and flourish, becoming the biggest employer in Lynn until the growth of food processing. Today split roller bearings produced by Coopers are put to a multitude of uses. Recent years have seen the company change hands, in 1987 by a Scottish consortium Clairmont and in 1991 by the American-based Kaydon Corporation.

Fruit and vegetables grown on the Fenlands and West Norfolk made the town an ideal centre for the food processing industry. Modern refrigeration techniques resulted in a decline of the canning industry. Typical was the arrival in 1973 of a Swedish company Frigoscandia formed in 1949 and operating cold stores in a variety of countries. It built the biggest freezer store in Europe on a 45-acre site on the Hardwick Estate with a substantial fruit and vegetable processing and packaging plant.

Campbell and Masterfoods, both heavily committed to the production of convenience foods and ready meals, established large factories during the Fifties and Sixties. Campbell's arrived in 1959, attracted by the readily-available local supply of meat, poultry and vegetables, plus the port facilities. The workforce soon numbered more than 500, rising to about 1000 until mechanisation saw this slowly reduced. A year after Campbell's put down its roots, another large North American firm was to settle in Lynn. Dow Agrochemicals built the largest factory of agricultural chemicals in Europe. And like Campbell's it had the opportunities offered by the EEC very much in mind.

The company suffered a setback in 1976 when an explosion at its works killed one man and caused £1.25 million damage to the property. But expansion was the continuing theme as new complexes were built and brought into production.

Today it is the variety of business being carried on which is the town's strength. They include such names as Porvair, makers of microporous plastics, Bespak producers of plastic valves for the pharmaceutical and other industries, Berol makers of pens and high quality arts material, Foster UK and Williams, makers of commercial refrigeration units and both selling their products world wide.

**The arrival of world-famous soup-makers Campbell's to King's Lynn was an enormous boost in attracting new industry – and good news for local farmers and the jobs market.**

Whatever the fortunes of Norwich's economy over the past 100 years or more the city's role as a financial centre has invariably proved a buttress during difficult times. Today this service industry remains as prominent as ever with the last thirty years of the twentieth century witnessing continued growth as more companies from the financial sector have looked to base themselves in the city.

That is growth from seeds sown more than 200 years ago by the enterprising Gurney and Barclay families, who created a banking empire. Meanwhile the late eighteenth century also saw Thomas Bignold creating the foundations of what was to become Norwich Union by setting up the Norwich Union Fire Insurance Society in 1797 and the Life Insurance Society in 1808.

Norwich and area was a promising market for the emerging insurance business, largely to protect owners and traders against loss of property and goods in a rapidly-expanding economy. By the Thirties the Norwich Union Societies were employing 1300 people in the city. Not to be outdone Gurney's Bank, which had amalgamated with Barclays in 1896, had one of the largest branches in the country at Bank Plain in Norwich employing more than eighty staff in 1961. The Bignold family link with Norwich Union eventually came to an end when in 1964, Sir Robert Bignold retired after almost half a century of service. He was the fifth successive generation to head its fortunes.

Banking and the insurance companies survived the years of depression and expanded as conditions began to improve in the late Thirties. Norwich had also become a magnet to insurance and banking companies. Branches of all the main banks were to be

**Sir Robert Bignold (1892-1970) was the fifth member of the Bignold family in direct succession to serve the Norwich Union Insurance Societies. He was president of the Life Society and chairman of the Fire Society from 1943 in 1964. Upon retirement he was made an honorary life governor having served nearly fifty years with Norwich Union. Sir Robert was probably the most widely travelled of all Norwich businessmen and in April 1965 he visited Singapore and Japan during a 40,000-mile world tour.**
**At the age of 34 he was among the youngest Lord Mayors of all time and his spell as a Norwich magistrate, from 1928 to 1967, made him the longest serving in the city. Sir Robert also had links with other firms, including Morgan's Brewery, Anglia Television and Securicor.**

found in the area by the Fifties by which time sixty insurance companies were represented.

But they were small operators compared with the Norwich Union which had become one of the largest insurance organisations in the world, represented in more than sixty countries worldwide.

A major development came in the early Seventies when Bland Welch and Co, Britain's biggest international insurance brokers, announced plans to move a major part of its business from London to Norwich. Norwich was increasingly becoming a world focal point for insurance matters. It meant 150 new jobs and a £2 million office development in Queens Road. Two years later the company was renamed Bland Payne by which time the company was about to move its main office to Norwich. Before the Nineties were out there were merger plans being announced with Bland Payne and fellow brokers Sedgwick Forbes coming together to create Sedgwick with a workforce of 1000, a figure which steadily fell as the company strived to increase efficiency and merged divisions within its operation. In 1999 it was taken over by US-based giant J & H Marsh McLennan.

Another financial element in the city was the Norwich Building Society, which later merged to become the Norwich and Peterborough. The society has so far resisted the late Nineties trend for larger building societies to de-mutualise and seek a Stock Exchange listing.

The early Nineties also saw Norwich Union establishing a link with the Virgin Group, headed by high-profile entrepreneur Richard Branson. Virgin was looking to diversify into financial services through direct selling and chose the insurance giant as its partner. The decade was also to see Norwich Union following the same path taken by other financial institutions, namely abandoning its mutual status to become a public company. Eventually an announcement was made in October 1996 that the Norwich Union intended to float, a decision subsequently endorsed overwhelmingly by members in a vote. And Norwich Union later sold its stake in Virgin Direct which was now well established and by 1998 employed 800 people.

The theme of the relentless quest for diversity is echoed again and again in the Norwich industrial story. Twice the decline of the city's staple industry - weaving, then footwear - has created problems for its economic well-being. Nowadays Norwich's business interests are more broadly- based than they have ever been.

In 1856 the milling firm J and J Colman moved from Stoke Holy Cross to the Carrow Works in Norwich, attracted by the labour supply and availability of rail transport. By the turn of the century they were a major business in the city employing 2200 people and engaged in the production of a variety of food and drinks, mustard and starch. The business was to be sold off by parent company Reckitt and Colman in the mid-Nineties. Four years after Colman's put down roots in Norwich, another food company, A J Caley, followed their lead. They produced mineral water and later cocoa, chocolate and Christmas crackers. By 1918 their workforce was in the region of 2800, and in 1932 it was bought by J Mackintosh and Sons.

A business union in Victorian times of William Boulton and Dawson Paul saw the birth of Boulton and Paul who initially produced a variety of agricultural, horticultural and household goods. By the end of the First World War - during which it produced aircraft - it employed 3000 on a Riverside site and structural steel was to become a main product. Barnards invented a machine for weaving wire-netting and both it and Boulton and Paul were producers.

Meanwhile the late 1880s witnessed a company Laurence, Paris and Scott, forerunner of Laurence Scott and Electromotors, being developed by a young engineer William Harding Scott. Supported by Colman's, who helped him establish the business, he began to make his own dynamos and in 1888 was joined by Reginald Laurence, the son of a stockbroker, who invested £6000 in the business which was steadily expanding. It concentrated on the manufacture of electrical machinery and before the First World War began producing equipment for shipping.

**The Norwich Union head office was built in 1905 and modelled on the old Amicable House in London's Fleet Street. Its famed marble hall was where the public came to pay their premiums to cashiers seated on high stools behind the counter. Norwich Union has grown to be one the country's biggest companies and investors in industry.**

Then in 1927 it amalgamated with Electromotors based in Lancashire. Another electrical engineering company was Heatrae, founded in 1920.

Printing, bookbinding and photography was another manufacturing industry to be established in the area. One company which moved to Norwich from Suffolk in the early years of the nineteenth century was Jarrold and Sons which in the years which followed were to make a substantial contribution in this field.

But the Second World War inevitably had its effect on Norwich's industrial life with much capacity being switched to meet the needs of the military, and air-raid damage.

Hindes and Sons, one of Norwich's few remaining textile business, had produced silk for parachutes during the war years. By 1960 it employed 275 people, had expanded and diversified to produce synthetic fibres and silk. In 1964 the company was take over by Courtaulds but it was finally closed in 1980.

One major newcomer which began life on the city fringe was chemical company May and Baker, engaged in making products for agriculture. In 1957 it opened its factory on Sweet Briar Road having outgrown its 64-acre site at Dagenham. In 1988 the name was changed to Rhône-Poulenc, the French multinational parent company. By 1996 it employed more than 4000.

The Sixties saw Her Majesty's Stationery Office resited in the city. So too did the Civil

**Robert Carter (1892-1966) was the founder of what was to become East Anglia's largest firm of building contractors and remains a household name in the region. Born at Drayton, he started the business using money saved from his pig-keeping sideline, a £1000 legacy and a bank guarantee from an uncle.**
**The firm RG Carter, started as a one-man business in 1921, developed over the years into a concern with a turnover worth millions of pounds and employing hundreds.**
**He also farmed about 1000 acres and had a host of other interests involving service on the county and rural district councils, British Legion and YMCA. Despite his business success he described himself as "a plain tradesman and proud of it". Contracts have included prestige projects such as restoration work on Blickling Hall, construction of the County Hall in Martineau Lane, the Stationery Office, extensions to Anglia Television and construction of Wayland Prison.**

Service Central Computer Agency. Other arrivals included Anglia Television, the University of East Anglia, the Food Research Institute and the John Innes Institute.

Some businesses have seen expansion followed by shut down, others have continued to thrive. F W Harmer continued production post-war with new premises in Mile Cross replacing the city centre site. At one stage the company was turning out more than 20,000 garments weekly, but closed in 1989 with the loss of 300 jobs. Long-established Barnards, taken over by a Sheffield company in the mid-Fifties, ceased trading in 1991. A major blow to the city's economy came in 1996 with the closure of confectioners Nestle Rowntree, with the loss of 900 jobs, although there was some consolation when a group from the firm set up their own operation and revived the original "Caley" name. Soon afterwards it was the turn of another long-established Norwich business to disappear. This time Christmas cracker maker Tom Smith closed in July 1998, costing 175 jobs. Another business to close has been R J Read, the grain milling company.

However against the losses have to be set the gains. Autowrappers were among the companies set up after the war, while more recent arrivals have included United Closure and Plastics, Diamond H Controls and Anglian Windows. A host of smaller companies can be found on the city's industrial estates as the end of the twentieth century approaches.

Long-established business such as Boulton and Paul and Laurence Scott have been the subject of change. In 1993 Boulton and Paul moved from the Riverside site it occupied for 73 years to Sprowston. This followed a two-thirds fall in the workforce to 130 after pulling out of constructional steel and concentrating on joinery manufacture. A year later it was the subject of a management buy-out. Laurence Scott has twice been involved in take-overs. In 1980 it was acquired by MS International who in 1986 sold the Norwich operation to FKI.

A major employer during this period was the construction industry, represented by a number of quite substantial concerns. By far the biggest was Drayton-based R G Carter employing more than 900 in the early Sixties. Founded pre-war by the late Robert Carter it continues to be the major player among local building companies.

An important development during the last decade has been the launch and development of the Norwich Research Park at Colney, employing hundreds of scientists, researchers and technicians involved in plant and food sciences.

Yarmouth has come a long way since herrings and holidays were the backbone of its prosperity. And though this vigorous resort is still sometimes labelled the Blackpool of the east coast, its industrial base has broadened dramatically during the last forty years of this century. Instead of the two Hs, it is the Es – electronics and engineering – which are contributing significantly to the year-round wealth of the area.

Fishing still provided the town's prosperity for the early part of this century. During the first ten years of the twentieth century, nearly a thousand boats landed their catches at Yarmouth during the season.

But the First World War closed overseas markets which never really revived after the fighting ended. Catches, too, declined and new ways of maintaining the town's economy were needed. One early business set up in the early nineteenth century was Grout and Co. who became well known as manufacturers of mourning crepe.

But the years between the wars were ones of stagnation, the growth in the holiday industry failing to make up for the loss of activity generated by fishing and the port. The state of the town's industrial structure was brought home in a 1943 report by the borough's planning officer Mr K K Parker. He warned that the geographical position of the town and other handicaps made it extremely unlikely that "basic" industries could be attracted to

**The Yarmouth Birds Eye factory pictured in August 1959. Its closure was described as "the blackest day in the town's history".**

"basic" industries could be attracted to Yarmouth by natural means.

Any efforts to attract industries should be targeted at those with natural affinities such as a boat building and repair industry connected with the Broads, a canning industry connected with fishing and agriculture, a furniture industry allied to the timber trade and animal feeds and manure linked to the agricultural hinterland, he suggested. It is possible Mr Parker's advice was heeded, for as the holiday industry reaccustomed itself to peacetime, so too new light industries were establishing themselves.

Canned fish, textiles, oil skins, radio parts, bread, moulded pulp articles, sacks, frozen foods, jewellery and furniture were some of the products leaving factories, some long established, others post-war arrivals. Greatest growth began to establish itself in the South Denes area, a stretch of grassland on which fishermen had dried their nets since the days of Edward the Confessor. Construction of a power station meant the town was generating electricity and the Hartmann Fibre Company set up after the war was extended to provide work for another 200 people.

North of the power station, post-war development saw Birds Eye Foods frozen foods processors being established. Johnson and Son were producing a wide range of clothing while elsewhere in the town Grout and Co were now producing crepe bandages for a world market. And there was also Lacons brewery, Smiths potato crisp factory, the timber yards of Jewson, Palgrave Brown and R H Porter at Cobholm. The range of products was growing at an impressive rate.

An industrial survey showed they included scales, precision instruments, chemical cleaning materials, machine tools, soft drinks and fertilisers, basket makers, ski and sledge producers, precast concrete, net makers, glass bottle and jar manufacturers, television sets and baking powder.

Towards Marine Parade could be found the buildings of a light industry that brought work for many people, Erie Resistor, makers of radio equipment. The company spawned a series of firms which went on to make up one of the most significant concentrations of electronics expertise in the UK. Names included Norfolk Capacitors, Alison Microwave, Placepower and Beck Electronics.

Despite this healthy state of affairs much of Yarmouth's engineering industry maintained its search to market their skills in new areas.

Brewers Lacons closed their doors on three centuries of brewing in 1968, bakers Matthes closure in 1978 was rated a "catastrophe", while 1986 brought the biggest blow of all. *"Blackest day in the town's history"* proclaimed a newspaper headline in June 1983 with the news that Birds Eye was to shut its South Denes factory within three years. When it did finally close 900 people joined the dole queue. A lucky 340 were transferred to the company's Lowestoft operation.

Poor road and rail links were blamed by Norfolk Line, the international haulier, when in 1991 it announced it was pulling out of Yarmouth and switching operations to Felixtowe. But Pasta Foods, producer of high quality wholemeal spaghetti which opened a factory at Yarmouth in 1972 has continued to enjoy growth and even exports to Italy.

Pressure on Whitehall saw Yarmouth eventually granted "assisted area" status. The final years of the century saw four initiatives which should ensure Yarmouth's economic progress. Plans by a consortium of private business interests are well progressed for a third power station to emerge on the South Denes site where earlier versions stood. This will be fuelled with gas piped underground from the Bacton terminal by 2001.

And more power could be generated two miles off the coast at Yarmouth when a wind farm begins to emerge early in the next millennium. Estimates are that it could produce enough electricity to meet the needs of a town bigger than Yarmouth. An exciting prospect is a long-awaited outer harbour for Yarmouth. Feasibility of the venture costing in the region of £33 million was being undertaken during 1999.

Yarmouth has been identified as being part of the Trans-European Road and Rail networks. Additionally the town announced early in 1999 it had joined forces with Dutch port Ijmuiden to launch a new freight ferry service across the North Sea. Attracting hi-tech businesses to Yarmouth is the aim of the borough council. The hope is that a new sixty-acre business park in south Gorleston could be bristling with small but progressive companies.

Harvesting the fruits of the North Sea has been a traditional way of feeding the people and economy of Norfolk and Waveney for many a decade. So the discovery in 1966 of the Leman gas field off the Norfolk coast triggered the birth of an industry which more than filled the gap left by the declining fishing industry.

The building of the Bacton terminals in 1968 to handle the gas from Shell's Leman field, at the time the world's biggest field, sparked a major boom in Norfolk and Waveney with a big demand for labour and support services.

Jobs were plentiful as buildings went up and a 100-mile pipeline was laid across the region to link it with British Gas' national grid and feed the ever-expanding number of gas appliances being converted to natural gas. It could not last, it was said, because the gas was supposed to run out 25 years later. But that forecast took no account of the rapid pace of technological change and the determination of the big operators to squeeze as much gas as possible from one of the most demanding working environments in the world.

And even as Prince Philip opened the Bacton complex in 1969 Shell's competitors were working hard to find enough gas to keep their own terminals fully occupied. In the same year Phillips Hewett, Mobil Galahad and Amoco Leman fields came on stream and the process has continued ever since. True, the emergence of Aberdeen as the United Kingdom's oil capital eventually led to some operators moving their bases from Yarmouth to Scotland but most still have links with Norfolk and Waveney.

Through a mixture of high technology and hard-nosed business decisions the lifespan of the industry has been extended well into the next century. In 1994 Shell announced it was planning to bring a new gas platform on stream every year for the next five years. Two years later Phillips was predicting another twenty years at Bacton as technologies like extended reach drilling have given operators the ability to link new fields into existing pipeline systems in established fields.

Three-dimensional seismic surveying has given them a better understanding of what gas reserves can be tapped and many millions of pounds have been spent on equipment designed to get the most out of ageing fields. It is estimated that, even after huge cost-cutting exercises have taken place, 400 companies and 5000 jobs in the Yarmouth area alone rely on the industry for their income. Apart from the multinational energy giants who plough hundreds of millions of pounds into the economy the North Sea boom prompted big fabricators such as Amec Process and Energy, Kvaerner Oil and Gas, Grootcon and supply service operators such as Wood Group (now Asco) to set up bases in Yarmouth. Over at Lowestoft, Odebrecht SLP is well-established and locals hardly spare a second glance for the huge structures dominating the skyline on its harbourmouth site. Also at Lowestoft, trawlers were converted to offshore support vessels and a whole new industry grew up so that Boston Putford employs 750 people and has a fleet of vessels developed specially to meet today's strict safety standards.

**A North Sea gas platform in action. The offshore industry has provided a huge boost to the Norfolk economy, particularly around Yarmouth, since the Sixties.**

Together these companies soak up a large proportion of the workforce but then there are a huge number of smaller businesses that have blossomed around the industry; in many Norfolk villages there will be some expert working on a piece of sophisticated kit.

At the next level there are those firms not directly involved in the industry who owe their expansion to it. Taxi firms are hired to deliver parts around the country, caterers are signed up to feed the workers, and printers to print the brochures - the list is almost endless. For instance, in August 1992, the EDP reported well over 100 construction workers would be involved in a £200 million-plus scheme to link the Phillips gas terminal to two new Mobil fields. In October 1993, Amoco announced that, as part of a £160 million investment in the Indefatigable field, the Bacton terminal would be modified creating more jobs. But the area has benefited in ways not always appreciated. Pressure to find better, safer and more economic ways of bringing in the gas has led to the emergence of new innovative companies who are winning work across the world.

Even in the quieter times, when offshore activity is at its lowest, they have found their expertise in demand. Rather than close down or move out they have adapted their services to meet the needs of other industries. Thus some have diversified into the water industry and others into chemicals and telecommunications. So, even when North Sea gas is exhausted its effects will still be felt through the companies which were founded on the back of gas and have gone on to flourish in other industries.

A further milestone in Norfolk's gas industry history came when the Duke of Edinburgh returned to Bacton thirty years after his first visit to officially open Britain's gas link to the Continent - the £400 million Interconnector pipeline to Zeebrugge. The opportunities it offered for exporting gas to the rest of the world was instrumental in encouraging the Shell and Elf energy giants to build a second pipeline giving Norfolk its first direct link with fields off the Scottish coast.

That in turn opens the door to other operators to ship gas from far-flung parts of the North Sea and ensures Norfolk's place at the forefront of the UK's gas industry. Shell terminal, for instance, already processes ten per cent of the nation's gas and the new pipeline gives it the potential to double its output.

Despite all these positive developments there have been some unwelcome forces at work in the energy industry which have put pressure on the North Sea industry. All the energy giants with an involvement in Norfolk and Waveney have been shedding jobs as they try to compensate for the falling price of oil which sank to $10 a barrel in 1999. In 1998 Shell blamed low oil prices when it announced that, although it was to invest £1 billion at its Lowestoft base and stay for thirty years or more, it was cutting 140 jobs. Massive industry consolidation also had its effect and more jobs were lost when BP took over Amoco, although most of them were outside Norfolk. BP subsequently agreed to buy Atlantic Richfield (Arco) which controls its Southern North Sea production from Yarmouth.

Norfolk's commerce and industry enters the new century in good shape. Firms such as Anglian Group (window manufacturers), Bespak (medical drug delivery valves), Jeyes (household goods), Norcor (corrugated board), Porvair (synthetic materials), Wensum (clothing) and Waste Recycling are among Britain's top companies. And Bernard Matthews has proven that a company based on the county's traditional agricultural base can become a major international player.

The importance of small businesses to the county's economy continues to be vital. In 1995 the EDP affirmed: *"Small firms hold the key to future employment growth. Three-quarters of Norfolk's 17,000 businesses employ five people or fewer. If they were able to take on one additional member of staff, the county's dole queues would be halved."*

The most dominant force in the county's economy is Norwich Union, which at time of writing owns 1.3 per cent of all British industry with assets topping £50 billion worldwide. It has increased its number of employees in the county to more than 6000 and is in the list of Britain's Top 30 listed companies.

The company, like many others, has moved into direct marketing via phone and, increasingly, internet links. The success of the pioneering Direct Line insurance agency sparked a Nineties revolution and paved the way for such developments as Virgin Direct, which has been one of Norfolk's best success stories of the late Nineties. Nor should one overlook the impact of firms such as Gorleston-based Worldwide Travel, which has brilliantly exploited the demand for teletext holiday booking services, and the call centre for Dutch airline KLM, opened at Norwich International airport in 1998 and planning to employ 300 by the year 2000.

The significance of these firms is that they could be based almost anywhere in the country. At a stroke, the arguments about dualling the A47 or A11 could become as meaningless as the Thirties debates about Empire Free Trade. What will increasingly count in the next century is telecommunications, not communications.

With a healthy stable of financial players based in and around the city already, the area needs to emulate the self-perpetuating wealth-creating story that is Cambridge's Silicon Fen. Success breeds success, and there is no reason to believe that view will change in the next century's business environment.

Silicon Broads, anyone?

# CHAPTER 10

# *The Families*

CHARLES ROBERTS

*The Hunt Ball at King's Lynn - Such fun this was, with, of course, about thirty Buxtons and as many Barclays and almost as many Gurneys. Lady Townshend's Raynham Hall party included pretty Miss Cicely Thorpe, that clever American sportswoman, Miss Rothermel, and Major Noel Sampson, the polo player. Lady Edward Hay and her husband and Miss Vickers were with the Birkbecks.*

From The Lady, April 11th 1929

Bright lights and gaiety reigned at the 1929 Hunt Ball at King's Lynn. Outside was the grey reality of depression, which for land-owning county families meant a continuing, nail-biting struggle to preserve their inheritances. By 1929, many had already lost the fight.

The Buxtons, Barclays, Gurneys and Birkbecks were - and remain - land owners too. But first and foremost they were bankers, who had led the way in teaching a hard lesson which gentry, squirearchy and nobility were having to learn. In short: if you would maintain your ancestral halls and acres, then educate your heirs to a productive job away from the land, to provide income to subsidise the home front; or send them to agricultural college to acquire the skills of estate management and business acumen.

In truth, the golden days of huge income from agriculture and land had passed half a century earlier, when high prosperity crashed into the crippling agricultural depression of the 1880s and 1890s. Families who had long been used to living richly off the income from their estates were suddenly reduced to what was, for them, near poverty.

For those fortunate enough to own London property, that was a buffer against adversity. Through into the Edwardian period, others sold off their libraries, pictures and any treasures likely to raise useful capital. And onward through the decades, right up to the Nineties, estates great and small in Norfolk have followed the same path.

A crushing further blow was the introduction in 1894 by Sir W Vernon Harcourt of an Act to replace Probate Duty by a new, so-called "Death Duty" on all property passing to the heirs on the death of the owner. It was to seal the fate of many estates, here in Norfolk and nationwide, and remains a potent threat.

With the opening years of the twentieth century there was some improvement in farming profits after 1906. The Great War brought a few boom years, to be followed by another ruinous depression through the Twenties and Thirties, a lift again with the Second World War and the essential need for home-grown food; and again a dip in fortunes through to the late Fifties. It was then that the future for land ownership, agriculture and country houses markedly improved and did indeed bring some good years. But yet again, the end of the century, as it did a hundred years ago, has brought dire times for agriculture.

In her incisive doctoral thesis, Norfolk Landowners Since 1880, UEA graduate Pam Barnes listed 32 Norfolk estates in 1880 of between 2000 and 3000 acres. A century later only five of these had retained 1000 acres in the ownership of their original families. In 1884, she records, there were eleven estates in the county of 10,000 acres or more. One hundred years on, eight of these were still in the hands of the original families.

She makes the point, nonetheless, that at the end of the nineteenth century, even the great landed estates, such as that at Holkham, did not escape unscathed. At that time the Earl of Leicester owned 43,000 acres. Yet his gross annual rental fell from £51,908 in 1880 to £31,393 in 1900. For the average Norfolk landowner in that period, says Miss Barnes, *"landed property had become a liability, for the pressures of ownership and management increased while revenue from the land fell drastically, sometimes disastrously"*.

But the inter-wars slump was equally punishing, when it was said that the banks owned virtually half of Norfolk as a result of foreclosures.

The feeling of the time was reflected in the EDP in September 1936 as it pondered *"the growing host of people who have been watching with anxious eyes and with sad hearts the diminishing number of beautiful country houses and estates"* which until that time had been maintained *"in the hands of enlightened and public-spirited owners"*.

Holkham today, under the committed and highly-professional management of the present Lord Leicester and his son Tom, Viscount Coke, has 25,000 acres, making it the biggest estate in Norfolk.

The size of its estate enabled Holkham to weather the opening years of the century, and the dark period of the Twenties and Thirties. "Though this family, unlike many great families in England, didn't own London property," says the Earl. "We had only the land here. So it was a fairly steady downward trend, and as rents fell, less repairs and improvements were carried out.

"I presume that in the inter-war years the family must have borrowed a lot of money to keep the place going. They must have trimmed their lifestyle a bit too. I mean, 25 to thirty servants living in! Consider that in 1776 the estate was getting 8s 6d an acre rent from its tenants. In 1935 it was getting 5s."

Lady Silvia Combe, daughter of the 4th Earl - a vital, energetic lady who this year (1999) celebrates her 90th birthday - recalls childhood visits to the great house, when the place was full of servants, who daily at 9am lined up - men one side, women the other - for morning prayers read by her grandfather, the 2nd Earl. His Lordship then took a hearty breakfast, rounded off with an egg which he boiled himself, on a plated egg boiler, for precisely three minutes. "He always poured cream over the top of his egg, after which he ended with a scone."

In 1934, to supplement the rents - quite apart from the hordes of servants and the large breakfasts! - Holkham sold a very fine Titian for £34,000, and the medieval Holkham Bible Picture Book. Both are now in New York. To meet substantial death duties in 1941 and 1948, some 16,000 acres of land were sold. For the 4th Earl, one answer was to give house and estate to the National Trust.

James Lees-Milne sat next to him at dinner in June 1947 and recorded in his diary: *"His last words to me were - 'If you can find any means whereby the Trust can take over this house and its contents, I shall be prepared to leave it, should my not staying on make the transfer easier'."* Such a transfer, as it happens, was not possible because of the family entail on the property.

When the present Lord Leicester came to Holkham in 1973, he went on record as saying that, as long as he was there, not one square foot of Holkham land would be sold - in fact, he has added to it. "That," he smiles broadly, "was in the arrogance of youth. We sold things like medieval manuscripts and the Leonardo notebook, on the basis that neither we nor the public saw them - and that they don't earn any income, whereas land does."

He admits that he "got a lot of flak from the heritage establishment... Of course one sympathises with their aims - but they don't tell you how to keep the roof over your head.

"Up to the early Seventies, the advice to owners was to sell off the old cottages on the estate because they were just a drain; and sell off land to reduce borrowings. I did neither. I didn't sell cottages or houses because I had then, and still have, a social conscience.

"We have about 300 cottages, all nicely modernised now so we can charge proper rents, which are a very big earner for the estate. But the criterion for anyone having a cottage is that they must work in Norfolk all the year round."

**The Earl of Leicester at Holkham: "I got a lot of flak from the heritage establishment... Of course one sympathises with their aims – but they don't tell you how to keep the roof over your head."**

Both great house and estate have been brought up to first-class order through the last 25 years to prepare them for the 21st century. The park around the house is open to the public each day; as are numerous footpaths and bridleways through other parts of the domain. The house itself is open ninety days a year, attracting some 30,000 visitors, whose entrance fees are another important element in the estate's finances. Lord Leicester is confident that the house could take twice the number.

Running the estate (of whose 25,000 acres he himself farms 5000) he regards as very much a team affair - thus the portrait hanging in the hall of himself with all his heads of department. This year the same artist, Andrew Festing, will be painting all 21 of the farm men, in a conversation piece; to be followed by the building department, to create a complete working record of all the estate workers in the year 2000.

Country houses authority John Cornforth perceives a pattern which *"confirms the impression that the great houses belonging to the higher ranks of the aristocracy have survived best, and it suggests that comparatively few of the houses that have come to the National Trust would have survived in private ownership, either because there was no son or obvious heir to inherit or because there was not sufficient land to support them in the future."*

In a county long used to "dewin' diffrent",

**Team affair: Lord Leicester with his heads of department. Artist Andrew Festing is now working on a new painting for the estate.**

the three major Trust properties in Norfolk are firmly individualist in how they came into the NT's care. In the case of Blickling, a hugely important precedent was also set, for this was the first house and estate to come to the Trust under the Country Houses Scheme, a system whereby, in place of death duties, whole houses and their contents could be left to the nation intact with their estate income as an endowment. Philip Kerr, last owner of Blickling, became 11th Marquis of Lothian and inherited the estate (plus a handful of others) in 1930.

Four years later he addressed the Trust's annual meeting - and set out the basis of the future Country Houses Scheme, which was enacted by Parliament in 1937. On his death in 1940, the great house and its considerable estate came to the Trust in December of that year. "Blickling was thus the prototype for one of the most important conservation initiatives of our times."

Felbrigg is a great twentieth-century rescue story by a father and son who brought it back from the edge. Robert Ketton inherited the estate in 1872 and was to be its master for forty years. It started well. He was an enlightened employer and clearly so proud of the place, where he lived in contented bachelorhood with his two spinster sisters. They died in the closing years of the 19th century, and Robert stayed on alone, reclusive, increasingly eccentric and increasingly careless of his inheritance. R W Ketton-Cremer, last owner of the house and known to all in the locality as The Squire, recorded poignantly in Felbrigg: The Story of a House, what happened:

*"The light had gone out at Felbrigg, and for the next quarter century it was a house of solitude and gloom... The estate began to go downhill. Repairs were neglected, to farmhouses and farm buildings and cottages alike. Land was undrained, watercourses became choked, nothing was done to the drives or roads."*

In the house, damp was soaking through the neglected roofs. Shrubberies, lawns and gardens were overgrown. Across the park, the church fell into appalling decay. There were no financial reasons for this indifference, wrote The Squire. *"It was as though he had just lost heart."*

He also grew unpredictable. When after the First World War he needed money to pay off a small family trust, he sold a treasure trove, first of superlative Oriental porcelain, Sèvres and Meissen, then of irreplaceable books - and all for very poor prices at auction.

The Squire's father, who was in line to inherit, watched all this helplessly. When he did take over, he and his wife pitched themselves into the mighty task of restoring house, gardens, park, woodlands and church, and in his turn their son continued the work. Thus when The Squire bequeathed hall and estate to the Trust in 1969, plus the entire contents of the house, he handed on a jewel of a property which enchants all who get to know it.

There are no longer Lothians or Ketton-Cremers amongst us in Norfolk. But over in the west, in the Trust's third major property in the county, Oxburgh Hall, the ancient Bedingfeld family is very much alive and in residence. The Bedingfelds came over from Normandy in the time of the Conqueror. Sir Edmund Bedingfeld built the romantic, castellated manor house, within its surrounding moat, in about 1482. Save for the odd gap, they have been there ever since. But in 1952 that enduring association came perilously close to an end.

In that year Sir Edmund Bedingfeld sold house and estate to a property company. It was divided into seventy lots for auction, with the house fated to be demolished for rubble and materials. Park and estate, 5000 acres in all, went under the hammer, most of the tenants each buying their own farms. Down came fine standing timber. But the baronet's mother, Sybil, Lady Bedingfeld, stepped in with the help of family friends and bought back house and garden. When the news was announced in the auction room, the whole company cheered and applauded. Not long afterwards, with the help of several trusts, Lady Bedingfeld was able to give the house to the National Trust. But the family stayed on.

"My grandmother bought back the house on a wing and a prayer - mostly a prayer, literally," says Henry Bedingfeld, heir to the 9th Baronet, who lives with his wife Mary and family in Oxburgh's east wing. "She ran the house, and looked after it for a year or two with the help of Fred Greef, the gardener, a loyal man who worked here for many years and is still alive, turned ninety, a bit deaf, but very clear-headed. But she realised she couldn't really cope. Then she heard from a neighbour about the National Trust..."

So in due course the transfer took place. "At first only the towers were open to the public. Fred would sell tickets at the entrance and grannie would be joined by cousin Vi and her companion who came during the summer to help out, selling tickets and giving guided tours. Grannie was still running the place although it was owned by the Trust. Gradually the Trust took over the responsibility. But it wasn't until about twenty years ago that we had an administrator."

Was it difficult, one wondered, to get used to the idea of the gardens and house being full of people on sunny days? Mr Bedingfeld, who has a wry and straight-faced sense of humour, considered the question: "My ancestor who built this place was extremely wise in putting a moat around it. So we don't get noses pressed against the windows. You would have to get extremely wet to achieve that."

Nonetheless, he tells the story of one man who rolled up his trouser legs, sat on the edge of the moat and happily splashed his feet in the water for hours - immediately opposite the Bedingfelds' main drawing room window. "But my grandmother's attitude, which I have inherited, is that if it were not for the public coming here, we would not be living here."

He ponders, even so, on the fact that he is the first Bedingfeld in 900 years not to own land. "The loss of the land I mind, in many ways, rather than the loss of the house," he concedes. "But if we still owned the house, we would still have to open to the public in order to get Government grants to maintain the place."

And what of the 1000-year family history of which he is the inheritor? "I am very grateful for, and fascinated by it. Sometimes I am astonished that I am me with this incredible history. But it doesn't make me grand. And it doesn't make me rich. It is quite a lot to live up to, I suppose. But I certainly don't feel important about living here and I don't think

**Sybil Lady Bedingfeld, who was able to buy back the house in 1952.**

**Henry Bedingfeld at Oxburgh Hall: "Sometimes I am astonished that I am me with this incredible history. But it doesn't make me grand. And it doesn't make me rich."**

Mary does either. I can show that I am descended from various kings. But that is just accident of birth. It doesn't make me important."

But family history is not only in the bloodstream of Henry Bedingfeld. It is his occupation too as an officer of the College of Heralds, with the resonating title of Rouge Croix Pursuivant of Arms. "The older I get the more I realise what my family and its history and Oxburgh mean. Even as a child and young man I adored coming here, coming back to my roots.

"As years roll by, more and more people come to see this house, about 55,000 of them a year. More and more people hear of the Bedingfelds. We seem to have acquired a higher profile, not because of anything we have done, but purely because the house has been opened to the public. It is an odd turn of fortune in a way."

He notes that many who visit Oxburgh like coming to it because it is a home that is occupied by its original family. At which point that laconic sense of humour surfaces again: "So I have become a museum piece."

The frothy socialite writer in The Lady, quoted at the beginning of this essay, went on from the jolly hunt ball at Lynn to Hunstanton. *"I was taken to lunch at the hall, where the Le Strange family have been ever since Norman times without budging!"* she warbled. *"Its owners are two young bachelors with modern tastes and habits, but a real love of their dwelling."*

Yet just twenty years later that unbroken line of great house and family was to be sundered, for in 1949 came the poignant sale announcement: *"Mr Le Strange will be obliged to sell Hunstanton Hall and gardens. His family has been in unbroken ownership for very nearly 1000 years. The break is due to the impossible burden of taxation."*

The sale went through that same year. Two years after that, for the second time in a century, the mansion was ravaged by fire. With the death of Hamon le Strange in 1993 the direct line of descent came to an end. The inheritance passed to Michael le Strange Meakin, whose mother was the daughter of the second son of the final family line.

To him came 3500 acres, in widely varied use today from sites in Hunstanton town (car park, leisure centre, caravan site, golf course leased privately and to the borough council) to agricultural holdings and forestry. As a young man he joined the estate office as deputy to his uncle Hamon le Strange, since whose death he has administered the estate alone.

He admits freely that he is not affected by the weight of the distinguished history and lineage of the Le Stranges. "I have been working in this office for 32 years. It is a job," he says simply. "The ownership doesn't seem to make a lot of difference. To me it is just a job you get on with." Mr Le Strange Meakin, who lives modestly in a Victorian, end-terrace villa in the town, has a son and heir, Charles, who is an accountant with a leading firm in London, and lives in Swindon. He is, says his father, interested in the family background, "but I don't know whether he would ever come to live in this area".

Nonetheless he feels an obligation to keep a traditional management in place: "The old people who remember the great days before the end of the family at the hall are coming to an end themselves now. Ten to twenty years ago there was still a feeling for the old village-to- hall relationship. But once you lost the big house as a focal point, things were bound to deteriorate in that respect."

When he first came to work for the estate in the Sixties he recalls, there were still some old retainers about. "There was one old boy of ninety who had been a gardener at the hall. When he first joined the estate, which must have been about 1880, when they gave out the Christmas presents he was at the end of the line of eighty outside staff, and there were another fifty in the hall."

Like his predecessors for centuries as head of the House, Mr Le Strange Meakin bears the splendid title of Lord High Admiral of the Wash, along with which goes ownership of the nine miles of foreshore between Wolferton Creek and Thornham, excluding the beach frontage of Hunstanton itself. Traditionally, the foreshore width is measured by a man riding his horse into the sea up to its belly - then hurling a spear. Where the spear lands is the limit of the Le Strange authority over whatever the sea throws up.

Ken Arnott relates in his book, Hunstanton, that when Mercedes Gleitz, the great Channel swimmer, became the first person to swim the Wash, she was greeted by Squire Le Strange with these words: "You do understand, Madam, that everything washed up on this beach belongs to me."

Next door to the Le Strange lands was another ancient Norfolk family, the Rolfes of Heacham Hall, celebrated for the marriage of John Rolfe, in about 1615, to the Princess Pocahontas, daughter of Powhattan, over-king of the Indian tribe in Virginia, who came back with him to England and became a great favourite at Court.

Before the turn of the twentieth century the family was already in trouble, with Eustace Rolfe living in Naples, desperately trying to live within his income while letting Heacham Hall to tenants. He wrote to his brother-in-law Holcombe Ingleby: *"I am worried out of my life over Norfolk and don't know what to do. The estate never brought me less and at the same time has never cost me more... Arrears (in rent) £818. I have held it within a few months of twenty years and paid for a lot of charges, but it gets worse and worse."*

The new Death Duty sounded the final knell and made it obvious that the hall would have to be sold. It was a huge relief to Eustace when Holcombe Ingleby proposed that he should buy the property himself, thus keeping it in the family on the female side. But by 1902 Ingleby realised that he could no longer afford to run Heacham either. He and his wife moved to the shooting lodge in the park and let the hall to an ex-rubber planter. Two years later Ingleby sold it to him and moved to the much more modest Sedgeford Hall a few miles away.

Eustace died in 1908, his brother Ernest barely six months later. Other members of the family lived long lives, but none produced offspring. By 1946 they had all gone. The long line of colonists, adventurers and country squires was at an end.

In his eloquent architectural study, The Country Houses of Norfolk, George Winkley surveys the great houses and the great men who built and lived in them, then places them, poetically, in their landscape with *"the host of smaller squires, with deep roots in their own parishes, not seeking a national reputation to emulate a Coke or a Townshend, but content to keep the noiseless tenor of their way in the quiet places of a still unspoilt rural county."*

A family who might well fit that lyrical description are the Cubitts of Honing who in the 1780s settled into the hall, with its elegant, pedimented south-front looking out over its park, and quietly husbanded their 2000 acres

**Bernard and Charles Le Strange of Hunstanton Hall pictured in a 1929 cartoon, "two young bachelors with modern tastes and habits, but a real love of their dwelling".**

HUNSTANTON HALL CELEBRATIONS

Le Strange Family's 850 Years' Occupation

Villagers Entertained

As a momento of this being the 850th year of the establishment of the le Strange family at Hunstanton Hall, employees of Mr. Bernard le Strange on Wednesday night made their squire a presentation. The gift was handed over by Mr. Frederick Wicks, the head gardener and oldest employee on the estate, during the festivities at a Coronation garden party in the hall grounds. At this party nearly 400 residents of Old Hunstanton were Mr. le Strange's guests, following a tea and sports he had provided for all the children of the village earlier in the evening.

Mr. le Strange, who has the title of Hereditary Lord High Admiral of the Wash,

**The EDP reported on May 23rd 1937 how the Le Stranges were celebrating 850 years at Hunstanton Hall. Less than 15 years later the link was to be broken.**

**Michael le Strange Meakin, hereditary Lord High Admiral of the Wash, pictured at the Hunstanton foreshore he owns, and (right) an old view of Hunstanton Hall, which is now no longer in the family's ownership.**

until the Great War brought terrible loss and shook the steady continuity of 130 years.

"We came through the twentieth century successfully and we are still here," says Thomas Cubitt, who with his wife Rachel has lived in the hall since 1976. "The two things that did make it enormously difficult to get through were the agricultural depressions and two world wars. The early Thirties depression nearly did finish the estate, and my grandfather died a very worried man."

Grandfather was 39 at the turn of the

century, and married with five sons and three daughters. "My father Randall was the eldest of the sons. Having finished his schooling and being the heir, I think he made it clear that he didn't want just to be his father's No.2 on the estate, but wanted land of his own. So an area was put at his disposal and he started up a fruit farm."

He was a pioneer in this field, and co-operated with other land owners such as the Blofelds of Hoveton. Honing became noted for its Bramley apples and, as we shall see, they were later to be the estate's saviour. Just before the Great War broke out, the youngest of the five boys died of meningitis. The three eldest boys joined up, all becoming officers in the 5th battalion of the Norfolk Regiment, which was sent to Gallipoli. On the same awful day of August 12th 1915, Randall and his brother Victor were killed. Eustace survived until April 1917, only to die, amid horrendous losses, at the second battle of Gaza against the Turks.

Randall's striking full-length portrait, in army uniform, hangs in the dining room at Honing. His son Thomas was born eight weeks after his death. But even the baby was not exempt from war. He was lying in his cot in his parental home at Ridlington, not far from Honing, when a Zeppelin passed over and released its load of bombs. The plaster in the ceiling above him cracked and collapsed, and crashed down onto the cot - but Thomas was unscathed.

"My grandfather died in 1933, which was a very difficult time for agricultural finances. I was the direct heir, as my father's eldest and only son. I was 17 and still at Marlborough. Grandfather had been advised that if he left the estate to me, a schoolboy with no resources of his own to put into it, it would have to be sold."

Thus on his deathbed the old man, concerned to safeguard the family inheritance, changed his will, leaving Honing to his surviving son Reggie - Colonel Reginald Cubitt, who in the early Thirties commanded the 5th Battalion of the Norfolk Regiment, in which his three brothers had died.

The Colonel - as he was known in the village and locality - pulled the estate through, though it was never easy. "The agricultural depression in the Thirties was much more severe than anyone had anticipated," says Mr Cubitt. "Yet there was an enormous reluctance to cut down the general standard of living here. My grandmother didn't understand at all what was going on, I think. But after my grandfather's death they had to accept reality and lived much more frugally. There just wasn't the money left."

With the coming of the Second World War, matters improved and the fruit farm came into its own. Fruit was being sent to Birmingham and Leicester; and in Honing village baskets were made in which to send produce to market - and hampers to Fortnum & Mason.

Thomas Cubitt meanwhile carved out a life and career away from Honing. After Marlborough he read mathematics at Trinity College, Cambridge, then went on to accountancy studies in London. These were interrupted by the Second World War, when he was commissioned into the family battalion of the Norfolk Regiment. He was serving in Singapore when it fell to the Japanese. He spent three years as a PoW, most of it as a slave labourer on the notorious Burma Railway, The Railway of Death. It was there that he was struck down by a bout of cerebral malaria. Against the odds, he survived to return home - and passed his final accountancy examinations just 15 months after his release. He was to become a partner in the chartered accountancy firm of Robson Rhodes.

Uncle Reggie died in 1976 and Thomas took over responsibility for Honing. Being by now in his sixties, he arranged for ownership to miss him and to pass directly to his three sons, two of whom are university lecturers and the third, CO of a battalion in the Irish Guards. The three take a keen interest in Honing and are kept fully informed about its affairs through its land agents, and by fairly regular family meetings held with their parents. Today's estate is entirely arable, with woodlands, a couple of wetland Sites of Special Scientific Interest; and work has been going on to restore heather to a piece of heathland which had been overtaken by gorse. "We are very fortunate that there is a great variety of landscape and wildlife here," says Mr Cubitt. "We try very hard to plan for wildlife generally – tree planting, set-aside strips and hedges, either restoring them or planting. We have been opening up a few more footpaths to supplement the official ones, to encourage people to come."

Looking to the future, he sees the problem as producing enough farming income to make living in the house an attractive proposition: "We are all agreed that we want to keep it a family estate. I think there is a strong possibility that the house will remain a family home for a long time to come – but one can't be certain."

On the far side of the county, near Downham Market, the Bagge family was established in Stradsett Hall three decades before the Cubitts were at Honing. But the Bagges go back, it is believed, to Viking days in the early ninth century, though no official record exists until 1168 when they were merchants in Lynn. In 1751 they acquired Stradsett through marriage. At the end of the last century the estate was hit not only by the disastrous agricultural depression of the time, but by two swingeing sets of estate duties in a short period.

Fortunately the Bagges were in the ideal position of not relying exclusively for their income on land. At the turn of the century they had in Lynn a brewery, a whaling fleet, a fleet that brought in coal and wine and, with other families, controlled the wharves. So as the twentieth century began they weathered the storms which had beggared others. For a time, nonetheless, the hall was let, as Sir Alfred Bagge chose to live at Crimplesham Hall, built by his father-in-law as a wedding present to him and his bride. The family came back in 1911. But only in the summer. In winter they migrated to their town house in Lynn, because it was warmer, says the present baronet, Sir Jeremy.

Through the great depression of the Twenties and Thirties, Sir Jeremy's great-uncle reigned at Stradsett. He was a barrister who became Recorder of Norwich, returning to Stradsett at weekends. "But he still maintained a butler, footman, housekeeper and 13 gardeners – though I don't think the estate provided any income at all."

Sir Jeremy took over from his father, who had inherited during the war, in 1985. He then promptly arranged for ownership to pass to his children, thus avoiding death duties when his time comes. Duties were of course payable following his own father's death – and are in fact still being paid. As a working farmer, he is keenly aware of the problems and concerns of modern-day estates. Stradsett has 2000 acres, of which one-third is tenanted and he farms the rest – and pays rent for the privilege to his children's Trust.

"It is now a very worrying period for farming," he says. "If we got no form of subsidy from the government, we wouldn't be here. I don't even pay myself for the job I do. Usually there is something to keep us going. If it's a bad year for cereals it's a good year for potatoes. Sugar beet was always a solid rock behind us. Then two years ago British Sugar cut the price to us by twenty per cent. By that time everything was in the ground and we had to go ahead. Yet the price of sugar on the shelves has not come down."

He points out that in the agricultural depression of a century ago, landowners were having to pay their tenants to farm. The wheel appeared to be coming full circle. "To keep these places running now requires an awful lot of working capital. Someone said to me the other day: 'I don't reckon it will be long before we are having to pay people to graze our parks, rather than hiring out the grazing'. A farmer has sheep on about 110 acres of the park here. But who is making any money on sheep at the moment? And if he doesn't make much money out of it, how long can he go on paying his rent?"

Apart from 26 cottages and farmhouses which Sir Jeremy's father modernised, another source of income is the local pub, which the estate owns – and draws a rental of £23 a year! It was fixed a little under fifty years ago, and will soon be up for renewal. The third of the estate which is tenanted is due back in 12 years: "So my son will be farming not 1350 acres but 2000, which will make it a much

**Sir Jeremy Bagge outside Stradsett Church: "At the moment it is impossible to project what the future holds."**

**Robin Combe of Bayfield Hall: "It is, I think, a very beautiful estate," he says, "and I am extraordinarily proud of it."**

more viable unit. "At the moment it is impossible to project what the future holds, because we just don't know what the fortunes of agriculture are going to be. It can't be allowed to get much worse, or everyone will get out of farming and all food will have to be imported.

"Of course the future of the house is dependent to a large degree on the income the estate provides. I qualified as a chartered accountant and have interests in London, where I spend about three days a fortnight. You have to look to other resources to bring money in to help maintain these places."

On home ground, Sir Jeremy takes a personal concern in the people who live and work on the estate, and in the welfare of the village. He and his brother James, a solicitor in London but back at the hall most weekends, take a positive interest in the little parish church in the park - so much so that when there is no clergyman available, they take the services themselves, which attract about 12 people each Sunday; and double when a retired cleric comes to take communion. "It would be tragic if the church closed down here. Other than the pub, it is the only other focal point left in the village."

Recently they received from the Charity Commissioners a form to fill in. One of its questions was: "What is your mission statement?" Sir Jeremy, no doubt thinking as much about the estate as about the church, wrote succinctly: "Survival!"

Ensuring the survival of estates comes in different ways. At Bayfield, near Holt, owner Robin Combe and his son Roger are taking a route which appeals as much to their inclinations as to the plain facts of financial stability - the ecological route towards encouraging all kinds of wildlife, flora and fauna, fur and feather; and equally to encouraging public access so that people can enjoy their land with them.

Bayfield came to Robin Combe in a wholly unexpected manner. Roger Coke, of the Holkham family, lived alone at Bayfield, never married, and died in 1960. It was anticipated that he would leave the estate to his friend and nephew Angus Ogilvy, Princess Alexandra's husband, who often stayed there for shooting weekends. Instead, he left it to his great nephew, Robin Combe (his mother Lady Silvia, quoted earlier in this essay, is also a Coke, being daughter of the 4th Earl). Mr Combe was in Wales when his father sent him a telegram – to tell him he'd inherited a hall and 1800 acres.

"I was 26 years old and wasn't prepared for it or trained for it," he admits. Also he felt he had a management career at Watneys (The Combes were an old brewing family). The result was two decisions he was to regret. Firstly to let more than half the Bayfield land to a tenant farmer. Secondly, to let the hall on an 18-year lease which was later extended to 25 years. So it was not until 1985 that he took up his inheritance – and suddenly realised what an amazing place had been granted to him and how much he had been missing. Story has it – and Robin Combe has not denied it – that in the exhilaration of that moment he tore off his clothes and raced, naked, three times round the outside of the house in exuberant celebration. "It is, I think, a very beautiful estate," he says, "and I am extraordinarily proud of it."

It is a pride which shines out of him, especially when he shows a visitor his woodlands. "We have more than sixty veteran trees, more than anywhere else in North Norfolk," he says. "Our oldest oak goes back to 1442, we have several Elizabethan trees and some very old beech and chestnuts. I've planted a tremendous number of trees, and I try to think in terms of what is going to happen in a hundred years' time, and not just now."

Bayfield offers eight and half miles of walks, all signposted, and ten and a half miles of bridleways for horses. With so much delicately balanced wildlife around the lake, including otters which were reintroduced with the help of otter expert Philip Wayre, paths carefully skirt it, but still allow walkers good views of it. The same happens in woodland and other areas where wildlife would suffer from human intrusion – a well-concealed badger sett, for instance. No fewer than 93 species of birds have been identified on the estate, among them several flourishing families of barn owls and a healthy population of skylarks.

"One has got to examine one's assets and see how they can best be exploited in the context of the environment and what the income resources are, which are getting less and less from agriculture and more and more from caring for the environment."

An altogether different element of conservation is Robin Combe's work to convert redundant farm buildings into workshops, which have been let for a remarkable range of businesses, from manufacturing high-specification lathe-made parts for Ministry of Defence use, via hi-tech guitars and sound systems to, side by side, a furniture upholsterer who has done much work for the Marquess of Cholmondeley's Houghton Hall and for the National Trust; and a furniture restorer who is also used by the NT.

But Robin is especially pleased with an enterprise called Natural Surroundings, which occupies 11 acres of varied land, from woodland to river wetland, tucked away behind the hall. Its objective is to teach young people in particular, but adults too, the variety of natural life, which its creator Peter Looseley illustrates through the ninety species of plants, including wild orchids, which he has found or planted. Last year he had a remarkable 20,000 visitors – and won the David Bellamy Award for education of young people in nature and conservation.

It is in line with this wide field of conservation that Bayfield is looking to Heritage Relief, and a thirty-year plan covering all the aspects which already are so dear to the Combes, father and son. "This will ensure that my son will be able to inherit, and that the estate is free of death duties, which is the only way that a beautiful estate like this, which really is a gem, can be preserved for the pleasure of thousands of people a year. We have agreed to go on this environmental route to make it a showpiece for North Norfolk, which it nearly is now."

This love for its own sake of the land and its plenitude of natural life is far more prevalent among land owners and farmers than might be apparent. Equally, without the need of bludgeoning "Right to Roam" legislation, a fair number in Norfolk actively encourage the public onto their estates. They accept that only in this way can city dwellers in particular be educated into appreciating the delicate balance between wildlife, agricultural needs and public access.

Frederick Forsyth, one-time EDP journalist and all-time celebrated novelist, has talked about the countryside being content for years to abide by the adage, "Never excuse, never explain." Those days, as he says, are long gone by: *"Slowly, I believe, the case for the countryside is being made, not by shrill assertion but by reasoned explanation. Townspeople are beginning to realise that there is no 'you' and 'us' in this matter, for the landscape of Britain is part of all our heritage."*

Lord Leicester and Robin Combe, as we have seen, would assuredly go along with that assertion. So too would Lord and Lady Walpole, of the Mannington and Wolterton estate near Aylsham, where the family has been established since the 1720s. The whole estate of 1500 acres is a rural conservation area, as is the National Trust's neighbouring Blickling estate. It has 25 miles of public footpaths, all waymarked and on the definitive map of the county, and with discreet interpretation notices so that walkers know what they are seeing. The beautiful formal gardens around the Walpoles' picturesque moated manor house at Mannington are regularly open; as is Wolterton Park daily from nine to dusk and Wolterton Hall on selected days.

"People talk about circular footpaths as if they are something new," beams Robin Walpole through the slight sheen of his pipe smoke. "We have been doing them here for 25 years and have a network which people use regularly." He is confident that waymarked paths are most user-friendly for walkers, rather than relying on an OS map; and that explanatory material, "telling people what they are looking at and the problems and niceties of it all," makes for fuller enjoyment, quite apart from encouraging a respect for habitat.

He illustrates the point with a Mannington success with skylarks: "We have one area here where you can guarantee to go and listen to skylarks, which is quite amazing. This was not easy. We used a piece of set-aside. Certain people thought it a quite ideal place to take their dogs for walks, and not on leads. But since we have put up notices, explaining what is happening and why they shouldn't walk across the field, they no longer do so - and several pairs of skylarks are nesting."

With the same enthusiasm he discourses about owls: "We actually know where seven pairs of owls are nesting on this estate. We are not just lucky to have them. We have them because we have managed certain meadows so that owl food - moles, voles and the like - are happy to live there and owls are able not only to sustain themselves, but also to reproduce themselves in increasing numbers."

Robin and Laurel Walpole firmly believe that countryside appreciation should start young. Thus, with that very purpose in mind, they run an organisation called The Mannington Minnows, open to membership aged six to 16. "Some of the older ones have stayed on after 16 because they just couldn't stay away," says Lady Walpole. "So they come and look after the youngsters and become so knowledgeable that they can tell the younger ones the names of wild flowers and butterflies and so on.

"The good old Victorian monitor system," declares the Baroness cheerfully, "works well on Mannington Minnows!"

Running an estate which encourages considerable public access, and not least with two Grade I listed halls upon it to be sustained, brings its problems. Thus the Walpoles are, at the time of writing (spring 1999), engaged in trying to set up Wolterton and its park as a separate Trust, with the support of the Heritage Memorial Fund. The

**Lord and Lady Walpole: "I don't think estates such as this are ready to face the coming century, unless they have very considerable help."**

aim is to promote conservation and landscape management, side by side with public access and recreation on the estate. Under the terms of the Trust, the hall would be open for at least 100 days a year. Visitors would see all the first-floor state rooms, which contain a nationally important array of family portraits, including the largest number of representations of Sir Robert Walpole, Britain's first Prime Minister, in any known collection.

While this project is being approached with optimism, Lord Walpole looks to the future of estates like his with caution: "I don't think estates such as this are ready to face the coming century, unless they have very considerable help. If you started an estate at square one and did all the things you have to do, and everything worked successfully, you are still left with the things which I think are essential, like being involved in education, and in helping people to understand the countryside.

"That is something which, quite honestly, you have got to be incredibly rich to sustain for ever. I think that is a part of it, and a part that should be done, but one can't continue to do it without help."

A notable and recurrent feature of the county families is their sense of service to the community. Lord Leicester, when Viscount Coke, gave considerable time to his role as Leader of King's Lynn and West Norfolk Borough Council; Robin Combe is the longest-serving churchwarden in the Glaven Valley, vice-chairman of his parish council, Trustee of the Shell Museum in Glandford village, and much involved with the Council for the PRE and Country Landowners' Association; Lord Walpole has a firm track record of service on local authorities and on numerous county and regional bodies dealing with education, the arts and tourism, and will, up to its demise in its present form, continue to take his seat two or three days a week in the House of Lords.

A firm believer in this concept is John 'Tiggy' Birkbeck, a well-known name and personality in county and district councils, a former High Sheriff of Norfolk and a devoted member of his local church, whose family, who were bankers, came down to Norfolk from Westmorland in about 1750. He and his wife Hermione acquired Litcham Hall in 1967, with a spacious garden and small paddock. The family land, to his chagrin, went elsewhere, though his second cousins, the Birkbecks of Westacre High House, maintain the tradition in farming a considerable estate near Castle Acre. It came to this branch of the family through the marriage in 1849 of Henry Birkbeck of Stoke Holy Cross to Mary Anne Hammond, whose family had been there for nine decades.

Tiggy Birkbeck was brought up at Little Massingham in the spirit of service to the community, with his parents as busy exemplars and his father very much in the mould of the country squire. "That upbringing, quite subconsciously, rubs off on one." The idea of "the squire" might be out of date. But he is convinced that every village needs a figurehead, someone who is, if possible, going to be philanthropic. Anticipating the obvious question he chuckles: "My view of being a squire is that (a) you have to be there for a long time, say about 200 years; and (b) you need a bit of cash, and I don't fit into either of those categories." Nonetheless the hall is frequently host to local events.

He joined the local rural district council in 1969 and subsequently of its successor, Breckland District Council, until he lost his seat in 1995. Save for a four-year gap, he has been a member of the county council since 1970. As he reflects ruefully on not having become the land owner/farmer he had expected to be, he observes that the old families in the county who have really kept their position are those who have hung onto their land: "There is an old saying, 'Sell everything in the house if necessary, but never sell land'. Land goes up and down but it always comes back in the end."

There are numerous other families, some landed still, others divorced from their domains, who have a place in the full story upon which this chapter touches. But it comes to an end with representatives of two of the old banking families with whom it began, the Birkbecks and the Gurneys. In

**Tiggy Birkbeck of Litcham Hall: "There is an old saying, 'Sell everything in the house if necessary, but never sell land'. Land goes up and down but it always comes back in the end."**

**The fate of Costessey Hall is one which sums up the story of those Norfolk landowning families who did not survive the rigours of the twentieth century. The hall, pictured above in 1913, was an astonishing confection of styles, built on such a lavish scale over the centuries that historians saw the Jerningham family as sowing the seeds of its own ruin. The eccentric Sir Fitzosbert Edward Stafford-Jerningham, the 11th Lord Stafford, who succeeded to the estate in 1892, owned 3200 acres in the county and 6800 outside. He died in 1913 at the other family seat, Swynnerton Park in Staffordshire. The rambling Costessey Hall was commandeered by the Army in the First World War and in November 1918 the estate was put up for sale. Now only a fragment remains, the merest hint at former glories.**

**David Gurney, ready for another horseback survey of his Bawdeswell estate: "I'd love my grandfather and father to come back and see what we've done and achieved. They'd love it."**

David Gurney, of Bawdeswell Hall, the three elements come together of real love of the countryside, of tenaciously holding on to land, and of a belief in duty and service.

By the turn of the twentieth century, there were Gurneys already established with mansions and estates all over Norfolk. In the great late nineteenth-century agricultural slump, as many farms crashed, the Gurney bank foreclosed on them and often the land came into Gurney family hands, and Birkbeck and Buxton hands too. David Gurney's grandfather added to the family holdings when he bought Bawdeswell in 1912 with 230 acres.

The banking interests inevitably shielded them from the desperate problems of the Depression and put them in an unassailable position: "In the Thirties my grandfather was offered land at 11s. 6d. an acre and refused to take it because he said it wasn't worth it."

The heart-breaking situation comes to mind, quoted by Barnes, of Edward Lee Warner being forced to sell for a knockdown price in 1930 his 1200-acre Wormegay estate near Lynn, which in that year recorded a net annual income, after expenses, of £34! Lee Warner wrote bitterly:

*"The time of good offers has gone for an indefinite period. There is no recovery in sight... Let us take the miserable offer and be done with it. Would any of us accept*

*Wormegay as a gift? Not I for one."*

David Gurney now farms 1000 acres around Bawdeswell Hall, and another 1300 acres in packets around the county, including a 550-acre farm at nearby Billingford which he acquired six years ago. Every morning he rides on horseback around his domain: "I keep a pretty close eye on what is going on. Even when I was going off to the bank every day, I still rode out each morning so I could see what was happening to the land. At the same time I'm looking for birds and animals and anything unusual.

"One of my friends said to me: 'You have to be a real peasant to love the land like you do'. Well, perhaps."

His grandfather, he says, was a great naturalist who loved his farm and land, and he often as a boy went on walks with him and learned a lot. "When I took over the Billingford Farm it had no woods or hedges. I planted five woods, mostly deciduous. That is putting something back into the environment. I won't see these woods mature. But I will see them, I hope, as reasonable trees.

"I'd love my grandfather and father to come back and see what we've done and achieved. They'd love it. Father modernised and I have taken it the next step forward. No doubt when I hand over to my son Robert he will take it a great step on again."

In his view of the land, of handing on through primogeniture, of looking after the financial future of his daughters, of his belief in duty and obligation to the present and the future, he admits that his attitude may be a nineteenth-century one: "I think there are massive changes yet to come, perhaps under New Labour. It is very difficult to see the way forward, but I think people will always rise to the occasion. I foresee that a couple of hundred years on, we will live in a very different world, but many of the old circles will have been re-formed. I don't know where my great-great-great-grandchildren will be by then - but I hope they will have the nous to be somewhere near the top."

And the future of country houses and estates? Lord Leicester, this year's President of the Historic Houses Association, has an optimistic view: "I think there is now an enormous awareness of the value of the English countryside and its symbols... of the things which are quintessentially English. Something like 73 per cent of foreign tourists come to see our built heritage. They are not interested in theme parks, they have got all that where they come from.

"About 11.5 million people a year visit the 332 open houses in the HHA. That is why I think these houses will survive. Because they will be seen and perceived as of value in the scheme of things."

## Chapter 11

# *The Sea*

**TREVOR WESTGATE worked as a staff reporter for the Eastern Daily Press and associated papers from 1952 to 1999. Born and educated at Great Yarmouth he moved to Lowestoft in 1958 after commissioned service with the RAF. He was passionate in defence of the distinctive character and environment of East Anglia. He was author of EDP Images of Lowestoft and other publications on historical themes, and a regular broadcaster on local radio. Married, with three children, he died in 1999 soon after completing this, his last major work.**

In October 1957, in a brave show of strength that was in truth failing fast, some 150 drifters took part in what was planned to be the first review of the East Anglian fishing fleet. In retrospect it proved to be something of a swan song for a way of life that has left an indelible mark on the maritime heritage of the region.

The drifters sailed in line astern through Yarmouth Roads, passing within a few hundred yards of the shore as they passed between Britannia Pier and the HMS Wave, from which the C-in-C Nore, Admiral Sir Frederick Parham, took the salute from a platform on the bridge. A score of longshore boats, also dressed overall, accompanied the drifters during the hour-long review.

As the fishing vessels passed HMS Wave four fishermen in oilskins stood on each foredeck. One in each drifter saluted Admiral Parham. The Fraserburgh motor boat Stephens, joint holder of the Prunier Trophy awarded for the largest single night catch of the season, led the boats from Great Yarmouth. Boats built at local yards were prominent in the Lowestoft section of the review, led by the drifter Silver Seas. The Scots from Lowestoft were led by Livelihood.

The review might have marked a new beginning. But an era of increasingly uncertain catches, changing demand at home and overseas and a dwindling fleet of drifters meant that the East Anglian herring voyage was inevitably passing into history even during the final years that brought some of the biggest single hauls on record.

The century which opened as steam began to oust sail in the huge fishing fleets once based at Yarmouth and Lowestoft is ending with only one of the rival East Anglian ports sustaining a major trawling presence in the North Sea. Yarmouth, which enjoyed centuries of pre-eminence in the autumn herring fishery, now supports only a relative handful of inshore vessels, and commercial shipping dominates the busy harbour scene at the Norfolk port.

Those of us who grew up among the sights, sounds and smells of the home voyage at Yarmouth still find it hard to believe that such an immense enterprise is now no more, represented only by the continued presence as a tourist attraction of the last of the steam drifters, the Lydia Eva. The distinctive herring "swills" that were once stacked in countless rows along the quays have gone, and rather more than a generation has passed since small boys darted among the busy fishermen to pick up any herring that fell to the ground during unloading. Such fish were fair game for the urchins of the town, and were threaded on a stout piece of twine to be carried like a bunch of silvery grapes.

The final link with a Yarmouth-based trawling enterprise was broken a few months before the outbreak of the last war when the smack Boy Leslie left Lowestoft to become a cargo carrier around the Norwegian coast. She was the last vessel to have sailed with the famous Hewett fleet of smacks, the Short Blue, which had a considerable presence at Gorleston and at one time employed 500 fishermen and boys. The enterprise marked the final years of "fleeting", when the catching vessels stayed at sea for long periods, transferring catches to fast cutters to be taken to market. The hazardous nature of this work was one of the factors that led to the establishment of the Royal National Mission to Deep Sea Fishermen, whose own smacks went to sea to minister to the needs of the fishermen.

The Short Blue fleet was dispersed just after the turn of the century and the Boy Leslie had been fishing out of Lowestoft for many years. Lowestoft, which challenged its Norfolk rival port with increasing success after the creation of its own harbour in the 1840s, has also long lost the herring industry that once provided jobs for many hundreds of local people at sea and in supporting roles in a variety of shore occupations. Lowestoft, however, has clung tenaciously to a tradition of trawl fishing throughout the year, and that aspect of the industry continues to provide a major plank in the local economy.

The present generation of skippers and fishermen, like their immediate predecessors, have had to come to terms with an unparalleled shift in fishing methods and have to cope in addition with a mass of paperwork and rules and regulations unknown a century ago. They remain, however, masters of their kingdoms in the sense that a trawler at sea is a self contained unit and the lives of all depend upon the sturdiness of the ship and the knowledge of the men aboard.

That is as true for the big beamers that now sail for trips of around ten days as for the smaller boats of the inshore fleet that still provide a sizeable contribution to fish supplies reaching the local market. Inshore fishermen are a tough and adaptable breed, prepared to go for such catches as come within range with net or line according to season. In historical terms, the use of sail, continued at Lowestoft far longer than in some other ports around the coast but smacks using beam trawls were no competitive match for steamers equipped with otter trawls. Catches are nowadays landed into a substantial modern covered market on the Waveney Dock offering facilities that are a far remove from the shabby Victorian structures that formerly lined the open quays.

Where once, however, there were hundreds of vessels in individual and company ownership, today's beamer fleet of nine vessels is operated by just a single company, Colne Shipping. Recent decades have seen the departure from the port of fleets formerly operated by companies such as Boston Deep Sea Fisheries, Small and Company and Talisman Trawlers. The port of Lowestoft nonetheless holds to its proud place as the country's principal centre for plaice. That species alone accounted for around £5 million of the total catch of 5700 tonnes worth £8.3 million at the port in 1997.

Fishing vessel numbers have been dramatically reduced in recent decades, but port owners have always been ready to respond to changing needs, and traditional side trawlers working from Lowestoft have long since been replaced by sophisticated beam trawlers. Today's diesel powered vessels, equipped with every modern aid, are a far remove from those working from the port at the dawn of the 1900s. Hugh Sims, chief executive of the Lowestoft Fish Producers' Association, points out that there have been vast changes in catching capacity with the advent of larger and more powerful vessels. When he joined the industry an engine of 500hp was regarded as large, and most local trawlers had engines of around 350hp. "Now we are constrained to 2000hp and would like to go higher."

The process continues.The latest beamer to arrive at Lowestoft, the St Anthony, replaces two ships that were themselves in the forefront of design only a few years ago. She represents a £3 million investment that called for both confidence in the future and determination to maintain a viable trawling industry based at the port. For both Yarmouth and Lowestoft the turning point in fishing fortunes came with the rapid decline of herring stocks in the years following the last war. It seemed for a time as if nothing had changed. The immense shoals of herring that had brought such prosperity for a thousand years or so continued to make their autumnal migration a few miles off the Norfolk coast. Grounds such as the famous Smith's Knoll, the Brown Ridges, and Dowsing seemed as inexhaustible as ever.

But the introduction of more efficient catching methods such as purse seining elsewhere made the drift-net fishery pursued by the English and Scots crews increasingly vulnerable. Catches began to show alarming variations, with a depressing long-term trend

**Harvesting sprats off Lowestoft in November 1968.**

of general decline. The scale of operations a few decades earlier almost beggars understanding, so vast was the home fishery, which ran from October to December. It was estimated that in 1911 the Lowestoft and Yarmouth combined herring catch totalled an astonishing 1,044,001,200 fish. In that year Lowestoft alone was the landing port for 300 trawlers, 326 local drifters and 334 Scots drifters. The peak year for both ports came two years later, when the fishing attracted 1776 drifters, just over 1000 of them working out of Yarmouth. The total catch that year was 1,359,213 crans.

Demand during the early years of the century was buoyed by the rapid development of the "klondyking" trade of exporting fresh herring to overseas markets, primarily in Russia and Germany. More than 126,000 barrels of pickled herring were shipped out of Yarmouth in 1911.

Much of the second half of the fishing century for the region belonged indisputably to Lowestoft, where substantial investment in new trawlers and vessels bought in from other ports heralded a period of some prosperity. The presence of two major Lowestoft shipyards, Richards and Brooke Marine meant that many new trawlers were built by local craftsmen. Both yards have now passed into history, having been numbered among the many victims of change within the fiercely-competitive global shipbuilding industry.

Since the early Sixties, when Lowestoft supported a trawling fleet of more than 100 vessels, there has been a steady decline in fleet numbers. The port economy was reprieved with the coming of the North Sea exploration programme for oil and natural gas that brought a massive demand for stand-by and safety ships. Former trawlers proved to be ideally suited for conversion to this new role. Lowestoft was therefore spared the spectacle of seeing dozens of vessels remain idle and tied up or sent for scrap.

The era of "wooden ships and iron men" has long since slipped into affectionate memory, but at the threshold of the new Millennium the fishing industry based at Lowestoft is far from being a lost cause. Sophisticated modern beam trawlers call for very substantial levels of investment, and the port owes much to the faith and determination shown by the Colne Shipping Company, which took delivery in early 1999 of the latest vessel in a fleet equipped to compete successfully in the harsh waters of the North Sea.

Fishermen at the close of the century enjoy working conditions that would have seemed like an impossible dream to their fathers and grandfathers. The toughness of life aboard the sailing and steam vessels of the early years of the century has been widely chronicled, and accounts of individual fishermen illustrate the way in which things have changed in times of both peace and war.

"Young Sonny" Gower, who was born in 1912, served as a cook on a Lowestoft drifter-trawler between the wars. Like many other local people, he followed family tradition, for his grandfather was born in 1863 and also went to sea as a 14-year-old cook. In the mid-Nineties Mr Gower, who went to see in 1927 at 15, recalled: "His life was very different to mine. His version was that he was a deckhand who did the cooking. He was involved with everything like shooting and hauling the trawl, gear mending and splicing when needed. They had no cooking stove, but cooked meat, fish or whatever and it was all done under the small coal furnace under the boiler that produced the steam to power the capstan that hauled the trawl."

Young Sonny joined the crew of the most famous herring skipper of that time, Frank "Podd" Catchpole of the Constant Friend, LT1172, in 1928. "My duties as cook included working with the shooting of the two miles of nets. At around midnight the cook turns out to make a kettle of tea (teapot not involved), then takes his position down the rope room and there he stays till the fleet of nets are hauled. Then his cooking duties begin. The 50 herring he has to cook for breakfast having been scaled, gutted and notched by the stoker — second engineer — whose job it is.

"After the rest of the crew turn in the cook then clears the breakfast things, cleans up the cabin and does the washing up. Plates and mugs are all enamelled so no breakages are involved. Each member of the crew carries his own knife, fork and spoon and if a cutlery article goes over the side with the washing up water you are in trouble. The aforesaid cutlery is kept under the bed in the crew bunks."

The hard-working regime experienced by Mr Gower was typical of his generation: "Fresh meat lasted us till five or six days out, and then meat puddings would be made with corned beef. Norfolk dumplings were the main item of a gorgeous repast. They were cooked in a steamer that fitted on the beef kettle for about half an hour. The ingredients

were flour, baking powder and small amount of salt. Usually twenty were cooked and any left over were eaten with jam or syrup."

The writing was already on the wall for the traditional drift net herring fishery when one of the top Lowestoft skippers of his time, George Draper, was featured in a national magazine in 1950. Skipper Draper was a winner of the Prunier Trophy awarded for the largest single night catch of the home voyage with the drifter Dauntless Star. A few years later, as local owners Boston Deep Sea Fisheries sought to keep abreast of Scandinavian competition for a share of the silver harvest of the North Sea, he took command of the seiner Princess Anne, which had been brought to Lowestoft from Fleetwood. Local manager of the Boston company at the time was Peter Catchpole. "We were the first people in the British Isles to introduce purse seining," he recalls. "Skipper Draper got me to accompany him to the Shetlands where a mass of Danes and Norwegians were taking part in industrial fishing and catching beautiful fish that were going for meal. I persuaded the Boston directors we ought to do it and the Princess Anne was brought in. Skipper Draper went to Norway and did a trip on one of their seiners before taking command. He did extremely well and was really getting into the swing of it when he lost an expensive deep water net after being caught in a Force 10 off the Norwegian coast and the expense of

**The Golden Harvest of Fraserburgh braves a heavy swell to set off from Yarmouth in this classic EDP picture taken in the late Fifties or early Sixties.**

replacement gear was seen as too much."

Might the purse-seining experiment have proved worthwhile in time? Mr Catchpole believes that the shallow waters of the North Sea nearer East Anglia might have posed problems that were not encountered by Scots fishermen able to exploit deeper waters. The Princess Anne was not the only fishing experiment to be tried by the Boston company, which also introduced a class of "pocket" stern trawlers as the switch away from traditional side trawlers gathered pace. And before the decision was finally taken to end a long fishing association with the port of Lowestoft, there was even a bid to share in the shrimp fishery of the Wash.

As one of the most successful skippers of his era, Skipper Draper had by the age of 34 taken over the Sunlit Waters, one of the most modern drifters in the Lowestoft fleet. A man who made up with iron determination and unrivalled knowledge of the ways of the sea for his lack of height, Skipper Draper was a good man to have at the helm. Like many of his contemporaries he served in the Royal Naval Patrol Service during the war as skipper of a minesweeper, and he won the DSC when he took his ship alongside a burning merchantman to rescue the crew.

After the war he landed fish worth £10,000 in a matter of ten weeks when he skippered the Golden Miller. When the Sunlit Waters was commissioned in 1948, owner Fred Catchpole had no hesitation in asking Skipper Draper to take command.

Ten years later he was skipper of the Dauntless Star, and the trip I made with him to the famous Smith's Knoll ground off the Norfolk Coast remains an abiding fond memory of a "don" skipper and his crack crew. There was no "Prunier" shot for us that night. The nets contained only a sprinkling of herring when Skipper Draper called the crew out to haul in the small hours of the morning.

But he found time on the run back to harbour in worsening weather to talk about the life of a fisherman and recall such memorable moments as the time when he decided to shoot his nets over a patch of "milky" water and finished up with an above average haul of some 200 cran. Men such as Skipper Draper were part of a sturdy tradition of people born to a seafaring life and well aware from an early age of the need to treat the North Sea with caution and respect.

The sheer numbers involved in the fishing industry from Yarmouth and Lowestoft during the first half of the century in particular brought a strong sense of community. There was always an element of roistering during limited time ashore, especially among the younger crew members, but by and large fishermen were decent, honest and certainly hard-working. Their calling was hazardous and financial rewards were seldom great, but boys had no hesitation in following their fathers to sea. What other occupation, after all, could better answer the need of youth to experience adventure and excitement, with a hint of danger thrown in for good measure?

One Lowestoft fishermen, Jack Cook, who was born in 1897, reminisced late in life: "When I was four years old my father took me shrimping with him as it was, so I learned later, a real nice day. We were gone seven hours at sea, and I remember him telling me later that I cried for my Mum all that time. But I went many times after that. It came at last that my parents rented a house in the town and I was, like many others, not able to keep away from the fish markets. Ships and tall masts were everywhere, and I've heard people talk about it all my life. What a picture it was.

"I think I am right, by how I heard the elder folk say, there were about 300 smacks and about 250 drifters, steam and sail. The sailing ones were called luggers. During the autumn herring season there were 200 to 150 Scots herring boats, mostly sailing craft, and their tall masts made a real picture. I must admit my education was poor. What I did not learn at school I must have made up for by knowing so much about boats. It came for me to leave school the week I was 13 years old. I had got a job at a hardware shop, but my heart was not there. I wanted to be on a boat.

"The first week was nearly over, and it was about nine o'clock on the Saturday night. I was in the shop when I saw my mother outside. She beckoned to me, and I went

**Calmer waters in 1999 as the St Davids heads out from Lowestoft harbour to the fishing grounds of the North Sea.**

outside to see her. 'Give your notice in, your father has got a cook's berth for you in one of the luggers.' Boy oh boy, was I pleased. I gave in my notice and at ten o'clock home I go.

"My father gave me all the news. The boat was the Willing Boys, LT737. This boat, like a lot more, was now getting ready for the spring herring, the May mackerel and what was known as the summer herring season, a voyage of 12 to 13 weeks. There was no weekly wage in those days, but these boats always had a bit of stockerbait (bonus) every day you landed. It was worked in this fashion: In you herring nets the mackerel was your bonus. If you had mackerel nets, then the herring would be your bonus."

A harsh introduction to a life at sea for a young lad was doubtless quickly forgotten at the end of the voyage in June. "The crew were at the office at the appointed time and I can recall the owner, the skipper still there, saying: 'Boy, here you are. Here is your share.' It was nine sovereigns and some silver, and I think his words to me were: 'Put this in your pocket boy. Home you go. Give this to your mother, and don't stop running till you get home.' I did this all right."

The following 12-week voyage to North Shields, Hartlepool and Scarborough, following the herring shoals, was rather less rewarding. At the end of it our young hero's share was 12 shillings, just a shilling a week. Later on, Mr Cook transferred to the sailing smack Narcissus, LT 305 as cook at 12 shillings a week. Mr Cook went on to serve on a number of other fishing vessels, sailing as cook in the smack Athena in 1913 under skipper Edgar Sark — "the best and kindliest skipper

**Haul away, boys... a drifter brings in more herring in a picture taken probably in the early Fifties.**

that I've sailed with in my life."

A few months later he helped haul a fleet of nets that had come adrift from another vessel. Money from the salvaged gear and the fish they contained brought a welcome bonus, and Jack's own share came to just over £2. Like many another East Coast fisherman, Mr Cook soon found himself at sea in a different role, working on boom defences during the first war and seeing service at both Gallipoli and in the distant icy waters off Murmansk.

Throughout the century Lowestoft has been a leading centre in the science of fisheries research. The present imposing CEFAS laboratory complex — the initials stand for Centre for Environment, Fisheries and Aquaculture Science — overlooks the sea at Pakefield in the south of the town. Scientists based at the laboratory continue a research programme of great significance in our understanding of present and potential fish stocks and the factors that influence variations in catches down the years.

The work done at Lowestoft neatly encompasses the entire century, for the first local research centre was established in 1902, not long after the first English fisheries laboratory was set up in Plymouth in 1887. Current planning is for a £30 million state of the art environmental research vessel to replace the Cirolana in the CEFAS fleet, an exciting concept for the start of the new Millennium. Cirolana, which cost £1 million, was built in 1970 and was originally based at Grimsby before being transferred to Lowestoft in 1984. The need for an ordered scientific assessment of fish stocks was generally realised by countries bordering the North Sea during the 1890s with the growing realisation that steam trawling introduced a significant new element in considering future catch potential.

There were international meetings of interested countries in Stockholm in 1899 and in Oslo and Copenhagen in the two following years. A direct result of these meetings was the formation of the International Council for the Exploration of the Sea (ICES) which was set up to co-ordinate the research work done by member nations and provide a forum for free discussion of the results. Initially, each country concentrated on the species of greatest significance in its national catch, and the UK decided to investigate the state of the plaice fishery that has been a priority for Lowestoft fishermen throughout the past 100 years.

The Marine Biological Association opened a small unit in Waveney Road at Lowestoft in 1902. The late George Atkinson, later to become a leading figure in local life, was a member of the inaugural team, and could recall the time in 1906 when the unit moved to more spacious accommodation in a house in the Marina and was able to set up the first laboratory facilities in the town. Four years later this laboratory was also closed down, the Lowestoft-based research vessel Huxley was sold and work was transferred to London under the auspices of the Board of Agriculture and Fisheries, which had assumed research responsibilities in 1908.

Lowestoft continued to be used throughout the period from 1909-14 as a base from which chartered vessels, including the steam yacht Hiawatha, sailed on research voyages. The decision to set up a new fisheries research laboratory was taken during the first war and two houses on the Esplanade were taken over and used as a base from 1921-1939. The programme of fisheries research was developed during those years under Dr E S Russell.

Following the last war the new Director of Fisheries Research, Michael Graham, headed renewed research. Premises alongside the Hamilton Dock were taken over as a new radiobiological section and offices were found in Pekefield for the hydrographic section. Not until 1955 did the laboratory staff move into the former Grand Hotel site, where various extensions have since been added to house scientists and support staff.

There is still an element of surprise in records that tell us about some of the "discoveries" made by scientists, more especially in those early years when there was so much to learn. Fish migration was imperfectly understood, and Mr Atkinson could recall his delight in tagging an eight-inch long plaice in 1905 and seeing the same fish caught alive and well and returned to the laboratory 16 years later. The inter-war years saw a great deal of important work in fields such as forecasting likely future catch levels, and studying the system of currents in the North Sea.

More resources became available after 1945 with the development of a fleet of research vessels and an extension of interest to events in more distant waters such as the Barents and White Sea. Modern equipment has made it possible to achieve far greater precision in evaluating information that will help predict trends in fish stocks and in turn give invaluable guidance to European states as they work to achieve 'sustainable TACs (Total Allowable Catches).

That work will continue into the next millennium, as will a substantial research effort directed at protecting the maritime environment from pollution caused by industrial processes and the damaging impact of accidental oil spillages.

The short sea routes across the North Sea to ports in Northern Europe, Scandinavia and the Baltic are the arteries that feed the commercial shipping life of the ports of Yarmouth and Lowestoft. Friendly rivalry exists between the neighbouring towns, but in truth their activities are complementary and have developed along parallel lines.

The River Yare gave Yarmouth an important historical advantage, for it was not until the railway boom of the nineteenth century that a harbour was created at Lowestoft. The long quayside available on both sides of the river meant that Yarmouth had ample time and space to develop a major maritime infrastructure geared to the needs of both the fishing industry and commercial traffic, handling a variety of cargoes and adapting to changing circumstances. Timber and grain, scrap metal and fertilisers, even block ice from Scandinavia were among the staples shipped in and out of Yarmouth — along with countless thousands of barrels of herring.

Changes wrought by the passage of 100 years have transformed the very shape of much of the Yarmouth waterside, and my grandfathers who worked respectively as a stevedore and fish market coffee stall proprietor would be hard-pressed to recognise more than a handful of the buildings they knew. Mounds of timber are no longer stacked high on Bollard Quay, and there are few longshoremen left to boil up their catches of shrimps aboard boats berthed on the Gorleston side of the river. Gone too are the forests of masts that dominated the waterfront scene during the years of sail. Yarmouth has had to move with the times, and today's shipping is governed less by wind and the swift-moving tides of the River Yare than by the need to keep to tight loading and sailing schedules.

The fortunes of shipbuilding and associated industries have inevitably fluctuated, and the labour-intensive days of the early part of the century have gone for ever, but Yarmouth has been quick to seize new opportunities as they have arisen, from roll on/roll off container services to offshore supply ships. Today the port deals with some 12,000 ship movements a year.

On the brink of a new century the port of Yarmouth could be poised for an exciting new era, for there are hopes of developing a major new outer harbour, costing many millions of pounds. If that long-held dream is translated into reality, and linked to an improved regional road network, the potential under the guidance of the Great Yarmouth Port Authority is vast indeed. The outer harbour project would involve major land reclamation and the building of a 1200-metre breakwater from the mouth of the present harbour. The scheme would eventually make the port available to vessels of up to 20,000 dwt around the clock.

The present day operating base is substantial, with cargoes including minerals, fertilisers, forest products, dry and liquid bulks and cargoes related to the oil and gas industries. The port handles shipments totalling some 1.6 million tonnes in the course of a year. Yarmouth can accommodate fifty vessels at any one time, with unrestricted access to ships of up to 4.3 metres draught and about 4000 dwt at all states of the tide. Main berths are located downstream of the Haven Bridge and some four km from the harbour entrance.

New facilities include a £1.5 million container crane with a lifting capacity of 63 tonnes. A further £1 million has been spent on resurfacing and repiling the port's Atlas Terminal. New hydraulic cranes have been brought in to give added flexibility to handling capacity and a new quayside warehouse has added a further 2400 sq metres of covered storage space. There has been major investment from the private sector to boost cargo sectors such as bulk shipments of feedstuffs and fertilisers serving the region's agricultural industry. Important contracts running into the next century will ensure a continued major presence serving the offshore supply industry.

Lowestoft, which is owned and operated by Associated British Ports, has no comparable grand scheme of physical expansion — but remains confident in its ability to develop present strengths in general cargo handling, a substantial fishing base and a centre for specialist activities such as offshore structures, ship repair and a base for a growing fleet of tugs. The port handles some 5000 vessel movements each year, with a growing trend towards recreational craft using the newly-rebuilt Yacht Basin. Lowestoft is well placed to serve feeder routes to the Continent, and offers extensive storage and warehousing facilities, as well as modern handling equipment. There has been recent investment in railway freight facilities alongside the harbour, and the port boasts a purpose-built container terminal, equipped with two park-gantry cranes and extensive

The sea has been a source of many livelihoods to the families who live along the coast. And, of course, a source of great tragedy too. Without the courage and skill of Norfolk's lifeboatmen the loss of life would have been much greater.

More than 29 vessels have been totally lost since 1900 and incident of the Dutch tanker Georgia which ran aground and broke in two on the Haisbro' Sands on the November 21st 1927 illustrates the superlative seamanship and tenacity of the lifeboat crews.

First on the scene was the Great Yarmouth lifeboat the John & Mary Meiklem with Coxswain William Fleming who, before finally giving up the attempt and returning to harbour, had been at sea for 22 hours. Next the Cromer Number One lifeboat, H F Bailey with Coxswain Henry Blogg along with the Number Two lifeboat, Louisa Heartwell, attempted the rescue and, by the time they returned to harbour, had spent a total of 28 hours at sea. For their gallantry the RNLI awarded Coxswain Blogg the Gold Medal, Coxswain Fleming the Silver Medal, and members of the crew of the H F Bailey Bronze Medals.

Blogg was, according to the Rev D T Dick, "Cromer's greatest son", and the legendary lifeboat coxswain is justly celebrated as one of Norfolk's bravest men.

But Coxswain Blogg, a man of few words, would always play down his role. Cmdr T G Michelmore, a former chief inspector of lifeboats recalled in a radio programme after Blogg's death in June 1954 one such example. "On his return to Cromer after one particularly gallant rescue, and hearing the church bells ringing to welcome him and his crew he asked: 'What's all this fuss about?'"

**Henry Blogg, GC, BEM: "He was the very embodiment of the spirit of courage of the North Norfolk fishermen." (Lord Templewood)**

Another fine lifeboatman of the century was Coxswain John Swan, who, in common with Blogg and Fleming was awarded the RNLI's highest award, the Gold Medal.

One of the century's most moving stories happened off Caister on November 14th 1901 when the lifeboat Beauchamp was overwhelmed by a gale. The disaster cost nine lifeboatmen their lives and left 44 children fatherless. James 'Ol' Jimmy' Haylett help rescue three survivors. But the sea had taken its toll, including Ol' Jimmy's son and one of his grandsons.

At the subsequent inquest, the coroner asked if the crew had given up the rescue and were returning. Ol' Jimmy's words in reply that "going back is against the rules" were subsequently embroidered to create the lifeboat service's most stirring phrase: Caister men never turn back.

hardstanding. The terminal handles a variety of modern cargo vessels and more than 250,000 tonnes of import/export traffic each year. Shipments include paper, timber, steel, machinery and containerised cargo. Specialist timber imports are handled on the south side of the harbour for the waterside joinery plant of Boulton and Paul. A silo complex on the North Quay has been refitted to handle grain and cement, with storage facilities of 10,000 tonnes and 4000 tonnes respectively. Aggregates and fertiliser shipments are also handled. There is a 76-metre dry dock and a number of slipways.

The port is also home to the Shell Expro supply base for gas exploration and production in the Southern North Sea, and there is a substantial local fleet of oil rig safety vessels.

**PAT MIDGLEY, MBE, is a retired teacher. She and her family moved to Norfolk from Oxfordshire in 1968. In 1987 she retired from teaching and began to research the North End fishing community of King's Lynn. In the same year she formed a small group of fisherfolk to save and restore the last remaining fishermen's yard in the town. True's Yard Fishing Heritage Museum opened in 1991. It quickly became apparent that the collection had outgrown the facilities and she made a successful application to the National Lottery to purchase, and restore, the adjoining building. The extension was officially opened by Sir Paul and Lady Getty in 1998. In 1997 she was awarded the MBE for services to the fishing community and in 1998 was made a Paul Harris Fellow of Rotary International for service to the community.**

The vast coastline of Norfolk with its three ports of Yarmouth, Wells and King's Lynn has supported numerous communities who made their living from the sea. These include Lynn, Brancaster, Wells, Blakeney, Cley, Weybourne, East and West Runton, Sheringham, Cromer, Overstrand, Mundesley, Bacton, Caister and Yarmouth. In an effort to control the fishery at the end of the last century the Eastern Sea Fisheries Joint Committee was formed. Today, the area covered by it stretches from Donna Nook in Lincolnshire to Dovercourt in Suffolk. The present Lynn fishing industry is probably the largest in Norfolk and, in common with other industries, has been affected by the developing technology of the twentieth century.

Major advances in technology such as the change from sail to steam and improved navigation and fish finding equipment have steadily altered the methods of fishing throughout the whole of the century. Although the Wash fisheries are now mainly concerned with shellfish, the fluctuation of the catch has always been a problem with periods of boom and bust and the uncertainties continue to this day.

The weather still plays an important part but there are many other factors affecting the industry. The traditional small boats are gradually giving way to larger vessels, the introduction of dredging the shellfish from the sands where previously the cockles were handraked at low tide mean that larger quantities can be taken in a much shorter period. Pollution of the waters has become a problem which, in turn, has led to the introduction of more and more stringent regulations of the catch. The effect of increasing control from the EEC since the introduction of the Common Fisheries Policy in 1983 remains uncertain.

Few of the great traditional fishing families of Lynn, many of whom can be traced back to the reign of the first Queen Elizabeth, actively pursue the fishery today. Times have changed since the Lynn Election Petition of 1911 against the successful candidate Holcombe Ingleby when it was stated that he had bribed the electorate by holding picnics on his estate on July 23rd 1910 for more than 300 fishermen and, on the second day for 450 dock porters and longshoremen.

Today both industries employ a fraction of those numbers. Other traditions have also long gone. The Fishermen's Regatta held annually was an event which took over the River Ouse. The men would be up before dawn to prepare their boats and great rivalry took place to win the cup.

Many of the men did not return to fishing after serving in the forces in both world wars. These included virtually the whole of the Lynn Naval Reserve in the First World War when the three cruisers the Aboukir, Cressey and Hogue on which they served were sunk by a German U-9 submarine commanded by Kapitanleutnant Otto Weddigen on September 22nd 1914. The actions of Weddigen changed the conduct of war at sea. Previously it had been traditional for ships assisting in saving survivors to be spared but as the stricken Aboukir was sinking, first the Hogue and then the Cressey were torpedoed in turn as they frantically tried to pick up the men in the sea. A total of 1495 officers and men from the three ships were lost that day.

Those that survived, and many others returning after the war, had seen a different life and preferred to work on land. The hard

**The great Worfolk family built more than 660 vessels at King's Lynn in their long career. Many of the wooden boats built by them over the century have been restored and survive as leisure craft. Walter Worfolk and his family came to Lynn from Stainforth near Doncaster in 1899. His wife was the niece of William Lancaster, the landlord of the Hulk in Bridge Street. Both his sons, Gerald (pictured left, 1891-1981) and William (right, 1894-1994) married local girls and followed their father into the tradition of boatbuilding. Sadly, the boatbuilding tradition (apart from one small company) in the town has now ceased.**

existence working the dangerous and unpredictable waters of the Wash has always demanded a high price in injury and loss of life. On January 6th 1928 the fishing smack the Mystery sank in a gale off Heacham and three brothers; Percy, Jim and Matthew Smith, along with their friend Earl Massingham were lost. It was said that the old North End fishing quarter was never the same again after the loss of so many young men.

The shortage of manpower during the difficult years of the Second World War meant that many old men stepped into the breach and kept the vessels fishing. For example, according to a 1946 Ministry of Agriculture, Fisheries and Food Report, one old man of 79 commanded an inshore motor trawler of 35ft with a crew aged 73, 65, 56 and 51, having chosen them of a certain age, he said, "so that none of them would be called up." Another seventy-year-old skipper, asked by one of the Ministry's officers, how he was getting on replied: "Well Sir, not too good. Young Harry has joined the Navy and I have to take my uncle aboard, and he is 83 and not so nippy about the deck as I am."

Until the end of the nineteenth century the port of Lynn had been controlled by a number of organisations but, following the wreck of the Wick Bay which ran aground near Daseley's Beacon in December 1889 and prevented the navigation of other ships using the port, it became urgent that some sort of overall control and responsibility for navigation should be introduced. In 1898 the King's Lynn Conservancy Act of 1897 was passed to safeguard the river. The Board was to deal with lights, beacons, buoys, tolls and the removal of wrecks. (Local ratepayers faced a bill amounting £20,000 which, incidentally, the Council did not finally redeem until 1947).

To ensure that vessels may safely negotiate the narrow, twisting approach channel, which is subject to strong tidal streams, siltation and exposed to severe weather conditions, pilotage is compulsory for all vessels in excess of 35m LOA. It is interesting to note that recent research in Town Hall archives has shown that Lynn was the earliest place in the country to control pilotage (July 1736) and, at that time, nine 'Pylots' with their vessels had to be at sea at all times to bring ships into port.

Although one berth in the harbour, South Quay Six, is still used for grain cargoes all other traffic is through the docks which are owned by Associated British Ports, larger vessels use the new Riverside Quay, which was opened in 1992. Cargoes are mainly: grain, soya, fertiliser, animal feed, steel, stone, petroleum products, timber and scrap. Total tonnage is around one million tonnes annually carried in 600-700 shipments. The size of the vessels has greatly increased, from 84 metres in 1984 to a Volga class vessel of 140 metres which berthed at the Riverside Quay.

The arrival of gas and electricity for central heating and power, plus the railways, led to the demise of the big barges which were such a familiar sight along the coast of Norfolk with their cargoes of coal. Vessels such as the Mavis of Hull (later to become a fishing boat skippered by Frank Castleton), were regular visitors to the town. Lynn, due to its geographical location, was ideally placed to receive such cargoes. The coal would be off-loaded on to the lighters and shipped down river into the hinterland of the town. This trade has virtually ceased.

**RICHARD BATSON, 44, is a Norwich-born journalist who reaches 25 years service with the EDP in the year 2000. The (Eaton) City of Norwich School old boy worked all around the county at King's Lynn, Dereham, Swaffham, Diss and Yarmouth as well as spells in his home city at head office. He took his current role as chief reporter at Cromer in 1992 – and has settled on it as "the best place in the county to live and work".**

Fishing is woven into the rich fabric of seaside life in North Norfolk. Generations of local families have earned a living from harvesting the sea – sons following fathers into a harsh workplace through tradition, expectation, and a love of the independent lifestyle. A man and his boat hunting his prey; working alongside, and sometimes against, the natural elements. It is a basic human quest for food as old as mankind itself.

Tourists and trippers have enjoyed the industry's time-honoured trappings and its crops. Visitors to North Norfolk love beachcombing amongst the fleets of little boats lined up on the sands alongside their trusty rusty tractor tugs and piles of pots. They love tucking into a tasty crustacean as part of their seaside sojourn. Artists and photog-raphers satisfy their insatiable appetite for pictures among the atmospheric colours and

**Lynn Fisher Fleet, around 1910.**

shapes of the tools of the trade - with flint-faced cottages, scenic seascapes and harbours as a dramatic backdrop. But these are not "stage prop" trimmings for the tourists. They are still part of a working cottage industry that has been adjusting to a changing world, despite its timeless appearance.

Shapes of most of the fishing boats have stayed as constant as the shapes of the seafood they catch. The evolution has come in manpower, markets and machinery - with fewer fishermen using more efficient boats to haul as many pots and lines as ever, and finding fresh outlets for their products - with transport, refrigeration and factory processing forging links with the powerful ally of the supermarket shelf. Now the fishing industry in North Norfolk is reaching the palates of families all over the country, as well as the palettes of painters drawn to its shores.

At the last turn of the century the North Norfolk coast was riding high on the roller coaster of a tourism boom. Cromer was already a select watering hole - but the combination of the coming of the railways, and the newspaper writings of Clement Scott praising "Poppyland", brought the crowds flocking to once-quiet fishing towns and villages. The influx of trains and people also signalled a new era for the fishing industry, which had long supplied just local demand with its short-shelflife seafood that needed eating soon after it came ashore.

The rail transport meant fresh fish and shellfish could reach large local markets - such as Lowestoft, Norwich and Yarmouth - for the first time, so demand soared. There was also extra local demand from tourists pouring in from urban London and the Midlands wanting seafood as part of their seaside experience.

At the twentieth century began there were

around 250 boats working the area, as the fishing industry enjoyed its heyday, with Sheringham the "capital" with 100 boats to Cromer's fifty. But the tourism boom also led to a building boom. And its ripples washed across traditional fisher families, starting to break the mould of local life as opportunities widened beyond the fishing industry.

People whose lives were interwoven inextricably with the centuries-old pattern of going to sea began to see other sidelines and careers over the horizon. Some found it lucrative to hire out their homes to holiday families; others drifted away from the sea, preferring the less risky, all-year-round income of other jobs created in the wake of the awakening tourism industry – particularly in the building trade at a time when new hotels were springing up along the coast.

The drift was more pronounced at Sheringham, which began the century with a biggest fleet but has now been overtaken by crabbing capital Cromer. Some found different financial spin-offs from the holiday heydays – running pleasure boat trips, and hiring beach equipment from chairs and costumes to bathing tents windbreaks. At the turn of the last century fishermen made up a large slice of the local population – more than 500 men and boys between the two towns of Sheringham

Eastern Daily Press

5 a.m. Edition

No. 25,570 NORWICH, MONDAY, FEBRUARY 2, 1953 Price 2d.



NORFOLK GALE DISASTER

100 MISSING AND DEAD

Seas' Wild Rush into Towns and Villages

AT LEAST 100 PEOPLE ARE REPORTED MISSING OR DEAD IN FLOODS ALONG THE NORFOLK COAST, WHICH STARTED WITH SATURDAY NIGHT'S GALES AND HIGH SEAS. MANY HAVE BEEN RENDERED HOMELESS. THESE ARE THE WORST FLOODS WITHIN LIVING MEMORY IN THIS PART OF THE COUNTRY. BY LAST NIGHT 39 BODIES HAD BEEN RECOVERED ALONG THE COAST BETWEEN KING'S LYNN AND HUNSTANTON.

The worst flood centres are:—

HUNSTANTON.—It was reported unofficially this morning that 40 people, including many Americans, might have been drowned. Twelve bodies have been recovered, including those of three Americans and a child. Most of the bungalows between Hunstanton and Heacham, principally occupied by American families, were swept away. Salt water entered the town's water mains and the supply was cut off. It was also stated unofficially today that 20 might have been killed at Snettisham.

KING'S LYNN.—Fifteen bodies have been recovered. Between 1000 and 1500 people have been evacuated from South Lynn housing estate, where the houses are standing in several feet of water. Part of the town's electricity supply has been cut off.

SEA PALLING.—The sea broke through a 100-yard gap in the dunes, washing away houses and causing the deaths of seven people, including three children. Some of the inhabitants in the bungalows were still refusing to leave their homes.

**Floods of tears: How the EDP reported the century's worst floods in 1953.**

Floods have cost Norfolk dear during the century. But none were as bad at the terrible storms of January 31st 1953 when a huge gale made a deadly combination with an abnormally high tide.

The two factors meant that sea defences were exposed as pitifully inadequate, with breaches all along the coast. Bungalows were swept away, streets inundated and other buildings smashed by the waves. One hundred people lost their lives in the county and more than 5000 homes were damaged. Lynn was the first place in the county to suffer, seeing a predicted 22ft 9in tide actually reach an astonishing 31ft, flooding a fifth of the town and killing 13 people.

Along the coast it was even worse: 32 died at Hunstanton and Heacham, including many members of the families of US servicemen billeted in the area. Salthouse, Snettisham, Cley, Sheringham, Sea Palling, Lowestoft and Yarmouth were also badly affected. The Yarmouth situation was made worse by the town's exposed situation on a spit of land. More than 3500 homes were flooded and nine people lost their lives when a wall of water six feet high poured through the town's streets. The clearing-up and coastal defence strengthening operations for the area took years, costing untold millions of pounds in today's terms and were a devastating blow to a country only just emerging from post-war hardship. But the many tales of heroism from that dreadful night made people realise that, though the loss of life was on a terrible scale, it could have been much worse.

By contrast, the death toll in 1978 was in single figures, thanks to the stronger coast defences and better warning systems in place. Places as far inland as Wisbech were affected. At Lynn more than sixty patients had to be evacuated as the flood reached the London Road area of the town. And families were evacuated from seafront houses at Hunstanton, Burnham Overy Staithe and Blakeney.

Hundreds of caravans and beach huts were swept away at Heacham and Snettisham. Off Lowestoft a Greek coaster went down, costing several lives.

And one of the saddest property losses was the destruction of the much-loved Hunstanton pier. It has never been rebuilt.

**Cockling on the sandbanks of the Wash in September 1974. The old hand-raking from small boats is now being supplanted by larger vessels using dredging to harvest the shellfish.**

and Cromer alone. A survey in 1913 shows Sheringham still had 75 boats to Cromer's 25.

Today there are still around 100 boats in the whole area – with Cromer and Wells the main centres, backed up by boats at Blakeney, Cley, Salthouse, Weybourne, Sheringham, the Runtons, Overstrand, Trimingham, Mundesley, and Bacton all communities long associated with fishing. A major sea change has come in the areas of efficiency, patterns of working, and outlets for the harvest of the local seas. Fishing has always been an industry ruled by nature and the seasons. But in the early part of the twentieth century the pattern of prey was different.

Today's main catches of crab and lobster were just a sideline, sandwiched between seasonal lining for cod and drifting for herring. The crustaceans came to the fore as over-fishing to meet rising demand killed off stocks of cod and herring. Crab and lobster now flourish year-round on a chalky, flinty seabed littered with wrecks. Ironically they are at their lowest ebb during the height of the tourist demand in August when they scuttle off to shed their shells and breed in rocky "wurry holes".

Herring stocks have since recovered but the market is much reduced. Cod stocks have surged again – to the joy of beach fishermen – but are no long a major quarry for the local fishing boats. Traditional double-ended clinker-built crab boats – whose shape mirrors ancient Viking longboats – had lug sails and oars before the first motorised vessel was introduced by Sheringham's Robert Emery in 1914. Sheringham's early century dominance went hand-in-hand with its role as the major boat-building centre. Museums in the town house a boat and tools which are testimony to skills which saw craftsmen such as Lewis "Buffalo" Emery build boats by eye rather than to any pre-drawn plans.

Motorisation however was originally too expensive for many fishermen – so the move into the engine-driven era was gradual rather than overnight. But it signalled the start of mechanisation, which brought increased efficiency to an industry which previously relied on the powerful arms and gnarled hands of its men of steel. Heavy engines however meant boats, once light enough to carry up the beach using their oars, had to be hauled by winches – and later tractors on beaches whose slope and surface allowed.

Hydraulic haulers introduced in the mid-Sixties meant the declining fleet of boats could bring in more pots than when hundreds of vessels were working at sea. Two-man crews can today effectively haul, empty and re-bait some 6000 pots a year in North Norfolk, compared with 4000 a century earlier, records reveal. Boat design has changed little, but materials have, with today's fleet more fibre glass than wood. More efficient, escape-proof "parlour pots", and electronic navigation systems have also made a hard job a little easier for the fishermen.

Fishing is a vulnerable industry at the best of times, held to ransom by powers outside its control, normally weather and nature, giving rise to rollercoaster good and bad days, months and years. But man-made disasters such as strikes and war have also put troughs in its graph of twentieth-century fortunes. The General Strike of 1926 took away lifeline rail links, meaning catches had to be sold in local markets using trucks, badly hitting incomes.

Between the two world wars there were fishery problems as the nation kept up its defences and military training. Bombing ranges at Weybourne had a major impact on the grounds – hitting the freedom to fish, as shown by a 1936 audit of landings which saw 26,690 more crab at Cromer, and just another 4832 at Sheringham, which was nearer the target area. During the Second World War the industry was hit hard, with fishermen called up to Service, blackouts for night boats, and a 1942 directive switching fishermen to farmwork, a decision which was later partially overturned following a protest.

Whelks were a victim of changing trends and tastes. Wells and Sheringham's whelking industries saw wagon-loads of the shellfish dispatched by rail and road to London and other markets. The shellfish was originally caught just as fishing bait.

But it struggled from the mid-Twenties as prices plummeted, and crabs took over the

**North Norfolk fishermen check their pots are in good order at the end of another busy day during the crab season.**

whelk grounds, and modern tastes, widened by foreign holidays, saw tourists demanding something more sophisticated than cockles, winkles and whelks. There was a brief whelking revival this decade when the sea snail's feet became a popular aphrodisiac in Korea, but the bubble burst when the Far East economic collapse saw demand plummet before it could have any lasting benefit to local fisheries.

But the fishing industry is hardy by nature and it has continued despite the hurdles put in its way. Fishing families are like limpets on a rock when it comes to prising them from their traditional livelihoods. An equally tough link to break is the expectation they would man the local lifeboats like their forebears.

The rescue connection, so closely intertwined with the local fishing fraternity, exists today – though the service is gearing up to train coming generations of recruits drawn from non-seafaring backgrounds as the size of the fisher fleets and families decline nationally.

Another tradition which is also dying out is families giving sons their father's first names, which spawned shoals of colourful nicknames added to avoid confusion. Alas, the days of people called Shrimp, Tuna, Downtide, Joyful, Teapot, Fatty, Gofather, Nuts and Squinter will die out when they do.

The seasons also traditionally brought a winter lull for fishermen. Offshore boats, such as those working out of Wells, keep pots going all year. But the inshore men still tend to stop in the winter as lower water temperatures drive the crabs further out to sea. Today some are forced to find other work, such as building, or face the dole queue until nature brings a new crop to harvest in the sea.

A winter ritual at Sheringham in the first half of the century was flint picking off the beaches, a useful out-of-season income for many fishermen and their families. The stones were milled down for use by Stoke potteries, and needed an army of people putting stones into boxes and buggies. It was a nice little sideline for them during the close season, and continued until the Sixties, when the council realised it was harming the town's sea defences.

Fishery protection work has continued throughout the century. Early measures controlled crab sizes to preserve stocks for current generations. Similar restrictions today have the general support of the local fishermen who realise protecting young and breeding stock is vital to sustaining the industry into the future. The year 2000 is signalling a fresh clampdown on shellfish sizes aimed at preserving stocks into the new millennium.

Good news for North Norfolk was that the Cromer crab was singled out for special attention. There were fears a blanket European minimum size would hit the fishery hard, but bureaucrats have recognised the Cromer species as being smaller than the European average and have given it a special size limit – without a fight. Short-term bad news is a tighter lobster restriction which could hit income for some local boats. The move is necessary to protect a population, whose trend towards younger breeding females, is a sign of pressure if not crisis.

Fishermen are, however, finding more and more people muscling into their "manor". Pipelines, cables, windfarms, and aggregate dredging have made inroads into areas where fishing boats had free rein for centuries. Consultation and compensation has improved but there are still fears that big business can get away with doing more environmental damage offshore, out of sight of landlubber officials. High-profile recent battles have centred on fighting dredging threats, which began in the Seventies and escalated through to the Nineties with millions of tonnes of offshore seabed sand being sucked up for sea defences.

The biggest storm came in 1994 when fishermen battled to beat off plans for new dredging at the Race Bank north of Wells to shore up Lincolnshire's coastline. Fishermen feared the plume of disturbed sand would have choked crab and fish breeding grounds – and the local fishing industry along with it.

They won the day and current fisheries minister Elliot Morley says his department, which also controls dredging and coast defences, says it will not grant dredging licences if there is a threat to fishery grounds. Fishermen however, who have seen changes of ministers result in changes of minds, are keeping up their vigilance against the dredging threat, according to North Norfolk Fishermen's Association chairman Ivan Large, who says the fishery is best protected by minimal ministerial interference and best left to regulate itself.

The minister however says the stability of the North Norfolk fishery, compared with decline in other parts of the country, is encouraging, along with a growing reputation for the area producing quality seafood now reaching a wider audience. The North Norfolk fishery has long fed two markets. There is a local demand, heightened during the holiday season, especially for crab bought from quaint front window-style shops.

But there is now a factory-led market reaching farther afield. Time was when the factories were a dumping ground, with rock-bottom prices, for leftover products which ended up as crab paste. Now they are a major area for growth, providing major and growing employment for an industry which is at best stable after a century of decline. The factories have added supermarket, catering and export potential on to a local market that has little room for growth.

Few modern-day families, used to convenience foods, know how to dress a crab. They demand healthy food, ready to eat or cook, from a source where food hygiene with

**Just as the West family have been associated with Sheringham fishing for generations, so the Davies name has been inextricably linked with Cromer. This picture, taken in February 1975 shows J J Davies and his grandson John. John's father – and sixth-generation fisherman – Richard is typical of the fiercely independent race of beach boat men proud that they work hard for a living. He has been connected with the family business all his life, and opened his famous wet fish shop with wife Julie in Garden Street 25 years ago.**
**Richard, 55 just before Christmas 1999, has also been coxswain of the lifeboat for 23 years, taking over from his second cousin Henry 'Shrimp' Davies in 1976 – and combining the two roles like many generations before him. He is also a well-known as an exponent of clog-style dancing imported into Cromer by visiting fisherfolk – but which he has pushed into the wings "since Riverdance really showed what can be done". He and son John caused a stir when they introduced a modern catamaran-style boat to Cromer beach working alongside the traditional double-ended boats – but it could be the shape of things to come.**

a potentially volatile product is guaranteed and done through a supermarket label. But getting on to the shelves of chain store supermarkets across the country only came in the Eighties.

The breakthrough was made by the Cromer Crab Company, started by two local fishermen John Williams and Reg Parkin who were selling shellfish in local pubs and saw scope for more outlets. In 1985 the factory, which takes a blend of local and imported shellfish, got frozen products into the major stores, followed by chilled ones in 1992. It is now poised to expand to a new factory adding another 165 jobs to the existing 100, and looking at ready-to-cook chilled products such as crab cocktail and mayonnaise.

Its sister factory at Sheringham, Norfolk Shellfish, specialises in supplying caterers, and also exports more than half its output to countries around the world including Spain, France, Greece, Italy and Portugal. It has also grown from a dozen to fifty workers since it was founded in 1982 by Frank Dankester. A fifth of the factories' supplies come from local beach boats, and a quarter from a growing fleet of bigger offshore boats working farther out to sea.

Health and hygiene regulations, which go hand-in-hand with the modern fish trade, can be a bone of contention among fishermen who point out a Cromer crab never killed anyone. But they are here to stay and have helped get the catches into the supermarkets, as bureaucrats try to strike a balance between public safety and not penalising a cottage industry, says Mr Morley. And the inshore crab and lobster fisheries escape relatively lightly in the red-tape jungle, compared with their deep water colleagues.

Public confidence in seafood is crucial. A shellfish poisoning scare off Scotland in recent years had the same kind of devastating effect across the industry as the salmonella in eggs and mad cow beef crises. Even though the problem was at the other end of the country, the North Norfolk fishery suffered from plummeting prices for several seasons, until the storm blew over. New shellfish hygiene standards in 1993 hit an already much-reduced fishery for oysters, mussels and cockles in North Norfolk. It meant only the very best products could be sold direct to the public without cleaning and cooking treatment. It coincided with a minor pollution problem at Blakeney harbour, which has meant big equipment investment for the handful of mussel producers left in a port which had 100 vessels a century ago. Other threats over the years have included lobster fishing by "cowboy" divers and hobby fishermen, imports of Russian tinned crab, and clampdowns on using crab meat bait in lobster pots.

Modern-day pressures on the North Norfolk fishing industry have been identified in a report prepared by the district council's economic development officers. The council was concerned that the independent and disjointed collection of fishermen along the coast had not voiced their problems very well over recent years. It highlighted fishermen's frustrations at feeling second-class citizens to "incomers" – eloquent second-home owners, and retired folk, raising planning objections to expansions of time-honoured fishery businesses. Newcomers complaining about the sounds and smells of country industries are not new – but the council is now trying to ensure their comments are balanced against the need to preserve and grow a local industry, which lands £1.6m worth of catches a year, and generates £10 million worth of income along with more than 400 jobs. An industry which has dominated North Norfolk's towns, villages, landscape and lifestyle for centuries is continuing its evolution, with the supermarket revolution offering a pot of higher prices at the end of its rainbow, although it is a prospect which sees fishermen sharpening the claws of their natural scepticism.

Cromer fisherman Richard Davies has seen the number of inshore boats on the local beach double in the past thirty years, and says families are making a good living from the sea. Local boats supplied both the cottage and factory markets, and the growth of the factories was a help, he added.

And if anyone questions the cost of the crab on their dinner plate, there is a stark answer from his relation, old timer "Shrimp" Davies. He has lost two brothers, two cousins and three good friends in fishing drowning accidents over his 85-year lifetime in the kind of seafaring accidents that can still happen today despite all the latest maritime technology.

"That," says the phlegmatic former fisherman, "is the price of crabs."

## Chapter 12

# *Social affairs*

No century has changed the lives of Norfolk people more comprehensively than the twentieth - for better or, some would say, for worse. The quality of life has improved beyond all imagining. Norfolk people are better off, better educated and in better health than ever before. At the same time, however, local government has moved steadily further away from the parishes, where it used to reside, and many village shops, pubs and schools have disappeared.

Old photographs, which provide a keyhole through which we peep at the past, give the impression of a sepia-tinged county of trees, hedgerows, horses, carriages and traffic-free country lokes. A society in which the pace of life was mercifully so much slower than it is today. But it is the viewer who applies the colour by wearing the rose-tinted spectacles of nostalgia. Take them off and you see the blemishes. The personal memories of our senior citizens are often selective. They tend to discard the more discomforting recollections of grinding rural poverty, drudgery and disease in the undemocratic society which was rural life before the Second World War.

Take a closer look at any old photograph of a village school. The girls and boys had been dressed by their mothers in the best clothes the family could afford, even if they were only "hand-me-downs" passed on by older, and larger, siblings. A right to elementary education had been enshrined in the Education Act of 1870, but village schools, often run by the Church through local boards of governors, offered little more than the basic four Rs - Reading, 'Ritin', 'Rithmatic and Religion - and not necessarily in that order!

Education, it was believed, only gave working-class children expectations which they had little hope of fulfilling. Working people knew their place. What prospect could they realistically anticipate other than a working life on the land?

Yet agriculture was in recession, wages were low, and for those who had no work there was little alternative but to throw themselves on the charity of the parish. For many proud families poverty was a reason for shame, and the thought of accepting charity, in the form of the spartan existence offered by the workhouse, was almost too awful to contemplate.

Almost all aspects of daily life were administered via the parish, and some workhouses had already been functioning for almost 200 years when the Poor Law Amendment Act of 1834 enabled parishes to link up in 'unions' to appoint a board of guardians for a shared workhouse. In the early years these Poor Law Unions, numbering around 25 across Norfolk, varied in size from 21 parishes in Guiltcross (South Norfolk) to sixty in Mitford and Launditch (Dereham area).

Workhouse accommodation was sanctioned by the Poor Law Commissioners and the number of places available for paupers varied from 150 at Gayton to 450 at Docking. The work ethic had been almost a religion for the Victorians who saw their "houses of industry" as being no place for idlers. Paupers were expected to work for such meagre charity as was dispensed, and to be punished if that work was not done.

The sexes were rigorously kept apart, and the cruelty of splitting families is vividly illustrated in the recollections of Sidney B Smith, who was one of a family of orphans admitted in 1900 to the Loddon and Clavering

**TONY CLARKE was born at Attleborough and educated at Thetford and Bungay Grammar Schools. He joined the Norfolk News Company in 1954, working in Thetford, Norwich and Wymondham. More than forty years with Norfolk's newspapers were interrupted only by National Service in the RAF and a three-year spell as assistant editor of Navy News, based in Portsmouth (1969-1972). He was chief reporter at the ECN branch office at Beccles for 25 years up to 1997. Married with three children and five grandchildren, his previous books include Sea of Memories, the story of friend Stan Smith's career in the Royal Navy, and Mighta Bin Wuss, Tales of the Boy Jimma.**

Union's workhouse at Heckingham where he stayed until 1907.

*"The institution was a large establishment divided with the males on one side and the females on the other,"* he later wrote. *"Frank was in another wing so I was all alone as far as my brother and sisters were concerned. My recollections of the Union are very unhappy. To be separated from my loved ones was terrible. I played with a dozen or so boys during the day and my school work kept my mind occupied, but I cried myself to sleep night after night.*

*"Most of the inmates of the institution were there because of unfortunate economic conditions; some were ne'er-do-wells and others were moronic, able only to do simple chores but unable to take care of themselves. Many had chosen the seamy side of life and were alcoholics or perverts of the worst kind who had a very sinister influence on the young boys who were forced into their company."*

By 1962, when Mr Smith returned from his home in Canada to revisit the scene of his unhappy childhood, it had become Hales Hospital.

Workhouses were formally designated as poor law institutions in 1913, but even though the Local Government Act of 1929 abolished unions and boards of guardians, and encouraged local authorities to take over these poor law institutions as hospitals, a bleak atmosphere lingered over them for many years in the minds of Norfolk people.

Workhouses finally disappeared in the 1948 National Assistance Act which provided that "the existing poor law shall cease to have effect". Norfolk County Council inherited the responsibility for providing residential accommodation for all persons who needed it "whether by reason of age, infirmity or any other circumstances", and to provide temporary accommodation for people in urgent need. By 1958 the county council had enough homes to provide 883 beds.

The 1948 Act also made the county council responsible for maintaining and supervising children and young people who had no parents or whose parents could not provide them with a home. Ten years after the Act the county council had two nurseries, seven children's homes, a hostel for girls aged between 15 and 18, and a boys' remand home at Bramerton.

In 1970 the county council's welfare work was combined in the new social services department which had a budget of £2.3 million in its first year, including £1 million for homes for the elderly and infirm. Twelve years later care for the elderly accounted for almost sixty per cent of the department's £31 million budget. In 1987 the department had 800 children and more than 1750 elderly people to look after, as well as its responsibilities towards blind people and those who had mental or physical disabilities. In the Nineties rising costs have forced the county council to close or re-group some of its smaller and less cost-effective homes while the private sector has taken increasing responsibility for looking after Norfolk's older generation.

Meanwhile, some of the old workhouses, by contrast with their original function, became highly desirable residential developments while others were turned into museums, farm buildings or offices. Some of the Poor Law Unions left another legacy - their colourful and ancient names. Wayland, Forehoe and Henstead, Mitford and Launditch, Depwade, Loddon and Clavering all dated back into the mists of history as ancient administrative areas known as "hundreds". They still featured as the names of rural districts whose councils disappeared in the massive reorganisation of local government in 1974.

For much of Queen Victoria's reign county administration in Norfolk had been largely in the hands of the Church or unelected justices of the peace. It is tempting to suggest that the emphasis placed by the Victorians on discipline is revealed by the fact that the formation of a Norfolk Constabulary in 1839 pre-dates the advent of universal elementary education by 31 years!

In fact, the law enforcers were pounding the Norfolk beat fifty years before the birth of a more or less democratically-elected county council. The phrase "more or less" is appropriate here because the authoritarian nature of Victorian life overflowed into the twentieth century and a huge proportion of the population, including the female half, was still denied the vote.

Norfolk County Council had been founded in 1889 to administer such services as road and bridge maintenance, public health and sanitation over an area excluding the city of Norwich and the boroughs of King's Lynn, Great Yarmouth and Thetford. But what sort of a county was it at the turn of the century? Steam engines and a few primitive motor cars were frightening the horses on Norfolk's country roads, and the railways were only just beginning to realise their potential for carrying people and freight long distances.

For most country people, however, the only means of transport were their own legs, and journeys outside their self-sufficient villages were major undertakings. Even the horrors of the First World War provoked few improvements to their lives during the recession-hit Twenties and Thirties, despite the sad memorials erected by every proud village to commemorate a lost generation. It was not until after the second war that the pace of change began to quicken. Norfolk villages were still without electricity or mains sewerage, the privy being at the bottom of the garden. Even in a town such as Thetford as late as the Fifties the local newspaper reported a road accident involving the "night soil cart", a malodorous though very necessary vehicle which toured the town emptying the pail closets which were the only sanitary provision which most households possessed.

We tend to look back on the Norfolk "privy" with some affection. But that same old selective memory masks the nauseous reality of a world in which, at the dawn of the twentieth century, diseases such as typhoid, scarlet fever, diptheria and smallpox were a fact of life - and death. In 1921 district councils, who ran their own primitive "fever hospitals", rejected as too costly a county council plan to build an isolation hospital at Dereham to serve the whole county.

After 17 years of procrastination it was not actually built until 1938, after which it treated all contagious diseases except smallpox for which part of the old Walsingham workhouse was set aside in the event of an outbreak.

In 1908, when Norfolk County Council appointed its first medical officers of health, both for the adult population and for schools, the main killer was consumption (tuberculosis). Throughout the Twenties and Thirties, Norfolk waged war on tuberculosis with the aid of special treatment at the Norfolk and Norwich Hospital and residential sanatoria at Stanninghall - where the British Red Cross Society bought a 700-acre estate for the county's use - Kelling and elsewhere.

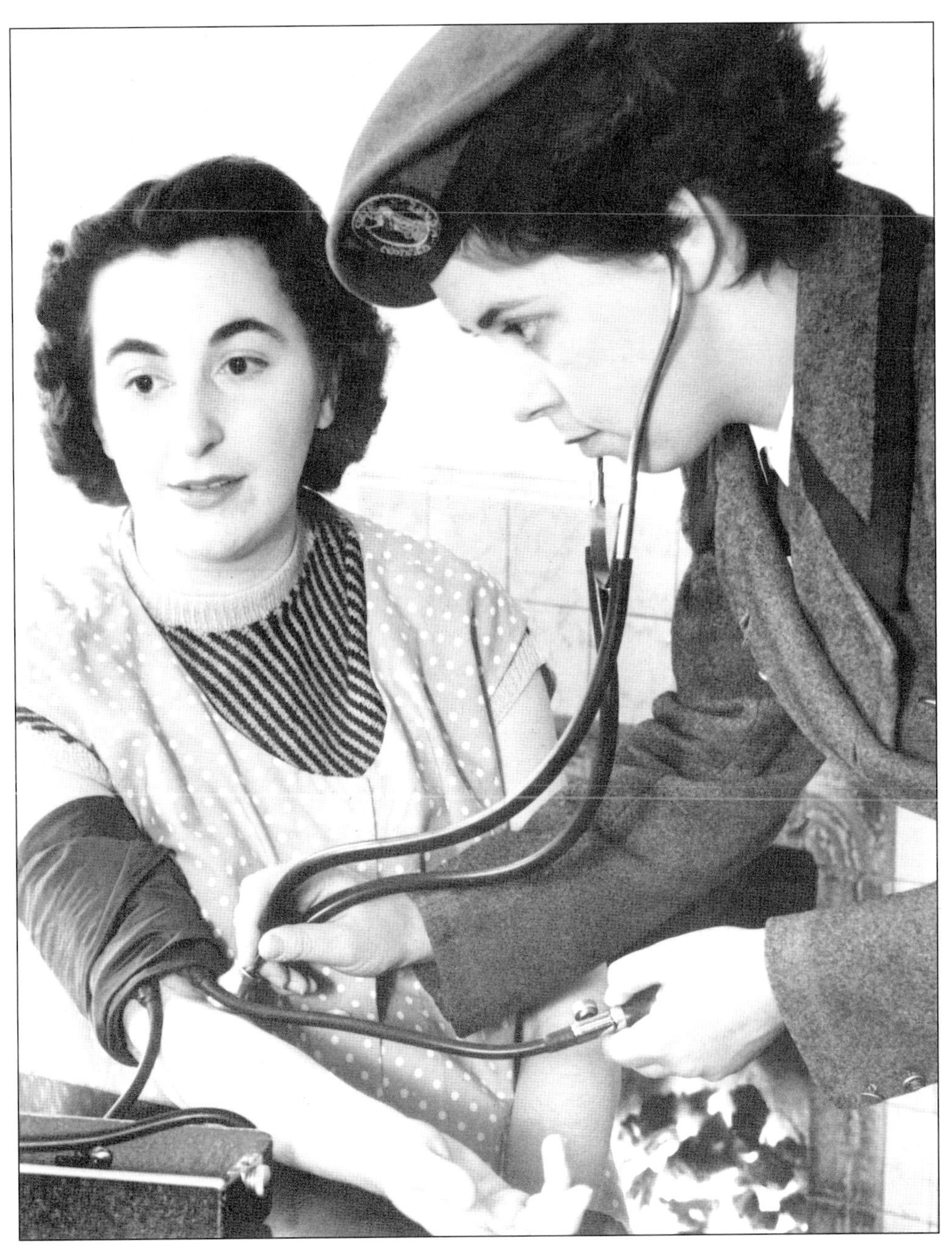

**Help for mothers-to-be had been put on a firmer footing with the Midwives Act of 1936. And by the time this picture of a Norfolk district nurse's visit was taken in 1958, the benefits of the National Health Service were making themselves clear.**

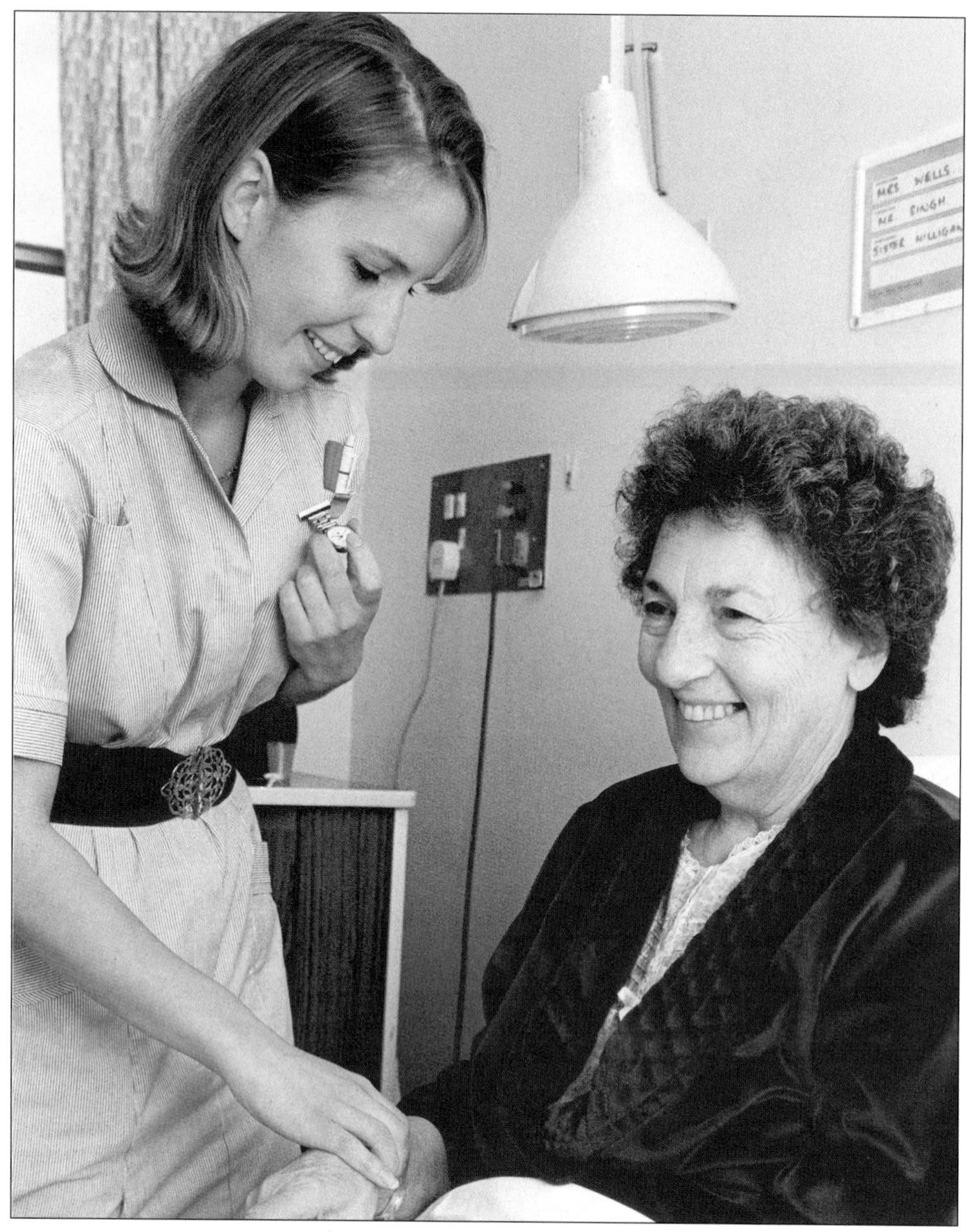

**The NHS may be more than half a century old, and handling sophisticated medical treatments in a way which would have astonished our forebears – but at the core is still the staff-patient relationship. Here staff nurse Elaine Greig takes the pulse of patient Jean Wells in the surgical ward at the Queen Elizabeth Hospital, King's Lynn.**

Despite the development of a vaccine, TB treatment still accounted for more than £30,000 of county council spending in 1935, the year the Stanninghall centre was sold.

On the threshold of a new and presumably more enlightened millennium it is an odd thought that Norfolk County Council's many responsibilities during the first half of the twentieth century included the management of St Andrew's County Asylum at Thorpe. This forbidding establishment was built in 1814 and had more than 1100 beds in 1930. There was also a "mental deficiency colony" at Little Plumstead Hall. Norfolk people were delivered into the world by midwives employed by the county council. The Midwives Act of 1936 required every parish to be covered by maternity nursing services. On January 1st 1935, the county council took over Melton Lodge, on Marine Parade in Yarmouth. This was an orthopaedic hospital where abnormal feet and dislocated hips were straightened, reducing the need for leg-irons and long periods of residential treatment.

The Education Act of 1918 not only provided for the education of physically and mentally handicapped youngsters, but also made the county council responsible for the health and welfare of all school children.

This must have been a thankless task. There had been a terrific spate of school building in the second half of the nineteenth century and a huge number of those Victorian schools survive today, though some of them have been modernised and many more have been closed and turned into private homes. The problem was that, even before the First World War these school buildings were overcrowded and poorly ventilated, and their sewerage and water supply systems were hardly - well, sanitary.

It would be impossible to estimate the huge sums which Norfolk County Council has spent throughout the twentieth century on the never-ending task of making outdated school buildings habitable. A Norfolk person does not need to be very old to remember schools with outside toilets which froze up and became useless in winter. Before the Second World War village schools were fertile breeding grounds for germs. They frequently closed and sent the children home at the slightest sign of an epidemic. Influenza closed virtually all the county's schools temporarily in 1918.

For elderly Norfolk people the least appealing memories of schooldays may feature the activities of the "nit nurse" or the drastic treatment meted out to sufferers from "the itch" (scabies). The latter involved three days of hot baths and the application of sulphur ointment. The treatment for ringworm was even worse. It involved cropping the hair, applying an ointment and wearing a large cap.

Such was the poverty of many families, especially in the depressed Thirties, that the school nurse often carried jars of "patent food" for distribution to children who were malnourished. The fact that head teachers recorded all illnesses in their school log books enables us to discover that 1929 was an unhealthy year for the pupils at Trimingham. In February more than half of them were absent with 'flu, in May it was mumps, and in July measles kept two-thirds of them at home. It is a wonder they had time to learn anything.

With the world on the brink of the First World War, Norfolk County Council found time to think about children's teeth. Today the word "mobile" has a new meaning to do with pocket-sized telephones, but to a school dentist in 1914 it meant Norfolk's first horse-drawn caravan to be used as a mobile surgery. By 1930 all the six dentists working for the Schools Health Service had their mobiles, and the following year the first motorised turn-out consisted of a trailer towed behind the dentist's car. But the horse-drawn mobiles did a fine job. They were still being used in Cromer and Lynn districts as late as 1938, three years after the service had opened its first "fixed" clinic at Aylsham.

In view of the criticisms which have been levelled at the National Health Service in the last two decades of the century - not least over the low pay of nurses and junior hospital doctors - it is worth remembering that the "baby" which was born in 1948 has served Britain well for half a century. During this time there have been numerous changes in its administration and unprecedented advances in medical and surgical techniques.

In the immediate post-war years an attack of measles could still be fatal, 400 cases of scarlet fever were reported in Norfolk in 1945, vaccinations for smallpox, diptheria and whooping cough were only just becoming commonplace, and as late as 1962 a national outbreak of smallpox prompted more than 11,000 Norfolk people to get themselves inoculated.

At the same time lung cancer was becoming a major cause of death. In 1960 the county medical officer remarked: "One wonders when the public will heed the warnings regarding excessive cigarette smoking." He might well wonder. Four decades later lung cancer clearly demonstrates how lifestyle has taken over from poverty as a major cause of death in the twentieth century.

The office of county medical officer of health disappeared in National Health Service reorganisations of the early Seventies when the county council lost virtually all its remaining public health responsibilities. Ever since its formation 85 years previously the county council had waged war against two of the main causes of disease, contaminated water supplies and poor sanitation. But progress had been slow.

For more than half the twentieth century, much of Norfolk was a largely unsewered world of "honey carts" and pail closets, privies and cess pits. In 1930, in the whole of the Swaffham district, there were only six houses at Shingham and two at Bury's Hall which had piped water supplies. Melton Constable was more fortunate. Known as "the Crewe of North Norfolk" this railway town set in the heart of the countryside was the headquarters of the Midland and Great Northern Railway. People in Melton Constable did not subscribe to the "Muddle and Get Nowhere" nickname bestowed on the M & GN by the rest of Norfolk because they enjoyed the benefits of piped water supplied by the railway company.

By 1930 all the county's market towns had piped water systems, except Wells which - appropriately enough considering its name - relied on 350 wells, many of which were susceptible to pollution.

In 1944, Norfolk's dubious claim to fame was to come top of a "league table" of counties without piped water. Almost 400 parishes were still dependent on wells. Spurred on by the 1944 Rural Waters Supplies Act, rural district councils got to grips with designing networks of water mains and sewer pipes, and submitting their schemes to the county council from which they received advice, grants and technical assistance.

Even so, despite a concerted effort in the first five years after the war, 37 per cent of

**Often outspoken and sometimes controversial, Norwich-born Sir Arthur South was the youngest councillor in Britain when he was elected to Norwich City Council in 1935 aged 21. His council service, interrupted only by the wartime requirements of the RAF, continued until 1978. He served as chairman of all the council's major committees, Sheriff and Lord Mayor of Norwich and, for almost twenty years, leader of the council. A member of the promotion committee which campaigned for the UEA, he was on the University Council from 1964 to 1980. His wide range of appointments included chairman of both the Norfolk District and East Anglian Regional Health Authorities, a magistrate, chairman of Norwich City Football Club and a member of the Football League management committee. Knighted in 1974, he received the Freedom of Norwich three years later.**

**Millions of people in the world have cause to be thankful for the pioneering work of Norwich surgeon Kenneth McKee. Mr McKee arrived at the Norfolk and Norwich in 1935 and started working on artificial joints in 1938. In 1952, the East Anglian Regional Hospital Board approved research funds of £1000 for Mr McKee's work. In 1960, Mr McKee was joined by John Watson-Farrer and the durable cobalt-chrome ball and socket joint was developed. It was first used in March 1961 but the discovery was kept under wraps while developed further. In 1965, they published a paper, regular operations began and surgeons from around the world descended on Norwich. Up to his retirement in 1971, Mr McKee had performed 1000 hip replacements. In 1971, he said of his work: "Someone said that if Florence Nightingale had been confronted with it, she would have dropped her lamp." Fortunately such pessimism was not founded. Now more than 50,000 patients in Britain and a million-plus internationally are given hip replacements every year.**

Norfolk households still had no piped water by 1951 (England average 17 per cent); forty per cent did not have their own WC (21 per cent) and 59 per cent still had no fixed bath. No wonder many Norfolk people can still remember the era when the tin bath hung from a nail on an outhouse wall, and the family's head-to-toe ablutions were confined to a once-a-week bath night.

Each member of the family would take a turn in the bath which, in winter at least, might be placed in front of the kitchen range in which a roaring fire would glint angrily from the tiny grate. It was as difficult to regulate the heat from the fire as it was to control the temperature of the hot water which Mother ladled from the copper with a saucepan. Memories of bath night are therefore populated by a cast of extremely red and wrinkled individuals who were only too relieved to get dried off and into bed, there being very few homes in those days with television to keep them up late.

In 1959 the county council set up its own public health engineering department which was to provide modern sewage disposal to more than fifty villages. And, by 1974, when sanitation and water supply were removed from the county council's list of obligations and handed over to the Anglian Water Authority, only tiny "pockets of resistance" remained of the once vast area of unsewered Norfolk.

Much the same could be said of the area health authorities and hospital healthcare trusts which now strive to maintain the standards of care required by the Government in its Patients' Charter. The various levels of health service administration cross county boundaries everywhere. For people living in areas bordering other counties, the general practitioners and community nursing services are still on their doorstep, and working closely together as co-ordinated teams, known as "primary care groups".

Their patients go to the nearest district hospital, whichever county it is in. And in an emergency a patient might have to be sent further afield, wherever a bed is available. Today's surgeons regard as commonplace surgical techniques which would have been unheard of in the Sixties. There is even a voluntary organisation, the aptly-named Norfolk Zipper Club, whose members have all had heart surgery, including multiple bypasses or even transplants, at Papworth Hospital, Cambridgeshire. In appreciation of each new day of a better quality of life, they dedicate their voluntary efforts to raising thousands of pounds to buy costly life-saving equipment for the hospital.

Modern medical services – and the costs attached to them – are a far cry from the situation at the King's Lynn and West Norfolk Hospital when the house surgeon was keeping detailed statistics in 1901. The average stay of each in-patient was just under thirty days – far longer than it is today. But the average total cost of each in-patient was around £3.16s.2d (about £3.81), making the daily cost a modest 2s.6d (13p).The symptoms treated by the hospital could often be attributed to the poor living conditions of large families. Typhoid, pulmonary tuberculosis and heart disease accounted for the majority of deaths.

Today the major medical and surgical services in Norfolk are concentrated in the three main centres, Norwich, Lynn and the Yarmouth-Lowestoft coastal patch. However, first point of contact with the patient is still the general practitioner and community nurse, while private medicine is centred on the Bupa Hospital at Colney, near Norwich, and the Sandringham Hospital at Lynn. It seems that public money is always short, no matter whether services are run by the county council, as they were in the first half of the century, or by local administrators responsible to a National Health Service.

All hospitals, great or small, need the fund raising efforts of the communities they serve to keep them at the "cutting edge" of surgical technology and to finance research. As the clock ticks towards a new century, cancer, in its many forms, is still the most feared killer. The Norwich-based Big C Appeal, launched in 1980, has raised a colossal £5 million from its charity shops, legacies and the voluntary fund raising efforts of Norfolk people, to help pay

for the know-how and technology needed to fight the disease in the county's hospitals.

For the National Health Service, the need to release precious public funds with care sometimes creates the impression that progress happens at a terribly slow pace. Yet the foreshortening effect of hindsight offers a slightly different perspective. The hospitals at Lynn and Gorleston have both been completed within the last twenty years of the twentieth century, and the Norfolk and Norwich Hospital is currently being replaced in a £214 million development which amounts to Norfolk's biggest-ever hospital construction scheme.

Mind you, all this activity has been a long time coming. As long ago as 1948 the people of Lynn knew that their 113-year-old hospital was more than ready for replacement. While various extensions were being added to the old hospital land was bought on the edge of town as early as 1958 although the first part of the new hospital, a maternity block, did not arrive until 1971. Nine years later, when the rest of the Queen Elizabeth Hospital was coming into service, the people of Lynn must have been more convinced than ever that good things do not happen overnight in the NHS.

At the same time, on the opposite side of the county, the problem of outdated hospitals in the busy resorts of Yarmouth and Lowestoft was tackled by putting a modern two-storey building on a forty-acre greenfield site at

**The new Norfolk and Norwich hospital at Colney, pictured under construction in 1999, represented the biggest-ever capital investment in Norfolk healthcare.**

Gorleston, midway between the two.

The building work was carried out over a shorter period than at Lynn, phase one being completed in 1981 and the second phase four years later. The hospital was named after the locally-born nineteenth-century surgeon Sir James Paget, whose distinguished achievements in medicine earned him the title of Surgeon Extraordinary to Queen Victoria. The 'JPH', as it quickly became known, provides general hospital services to an area of East Norfolk and North East Suffolk which not only has a population of more than 200,000 but also contains holiday camps, caravan parks, camp sites, beaches and tourist attractions which come alive in summer, inevitably adding to the hospital's workload.

Meanwhile, hundreds of building workers are currently involved in the massive four-year construction of Norfolk's new hospital at Colney, a huge building project which will change the face of this part of Norwich in the first decade of the new century. Over the past few decades the original Victorian Norfolk and Norwich Hospital has undergone many extensions and improvements. Although nobody denies the urgent need for a completely new hospital - and the streets around the present city centre site have been a parking nightmare for years - there is some regret that the hospital is moving outside Norwich.

This massive development is funded through the Government's Private Finance Initiative. In turn for financing and building the new hospital, the Octagon Consortium will receive annual rental payments from the Norfolk and Norwich Healthcare NHS Trust amounting to £1.368 billion over sixty years. Meanwhile, the University of East Anglia and the county's major hospital and community trusts have also submitted a multi-million pound bid to the Government for the go-ahead to establish an undergraduate medical school based around the UEA's School of Health.

It is a far-sighted and inventive initiative which would train 110 doctors a year and is supported by more than sixty GP practices, two acute general hospitals, a mental health care trust and a community trust. Successful or not, it proves that Norfolk is looking to the future rather than over its shoulder at the past.

Norfolk people have never been afraid to fight for their rights, especially when they sense injustice.

In 1914, with the black clouds of war hanging over the world, a tiny South Norfolk village was the flashpoint for a social conflict which reverberated throughout the land and led to England's longest-ever strike. It put the name of Burston into the national headlines and carved a special place in history for teacher Annie Higdon and her husband Tom.

The couple, committed Christian Socialists, had moved to the village from Wood Dalling. Annie became head and Tom assistant teacher at the village council school. Tom got involved in a dispute over low pay for agricultural workers and ousted the vicar, the Rev Charles Tucker Eland as chairman of the parish council. Shortly afterwards the county education authority appointed the vicar and four of his acquaintances on to a six-member board of school governors with Mr Eland as chairman. It was a classic recipe for parochial strife.

The school was hit by one of those epidemics which, as we have already seen, were commonplace in those days. After consulting the vice-chairman of the governors Annie closed the school. This action, plus an unsupported allegation that she had caned two Dr Barnardo's children and lit the school fire on a wet day without permission, was all the excuse the managers needed to sack the Higdons.

On April 1st 1914, a 14-year-old pupil, Violet Potter, became a strike leader simply by writing: "We are going on strike" on the classroom blackboard. All but six of the 72 pupils followed her on a protest march through the village in support of their much-loved teachers. The children refused to attend the council school, preferring to attend classes with the Higdons on Burston Common where a public meeting was also held to protest against the action of the managers.

The Higdons received whole-hearted

**A happy time at Bawdeswell Primary School for May Day in 1968. But for many Norfolk village communities the gloomy spectre of the closure of their local school in education reorganisation has been a dominant theme for the past generation.**

support from village families, despite prosecutions and fines for refusing to send their children to school, and the retaliation of the vicar who turned Higdon supporters off their church-owned land. The population was incensed. The strike attracted national recognition, rallies were held, and the strike school moved first into a carpenter's workshop.

Labour Party and union branches all around Britain woke up to the battle which was being waged in a sleepy Norfolk village, and a national committee was set up, with George Lansbury as president, to appeal for funds. In 1917 a strike school was built on the common where it still stands as a museum and memorial to the Higdons. A banner displaying the words "Love and Justice" recalls the school's motto and revives echoes of turbulent times.

The strike school prospered for 25 years. Memories of injustice refused to fade and many parents, faced with the choice of sending their children to the council school, preferred to entrust them to the care of the Higdons. Tom outlined his own view of the origins of the dispute in a book called The Burston Rebellion.

He had incurred the wrath of farmers by helping agricultural workers to form a trade union and then encouraging working men to become parish councillors at both Wood Dalling and Burston. He later became Norfolk county secretary of the National Union of Agricultural Workers.

The strike school continued until some time after Tom's death in 1936. Annie, who was remembered by her former pupils as "a lovely woman who would help anyone", died in May, 1946, sadly ending her days in the former workhouse at Swainsthorpe. It had been taken over by Norfolk County Council in 1930 and turned into a hospital for patients with senile dementia. But her legacy of love and justice lived on in the hearts and fond memories of hundreds of pupils who were caught up in an

**"Tidy larder and refrigerator!" urges the notice on the wall of the this domestic science class at Lakenham Girls' Secondary Modern School on December 6th 1957. Massive post-war investment had revolutionised both the structure of education and the facilities available to pupils.**

episode which has become part of the fabric of Norfolk education in the twentieth century.

The Education Act of 1902 enabled Norfolk County Council and Norwich City Council both to set up education committees the following year. It is recorded that Norfolk appointed Mr Lee Warner as its first education committee chairman with a salary of £600.

This was a rather more generous remuneration than that paid to Norfolk's 1400 teachers. An elementary school head received between £110 and £180, an assistant teacher between £80 and £110, and uncertified teachers, who made up more than half the total, between £60 and £70. So reluctant were some families to send their children to school that the county council offered attendance prizes, and when these did not work, employed "kid catchers" to round up truants and prosecute their parents.

The Education Act charged local authorities to see that their areas were "properly and adequately supplied" with secondary schools.

In both Norwich and Norfolk there already existed grammar schools founded centuries before by far-sighted benefactors, but, especially in the rural areas, few children expected to be educated beyond the age of 12. Education has always enjoyed a high priority in Norwich where an urban population perhaps nursed greater academic ambitions than the country folk.

A Higher Grade School had been opened in Duke Street in 1889 and a new technical institute started in St George's in 1901. Following the 1902 Act the higher grade school became a municipal secondary school, retaining both boys' and girls' departments until the City of Norwich School was established at Eaton in 1910 to take over the functions of the boys' department. The Municipal Secondary School for Girls continued until it became the Blyth School in 1929.

Another aspect of education and the welfare of children in which city was well ahead of county was in the establishment of a school meals service which dates back to 1906 in Norwich. The city's school medical service started the following year and in 1908 Norwich opened its first school for physically disabled children. The 1918 Education Act raised the school leaving age to 14 and in 1926 the Hadow Report recommended the provision of separate schools for all children over the age of 11.

With the junior scholarship examination in place, forerunner of the 11-plus, a system was set up which, reinforced by the 1944 Education Act, ensured that all children received secondary education, either in grammar schools or secondary moderns. Ancient grammar schools such as those in Lynn, Swaffham and Thetford, for example, had started life centuries before as centres of learning for their immediate neighbourhoods. Now they were required to take pupils who travelled in by train and bus from a wide surrounding area. And many are the wild stories those "old boys" tell of the dubious joys of travelling to school. At Thetford, for example, boys and girls mingled freely on the train only to be strictly segregated on arrival, their separate schools being on opposite sides of the road.

The Second World War inevitably put the brakes on educational investment. In September 1939 Norfolk was immediately faced with the major challenge of setting up temporary schools to cope with 11,000 evacuees from Britain's cities. By 1941 the number had dropped to around 5000 and two years later only three of the temporary schools remained.

Bomb-ravaged Norwich lost no time in trying to sort out its damaged education system. A far-sighted development plan, launched in 1946, saw huge gains, notably in the form of modern secondary schools sited in the Lakenham and Earlham areas to the south and west of the city where many new homes were being built.

The plan was to provide schools for secondary modern children which *"should equal in their facilities and amenities any provision which could be made for a similar number of secondary grammar school pupils"*.

At the same time further education was boosted in the city by the completion of the new buildings in Ipswich Road which were to accommodate the Norwich City College and Art School. The college had been planned in the Thirties but building work had been brought to a halt by the war. A structural steel skeleton stood on the site for the duration.

Norfolk's post-war development plan was greatly hampered by lack of funding from central Government. But the Education Authority made one of its best-ever decisions in 1950 when it appointed Dr Lincoln Ralphs who, as chief education officer from then until his retirement in 1974, conducted a passionate campaign to secure more funding and better resources for education, and to eliminate, finally, the all-age primary school. It was a period which drove Norfolk forward and earned the chief education officer a knighthood in 1973.

One unpromising investment was to pay off handsomely. It was in 1951 that the Education Committee bought a group of Nissen huts which had started life as a wartime American military hospital situated midway between Wymondham and Attleborough. The huts became Wymondham College, a state-run residential secondary school which was to establish itself firmly as an important part of Norfolk's education system.

Other residential schools were set up around the county to accommodate children with a variety of educational needs, and by 1965 the post-war reorganisation was almost complete. The county council wanted to turn its mind to the overdue matter of upgrading primary schools and building new ones.

Dr Lincoln Ralphs wrote: *"The post-war*

**First elected to Norfolk County Council in 1922, Sir Bartle Edwards, of Hardingham Hall, served for more than fifty years, 16 of them – from 1950 to 1966 – as the county council's seventh chairman. Serving in the Rifle Brigade from 1910 to 1921, he saw First World War action in France, Salonika and Palestine, was awarded the Military Cross and twice mentioned in dispatches. He farmed extensively and served both as president and chairman of the council of the Royal Norfolk Agricultural Association. His long public service also included forty years as a magistrate at Dereham, long service as a member and chairman of Mitford and Launditch Rural District Council, and chairman of the governors at the Norfolk College of Arts and Technology in King's Lynn. He was knighted in 1956 for public services.**

**A forthright and witty campaigner, Sir Lincoln Ralphs, chief education officer for Norfolk from 1950 to 1974, was knighted in 1973 for his services to education. He had a brilliant career at the University of Sheffield and teaching experience in Yorkshire before arriving in Norfolk in 1945 as assistant education officer. During his time as chief, 34 secondary schools and one grammar school were built in Norfolk, and he was a force in the establishment of Norfolk College of Arts and Technology, Easton School of Agriculture and the University of East Anglia, as well as the development of Wymondham College as the largest co-educational boarding school in Europe. Among numerous other appointments, he was chairman of the National Schools Council from 1972 to 1975. He died in 1978 aged 69.**

*priority given nationally to secondary school development has prevented much improvement to primary schools of all kinds.*

*"In Norfolk nearly half the primary schools are pre-1870; little more than ten per cent have been built in this century. Most are, therefore, inadequate in some particular, although the transfer of children over the age of 11 to new secondary schools has reduced the overcrowded conditions of many small schools and left a substantial proportion with an embarrassingly small number of pupils."*

Those who believe that pressure to close uneconomic village schools is a phenomenon of the late twentieth century would be surprised to learn that as far back as 1914 a correspondent in The Times Educational Supplement advocated their closure and *"taking the children to convenient centres where they can have better teaching and the stimulating companionship of numbers".*

In Norfolk the issue has traditionally two quite clearly defined sides. On one has been the widely-held view that village schools are an important part of community life, and that the children enjoy more individual attention from their teachers and thereby are better educated. On the other is hard economics and the belief that children are stimulated by larger schools which have greater resources and offer a more varied educational experience.

In 1960 Norfolk still had 77 schools with fewer than thirty pupils and 22 with only one teacher. Between 1974 and 1984, the county council, under pressure from the Government, closed 75 small village schools, losing 434 primary teaching posts. In 1985 a pressure group called KORS (Keep Our Rural Schools) was established after a successful fight to keep open the primary school at Great Cressingham.

The county council said it would be "sensitive to the particular needs of the local community" when considering future closures but the retention of a school with fewer than forty pupils would have to be strongly justified. A book entitled Centenary, A Hundred Years of County Government in Norfolk, published by the county council in 1989, prophesies rather gloomily: *"The problem of the village school is one which will obviously continue to bedevil Norfolk County Council during its second century."*

While Norfolk would have preferred to concentrate on upgrading its primary school system during the Sixties the mind of the nation at large was preoccupied with comprehensive education. Its supporters argued for the egalitarian ideals of a system which would at least try to provide a level playing field for each pupil, and would do away with a selection system which appeared to brand some children as failures at the age of 11. Opponents maintained that this argument under-valued the role of the secondary modern schools.They regretted the passing of the old grammar schools and forecast a levelling down of academic standards.

The year 1974 saw Norfolk's somewhat reluctant change-over to a comprehensive system. Norwich had embraced comprehensive education in 1972. Yarmouth's hitherto self-contained education authority had also submitted a comprehensive plan.The advent of one education authority to cover the whole of Norfolk, including Norwich, propelled Norfolk into a system which brought first, middle and high schools into being.

Education accounts for more than half the county council's annual budget yet Norfolk has often had to counter criticism, usually implying that school buildings are "shabby", textbooks in short supply or pupils' attainment levels could be better. The introduction of comprehensive education did not bring an end of controversy. All education authorities have had to deliver the best standards possible against a background of continuing change in the way education is funded or administered from Westminster.

In these days of constant self examination by teachers and pupils, with schools desperately keen to meet the approval of inspectors from the Office for Standards in Education (Ofsted), the particular problems of delivering an education which is free and fair for all in a rural area will probably remain a challenge well into the new century. One hundred years ago many Norfolk people did not see the need for "book larnin'". Today they can get it on the internet, and Britain has a Government which wants to give all teachers and pupils access to computers.

At the same time it has belatedly recognised the need to raise standards by returning to some of the traditional and well-tried teaching methods which might almost have been familiar to Annie Higdon. There are times when modern technology is out of place in the classroom.

Norfolk's first further education institute, the County Technical College at Lynn, had 63 full-time students in 1951 and 610 by 1960. By 1970, when it had become the Norfolk College of Arts and Technology, it had 1000 full-time students and 1300 on day release. In 1973 the Queen Mother opened new extensions costing more than £1.25 million.

In 1998 the college absorbed the Wisbech-based Cambridgeshire College of Agriculture and Horticulture to form the 16,000-student College of West Anglia. West Anglia's three main sites at Lynn, Wisbech and Milton, near Cambridge, plus its outreach centres at Fakenham, Swaffham, Thetford and Sheringham had a joint budget for 1999 of £18 million. Students from Norfolk, Cambridgeshire, Suffolk, Lincolnshire and Essex attend the new college.

Its confidence in the future was further underlined by a £2.3 million Faculty of Creative Studies, planned to open in autumn 1999, which represented the college's largest building project for forty years.

In 1974, when Norfolk County Council took over the education authorities of Norwich and Yarmouth, it also inherited the City College and the School of Art in Norwich, and the Yarmouth College of Further Education. With institutes of agriculture and horticulture, and a complex range of evening classes at school-based centres around the county, Norfolk people now had many opportunities to broaden their academic, technical and career opportunities while also expanding their range of spare-time interests.

The Sixties campaign for a University of East Anglia was, in its way, as significant an event as the Burston School Strike in that it was fought by people fired by the ideal that a university education should be available to all.

It was an era of much activity in the building of "red-brick" universities, so called to distinguish them from more ancient seats of learning such as Cambridge and Oxford. And

**The University of East Anglia: a fine university for a Fine City.**

**Peter Garland was the first Chief Constable of Norfolk after the police forces of Norfolk, Norwich and Yarmouth amalgamated in 1967. He had started his career in 1934 as a constable with the Metropolitan Police. Serving as a bomber-navigator with Bomber Command, he was flying his 26th mission over Germany on January 23rd 1944, when his Halifax was shot down. He was the crew's only survivor and was a prisoner for the rest of the war. He came to Norfolk as assistant chief constable in 1952 and was appointed chief four years later. Invested with the Queen's Police Medal in 1965, he was made a Commander of the Royal Victorian Order in the Birthday Honours list of 1969. He was president of the Norwich area St John Ambulance Brigade, and in 1956 launched an annual ambulance competition for the force.**

the imagination of the local population was gripped by the idea of Norwich becoming a university city. A site was earmarked at Earlham and in October 1963, only three years after the Government had given the go-ahead, the university welcomed its first 88 students. They were housed in a new "village" near Earlham Hall whose extensive park would accommodate the permanent university buildings.

By the time Sir Keith Murray officially opened the village as his last public engagement as chairman of the University Grants Committee, he was able to congratulate the region on the gift of 165 acres from the City of Norwich, a further 12 acres from an anonymous donor, an annual £60,000 promised by local authorities, and above all, the £1,400,000 subscribed to the university appeal by the people of Norwich and Norfolk.

The State, he said, "envisages an investment of over £6 million in buildings and an annual investment of some £1.5 million to £2 million by the time this university reaches 3000 students".

To those people whose work had turned the hopes and ideas of the past fifty years into reality, Sir Keith said: "When the Government made the decision that the time had come for some new universities your years of persistence in an ideal and of planning for its achievement came to fruition.

"Your University Promotion Committee, widely representative of all interests in your region, provided that foundation of local enthusiasm and interest for which the Government was looking."

Lord Mackintosh, the UEA's first Chancellor, said it had been decided to bring forward the admission of students as much as possible to increase the momentum of university promotion and make a significant contribution to the "crisis of the bulge generation".

With the university came the establishment by the Agricultural Research Council of a new food research institute which has consistently advanced knowledge in a vitally important and often controversial area of research. There is no doubt that the university has injected tremendous vitality into many aspects of life in Norfolk and Norwich.

Norfolk Constabulary had been in existence 61 years at the dawn of the twentieth century, run by a Standing Joint Committee of county councillors and magistrates. Separate police forces existed for Norwich, Lynn and Yarmouth. By contrast, fire fighting had been a function of individual parishes since the sixteenth and seventeenth centuries when, it seems, virtually all the towns of East Anglia were devastated by fire.

Each of Norfolk's 38 town brigades was so independent that, should it be persuaded to assist a neighbouring parish in dealing with a major blaze, it would charge for its services.

Some of the county's main employers, such as Colman's and Norwich Union, also maintained their own brigades. But in the days before mechanisation a fire had ample opportunity to take a firm hold while the brigade's horses were being rounded up and harnessed to the manual pump so that the fire fighters could gallop to the scene.

Meanwhile, the image of the village constable with his police house and his bike, giving miscreants a summary cuff round the 'lug', has passed into rural folklore as the law itself has become steadily more complex, crime rates have soared and both police and the villains they chase have become more mobile.

In the aftermath of the Second World War, when police resources were severely stretched, recruitment problems were eased by the amalgamation of the Lynn Borough Police with the county force. Such are the familiarities of life today that one learns with surprise that Norfolk's first girl police cadet was enrolled as recently as 1964 and the county's first traffic wardens appeared on the streets of Lynn in 1966. The same year officers on foot patrol, again at Lynn, were issued with personal radios.

On January 1st 1968 the inexorable process of centralisation saw the Norfolk, Yarmouth and Norwich forces combined under Mr F P C Garland who had been chief constable of Norfolk since 1956 after a meteoric career

**A policeman's lot: East Harling policemen and village folk pictured in 1900.**

which had started in 1934 as a constable in the Metropolitan Police.

The ambulance service in Norfolk was born during the First World War when the Norwich Transport Company, manned by British Red Cross Society volunteers, conveyed more than 41,000 repatriated soldiers, wounded in battle, to hospital. After the war the service was fragmentary until the 1946 National Health Service Act prompted a comprehensive reorganisation.

Even so, the service still relied heavily on Red Cross, St John Ambulance and other volunteers, and in 1960 it was run by a series of voluntary agency committees, some staff being employed full time and some being volunteers.

Highly-trained ambulance crews worked long hours on standby and had no national rates of pay. It was not until 1970 that the Norfolk County Ambulance Service came into being as a full-time professional service. As time went on, and with emergency vehicles linked by radio to a central control, the ambulance service grew into one huge East Anglian NHS trust. Later, following public concern, the return of chief officers for Norfolk, Suffolk and Cambridgeshire was seen as a move to improve management and morale.

A National Fire Service came into being during the Second World War, and Norfolk's firefighters and ambulance crews had their finest hour during the 'Baedeker' raids on Norwich in April and May 1942.

The Norfolk Fire Authority was formed in 1974 when the Norwich and Yarmouth brigades were merged with the county service.

Norfolk Fire Service, run from its headquarters at Hethersett, is a force of whole time and retained fire fighters deployed around the county and ready to tackle virtually any emergency ranging from Norwich city centre blazes such as those which damaged the Assembly House and destroyed the central library, to hauling a cow or a horse from a dyke in one of Norfolk's many grazing marshes.

**Norfolk firefighters find themselves in the thick of the action once again, this time dealing with a February 1996 blaze at Merton.**

There is probably no better example of the courage and commitment displayed by Norfolk's emergency services than the fire in an underground bunker at RAF Neatishead in February 1966. Started deliberately, it cost the lives of three fire fighters, one from Holt and two from Acle, and did £750,000 worth of damage.

The year 1974 keeps popping up in this narrative like the proverbial bad penny. The reason is that it was a time of cataclysmic change in the administration of the county of Norfolk - and everywhere else in Britain, for that matter. Before that year Norfolk and neighbouring Suffolk were a patchwork of rural districts, many still carrying the names of the ancient "hundreds". The market towns all had their own urban district or non-county borough councils. All these were replaced by a new level of local government, the district council. Critics loudly proclaimed that April 1st, the day the changes took place, was a very appropriate starting date!

Norwich and Yarmouth, previously county

boroughs, resented their loss of status while Lynn, proudly a municipal borough since 1894, became part of West Norfolk District Council. The smaller market towns were so incensed by their loss of powers and reduction from urban district to the humble status of parish that, as a concession, their councils were allowed to call themselves "town councils" and each to elect a "town mayor". It gave them a semblance of their former independence.

In the countryside many people felt that the new district councils would be unwieldy and that local government was moving away from the people. South Norfolk, for example, stretched from Costessey, on the outskirts of Norwich, to Diss. In 1981 West Norfolk District Council was granted borough status and changed its name to the Borough of King's Lynn and West Norfolk so, to some extent, honour was satisfied.

In North-East Suffolk the creation of Waveney District, based on Lowestoft, was preceded by a great debate as to whether the county boundary should be moved to enable Waveney - twice the distance from Suffolk's county town of Ipswich that it was from Norwich - to become part of Norfolk.

In the end, only a minor alteration was made and Waveney remained Suffolk's northernmost outpost. The furore died down, the parishes, once the hub of all community life, found themselves battling to get their voices heard in more remote corridors of power.

To bridge the gap, the county and district councils co-operated by staging local forums at which parish councillors and others could identify the specific needs of their communities. Rural planning and transportation are the favourite battlegrounds.

With Britain needing to build ever more homes for its growing population, the pressure to swallow up greenfield sites does not diminish. The country lokes of those sepia-tinted old photographs are now choked with cars. Where once the county council's main concerns centred on public health and sanitation, it now battles to cope with the scourge of the internal combustion engine. A new slogan - "traffic calming" - has entered the language of local government.

And in "dew diffrunt" Norfolk, where the people's natural instinct would be to declare unilateral independence, nobody is prepared to forecast that we will ever be free from the influence of meddlesome outsiders, or that the steady process of centralisation is ever likely to be reversed.

The poor old parish is not what it used to be.

## CHAPTER 13

# *Second World War and After*

Once it was a secret hideaway buried in the middle of a wood. A sunken cavern, solidly constructed of brick, concrete and metal, designed to store a cache of arms and explosive. Little more than sixty years ago, this hole in the ground on the edge of Norwich formed part of the country's "last ditch" defence from which a clandestine resistance movement would continue to wage war on an invading army.

Like so many crumbling clifftop pill-boxes, their foundations undermined by the sea over which they once stood guard, this relic of war has all but succumbed to nature's remorseless advance. The entrance is choked with leaves. The earth walls have sprouted a tangle of roots. And brambles trail down to pluck and scratch the unwary. But fragments remain. The arched concrete roof with its skin of metal, now rusted and ragged, has been laid bare. A thick layer of moss, like a coat of green velvet, smothers the earth bridge and, not far away, a chunk of brickwork lies almost swallowed by the undergrowth.

Few who walk this stretch of woodland know of its existence. Fewer still have any inkling as to its intended role as an embattled country and its people steeled themselves for the final battle that scarcely anyone had imagined possible.

As Europe slid towards war in the late Thirties, the notion that vast tracts of countryside might be churned into a battleground appeared risible. A sea-borne invasion seemed out of the question.

The most chilling threat, and one stoked up by a plethora of politicians, appeared to come from the air. The grim spectre of mass destruction being unleashed on civilian populations by vast air armadas bordered on the apocalyptic. As early as 1932, Stanley Baldwin had set alarm bells ringing when he famously declared: "I think it as well for the man in the street to realise that there is no power on earth that can prevent him from being bombed. Whatever people may tell him, the bomber will always get through..." It was a bleak forecast which the experience of Guernica and Nanking did nothing to dispel.

By 1937, the Air Staff were estimating that an anticipated all-out air assault by Germany would cost the lives of 66,000 civilians in the opening week of war. Home Office officials expected that around five per cent of all property would be laid waste within the first three weeks.

And someone came up with the grisly statistic that twenty million sq ft of seasoned timber would be needed each month to meet the demand for coffins. Each year these figures were amended upwards, provoking terrifying images of a rain of firebombs and a smog of poison gas engulfing entire cities in a Dantesque inferno.

To meet the perceived threat of a humanitarian catastrophe on a scale never previously witnessed, the Government acted, tentatively at first, by establishing in 1935 a small Air Raid Precautions Department at the Home Office. Originally tasked with making plans for large-scale evacuations of major cities, expanding fire services and promoting methods of protection against bombing and gas attack, its responsibilities were made law and handed down to local authorities two years later. The country was divided into Civil Defence sectors.

Norfolk became part of a vast Eastern Region which stretched beyond Chelmsford to the outskirts of Greater London and south-west as far as Bedford. Each council recruited

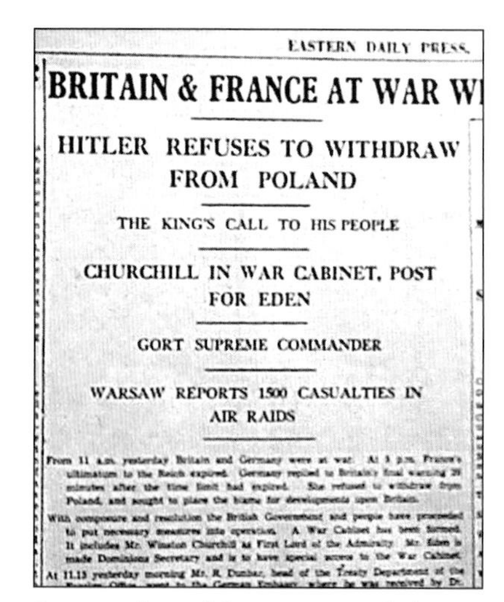

EASTERN DAILY PRESS.

BRITAIN & FRANCE AT WAR W

HITLER REFUSES TO WITHDRAW FROM POLAND

THE KING'S CALL TO HIS PEOPLE

CHURCHILL IN WAR CABINET, POST FOR EDEN

GORT SUPREME COMMANDER

WARSAW REPORTS 1500 CASUALTIES IN AIR RAIDS

From 11 a.m. yesterday Britain and Germany were at war. At 5 p.m. France's ultimatum to the Reich expired. Germany replied to Britain's final warning 20 minutes after the time limit had expired. She refused to withdraw from Poland, and sought to place the blame for developments upon Britain.

With composure and resolution the British Government and people have proceeded to put necessary measures into operation. A War Cabinet has been formed. It includes Mr. Winston Churchill as First Lord of the Admiralty. Mr. Eden is made Dominions Secretary and is to have special access to the War Cabinet.

At 11.15 yesterday morning Mr. R. Dunbar, head of the Treaty Department of the

**September 4th 1939, and the EDP reports the start of hostilities.**

**A line-up of Mk 1 Blenheims at Watton at the start of the war. The Blenheims sustained heavy losses in the early raids of the war.**

its own volunteer army of air raid wardens. Norwich appointed its first ARP officer in May, 1938 and, in the months following the short-lived respite provided by the Munich agreement later that autumn, work intensified on preparing the city for an unprecedented aerial ordeal.

As Europe stumbled from crisis to crisis, a network of warden posts and air raid shelters spread like a rash across the county. Defences ranged from huge subterranean shelters to the more numerous and far cheaper pre-fabricated Anderson shelters and included surface shelters and concrete-walled trenches. In Norwich, tunnels were cut into the chalk on which large parts of the city was built. One of the largest shelters of this kind was burrowed beneath Carrow Abbey meadow. To Reg Butcher, it resembled "a miniature attempt at a channel tunnel". He later recorded:

*"These tunnels had five entrances which extended 100ft back and were linked by a 12ft wide traversing tunnel at the rear. They were lined with H section steel ribs at 3ft centres covered with galvanised steel sheeting. Ventilated by 9in diameter shafts from above, they could accommodate 1000 people if necessary."*

As the dispute over Danzig escalated towards war in the summer of 1939, the wail of air raid sirens, designed to provide eight minutes' warning of attack, became ever more familiar.

But months of practice were soon to give way to the real thing. On August 31st mobilisation orders were issued. A ban was placed on all civil flying over the eastern half of England and local ARP controllers were told to assume duties.

The following day, as German tanks rolled into Poland, around three million women and children began to pour out of the country's most congested areas in an unprecedented mass evacuation. Norfolk, alone, was to receive 50,000 children, most of them from the London area.

There was still, in those last moments, an air of unreality about the preparations for war. As detachments of the civilian-manned National Defence Company occupied posts guarding Norwich's vital transport centres, holiday-makers at Lowestoft were enjoying the Queen of the East Beauty Contest. The town's annual regatta was in full swing, and, further along the coast, the incongruous presence of a pair of elephants drew crowds to Mundesley beach. But war clouds were gathering. Mountains of sandbags mushroomed around public buildings.

Windows were criss-crossed with tape to limit the dangers of shattered glass. And motor car and cycle lamps were covered. With the country teetering on the brink, the EDP declared: *"Our safety by night lies in our own darkness"* and on the last Saturday of peace the citizens of Norwich responded by buying up every last piece of black drapery they could find.

The following morning, at 11am, millions heard a weary, bitterly-disappointed Prime

**Donald Gould Bradford (1912-95), centre, was one of the most aggressive and successful of Coastal Forces' captains to sail out of Yarmouth, remembered by hundreds of naval personnel as HMS Midge. Bradford was given his first command in November 1942, and within a year he had won a DSC and been promoted senior officer in the 55th MTB Flotilla. With their distinctive shark teeth markings on their bows, Bradford's boats terrorised the Dutch coastal waters. Their crowning success came on September 19th 1943, when Bradford's MTB 617 torpedoed the 17,000-ton liner Strasbourg which had run aground off the entrance to Ijmuiden. In the fierce fire-fight which followed one armed trawler was sunk and another badly damaged as the Yarmouth flotilla, to use Bradford's words, "turned west and hared out of it!"**

Minister Neville Chamberlain gravely announce that "this country is at war with Germany". Anxiety was mixed with resignation.

The news came as Paul Banham's father was putting the finishing touches to his DIY air-raid shelter in the back garden of his house in Larkman Lane, Norwich: "Not for him... the ready-made (and freely available) 'Anderson' shelter. He had dug a circular hole some 6ft in diameter and about 3ft deep. It was lined with a single skin of bricks, like a well, and steps curved down to the bottom, making a quarter turn in the process - which means that he must have taken into account the danger of direct blast..."

Others were not so far advanced. John Mingay's family, huddled round the wireless in their Lingwood bungalow, had listened to Chamberlain's words "in complete silence - horrified".

His father, a veteran of the Somme, had stormed out into a nearby field where he was found "kicking the bank in frustration". Pulling himself together, he turned to his son and said, "Let's get back to the yard. We'd better start digging out a hole to make an air-raid shelter." It was a similar story across the county.

Roy Sayer had spent the morning preparing a shelter, and by the afternoon "people... were like bees when the sun comes out, ransacking their sheds to find bits and pieces to build shelters or make shutters for their windows..."

At various points around the county warnings were sounded, but they merely proved the first in a welter of false alarms. It was just as well. J A Walker was a territorial gunner in a Norwich-based anti-aircraft battery called up at the end of August:

"We had trained on a 3in ex-Naval gun and had been told that if war broke out we would take possession of a brand new 3.7in gun which was waiting for us at the depot in Cromer Road... We did not go to the Cromer Road depot, however, but to one at Arminghall which we had never heard of. There we collected a rather ancient Lewis gun and a small party... sallied off to West Beckham to what turned out to be a radar station.

"The security guards would not let us in at first and had no food for us... For the next few days we made ourselves as comfortable as we could and got rather sketchy training on the Lewis gun (of which we knew nothing). On the fateful day (war was declared) I was off duty and went to the Fighting Cock pub at West Beckham.

"There we heard the news... We relayed the information to the rest of the unit with much fear and foreboding as we were in no position to engage the enemy should he attack. The siren did go but we saw no enemy planes. I don't think the general public really knew how unprepared the country was for the war..."

Men such as Neville Painter, however, had a good idea. A bus mechanic and a member of 280 Field Coy, RE, a territorial unit based in Norwich, he had reported to the Market Avenue drill hall on Friday, September 1st:

"That evening, we had to go back home again because they hadn't sorted out any billets. We reported back at 8am the following morning... And after a makeshift meal in the roller skate rink opposite the old cattle market billets were sorted out for us in the Rose Lane and Prince of Wales Road area. Aubrey Punchard and I shared a large double bed in the front room at 1 John St; it was common practice from day one to share double beds... The next morning we were all lined up on the old cattle market - most of the Company had arrived by then - and the commanding officer read out the declaration of war. We then broke up and spent the rest of the day flitting between the drill hall, the mess hall and our billets. It was gone Monday before we had any semblance of order. There wasn't any sense of alarm. We'd all joined for the fun really and in any case we all thought the war was going to be over by Christmas..."

The people of Norwich were mostly in bed when the sirens sent them scurrying for the shelters at 2.42am on September 4th. The scare lasted 37 minutes before the all-clear was heard. It too had been a false alarm. *"During the next 10 months running to the shelter became a game that quickly lost its charm and the wailing note of the alert gradually became largely ignored,"* wrote Joan Banger in her history of the Norwich blitz. In the absence of the Luftwaffe, the well-intentioned efforts of ARP officials appeared pointless and, on occasions, to border on the ridiculous. Test alerts were often ignored or mistaken for the real thing. Such was the level of chaos in March 1940, that the authorities felt moved to announce: *"Unless the unexpected occurs there will be no cause for anxiety when the air-raid sirens sound in Norwich today. On Tuesday, when one siren only burst forth, there were many people who immediately feared the worst and some disorganisation, which in itself is costly, occurred in factories where employees were sent to their shelters... Today we shall expect to hear the steady note for half a minute, followed by a warbling for 25 seconds, and if by the strangest coincidence a real alarm has to be given at exactly midday the warbling will continue for several minutes..."*

In the face of so much apathy and not a little bewilderment, officials were in a quandary about how to ram home the ARP message without appearing alarmist. Posters were plastered over walls, booklets printed by the thousand, but the unpalatable truth was that hardly anyone seemed to be taking any notice. Bernard Storey, Norwich's ARP controller, felt compelled to declare:

*"A sense of unreality still appears to exist about air raid precautions. There are a few, but only a few, outward signs that we are at war. Other people are being bombed, not us. All of us are apt to get slack and careless about air raid protection. Don't. By the time this message is read we may need its service badly enough."*

Not for nothing were those early months known as the Phoney War. However, like all generalities, it was not wholly accurate. Indeed, aircraft from bases in East Anglia had been engaged, sometimes with disastrous results, from the very outset with Blenheims from Wattisham mounting the RAF's first bombing raid of the war on September 4th. That same day Wellingtons from Honington and Mildenhall made an unsuccessful sortie against the battle-cruisers Scharnhorst and Gneisenau at Brunsbuttel. Out of 14 bombers despatched, eight turned back due to bad weather and two of the remainder were shot down. No hits were recorded. Barred from bombing targets inside Germany, on political grounds, the RAF confined itself to costly attacks on German harbours and the safer, if futile, leaflet-raids, derisively dubbed by crews "bumf-missions". The war was three months old before the first British bomb fell on enemy soil, and even then it was by accident rather than design. "Hung-up" during a shipping raid, the bomb slipped from a Marham Wellington as it passed over Heligoland.

The RAF were not alone in their "sensitive" bombing campaign. The Luftwaffe restricted their operations to anti-shipping strikes, mine-laying and reconnaissances, although these too carried a measure of hazard. On December 6th 1939, three days after Marham's unintentional entry into the record books, a Heinkel He115 float-plane became the first enemy aircraft to crash in the region when it plunged into shallow water off Sheringham beach. The

**John Grix became one of the most famous of all Norwich's heroes of the blitz. Having lied about his age to be accepted as a Civil Defence messenger, he was 15 when the Luftwaffe raided Norwich in April 1942. During one attack, the scout leader was blown off his bike five times. Despite suffering acid burns, he worked throughout a night of heavy bombing. "It wasn't a case of being brave," he later remarked. "I just wanted to be involved and, to be honest, I didn't know what I was letting myself in for." He was awarded the British Empire Medal for gallantry and received an illuminated address from Australian Civil Defence workers. Grix later spent forty years working at Laurence & Scott. He always regarded his brief encounter with fame as a "nine-day wonder". He once admitted: "I feel embarrassed at the same time as feeling honoured by the medal they gave me... I did no more than what others did."**

aircraft, which had been engaged in dropping mines, had apparently struck the top of the 240ft high CH (radar) mast at West Beckham. All three crew were killed and, but for the fact that the machine landed just below the high water mark, it would have qualified as the first German aircraft brought down on English soil during the Second World War. Even so, it still excited considerable interest.

Bill Webdale, a young sapper who was on guard duty at Sheringham the night the Heinkel crashed, recalled: *"We didn't see it come down, but we heard it. It seemed to come over the sea and then head inland before coming back. It just missed the gas works, came over the golf links, nose-dived and hit a lamp-post before going into the sea. When we came off duty the following morning the pilot had been laid out on the promenade.*

*"There were a lot of air force officers from Raynham and a few of us had to wade into the water to carry the aircraft's wings out. The water was freezing. A little later they buried the pilot. It was quite an affair. The RAF sent an official party. They gave him a hero's send-off, firing three salutes over his grave..."*

At sea also, there had been considerable activity with many cruel losses, chiefly to submarine attacks and a deadly new weapon, the magnetic mine, which made its appearance along the east coast. Mounting losses, particularly in supply ships, and growing concern for the future prompted the Government to introduce food rationing on January 8th 1940. Shortages had forced similar action towards the end of the Great War, but it was on nothing like the scale of that adopted in the Second World War. Rationing was to become a way of life - with everything from clothes to petrol affected - which left an indelible mark on a generation who became reliant on an economy based on coupons and the black market. Initially, only bacon, butter and sugar were affected, but eventually the small buff books came to encompass virtually every food or drink.

Jessie Griffiths, who served as assistant food officer for Norwich, later recorded: *"The whole object of rationing was 'fair shares for all'. However, experience proved it essential to make concessions to specified categories of people. Then trouble started. Basically, so long as everyone had equal shares, however small, people were reasonable and philosophical but as soon as the man next door got extra milk and eggs for his ulcers or could exchange butter for meat coupons, etc doctors and food office staff were besieged by people who discovered new aches and pains for which they demanded extra rations. Quite the most explosive reaction of all time was to the special allowance of extra cheese permitted to some categories of workers..."*

Overall, Griffiths considered that rationing worked and proved "a great leveller". One unexpected by-product of food shortages was a healthier diet. Animal fats were kept to a minimum, thus reducing heart trouble. Severe sugar rationing made chocolate scarce and meant the sweet-toothed could not over-indulge. School children, however, received one third of a pint of milk a day - free. Griffiths recalled: *"Early thought was given to the necessity for young children to have a supply of fresh milk. A milk scheme was introduced but proved administratively clumsy and eventually it was absorbed into the evolving welfare foods scheme for expectant mothers and young children. In the midst of deprivations it was a great joy to watch the city's babies flourishing on vitamin orange juice, cod liver oil and the popular 'National Dried' milk..."*

As the New Year signalled a descent into an Arctic-like winter, there was considerably less joy to be found on the frozen Western Front where hundreds of Norfolk soldiers faced the prospect of enforced idleness. In almost four months of war the rival lines had scarcely budged. Casualties in the British army amounted to no more than a handful of men. It was not until January 7th 1940, that the army suffered its first officer fatality - Lieut P A C Everitt, of the 2nd Royal Norfolks. It was a strange war conducted, like the bombing campaign, according to a bizarre set of rules which bred nothing but frustration. Peter Barclay was a captain, serving in the snow-

**A dramatic view of the air raid on Yarmouth which damaged Grout's silk mill on February 1st 1941. Wartime censorship meant this EDP photograph was stopped from publication.**

**David Jamieson (1920-) was 23 when he earned the Victoria Cross for "superb qualities of leadership and great personal bravery" during the Normandy campaign. His was one of five VCs to men of the Royal Norfolk Regiment, a record for the Second World War. Educated at Eton, Jamieson joined the 7th Battalion in the spring of 1939. Considered too young to accompany the unit to France in January 1940, he was spared the disaster which overwhelmed the battalion at St Valery the following summer. Second in command of a company when the reformed 7th returned to Normandy four years later, he earned his VC during the defence of the Orne bridgehead when he inspired his depleted force to withstand repeated armoured attacks. He resigned from the army in 1948 to pursue a highly successful business career in Britain and Australia. A High Sheriff of Norfolk in 1980, he was also a lieutenant of Her Majesty's Bodyguard of the Honourable Corps of Gentlemen at Arms. He now lives in Burnham Market, the last surviving Norfolk holder of the nation's highest military award "for valour".**

covered Ligne de Contact on the Saar front. During his tour, he detected an enemy observation post sited in some stationary railway carriages on an embankment in No-Man's-Land. He later recounted: *"I thought, 'well, that's a jolly good gunner target!' So I ordered fire to be brought down by the French artillery 75s which were supporting us. Nothing happened to my indignation and I got onto Battalion HQ to find out why I wasn't receiving the response to which I reckoned I was entitled. They said, 'Oh, it's not a legitimate target - the only legitimate target you should know by now is a working party in the open'. Such was the 'Phoney War'."*

Shortly afterwards, Barclay stirred up sufficient "trouble" to earn himself a rebuke from his battalion commander and a Military Cross. It was the first such honour of the war.

Clashes, however, remained the exception rather than the rule. By the time the 7th Royal Norfolks, a pioneer unit made up of territorials and militia men, took their places in the Ligne de Contact in April it was as though an agreement had been reached not to extend the conflict beyond a few raids and ineffectual salvoes. There was a tacit understanding that neither side would shell each other's billets, while some units appeared set on conducting a war according to timetable.

Paul Hawkins, a company commander and a future MP for South-West Norfolk, recalled: "There was a Frenchman called Commandant Koch, who had a battery of horse-drawn artillery which would turn up about 3pm every afternoon in exactly the same spot, loose off six or seven rounds at a crossroad on the German side and then bolt off. It was just a question of showing the flag..."

The German blitzkrieg launched against Belgium and Holland in the early hours of May 10th 1940 changed all of that. In a matter of days, the war was transformed and the British army was fully engaged in a desperate struggle for survival as it fell back towards the Channel. The 2nd Royal Norfolks made contact with the German army on the banks of the River Dyle on May 15th. Over the course of the next 12 days the battalion was decimated in a series of bloody, defensive actions which culminated in the massacre of 97 men captured after a fierce fight near the French village of Le Paradis. Fewer than 100 men from the 2nd Royal Norfolks succeeded in escaping through Dunkirk and various other ports. Among them was Peter Barclay, who had been badly wounded during a bitter battle along the river Escaut in which his company-sergeant major had earned a posthumous Victoria Cross.

Paul Hawkins was not so fortunate. Along with the vast majority of the 7th Royal Norfolks, he was taken prisoner when the beleaguered port of St Valery-en-Caux fell to General Rommel. Barely forty men from the unit made it back to England, the biggest single party escaping aboard a fishing boat. By the time, Second Lieut Jim Walker marched the remnants back to Britannia Barracks on July 3rd, the disastrous campaign was over. Holland and Belgium had capitulated and France had signed an armistice. Britain stood alone, an invasion expected at any time with the beaches of Norfolk once more high on the list of likely landing points.

As early as June 18th, a fortnight after the last of the little boats had departed the smoke-wreathed beaches of Dunkirk and a day after it was announced that the French had asked for "peace terms", the people of Norfolk were being prepared for invasion. A circular issued by the Ministry of Information urged the civilian population to "stay put" in the event of a German landing by sea or air. It stated: *"Should parachutists come down near one's home, the best guidance is - 'Don't give any German anything. Don't tell him anything. Hide your food and your bicycles. Hide your maps. See that the enemy gets no petrol. If you have a car or motor-cycle put it out of action when not in use. The time may come when civilians will receive orders to block roads or streets in order to prevent the enemy advancing. In such an event they should be ready to help the military in any way..."*

In those dark days, Churchill had rallied the nation. As the remnants of a beaten and bedraggled British army retreated from France, his Shakespearean eloquence breathed defiance: "We shall go on to the end... we shall defend our island whatever the cost may be.

**George Swain's photograph of the removal of the Theatre Street bomb in September 1940 was one of the most dramatic images of the Norwich blitz. The 880lb UXB forced a large area of the city centre to be evacuated and took days to dig out. The courage of the bomb disposal team was later recognised by the award of the newly-instituted George Medal to three men.**

We shall fight on the beaches, we shall fight on the landing grounds, we shall fight in the fields and in the street, we shall fight in the hills; we shall never surrender." Stirring words, but the truth was that, so far as any land battle was concerned, Britain had precious little to fight with. The country's fortifications were pitifully weak. Along the Norfolk coast, considered to be a prime site for a diversionary attack, work had begun on bolstering the defences only at the end of May. By June, civilian contractors and army engineers were engaged in a desperate race against time. The task was an immense one. After visiting troops working on the defences, General Ironside, Commander-in-Chief, Home Forces, noted: *"...the guns and wire are being put up at all the likely points. Work will never end. It ought to have been begun months ago."*

The plan followed similar principles to those adopted during the First World War: to hold the enemy as long as possible on the shoreline before withdrawing to a series of fallback lines based on the rivers Ant, Bure and Wensum. Concrete pill-boxes were hastily built, trenches dug, anti-tank ditches excavated, bridges prepared for demolition and thousands of mines laid along a shoreline festooned with barbed wire.

Much of the work was carried out by East Anglian soldiers, territorials from the 18th Division. They included a workshop section of 251Field Park Company. From bases at East Harling and Shotesham Hall, they ventured out throughout the summer. Neville Painter recalled: "There were about four or five of us in our party and we were set to work building pill-boxes. We put one up at Sheringham,

**Douglas Bader (1910-82), one of the most famous of all fighter aces, was based at Coltishall when the Battle of Britain began in July 1940. A bold, bombastic leader, he had overcome the effects of a near-fatal pre-war crash which resulted in the amputation of both his legs. Posted to Norfolk to take command of 242 Squadron, he found a unit consisting mainly of Canadians low in morale and lax in discipline. Through dint of personal example, he quickly transformed the squadron. His Coltishall score opened with a Dornier shot down off Cromer and he added another which came down in the sea three miles north-west of Yarmouth on August 21st. That same day three pilots from Bader's squadron shared in the destruction of the only enemy bomber to fall on Norfolk soil during the battle. Bader was eventually shot down over France in August 1941, becoming a troublesome prisoner. A post-war biography and a highly successful film ensured his exploits were not forgotten. He was knighted in 1976.**

another at Trimingham and others at Elveden and East Harling. The one at Harling was built of sandbags which we then concreted round. I remember it was the first time we'd used a cement mixer. For the others we had to mix the cement by hand. The routine was much the same. We'd be given instructions to go to a particular site, selected in advance and marked on a map, and then we'd simply gather all the materials together on a lorry and head off. On arriving, the first thing you'd do was look out the nearest pub. You made the best of things. The pill-boxes were pretty much of the same design; slots on all sides and a blast wall to protect the doorway. But the positions were important, because you had to ensure the fields of fire were correct. We didn't have any special training, but of course we had skilled bricklayers in the section. And it took about ten days to a fortnight to complete each one."

In between building pill-boxes, Painter's unit busied themselves making thousands of duckboards for trenches, building barricades and ferrying landmines to be laid by other sappers. One of the men involved in this work was Bill Webdale: *"We went out to Sea Palling, Winterton, and mined all the beaches there. You had to dig the holes for them to be placed in a pattern. The idea was that if an enemy soldier landing missed one, he'd step on the next one. They were filled with explosives and the sergeant in charge would put in the detonators. There was barbed wire to keep people off the beach, but I heard there was at least one fatality. I think some fellow was blown up taking his dog for a walk..."*

As well as building defences, men of the 18th Division were also intended to play a prominent role in resisting any invasion. Bill Webdale's unit, 287 Field Company, were charged with the task of preparing for demolition a series of bridges along the line of the North Walsham-Dilham Canal and the River Bure. Webdale's sub-section was responsible for placing explosive charges beneath the Wherry Inn bridge, near Little London. Others earmarked for destruction "within three hours of receiving orders" in the event of a successful enemy landing included Aylsham's road and rail bridges together with other road bridges at Oxnead and Ingworth. Orders issued on July 13th 1940, stressed that demolition teams were to rejoin their unit at Cawston "immediately" and not to engage the enemy except in self-defence. The importance of these operations was plain: *"Demolitions are a vital part of military plans, and their failure will have the most adverse effects... It is therefore stated that on no account will a complete bridge be allowed to fall into the enemy's hands. Once the charge is laid and the bridge prepared the responsibility of completing the demolition at all cost must rest entirely with the demolition party."* Elsewhere, infantry units manned the newly-constructed fortifications, or were held inland ready to strike back. The 5th and 6th Royal Norfolks rotated between the coastal defences and Gresham's School, near Holt. The 4th Battalion had the task of defending Yarmouth and Gorleston from attack by air or sea or both. It was a daunting mission. The defensive line ran almost 22 miles and was somewhat unorthodox. As well as a tank trap cut across the golf course, much to the consternation of members, road blocks were constructed using herring barrels filled with sand and lashed with timber.

These were sited all round the perimeter, prompting complaints from the corporation transport manager for throwing out the bus time-table! Having mined the beaches, at the cost of two men killed, set up trip-wires and prepared floodlights to cover exposed stretches of shoreline, the 4th Royal Norfolks prepared for the most spectacular operation – blowing a gap in Britannia Pier. Lt Col Alfred "Knocker" Knights, who went on to command the battalion, recorded: *"The event was well-advertised, and a record crowd gathered to watch the display from a safe distance. Unfortunately, the windows of the houses on Marine Parade suffered rather severe casualties. The actual explosion was, however, quite impressive. It was then that one very important local person said to another very important local person (who happened to be one of the principal pier shareholders): 'Well, Tom, that's the first time you've seen so much of your money go up in smoke.' The Flag Officer in Charge (of the port) didn't think a real good job had been made of it and ordered a few torpedo warheads to be installed at the seaward end of the pier with an electrical firing connection so that, if enemy troops landed at the pierhead, it and they could be blown sky-high. The idea was undoubtedly good, but the switch for making the necessary electrical connection was installed by the side of the switch which operated the beach floodlights. It was always a tense moment when orders were received to test the floodlights in case the NCO in charge of the post closed the wrong switch..."*

Throughout the summer of 1940 the defences and the number of men manning them grew steadily. Fields once ripe with crops sprouted poles to prevent their use as landing grounds. As invasion fears mounted, there were increasing reports of "spies" and "fifth columnists". False arrests were frequent. Anyone with a foreign-sounding name or accent was suspected of being an enemy agent, while concern that the Broadland waterways might be used by the Germans to land spies or saboteurs resulted in the establishment of one of the war's strangest units.

The Broads Flotilla, based at Wroxham, was a sub-unit of the 30th Royal Norfolks, itself a successor of the National Defence Companies formed in the summer of 1939. Although crewed by regular reservists, the flotilla of armed motor-launches came under the operational control of the Royal Navy. Bill Smart, who commanded the waterborne force for a period during 1941, recalled: *"We had six motor-boats, all requisitioned from private individuals, and a cabin cruiser which served as a headquarters. The boats had Lewis guns mounted fore and aft and a crew of between four and six. It was thought that enemy seaplanes might land on the Broads in the evening or early morning, so we patrolled at dawn and dusk. But we never saw anything..."*

Most famous of all the units ranged against any would-be invader, however, were the Local Defence Volunteers, later re-christened the Home Guard and now more famously remembered as "Dad's Army". The new force, officially open to men aged between 17 and 65 although in reality the age range was far wider, came into being on May 14th 1940. The appeal for recruits was instantly answered. In Norfolk, around 6000 men prevented from joining the regular forces on account of being too young, too old or in reserved occupations, signed up in the first 48 hours and by the end of May that figure had risen to 30,000. Villages formed their own sections or platoons, depending on numbers. In time, these myriad volunteer units grew to form no fewer than 17 Norfolk Home Guard Battalions. Initial shortages of arms and uniforms did little to dampen their enthusiasm. Quickly dubbed "parashooters" by the press, some showed a

**Many East Anglian towns and villages suffered in the Luftwaffe attacks. Cromer was badly affected by the raid of July 22nd-23rd 1942.**

marked propensity for striking first and asking questions second. A school teacher who had volunteered for the Norwich Home Guard later recalled one such incident: *"We had to do night guarding at the Waterworks, and one night my companion and I heard somebody approaching. So, we gave a tremendous challenge and nearly knocked the wits out of our commanding officer who was taking his dog for a walk."*

Many such incidents would not have been out of place in David Croft and Jimmy Perry's splendidly comic evocation. Peter Ducker, who joined the Norwich Post Office Home Guard as a teenager, was among a small party abandoned in a railway carriage after their senior NCO forgot to inform them that the night exercise had finished hours earlier. He recalled another large-scale "scheme" which resulted in the capture of Norwich by an invasion force made up of British parachutists:

*"We were working in co-operation with the Royal Norfolks. I was a corporal and we took our Lewis Gun down Hall Road. We were guarding the entrance over the railway bridge... and we actually dug a pit in a little triangular grass plot. We went down on the Friday night, but we didn't see or hear anything. The people living round there supplied us with food and we were still there on Sunday.*

*"That afternoon we walked all the way back and when got to the Cattle Market the place was swarming with paratroopers. Many of the Home Guard were encaged in cattle pens. The Post Office had been captured and the police were all locked in their cells at Bethel Street. The paratroopers had taken complete charge of the city... I later learned that they had got into the city past the roadblocks by commandeering buses and laying on the floors, and, of course, the Home Guard didn't bother to check and just waved them through. As for me, the officer in charge of the paratroopers said, 'You look tired. You'd better go home'. A little while later he came up and said there was a vehicle waiting to take me. I walked out of the Post Office and there was a fire engine, complete with escape ladder, and a paratrooper as driver. 'He doesn't know Norwich, so you'll have to direct him,' said the officer, and off we went. I remember we went down London Street with me ringing the fire bell..."*

Of course, there was a more serious side to Home Guard activities, and none more than those carried out by members of No 202 Battalion. Part of a British resistance organisation intended to fight on in the event of a successful German invasion, the secret unit included, by 1941, some 200 men from Norfolk divided into 35 small auxiliary units with forty operational bases, mostly underground lairs hidden in woodland. These men were trained to wage guerilla warfare against an enemy army of occupation. John Fielding was one of those members of the Home Guard recruited into the clandestine force.

He later helped construct an underground base on the golf course at Earlham and, in an account given to historian Adrian Hoare, he recalled: *"The training we received was very good. I... received special instruction in sabotage techniques. These skills gave me a lot of confidence. We believed that we could create a considerable amount of mayhem for an enemy. We were certainly not frightened of the Germans and I looked forward to getting stuck in if they did invade us. We had been well-trained and were confident that we could do a lot of damage to an enemy by destroying vehicles, petrol dumps, etc."*

As the months went by without sign of any landings such hazardous operations appeared increasingly unlikely. By the winter of 1941-42 with German attentions focused on Russia, the main danger had passed. But the defences continued to be manned and the Home Guard remained in being. Norfolk had become one vast armed camp. Airfields freckled the countryside and Motor Torpedo Boats launched audacious raids against enemy shipping from their bases at Yarmouth and Lowestoft. From these same ports, fishing fleets, their crews reduced by call-ups, continued to ply their dangerous trade at considerable human cost. Between 1939 and 1944, 827 fishermen were killed. Little did the public realise (through the tight security of the period) at what immense risk to life and limb every pound of fish was brought to port. In spite of much of the fishing grounds of the North Sea being closed and the mine-belt all along the East Coast, thirty per cent of pre-war catches were maintained.

The coast of Norfolk also became home to thousands of new recruits undergoing rigorous battle training at specially established "finishing schools". Dennis Ensor was one such "pupil". Together with around 100 young soldiers, he found himself in a converted holiday camp at Bacton, where the chalets, ill-suited to winter weather, leaked to leave the occupants "almost floating in water". After four months training, Ensor, who had previously served in the Home Guard, found himself on coast defence work:

*"At no time were we... ever issued with live ammunition, 500 rounds being kept in a sealed box in the guard room for emergencies. Part of our duties, also, was to mount a heavy machine gun, dawn and dusk, to give a reception, and departure, to bombers visiting Norwich. While... we were issued with a box of ammunition, we were not allowed to load the weapon, which was a sensible idea, since the gun was not part of our armoury and I had never been shown how to load, much less fire it... What with no small arms ammunition and no training on the heavy machine guns, so Norfolk slumbered in peace each night, secure that their army watched over them..."*

Bert Fisher was stationed at Bacton at the same time. A young soldier from Norwich serving with the 7th Royal Norfolks, he too heard the drone of German bombers as they flew inland towards their targets. One night, in particular, remains fixed in his memory. It was late April, 1942: "You could see the sky towards Norwich all lit up with searchlights and flares. We'd heard the planes going over and naturally knew what had happened. There were a lot of us there from Norwich and we didn't wait for nothing. Most of us had bicycles at the camp and that night we just took off and biked home. The next morning when they had the roll call there was hardly anybody left. I should think nearly three-quarters of the battalion had gone. When I got to the city everything was in a terrible state. City Station got hit badly, and I remember my mother was covered in soot, but at least my family were safe. Father, who had a baker's shop in Oak Street, lost nearly all his customers..."

**Wighton Home Guard in good spirits outside the Half Moon at Walsingham. The photograph reflects the wide range of ages and the antiquated weapons available, with a Lewis machine-gun and First World War vintage Ross rifles.**

The aerial assault, for so long feared, did not actually materialise, so far as Norfolk was concerned, until May 1940. Shortly after Bernard Storey, Norwich's ARP controller, had warned people of the dangers of not taking precautions seriously enough, the first enemy bombs – 13 high explosive types – fell on open ground near RAF West Raynham half an hour into May 25th. It was another six weeks, however, before the brutal realities of war were fully felt by the civilian population. Around 5pm on July 9th, just as many workers were leaving off, two German bombers launched a deadly attack on Norwich. Ironically, after all the tests and false alarms, there was no alert. The first many people knew about the raid was the sound of bombs whistling down. Barnards' factory on Mousehold was struck first. Thirteen hits were registered, killing two and wounding five. Carrying on unhindered, the raiders dropped five bombs on Boulton & Paul's Riverside works, leaving the plant wreathed in a pall of black smoke and a casualty list stretching to ten dead and almost seventy injured. The neighbouring railway lines and locomotive sheds were also damaged, but the most harrowing scenes were on Carrow Hill where workers, many of them women, were heading home after their day's shift at Colman's factory. Caught in the open, they suffered grievously when a bomb burst at the top of the hill showering them with shards of shrapnel. All told, 27 people were killed that day in a raid notable not only for its horrors, but for the remarkable accuracy of the German bombers.

It was a rude awakening. Heavily censored reports of the time spoke of "not the slightest sign of panic". In reality, there was a deep sense of shock. Such was the anger at the enemy's ability to strike unannounced that workers threatened to down tools unless a new early-warning system was introduced. The level of resentment would, no doubt, have been still greater had they known of the findings of a secret inquiry which indicated that the enemy bombers had been sighted at least an hour before the first bombs fell without any attempt being made to intercept them. Even so, civic leaders endorsed the workers' grievances, arguing that the deaths were unnecessary. As a result, some firms joined forces to establish their own "plane-spotting" organisation.

July 9th 1940 marked the beginning of Norwich's long ordeal. The attack, carried out almost two months before London was bombed, was the first of 46 raids on the city during the course of the war. For the most part, these were small-scale, sporadic and seemingly arbitrary in their objectives. Only in hindsight does a pattern of sorts emerge for the Luftwaffe's assault on Norfolk... a pattern of destruction that progressed by turns from the hit-and-run raids to the Baedeker ordeal, from the so-called "Butterfly Blitz" to the low-level tip-and-run attacks carried out on coastal towns and from the Doodlebugs to the far more menacing V2 rocket campaign.

Initially the emphasis was clearly on military and industrial targets. In many cases these attacks were carried out by no more than a handful of raiders and while Norwich came in for its share of bombing, the brunt of the early assault was borne by the ports of Great Yarmouth and Lowestoft. During the first three months of 1941, Lowestoft was attacked on no fewer than 23 separate occasions. The tally for Yarmouth for the same period was 33 raids, four of them being recorded on a single day. Indeed, Lowestoft went on to claim the dubious distinction of being the not only the most bombed place in the UK but of having suffered the worst single air-raid incident of the war when four bombs from a lone Dornier fell on the town centre killing seventy and injuring almost 150. During the course of the 105 attacks, 192 civilians and 83 military personnel were killed, but the most startling statistic of all was the damage done to housing. Of the 11,830 homes in the Borough at the outbreak of war, a staggering 9433 were damaged, some on more than one occasion.

Nowhere was immune to air attack. Bungay, Cromer and King's Lynn all bore their share of suffering. Sometimes the scale of destruction was totally disproportionate to the number of bombers employed. In Lynn, for example, there were 57 air-raid victims among the civilian population throughout the war and, of these, 18, together with 24 servicemen, were killed by a single bomb which destroyed the Eagle Hotel on June 12th 1942. Geography also came into the equation. Caister was the most heavily-bombed parish in Norfolk – enduring 34 raids and having 139 high explosive bombs fall within its boundaries – simply on account of being situated next door to Yarmouth, the enemy bombers' intended target. Thus, by accident or design, the Luftwaffe left its mark, both physically and psychologically, on the collective memories of thousands of people in countless numbers of towns and villages across the region.

The air raids had brought the war home and in doing so produced a new breed of hero. Auxiliary firemen, wardens, fire-watchers, rescue workers and air-raid messenger boys were plunged into the maelstrom, often at night and usually after a day's toil. In these circumstances, ordinary people of all ages performed extraordinary acts of bravery and devotion. None more so than those men, who volunteered for bomb disposal work. Called out to deal with any number of UXBs, the earliest squads had little by way of training and no specialised equipment. Bertie Lawson was one of three members of a Norwich-based squad awarded the newly-instituted George Medal for their part in removing a 250kg delayed-action bomb which brought chaos to the city centre in September 1940. He recalled: *"It's no use saying we didn't think anything about death and what might happen when we went out on a job. It was always on your mind. This was OK at the beginning... but as time went on and Gerry (sic) kept bringing out new fuses and gadgets to deal with, it started to get more complicated. We also got more competent in handling the bombs. You had to. If you didn't keep up with all the information supplied to you then things would happen for the worst. Sorry to say that is why we lost so many of our comrades...*

*"One day (after helping remove and defuse some bombs which had fallen at King's Lynn) I arrived back in Norwich and as I drove up the driveway the section lieutenant was just getting into the utility van... He told me to come with them as one of the bombs had gone off and had killed some of the section near a place called Worlingworth. When we got to the site a man was standing on guard by the crater. His story was that he had gone over to the farmhouse to phone for the officer to come and defuse it, but before he got there the bomb had gone off, killing a local police officer and three of his section. This was my first encounter with death in the section. It was a terrible job searching that field for what remained of the fellows..."*

Later in the war, the widespread dropping of deadly 2kg anti-personnel explosive devices, nicknamed Butterfly bombs, brought fresh hazards to UXB teams. Dropped by the thousand over East Anglia, they were designed to inflict maximum disruption with the minimum effort. Ultra-sensitive to the slightest contact, the winged bombs which were scattered across open countryside posed a major threat to harvests and to local air bases. The campaign which came to be known as the Butterfly Blitz reached a peak in the summer and autumn of 1943. During that time, local bomb disposal teams made safe almost 270 of

ANTI-PERSONNEL BOMBS ARE BEING USED

On the night of June 13/14 1943 the enemy, in an attack on an East Coast town, used a large number of these bombs along with about 6,000 incendiaries.

**These three photographs show how the anti-personnel ("Butterfly") bomb actually comes down. If in the ceiling of a room, it may explode downwards and sideways with terrific force. Pending disposal of the bomb, the room concerned and those immediately above, below and on either side must be vacated.**

When an attack from the air develops and incendiaries are dropped in numbers, the police and Civil Defence services should use their handlamps freely to detect the presence of any anti-personnel bombs, and the N.F.S. and fireguards may remove the dimming material from their torches.

**EVERY WARDEN SHOULD MAKE HIMSELF FAMILIAR WITH THE INSTRUCTIONS FOR THEIR TREATMENT.**
(C.D. Training Pamphlet No. 1)

**DON'T TOUCH IT!**

NEVER TOUCH AN ANTI-PERSONNEL BOMB IN ANY CIRCUMSTANCES WHATEVER; THEY ARE LIABLE TO EXPLODE AT THE SLIGHTEST CONTACT.

Bomb has Penetrated Ground—Wings Left Above

Separated Wings

Body of Bomb

Bomb Caught in Roof—Looking Upwards

Bomb Detached on Floor of Loft—Wings Left in Roof

these devices. One officer dealt with 27 of an estimated sixty Butterfly bombs reported to have fallen around Caston. Six days later, the same man defused another 31 similar missiles which had brought Wells harbour to a standstill. His courage earned him a George Medal. For all its dangers, however, the Butterfly Blitz was as nothing compared with the devastating impact made by two attacks carried out in the space of three days on Norwich in the spring of 1942.

The Baedeker raids of April 27-28th and April 29-30th wrought havoc across a large area of the city centre. The carnage made a deep and lasting impression on all those who lived through it. Many people's abiding memories of the conflict were shaped by the terrifying sights of those two nights which reminded at least one First World War veteran of the ruins of Ypres and Armentières. Deliberately designed to provoke terror among the civilian population, the raids were part of a co-ordinated campaign waged against Britain's cultural centres as a reprisal for a heavy RAF assault on the historically-important German city of Lubeck. Post-war evidence reveals that British intelligence knew

**Although small in size, the 2kg Butterfly bomb was potentially the most dangerous of all anti-personnel weapons used during the Second World War. Scattered in their thousands over airfields, harbours and fields of standing crops, they caused wide-scale disruption and numerous casualties, forcing the authorities to issue dire warnings about the perils of trying to remove them.**

shortly before each attack the area to be targeted, but defensive measures proved lamentably weak in the face of a well-mounted and accurate assault. Prior to the first Baedeker raid, Norwich had endured 27 raids at a cost of 81 civilian dead. But these sorties had been ill-defined and small-scale. Furthermore, the city had not been attacked for eight months. People had become blasé about the threat. *"The... comparative calm,"* wrote Ralph Mottram, *"had induced a certain number of citizens to disregard the siren, and not to seek the shelters."* The local authorities had grown equally lax. So little used were some public shelters that the council had decided to lock them to prevent them being vandalised. Such complacency was to have fatal consequences.

When eventually computed, the casualty figures from the first raid revealed the heaviest loss of life of any attack carried out against an East Anglian target in the war. Altogether, 162 people were killed and more than 600 injured. The area around City Station, Oak Street and Dereham Road was particularly badly hit. Police later reported around 7000 homes damaged. In one of the most tragic incidents, a number of people were killed and others buried when a bomb scored a direct hit on a shelter in Chapel Field Gardens.

Rescue worker "Ossie" Osbiston left a vivid account of the desperate efforts to bring out the injured: *"The site was a bad one. Young and old were entombed in an underground shelter. Two sisters, about 15 or 16, were dead. An elderly man was in a sitting position with smashed legs. I was held by the legs upside down and after injecting morphine into his limbs I managed to saw through his seat and release him and he was passed up to the men above. The next thing was to get out twin children who were also trapped. Their mother was a big woman, I should think around 14 to 15 stone. We were told to keep our heads down because of the unexploded bombs, but about 7am the bomb disposal officer said we could carry on as the bomb was rendered 'harmless'..."*

After a while it was thought that all the casualties had been cleared. But Osbiston was not certain. Having made his initial report, he returned... *"We all took up positions in the crater and laid our ears to the ground. Immediately one chap said, 'Ossy, I can hear moaning'. I lay down beside him and heard it too. I said, 'Do not use any heavy tools, only the hands'. We soon came across a very beautiful young girl dead. She was suffocated, but she was lying on top of an old lady and this had saved her life. Part of a concrete reinforcement had gone through her hand. I cut the iron off and my First Aid man covered it and she was sent to hospital. She recovered, as did the chap with smashed legs..."*

Following a brief lull, the German raiders returned on April 29-30th in greater strength. Where around 26 aircraft had bombed on the first night, forty struck in a second raid in which the bombing was more concentrated on the city's commercial centre. Fires, fanned by a stiff wind, raged out of control, laying waste to department stores and Caley's chocolate factory. Ted Harvey, an NFS section leader, was called out to the Davey Place area: "There was a conflagration all around us. We weren't controlling anything. It was just a case of pouring water onto the flames, and in time the sheer amount of water reduced it. But by then the centre was devastated. Buildings had collapsed, particularly those of steel girdered construction. Timber-framed buildings, funnily enough, stood up to it better. In the end, it was a question of taking a stand and just trying to stop the fires spreading any further."

That night another 69 people were killed and a further 89 injured. The toll would almost certainly have been greater but for a mass exodus which took place between the two raids. Many families had trekked to shelters on the outskirts of the city and some had simply spent the nights in open countryside. An official report claimed that as many as 40,000, a third of the city's population, had taken part in the voluntary evacuation. "Whole streets and roads were deserted at nightfall for days and weeks afterwards. It was like living in a ghost town," declared one who chose to stay. It was not so much a case of mass hysteria, as simple common sense. "There was a quiet spirit of acceptance," one woman recorded,

**Coming home: B24s cross the Norfolk coast on their return from another bombing mission. The aircraft belong to the 458th Bomb Group which was based at Horsham St Faith, on the outskirts of Norwich.**

"and as they tramped out of the city in their hundreds in the evening, a few belongings in an old pram, tired dirty children, a setting sun... suddenly one picture people all over the world doing the same out of Lashio, out of Mandalay, out of Rostock. Everywhere. And in much worse circumstances, than dry, springtime Norwich..." The mass trekking only lasted about a week, which was just as well since a number of Civil Defence workers had left too. In one incident, a whole team of fire-watchers abandoned their post. The ravaged city became a breeding ground for wild rumours. There was talk of typhoid outbreaks, of panics and of widespread looting. Few of the stories proved accurate. "People were frightened, but not cowardly," one woman later told a survey into the blitz experience. Morale may have been dented, but it had not cracked. Indeed, there had been many instances of bravery, most notably by a 15-year-old messenger boy. John Grix had been blown off his bicycle five times by bombs as he pedalled between warden posts in the early hours of April 30th. Each time, he got back on and completed his journey. His remarkable bike ride earned him a British Empire Medal.

The Baedeker Blitz continued against targets in East Anglia through the summer into the autumn, although few of the raids proved as destructive. Poor marking and a fire decoy site at Bramerton conspired on one occasion to divert the bulk of the bombs intended for Norwich on open countryside around Poringland. A massive fire raid on June 26-27th resulted in an estimated 20,000 incendiaries raining down on the city. Fire-fighters were overwhelmed. More than 660 blazes were reported and, for the first time, the Cathedral was hit by incendiaries. Casualties were

**James Stewart (1908-1997) was already a major Hollywood star when he joined the US 2nd Air Division in Norfolk in 1943. Scorning offers of safe jobs and morale-raising assignments, the "tall drawl" amassed twenty combat missions from Tibenham and Old Buckenham. From squadron commander he rose to Group operations officer and ended the war as chief of staff of the 2nd Combat Wing. No other American film star had a comparable combat record. Lt Col Stewart was awarded the Distinguished Flying Cross, the Air Medal with oak leaf cluster and the French Croix de Guerre. He revisited his wartime haunts on a number of occasions and it was typical of his modesty that he always disdained special treatment.**

relatively light in this, the last of the Luftwaffe's major raids on Norwich, but damage to property was widespread. The aerial campaign finally petered out with an attack on Lynn in September. Thankfully, most of the bombs missed the target and no casualties were reported. It did not, however, mark the end of Hitler's assault on East Anglia.

May 1943 signalled the climax of a series of surprise attacks carried out by FW190 fighter-bombers, flying at extreme low level. In the worst tragedy, 24 ATS girls were killed when their seafront billet at Yarmouth suffered a direct hit. For the people living on the coast, these sudden raids were jarring on nerves already frayed by years of aerial bombardment. But the so-called tip-and-run raids were as nothing compared with the startling new campaign unleashed against Norwich in the autumn of 1944.

It began, inauspiciously, around 4.30pm on September 26th with a devastating blast in open country near Ranworth that left a crater 30ft wide and 13ft deep. Civil Defence workers were mystified. The missile seemed to have come from nowhere. However, by a remarkable coincidence, crews from 100 Group Liberators based at Oulton had witnessed *"a single trail... rising on a thirty degrees angle towards this country"*. A minute later, American airmen flying out of Thorpe Abbotts had caught a fleeting glimpse of a "long, solid trail of white smoke" which started at 18,000ft and rose to 45,000ft. Four minutes after their sighting came the explosion. Subsequent investigation showed it to have been a V2, code-named "Big Bens".

Such was the secrecy surrounding the new weapon, however, that the Civil Defence team attending the Ranworth incident listed it as a "plane crash", even though the first rocket had fallen on mainland Britain 18 days earlier. Confusion persisted even after three more V2 strikes in Norfolk the following day. Asked to confirm if they were "Big Ben" incidents, the puzzled authorities replied: "We can't confirm it's a 'Big Ben' because we don't have any information to tell us what a 'Big Ben' is." In fact, the short-lived campaign waged by Versuchs Artillerie Batterie 444 from their base in South-West Friesland was over by the time the world's first inter-continental ballistic missile was acknowledged as a reality of war. Not that it would have helped the people of Norfolk if they had known the truth. There was absolutely no defence against Hitler's latest and most lethal tool of vengeance. But fortunately for the people of Norwich, the only city in Britain outside of London deliberately targeted for destruction by rockets, accuracy was not the V2's strongest suit. Of the 46 aimed at Norwich during the 17-day campaign, 27 landed in Norfolk, four in Suffolk and none actually struck the city, although a few came frighteningly close. The nearest miss was on October 3rd when a rocket exploded on the Royal Norwich golf course at Hellesdon. Around 400 homes between the Dereham and Boundary roads were damaged and the shock was immense.

Incredibly, there were no reports of any injuries. The children of Rockland St Mary School were not so lucky when a V2 exploded near their village the following day. Twenty-one pupils were injured, although none fatally. That same day another rocket fell in open country at Crostwick, barely a mile from a bomb store at Rackheath. A potentially catastrophic yet ultimately futile chapter drew to a close on October 12th 1944, with an explosion that did little more than shatter the rural calm of Ingworth.

By then the balance of the air war had shifted overwhelmingly against Germany. Day and night vast fleets of heavy bombers filled the skies over a Norfolk so interlaced with airfields that someone likened the county to one enormous, stationary aircraft carrier. Miles of concrete strips, fringed by thousands of corrugated Nissen huts and huge hangars, freckled the countryside and the transformation brought with it a social revolution that would be remembered long after the war.

In September 1939 there had been just five military airfields (Bircham Newton, Feltwell, Marham, Watton and West Raynham) in Norfolk with three, at Coltishall, Horsham St Faith and Methwold, in the process of being completed. By the end of the war the number

**Airborne with the 'Mighty Eighth'. A spectacular aerial photograph showing B24 Liberators of the Hardwick-based 93rd Bomb Group, identifiable by their tail markings. The 93rd were part of the US 2nd Air Division, which was located entirely in Norfolk.**

had risen to 39, of which 15 were occupied by units of the 2nd and 3rd US Air Divisions in what is remembered as the "friendly invasion".

Prior to America's entry, and for some time after, the airfields of Norfolk were a British Commonwealth preserve, with a smattering of units made up of airmen from the occupied countries of eastern and western Europe. All sections of the RAF were represented, from the dashing heroes of Fighter Command, who included the aces Douglas Bader and Stanford Tuck, to the less glamorous though no less brave crews of Bomber Command who, first in Wellingtons, and then in Stirlings, Halifaxes and Lancasters set out from their bases in the west and north of the county in the war's longest and hardest-fought campaign. Arguably the most memorable and almost certainly the most costly contribution in the early days came from the light-bomber squadrons which made up 2 Group.

Flying under-powered and poorly-protected Blenheims from airfields, some of them no more than grass strips, they sustained some of the heaviest losses of any force during the entire war. Whole squadrons were virtually wiped out in gallant attempts to stem the German tide in 1940, and then again during a series of ill-judged strikes against heavily-defended ports and enemy convoys. So great was the sacrifice that Churchill compared it to the Charge of the Light Brigade. The Norfolk and England cricketer Bill Edrich, who earned a DFC flying Blenheims, never forgot one raid on Rotterdam in which six aircraft from his squadron were despatched from Watton. "I had laid on nine late suppers in the Officers' Mess, but only one officer got back," he recalled. "His supper remained uneaten." Tragically, such wastage was not exceptional. Of 12 Blenheims sent from Watton to attack a German airfield at Aalborg in Denmark on August 13th 1940, one aircraft aborted and the remainder were shot down. Today a twisted propeller salvaged from one of the wrecks recalls the desperate valour displayed on this and many other occasions.

In spite of such losses, Blenheim crews contrived against the odds to score a number of notable successes, including an attack on the Knapsack power station in Cologne and an audacious, low-level strike against Bremen which earned for its Swanton Morley-based

**Derek and Hugh Seagrim achieved the unique distinction of becoming the only brothers to earn the Victoria Cross and the George Cross, the nation's two highest gallantry awards. Sons of the Rev Charles Seagrim, the rector of Whissonsett-with-Horningtoft, they were educated at the King Edward VI School in Norwich and both joined the army – Derek entering the Green Howards and Hugh the 1/20th Burma Rifles. Derek Seagrim earned his VC for his courageous leadership during the assault on the Mareth Line in North Africa on March 20th-21st 1943, only to be killed in action three weeks later. Hugh, nicknamed "Grandfather Longlegs" on account of his height, was also posthumously honoured for an unorthodox campaign waged far behind enemy lines in Burma. When the Japanese began murdering natives for harbouring him, he gave himself up in the full knowledge he would be executed. In 1985, Whissonsett honoured its bravest sons by unveiling a new village sign dedicated to their memory.**

leader, Hughie Edwards, a well-merited Victoria Cross, one of five to airmen flying out of Norfolk during the Second World War. Eventually, the Blenheims gave way to Bostons, Venturas, Mitchells and Mosquitoes. New and improved aircraft brought a steady reduction in the loss ratio, although even as late as the spring of 1943 a New Zealand squadron based at Methwold was all but wiped out during a raid on Amsterdam power station. Such disasters, however, were increasingly out-weighed by the growing number of successes, from the spectacular raid on the Philips factory in Eindhoven in December 1942, to a whole series of pinpoint bombing sorties against Gestapo headquarter buildings across occupied Europe.

In the midst of all these forays was a mission outstanding neither for its scale nor its success, but for the participation of a small contingent of American airmen. The Independence Day raid mounted from Swanton Morley in the summer of 1942 marked the first involvement of the United States Army Air Force in the European campaign. Although all 12 Bostons bore RAF markings, six were crewed by men of the 15th Bomb Squadron against enemy airfields in Holland. It proved a rough baptism. Two of the American-manned bombers were lost and a third limped home on one engine. Leo Hawel, one of the pilots, wrote in his diary the following day: *"Everybody's feeling mighty rough, me included. We had a roaring party here at Swanton Morley last night. When you lose a bunch of good boys, you have to get good and drunk, otherwise you'll get pretty browned-off with the whole set-up..."*

In the months that followed, there would be more good men lost and many more parties as the heart of rural Norfolk was transformed into a vast American encampment. As the war progressed, Norfolk had seen a huge influx of building workers, who laboured on the construction of a network of concrete runways designed to take fleets of heavy bombers. Many of these were handed over to the USAAF and they quickly became temporary home to an army of thousands, ranging from airmen to admin staff, ground crews to medical teams and any number of engineers and assorted support units. The Liberator-equipped 2nd US Air Division was exclusively based in Norfolk, with the presence of Flying Fortress groups from the 3rd Division limited to three bases at Deopham Green, Snetterton Heath and Thorpe Abbotts. It was these aircraft with their shining silver liveries and irreverent names which filled the skies over Norfolk and provided one of the war's enduring images.

Yet, enormous as was their contribution to the war effort, with their massed daylight raids on industrial targets, oil refineries, port installations, U-boat pens and the like, it was their cultural and social impact on the day to day lives of thousands of ordinary people that left the greatest legacy. To a war-weary population grown accustomed to austerity, starved of almost all luxuries, the sudden invasion of thousands of young Americans was like a breath of fresh air. They brought with them a sense of excitement, an impression of glamour that was not always justified and, of course, money. Pubs and shops in villages dwarfed by neighbouring bases had never had it so good. Nor had the children, many of whom were befriended by homesick Yanks, and a good many young, and not so young, women. Eagerly-awaited parties on the bases and regular dances at such clubs as the Samson and Hercules left a trail of GI brides and broken hearts. The phrase: "Over sexed, over paid and over here" was soon coined. But it hardly told the whole story of a genuinely special relationship.

Pamela Standley, of Wymondham, remembered attending dances at Deopham Green on Wednesday evenings: "Sometimes as we arrived at the base, the B-17s would still be returning from that day's raid... I think it brought home to even the flightiest of us the seriousness of what was going on around us... Being surrounded by bases we were very conscious of all these planes taking off. We would watch as they circled, quite low at first and then higher and higher, finally forming up and heading off eastwards. It was quite different when they came back. Sometimes a squadron all together, but often just ones and

**Cheering crowds greet the arrival of more servicemen during Norwich's VE Day celebrations. But the war was to drag on another three long months in the Far East.**

twos. We could tell what sort of mission it had been by the way they returned. And if you had a special boyfriend it all seemed very close. You almost felt part of their lives..."

It was a mutual feeling. Contrary to the popular myth, life on the bases was no bed of roses. The wretched weather and freezing Nissen huts were a constant source of complaint. *"I don't believe I was ever really warm or without a cold the whole time we were there,"* wrote Kenneth Jewell, a pilot based at Shipdham. Another airman, Forrest S Clark, remembered: *"We all, or most of us, wore warm socks even in bed. Yet the dampness seeped into the quarters and into the beds and the wind rattled against the huts..."* According to Roy Jonasson, a mechanic serving at Hethel, *"one feels the cold here much more than in Montana where it gets colder."* The harsh conditions combined with a longing to be with their loved ones made many Americans all the more grateful to those people who welcomed them into their homes. *"The love and kindness was at times like an oasis in hell,"* recorded one airman befriended by a Norwich family. *"I will love this family and the English people as long as I shall live."* Many Americans were struck by local people's willingness to share the most meagre rations. Roy Jonasson treasured a memory of a Christmas dinner provided in Hethersett by two elderly women: "As I sat there eating, I thought of the many things they had gone through during the Blitz, yet they were so happy to have some Yanks in their home for Christmas..."

Such was the human face of the "grand alliance", the first chapter of which drew to a close in a shower of fireworks and flares as people marked VE-Day with mixed emotions. Many were sorry at the prospect of the departure of men who had become close friends. Pat Everson, a schoolgirl living on the edge of the Seething base, recalled her mother explaining that the war was over and the Americans would soon be returning home: "I remember sitting at the bedroom window windows crying as I did not want them to leave. They had really brought colour and excitement to the children around the base." Before leaving, however, they had one more important role to play. The Victory Parade through the crowded streets of Norwich was largely an Anglo-American affair with the men

THE KING OPENS PARLIAMENT

Over Quarter of a Million People Outside Palace

A GREAT DAY OF REJOICING

The joy and relief which the nation felt at the restoration of peace after six years found its most eloquent expression in the scenes that marked the State opening of the new Parliament.

World Reactions to News of Surrender

**It's finally over: The EDP reported on August 8th 1945 on the celebrations following the surrender of Japan.**

of the 44th Bomb Group based at Shipdham providing a large proportion of the marching units. Taking the salute on the steps of City Hall on that Sunday in May were Field Marshal Lord Ironside and Brig Gen Leon W Johnson of the USAAF. It was a fitting tribute to a spirit of friendship and a sacrifice - 6300 men of the 2nd Air Division alone lost their lives - which is remembered to this day.

Victory in Europe, however, did not mark the end of the "special relationship". Nor did it bring an end to the war or the suffering. The conflict against Japan in the Far East dragged on for a further three months, a source of particular anguish and anxiety for thousands of families across East Anglia.

As well as the hundreds of local men fighting in Burma, many more were engaged in a grim struggle for survival in prison camps in Singapore, along the Thai-Burma border and in Japan itself. These were the men of the 18th (East Anglian) Division, a force which included no fewer than three Norfolk territorial battalions as well as detachments of engineers and medics raised in the county. They had spent the first two years of the war training and guarding against an invasion that never came, before being shipped abroad in the autumn of 1941. Bound originally for the Middle East and a campaign for which they had prepared long and hard, they were diverted, for reasons more of political expediency than military advantage, to Singapore and a campaign many considered already lost. One brigade, including the 5th and 6th Royal Norfolks, were plunged, devoid of jungle training or experience of Japanese tactics, straight into battle. The last of the divisional units to arrive did so just ten days before the embattled island, teeming with ill-prepared British and Commonwealth soldiers, was ignominiously surrendered to a numerically inferior enemy.

A lucky few escaped just before the end, but for the overwhelming majority of the 18th Division a defeat Churchill called the "worst disaster" in British military history signalled only the beginning of an ordeal that all but beggared belief. During more than three years of brutal captivity around a third of the 20,000-strong division succumbed, victims of malnourishment, mistreatment and myriad tropical diseases. Of all the struggles endured by battalions of the Royal Norfolk Regiment, from the Calvados to Kohima, theirs was by far the worst.

"You didn't think about tomorrow and you daren't think of home because that would have destroyed you," recalled Fred Eva, a former member of the 6th Norfolks who worked at the famous Kwai bridge camp. "Survival was by the hour." Forced to slave on the notorious Death Railway linking Thailand to Burma, in the treacherous copper mines of Taiwan and the dockyards of Japan, many fell easy prey to beri-beri, cholera, dysentry, malaria and tropical ulcers. Denied basic medicines, they relied on the skills of their overworked doctors and simple comradeship to pull them through. Noel Duckworth, an army padre whose selfless work in captivity made him a legendary figure, later movingly wrote on his fellow prisoners: *"They were left to fight what turned out to be a better fight - that of sharing each other's ills, sorrows and meagre rations, and to wrest their comrades' lives from the very pit of hell... Having nothing of this world's goods, they possessed all things of inner strength and of the finest of human gifts - courage."*

Charlie Carpenter, a survivor of the Thai railway camps, put it differently: "Day after miserable day the majority of us dragged ourselves to work, because we knew that to give in would be fatal...We resembled human skeletons, but we still held our heads high, and even tried to laugh and make jokes. This completely baffled the Japs who thought we were bloody mad."

Theirs was indeed a victory snatched from defeat. But it has left painful scars which have yet to be healed. Many came home with the spectre of the labour camps locked forever in their minds. Others never fully recovered their health. No one will ever know how many deaths were hastened by their fearful ordeal. To this day, some of the survivors feel a deep sense of betrayal and injustice not only over the treatment meted out to them all those

**Lest we forget... Ex-serviceman Ray Riches wipes away a tear during the Norwich commemoration on May 7th 1995 of the fiftieth anniversary of VE Day.**

**Reis Leming, a young United States serviceman, was one of two Americans awarded the George Medal for their bravery in helping rescue victims of the notorious 1953 East Coast flood disaster.**

years ago, but in the many decades since. A long-running campaign for compensation looks like continuing into a new century. Peace, it seems, has not exorcised the demons of the past.

Years after the war, Herbert Widdows attempted to articulate the intensity of feeling: "It is possible to go on for ever about conditions and harsh treatment in the Japanese PoW camps but words cannot convey the atmosphere, the mud, filth and smells, the misery, degradation and suffering and above all the deaths of the human skeletons all around, every day and night. It is easy for anyone not affected to take a detached view of all this – they can never comprehend. But for those who were there it was a large part of their lives which can never be forgotten – or forgiven."

The land to which they returned in the autumn of 1945 was a very different place. Once again war had proved a powerful catalyst for social change. Churchill and the Conservatives had been swept away by a Labour Party committed to the most radical programme of State intervention of this or any other century. But victory had been won at a heavy price. It was to be an austere revolution in a country made weary by war, its coffers all but exhausted and its people still reliant on a rationed economy. To further darken an already gloomy picture, the construction of a "new Jerusalem" was to be carried on under the shadow of a new menace.The cataclysmic atom bomb blasts which ended the conflict ushered in the nuclear age and a peace that was to prove every bit as fragile as the health of so many of the prisoners of war the explosions had saved.

Tensions between the victorious allies, contained for the most part during the war, soon surfaced to threaten a world riven by ideological division. It was the beginning of a power struggle which would touch the lives of countless millions of ordinary people on every continent. The Cold War, as it became known, fuelled a spectacular arms race that was matched, in human terms, by a fresh call to arms. National Service was introduced. Volunteers were recruited into a new Civil Defence force. Even the Home Guard was briefly resuscitated. The signs of the worsening crisis were everywhere apparent, not least in a remote corner of rural Norfolk which found itself at the centre of an acrimonious wrangle in the spring of 1948.

The argument was over the rights of people from five Breckland villages to return to their homes six years after they had been requisitioned by the army to form part of a new training ground known as the Stanford Battle

Area. The wartime land grab involved 15,000 acres of land, fifty to sixty farms, five churches, four schools and about 1100 people, who were to be entitled to compensation and treated *"as if they had been bombed out by enemy action"*. Contrary to contemporary press reports, the decision announced in June 1942, was accepted without enthusiasm, which was hardly surprising given that the inhabitants of Stanford, Lynford, Tottington, West Tofts and Buckenham Tofts were given only a month to move. For the rest of the war, with the single exception of the harvest of '42, the battle area remained closed to the general public.

And so it remained into peacetime, even though a 1946 county council review concluded that *"the owners of the property... were promised by the Regional Commissioners that the area would be returned to them after the war"*. It was clear, however, that the military authorities had no intention of relinquishing their control. In fact, they were anxious to extend the training area by another 12,000 acres and to maintain it on a permanent basis. Battlelines were drawn and a public inquiry held. But it was all to no avail for the dispossessed villagers. Their plea for the Government to honour a wartime promise counted for nothing against the threat apparently posed by the Soviet Union. On July 19th 1948, villagers' hopes were finally dashed when the Minister of Town and Country Planning, Lewis Silkin, announced to the House of Commons that the Government was "compelled by circumstances to disregard the pledge given". The decision sharply divided public opinion. One commentator echoed the words of Dorothy Sayers in calling it "this damnable cat's cradle of bloody alternatives". To the villagers of Breckland it amounted to a betrayal which rankles to this day.

By the time the decision was reached, the Cold War was hotting up. A few weeks earlier the Russians had sealed off all land routes into the western sectors of Berlin, precipitating a massive airlift and the return of the United States Air Force to Britain. Even as the Stanford debate rumbled towards its bitter conclusion American bombers were landing at RAF bases in Norfolk. By December, the former wartime RAF base at Sculthorpe, near Fakenham, had been reopened, and by February it was accepting the first of many squadrons of B29 and B50 Superfortresses.

In the tense months that followed, training missions were flown complete with dummy A-bombs and rumours persist that live bombs, the first to arrive in this country, were stored at the base. Although their stay was to be a short one, the arrival of the bombers signalled the start of a post-war association even more deep-rooted than those special relationships

Eastern Daily Press

Telephone: Norwich 23231

NORWICH, MONDAY, April 23, 1956

**Открытое Письмо**

**г. Н. А. Булганину и**
**г. Н. С. Хрущеву**
**по случаю посещения ими района Норфолка**

Джентельмены — В момент разгара пыла военных лет рядовые граждане как Советского Союза так и Великобритании были охвачены верой в то, что элементарная гуманность заполнит брешь существующую между народом Вашей страны, и населением Англии. Однако, последовали годы, когда казалось несомненным, что таким надеждам не суждено сбыться; прения по разоружению не кончились ничем, не столько по причине самого вопроса о методах, как, главным образом, вследствие того, что обоюдные расхож-

**An Open Letter**

**to Mr. N. A. Bulganin and**
**Mr. N. S. Kruschev on**
**their visit to Norfolk**

Gentlemen—In the fine fervour of the war years ordinary citizens of Russia, as of Britain, rallied to the belief that common humanity might bridge the gap between your people and ours. In the years that followed any such hopes have seemed utterly shattered; disarmament discussions have foundered, not so much on questions of method as because the conflict between your beliefs and ours was too acute for there to be any basis of trust and confidence.

Of recent months you have been engaged in an agonising re-appraisal of the cult of personality; it may be that into your minds, even if not publicly expressed, there has crept a doubt whether

**One of the most celebrated EDP editorials of the century came on April 23rd 1956 when, to mark the visit to RAF Marham of Russian leaders Nikolai Kruschev and Marshal Bulganin, the paper's comments were translated side-by-side into Russian. During their visit to the base the Soviets saw new Canberras and Valiants and toured the home of a service couple. There were smiles at the question posed to Marshal Bulganin by their five-year-old son: "Are you Father Christmas?"**

forged in wartime. For where the old bases had been temporary, Sculthorpe was to become a permanent home for the USAF. By the end of the Fifties, it had become the largest and most important American airfield in Europe, complete with its own schools, shops and a shoal of bungalows dubbed "tobacco houses" on account of having been built by the British Government in return for tobacco. At its peak, the base population, including satellite "settlements" from Hunstanton to Cromer, totalled around 10,000 people. Not surprisingly, the area around Sculthorpe became euphemistically known as Little

U.S. airman aimed gun in nuclear suicide bid

A SERGEANT of the U.S. Air Force threatened to commit suicide by firing a pistol into a nuclear bomb on Sculthorpe U.S.A.F. base in 1958, a U.S. Defence Department spokesman said in Washington late last night.

The incident was one of several said to have brought about a tightening of regulations designed to prevent unstable personnel from handling nuclear weapons.

The sergeant was not identified, but was said to have been employed as a special weapons maintenance technician, with access to nuclear weapons. He was prevented from carrying out his threat.

The Defence Department spokesman said, "He did not complete his threatened action. Even if he had attempted it, the action would not have resulted in a nuclear explosion. It might have caused an explosion of a small amount of

POLICE TO GET SIX PER-CENT

**After years of rumours, it was finally admitted in November 1962 that a USAF master sergeant had threatened to detonate a nuclear device at Sculthorpe in 1958.**

America. Jim Baldwin, who witnessed and later chronicled the transformation, recalled: *"The impact of all this on the rather austere post-war economy of North Norfolk can be imagined. The Americans seemed to be involved in everything in Fakenham, from Youth for Christ to fights in pubs! It was just that they seemed to have everything. If you wanted a PA system for a fete they had one, if you wanted lights they had them. And if you shouted, 'ha' yer got na' gum, chum?' you were equally rewarded with a stick of Spearmint. They even had the first electric guitar to be seen in this part of the world."*

Much of the operational work carried out from Sculthorpe, including spy flights deep into Warsaw Pact-controlled airspace, was shrouded in secrecy, but two events during the Fifties brought the base to national prominence. The first was the devastating East Coast floods of 1953 which cost the lives of hundreds, including 17 Americans living in seaside chalets at Hunstanton, and produced a hero in the shape of a lean, young US airman called Reis Leming. Among a detachment of the 67th Air Sea Rescue Squadron hurried to the flood-hit coast, he helped save 27 people before collapsing with exhaustion. It was an act which earned him one of two George Medals awarded to American airmen. The second major incident, five years later, was of an altogether different nature and, if some accounts are to be believed, threatened to achieve something the Soviet Union never attempted - the nuclear destruction of one of NATO's most important installations.

At the centre of the extraordinary drama was Master Sgt Leander V Cunningham. Beset with personal problems, he took a .45 pistol, locked himself in a nuclear bomb store and threatened to blow himself and a large chunk of Norfolk to "kingdom come". The stand-off lasted two hours before Cunningham surrendered. Official American denials about his ability to activate the weapons have been periodically countered and the arguments about how close Norfolk came to a nuclear catastrophe have raged ever since.

There were other alarms which found their way into the public arena: notably an accidental explosion at Marham in 1954 which damaged 11 Canberras, putting six of them out of action, a fire which tore through one of Fighter Command's key radar bunkers at Neatishead and innumerable aircraft crashes. The Cold War also brought its domestic flashpoints. North Pickenham's Thor missile base was the scene of prolonged and sometimes turbulent protests during the late Fifties into the early Sixties. But these were the exception to the rule. Given the extent of the arsenal of weapons sited in Norfolk, from V-bombers to Meteors and Lightnings to Bloodhound missiles, it seems, in hindsight, surprising that the disturbances were so few. As it was, the great threat to world peace, the most damaging and dangerous of all the Second World War's legacies, proved an illusion. The fall of the Berlin Wall in 1989 marked the end of a conflict which bore comparison with the Phoney war and the invasion scare which followed. In its wake came a series of military cutbacks. Nuclear bunkers were sealed and sold off. Air force bases were closed. Among those to go were Swanton Morley (handed over to the army), Watton and West Raynham.

By the Nineties the huge American commitment at Sculthorpe was already a distant memory. The last major unit had flown out in the spring of 1964, but in the years after they had maintained a small presence. A million pounds was spent in 1977 on improving a runway which remained the third longest in Europe and there were plans to upgrade the base. But on a fine autumn morning in October 1992 the USAF finally severed its Norfolk links with a short ceremony culminating in the Stars and Stripes being hauled down for the last time.

Jim Baldwin recorded: *"In the small crowd of onlookers was a man in overalls carrying a spanner and some keys.*

*"When everyone had gone, he turned off the water and locked the gate..."*

# Chapter 14

# *Sporting Norfolk*

When schoolmasters Robert Webster and Joe Nutchey called a public meeting at the Criterion Cafe in White Lion Street, Norwich, on Tuesday, June 17th 1902, they could scarcely have imagined the long-term consequences of their decision to press ahead with plans for a new football club in the city.

They argued "that the time has now arrived when it is desirable to form a Norwich City Football Club" - and when the motion was carried, it kicked off nearly a century of triumph and tragedy, delight and dejection, buoyancy and near-bankruptcy, celebration and controversy in the life of a club whose fortunes have since touched the lives of so many thousands in Norfolk and far, far beyond.

The immediate effects of the club's formation were the upstaging of the Church of England Young Men's Society as the major force in Norwich soccer, the capture of the Norfolk & Suffolk League title within three years, bringing crowds of 6000 to home matches at their Newmarket Road ground, and, in 1905, after the FA found the club guilty of making payments and incurring expenses not compatible with their amateur status, the move to professionalism and election to the Southern League.

It was another three years before the club moved to a new ground, The Nest, fashioned out of a disused chalk pit in Rosary Road, Norwich. It was the Canaries' home for more than a quarter of a century - until, in fact, the stadium was declared unsafe following a record crowd of 25,037 for the FA Cup visit of Sheffield Wednesday in February 1935.

The Nest was a daunting sight for visiting teams with a 50ft concrete wall at one end of the ground, holding a cliff topped by a row of terraced houses. Less intimidating for the opposition, it seems, were the Canaries, whose progress on the field was modest except for the occasional FA Cup upset - and whose off-field ailments were very nearly terminal.

Debts of £3000 incurred during the First World War forced the club to be wound up in December 1917, but a new company was formed in February 1919 and six months later, City were back in action in the Southern League, albeit briefly. They were admitted to the Football League in May 1920 after the Southern League first division clubs came up with the proposition that they become the Football League's new third division. The idea was accepted and a 1-1 draw at Plymouth in August 1920 marked City's Football League baptism. But in the Twenties City did not make startling progress, finishing no higher than 11th in Division Three South. That was in 1923-24, and it was to be another ten years before Norwich climbed further up the league ladder.

**DAVID CUFFLEY was born at Caister, and educated at Caister Junior School and Great Yarmouth Grammar School, joining Eastern Counties Newspapers as a trainee reporter in 1979. He joined the Eastern Daily Press sports desk in 1985, covered Norwich City matches for six seasons for the EDP and Evening News, and still writes on the club's affairs. He became Evening News sports editor in 1995. Married with two children, he lives in Norwich.**

**Norwich City football club 1909-10, pictured at The Nest, off Rosary Road.**

**Born at Sheringham, Joe Hannah made his Norwich City debut in their first season in the Football League, 1920-21, and went on to make a pre-war record 427 appearances for the club. Hannah, who later became captain, was still a key figure in the Canaries' first-team line-up in 1933-34, playing more than half the Division Three South programme as City clinched the championship and a coveted place in Division Two. He played mostly at right-back or right-half, and was such a perfectionist that on one occasion, greatly dissatisfied with his own performance, he sentenced himself to walk 25 miles home to Sheringham. A knee injury effectively ended his career at the age of 35. He was later City trainer. Only four players since the war have passed his appearance total. Hannah died in 1975, at the age of 76.**

Third in the table in 1932-33, a season marred by the death of Jimmy Kerr, their most successful manager of the period, the Canaries finally gave their supporters the prize they had been waiting for in 1933-34. With former Southampton and Arsenal full-back Tom Parker as manager, the Canaries stormed to the Division Three South championship by a margin of seven points, booking that coveted place in Division Two. And, a year later, with The Nest declared unsafe, came the move to Carrow Road, Norwich City's home to the present day, and the start of a rollercoaster ride through six and a half decades of joy and despair for all of the Canary faith.

There have been glorious days and nights when the Canaries have thumbed their rustic noses at the aristocrats of English, even European soccer, and shaken the football world. And equally there have been days of utter despair to tax the loyalty of even the most ardent supporter. Norwich City, it must be said, are almost unrivalled as football's masters of the anti-climax.

But it is the good times that sustain supporters on long journeys to Carlisle, Exeter, Newcastle and Wrexham – heroic occasions that bring a lump to the throat and a tear to the eye and remind us why thousands stay committed to the cause in the hope that their loyalty and sacrifice of time, energy, hard-earned cash and irreparably frayed nerves, will once more be rewarded.

So it is fitting, at the end of nearly a century of Canary history, to reflect on the golden days and to pose the question that supporters must frequently ask – just when was Norwich City's golden year? What was truly their finest hour?

It would be unfair in such a debate to dismiss the highlights of the period between the wars, particularly the achievements of Parker's Canaries in 1933-34, when they topped Division Three South for 28 out of 34 weeks and the goal-scoring feats of Jack Vinall and Billy Warnes helped pull in record crowds at The Nest, including 22,363 for the Easter Monday game against Newport County.

Nor should one ignore the claims to a place in City's hall of fame of men such as Sheringham-born Joe Hannah, who made a pre-war record 427 appearances for the club, or goal-scoring heroes such as Vinall, who scored 80 times for City – fourth in the all-time list – and before him, Percy Varco, the Cornishman who scored 47 times in 65 matches between 1927 and 1929 and then joined Exeter on a free transfer! But the Canaries were relegated from Division Two at the end of 1938-39 and it is only since the war, and more precisely in the past forty years, that Norwich City have made a name for themselves outside Norfolk, and not just as another name on the pools coupon.

And from those last four decades, most supporters would probably pick their proudest moment from one of four years – 1959, 1972, 1985 and 1993.

The FA Cup had brought out City's giant-killing instincts in half a dozen major upsets even before the exploits of Archie Macaulay's legendary team of 1959.

Three of those triumphs came before the First World War. In January 1908, Norwich's final season at Newmarket Road, they beat FA Cup holders Sheffield Wednesday 2-0 in the first round, and the following season they beat Liverpool 3-2 at Anfield. Sunderland were another major scalp, beaten 3-1 at The Nest in January 1911.

First Division Leeds were knocked out in a fourth round replay in 1935, and the early Fifties saw further heroics. In 1950, the Canaries drew 1-1 with League champions Portsmouth at Fratton Park, but should have won – Pompey's Lindy Delapenha later admitted he had scored the equaliser with his hand. The replay set a new Carrow Road attendance record of 43,129, but Portsmouth won 2-0. In 1951, with Norman Low as manager, the Canaries wrote another giant-killing chapter with a 3-1 home win over Liverpool in the third round, and in 1954 came an even greater shock, a 2-1 fourth round win at Arsenal thanks to two Tommy Johnston goals.

But even this catalogue of conquests was put in the shade by the extraordinary events of nine and a half weeks in early 1959, when Norwich became only the fourth Division Three side to reach the FA Cup semi-finals, and the whole of Norfolk was gripped by football fever. Their achievement was all the more remarkable in that it came just two years after the club was threatened with extinction. It was during Parker's second spell as manager that City went 25 League games without a win, and gates in 1956-57 dropped below the 10,000 mark.

The Norfolk News Company, publishers of the Eastern Daily Press, paid one week's £500 wage bill before a public appeal led by the Lord Mayor of Norwich, Arthur South – years later to become City chairman – raised £20,000 to rescue the club. A new board was formed under the chairmanship of Geoffrey Watling, and one of his first acts was to recruit former Scotland international and Dundee coach Macaulay as manager, a masterstroke and a turning point in club history.

Even so, there had been little in the first half of the 1958-59 season to suggest that City were about to take English football by storm, but all that changed with a thrilling 3-0 third round victory over Manchester United's post-Munich Busby Babes at snow-covered Carrow Road in front of the first of four capacity 38,000 crowds in the competition that season.

Victory was given additional local flavour since two of the goals came from Fincham-born 23-year-old centre-forward Terry Bly. By the time City had made their heroic semi-final exit, Bly had bagged a further five goals in the competition and earned himself a permanent place in Canary folklore.

By the standards of the day, Macaulay's magical team, roared on by the distinctive club anthem "On the Ball, City", was distinctly cosmopolitan, blending a Canadian, two Irishmen, a Scotsman and later a South African with seven Englishmen, led by skipper Ron Ashman from left-back. Cardiff were beaten 3-2 at Norwich in round four, and an estimated 20,000 City fans were at Tottenham on St Valentine's Day as a freak last-minute equaliser from Cliff Jones cancelled out Terry Allcock's goal and gave Bill Nicholson's glamour team a fifth round replay at Norwich – a brief reprieve as Bly's second-half winner put City into the last eight.

There followed at Bramall Lane, Sheffield, arguably the bravest individual performance in the Canaries' history, goalkeeper Ken Nethercott playing the final half-hour with a dislocated shoulder, during which time Canadian winger Errol Crossan scored to earn a quarter-final replay against Sheffield United.

The injury marked the end of England B international Nethercott's first-team career, and it is to City's eternal shame that the brave Bristolian was never granted a testimonial in recognition of his 416 games for the club.

The Blades were beaten 3-2 four days later

**Goalkeeper Ken Nethercott leaves the field at Bramall Lane in 1959 after his heroic FA Cup performance against Sheffield United.**

**No player has donned the Canary yellow shirt with more pride and distinction than Ron Ashman, whose playing career with Norwich City spanned 16 years before he became acting manager, then manager. Ashman's total of 662 first-team appearances has been beaten only by Kevin Keelan, the goalkeeper he signed in July 1963. Whittlesey-born Ashman started out at centre-forward and scored 56 goals for the Canaries, but reverted to half-back for much of the Fifties and finally to left-back in his last few memorable seasons with the club, skippering City to the FA Cup semi-finals in 1959, promotion to Division Two a year later, and the Football League Cup in 1962. As manager from December 1962 to June 1966, he made some astute signings, including Keelan and star goalscorers Ron Davies and Hugh Curran. Few men have inspired such affection among City supporters as Ashman, who earned an FA twenty-year long service award.**

in a thrilling replay as the brilliance of outside-left Bobby Brennan and two more goals from Bly saw City home, with South African keeper Sandy Kennon making his debut in place of Nethercott. It was Brennan again who kept the Wembley dream alive with a semi-final equaliser on his 34th birthday against Luton at White Hart Lane, but the replay at St Andrew's, Birmingham, marked the end of the road when the Hatters went through to the final with a second-half goal from Irish international winger Billy Bingham, despite City dominating three quarters of the game.

Macaulay's work had only just begun, and a year later, he steered the Canaries back to Division Two as Division Three runners-up to Southampton. They even finished fourth in their first season back in Division Two in 1960-61, before the manager with the Midas touch resigned to take over at West Bromwich Albion.

Successive City teams of the Sixties struggled to live with the legacy of the Macaulay era. There were further FA Cup upsets - a fourth-round replay triumph over Ipswich at Portman Road in 1962, just a few months before Alf Ramsey's team won the League championship; a superb run to the quarter-finals in 1963 which ended when Leicester won 2-0 in front of a record crowd of 43,984 at Carrow Road; and, most astonishing of all, in 1967, a 2-1 victory at Old Trafford for Lol Morgan's Canaries against a Manchester United team including George Best, Bobby Charlton, Denis Law and Nobby Stiles.

City also won the Football League Cup in 1962 during Willie Reid's short reign as manager, beating Rochdale 4-0 on aggregate in a two-leg final, but First Division football remained a remote prospect for most of the decade as Reid, George Swindin, Ashman and Morgan tried and failed to find the formula for success. Remote, that is, until the arrival of Ron Saunders from Oxford as manager in July 1969. A tough centre-forward in his playing days, he nevertheless believed in laying solid defensive foundations - with goalkeeper Kevin Keelan and twin centre-backs Dave Stringer and iron man captain Duncan Forbes the triumvirate around which he built his underrated team, gradually adding more invention with such shrewd acquisitions as midfielders Doug Livermore and Graham Paddon, and strikers Peter Silvester, David Cross and later, Jim Bone.

It was in 1971-72, Saunders' third season in charge, that the Canaries - until then criticised by fans for a sterile approach under their no-nonsense boss - finally delivered the goods. Top of the table for most of the season, unbeaten at home and losing just six matches on their travels, City clinched promotion with a 2-1 victory at Orient on an emotional night on Monday April 24th 1972, courtesy of a goal from fans' favourite and leading scorer Ken Foggo and a penalty by Paddon.

Five days later a goal from player of the year Stringer was enough to secure the championship in a 1-1 draw at Watford. Saunders' successful formula continued to work as City began life in Division One impressively, beating Derby, Arsenal and Tottenham early in the season before reaching Wembley for the first time, losing 1-0 to Spurs in a disappointing League Cup final in March 1973. But the real drama had come in earlier rounds with a 3-0 victory at Arsenal in the quarter-finals - when Forbes suffered a punctured lung - followed by an agonising semi-final saga with Chelsea, in which the second leg had to be replayed because of fog. City, leading 3-2 on the night and 5-2 on aggregate, were less than six minutes from Wembley when thick fog enveloped Carrow Road. Thankfully they won the replay 1-0 with a goal from Forbes' replacement, Steve Govier, to go through 3-0 on aggregate.

Either side of Wembley, City had slipped alarmingly into the relegation zone, and it took an injury-time goal from Stringer in the final home game against Crystal Palace to secure a 2-1 win and Division One survival. Saunders' days were numbered, however, and he resigned in November 1973 - just a few months after the resignation of Watling, the chairman he admired so much. The 14 years following Saunders' departure saw a different kind of revolution for the Canaries - with two graduates of the West Ham soccer academy

**The best of times... (above) Norwich City players Graham Paddon and Ken Foggo celebrate their goals against Orient in 1972 which took the Canaries into Division One for the first time, and (left) celebrations after the Milk Cup victory at Wembley in 1985.**

**It is unlikely Kevin Keelan's record of 673 first-team games for Norwich City will ever be beaten. No wonder Ron Ashman, the manager who signed him from Wrexham for £6500 in July 1963, described him as the "bargain of the century". Calcutta-born Keelan's City career spanned 17 years, his final appearance coming at the age of 39 against Liverpool in February 1980. A brave, agile and, at his best, spectacularly brilliant showman with an occasionally fiery temper, Keelan was twice voted Player of the Year, twice played in promotion-winning City teams and twice played in League Cup finals at Wembley, performing heroically in the second of them against Aston Villa in 1975. He broke Ashman's club appearance record in his final season. Now an American citizen, living in Florida, Keelan made an emotional return to Carrow Road in 1997 for a City "team of legends" dinner.**

directing operations at Carrow Road. John Bond replaced Saunders as manager from November 1973 until October 1980, when he resigned to take over at Manchester City, and was succeeded by his assistant, Ken Brown. Both had played in the highly successful Hammers side of the early Sixties, and brought with them a belief in the same brand of attacking football. City were relegated in 1974, six months after Bond's arrival, but were promoted again a year later, also reaching the 1975 League Cup final. After a stirring run to Wembley, they performed miserably on the day – Keelan, Stringer and Forbes apart – and lost 1-0, ironically to Saunders' Aston Villa.

Under Bond, City were at times breath-takingly brilliant, and his signings included such top-class performers as temperamental striker Ted MacDougall, who scored 28 goals in 1975-76, World Cup winner Martin Peters, England centre-forward Joe Royle and striker Kevin Reeves, the first of City's £1 million exports. The capture of Peters for £40,000 from Spurs in 1975 ranks as one of the Canaries' best pieces of business, and he repaid them with 232 games and fifty goals in the twilight of his career. Bond also established a youth policy which produced a crop of future first-team regulars, among them ex-boxer Justin Fashanu, another £1 million striker.

But his teams had a defensive frailty which went hand-in-hand with their adventurous style of play, and though they held their own in Division One, there was seldom any likelihood of winning a trophy. The Canaries were just as unpredictable in Brown's seven-year reign.

Relegated twice, promoted twice, they again bounced between the divisions, but Brown and coach Mel Machin – one of Bond's first recruits in 1973 as a polished right-back – at least got their hands on some silverware.

The most memorable day of Brown's managerial reign, though by no means the most outstanding victory, was the Milk Cup final against Sunderland on Sunday March 24th 1985. City booked their place at Wembley with the sweetest of semi-final successes, beating Ipswich 2-0 at home in the semi-final second leg to earn a 2-1 aggregate win over their old rivals, courtesy of a first-half goal by John Deehan and an 88th-minute winner from defender Steve Bruce, his first goal for the club. It was one of Carrow Road's great nights, with three sides of the ground a veritable cauldron of noise and the fourth almost eerily empty – the crowd restricted to 23,545 because of the fire which had destroyed the Main Stand five months earlier.

Bruce went on to earn the man of the match award at Wembley, but it was one of City's veteran performers who was credited with the goal which decided the game. At the start of the second half, 34-year-old former Scotland international midfielder Asa Hartford's close-range shot took a big deflection off the chest of Sunderland's Gordon Chisholm and flew into the net. Some 12 years earlier, Hartford, then playing for West Bromwich Albion, had been fined £50 for spitting in the face of a Norwich fan at the end of a match at Carrow Road. Perhaps the fan in question accepted Hartford's Wembley winner as a belated apology.

Sunderland's Clive Walker missed a penalty three minutes later, ensuring that Dave Watson became the first, and so far only, captain to collect a major trophy for Norwich City in the Royal Box. The match was also dubbed the "Friendly Final" for the excellent rapport which existed between the two sets of supporters. Hartford and 36-year-old former England international Mike Channon were the old stagers in the team which received a heroes' welcome at City Hall the following night, but the side also included four of the club's own youth products in Paul Haylock, Mark Barham, Peter Mendham and Louie Donowa.

City's Wembley joy was short-lived as their form nose-dived and within weeks they, like Sunderland, were relegated from Division One as well as robbed of their hard-earned UEFA Cup place when English teams were withdrawn from Europe following the Heysel Stadium disaster.

Brown's rollercoaster reign continued. His re-shaped side cruised to the Division Two championship in 1985-86 and the momentum continued as they finished fifth in Division One a year later, then City's best top-flight position. But Brown was sacked in November 1987 when, after Machin's summer resignation, City found themselves deep in relegation trouble. The manner of Brown's sacking led to City supporters' first show of public disapproval at club chairman Robert Chase, who had succeeded Sir Arthur South at the head of a completely new board of directors in January 1986. Chase had more than ten years in the chair - and was to face the fans' wrath time and again over such issues as the sale of top players, abolition of the terraces and the club's perilous finances before he eventually resigned in May 1996, the Canaries having lost their precious top-flight status and battling to reduce debts of around £7 million. Yet for much of his reign, City prospered on the field as never before.

Dave Stringer, appointed manager in place of Brown, swiftly led them to safety in 1987-88 and in his first full season in charge, 1988-89, the Canaries threatened to pull off an amazing double. Skippered by Michael Phelan, City led Division One at Christmas thanks to a supremely polished brand of football, which brought handsome wins at Old Trafford and Anfield, and they were serious title rivals to Arsenal and Liverpool until Easter, after which their season collapsed. City still finished fourth, then their best-ever position, and reached the FA Cup semi-finals for only the second time in club history, losing 1-0 to Everton at Villa Park on the same day as the Hillsborough disaster.

Gradually, some of the key players from the 1989 side departed in seven-figure moves, among them defender Andy Linighan, midfielder Andy Townsend and Caister-born winger Dale Gordon, but Stringer again took City to the FA Cup semi-finals in 1992, only for them to lose tamely 1-0 to Division Two strugglers Sunderland at Hillsborough.

City only narrowly avoided relegation in Stringer's last season in charge, but as if to prove that it is always darkest just before the dawn, the next 18 months saw the Canaries scale unprecedented heights. Reserve team boss Mike Walker was appointed manager, with Deehan recruited from his coaching role at Barnsley as his assistant, and together they transformed their squad - supplemented by the signing of Manchester United striker Mark Robins - into title challengers in the newly-formed FA Premier League.

City had an eight-point lead at the top in early December but in the end, it was United who took the title for the first time in 26 years. However, by finishing third, Walker's men at last booked a prized European place, albeit with a little help from Arsenal, who won both domestic cup competitions to create the extra

**It's there: Arguably Norwich City's most famous goal of the century came from Jeremy Goss on the night of October 19th 1993 when this volley sparked off the shock defeat of Bayern Munich at the famous Olympic Stadium.**

**Chris Sutton became the most expensive player in British football when Blackburn Rovers paid Norwich City £5 million for his services in 1994. It was a sound investment. Sutton, who scored 28 goals in his last season with the Canaries, and was voted Player of the Year, helped Rovers win the championship in his first season at Ewood Park, their first title since 1914. Sutton, whose father Mike played for City in the Sixties, scored 43 times in all for City before his transfer. His strike rate was all the more remarkable since roughly a third of his 127 senior appearances for the Canaries were as a defender. Nottingham-born Sutton, who attended Horsford and Hellesdon schools, won his first England cap in 1997 before a dispute wrecked his chances of a place in the 1998 World Cup squad. He was transferred from Blackburn to Chelsea in July 1999 for £10 million – resulting in a £525,000 sell-on fee windfall for the Canaries.**

vacancy in the UEFA Cup. The Canaries' European adventure brought them the kind of nationwide acclaim they had not enjoyed since 1959.

Their 3-0 home win over seeded Dutch club Vitesse Arnhem in the first round, first leg - the sides drew 0-0 in the second leg - should have sent alarm bells ringing through Europe, but German giants Bayern Munich clearly were not listening, and the Canaries followed up with an historic 2-1 win over No 2 seeds Bayern in the Olympic Stadium in the second round, first leg on October 19th 1993. City inflicted Bayern's first home defeat by an English club in a European tie thanks to first leg goals from Jeremy Goss and Mark Bowen and some goalkeeping heroics from Bryan Gunn, and the equaliser from Goss in a 1-1 draw in the home leg 15 days later was enough to clinch an aggregate win.

It was top seeds and eventual trophy winners Inter Milan who ended Norwich's Euro dream in round three, winning each leg 1-0, though injury-hit City's performance in the second leg in the San Siro must go down as one of their greatest ever. Alas, a taste of Europe did not signal the end of the beginning for City so much as the beginning of the end.

A month after the Milan defeat, Walker resigned to take over at Everton, triggering a downward spiral of events which brought the sale of more top players - four of them strikers, including Chris Sutton to Blackburn for £5 million in 1994 - and, with Deehan then caretaker-boss Gary Megson at the helm, relegation in 1995. Despite a further four changes of manager in four years, with Martin O'Neill, Megson again, Walker again and Bruce Rioch all attempting to revive the club's fortunes, the Canaries have hit something of a plateau in mid-table in the new Nationwide League Division One. Even the goal-scoring feats of Welsh duo Craig Bellamy and Iwan Roberts were not enough to push City into a play-off place in 1998-99.

All the more reason, then, to salute City's past achievements. But as for their finest hour?

In terms of public fervour and hero worship, those nine and a half weeks in 1959 will probably never be surpassed. As Terry Allcock once said: "We were treated like gladiators." The 1985 Milk Cup remains City's one major trophy, and their only Wembley triumph - and it was certainly a memorable occasion. But the Canaries' route to the final was not the toughest, and one might argue that given such a favourable draw, it would have been disappointing not to have won the trophy. Victory celebrations, too, were swiftly tempered by relegation and exclusion from Europe.

In terms of prestige, Bayern Munich must be rated City's outstanding scalp, though Bayern were probably no better in 1993 than the top Premiership teams City were meeting, and quite often beating, around the same time. But in cold, hard statistics at least, their best-ever league position and their first-ever European victories ought to make 1993 the undisputed golden year.

All of which leaves Saunders' trail-blazers of 1972. They were probably the least glamorous line-up, arguably played the least attractive football, and have almost certainly had less lasting acclaim than the players of 1959, 1985 and 1993. Yet in many ways, Saunders' achievement on limited resources was the most important of all, in that it had the greatest long-term significance. It was by winning Division Two that the Canaries were, for the first time in seventy years, propelled into the top flight of English football, there to remain for most of the next 23 years. Was this not, in many respects, Norwich City's finest hour?

Not all the greatest players in City's history were fortunate to share in one of the club's major triumphs. But no tribute would be complete without reference to Johnny Gavin, the outside-right from Limerick who still holds the club's all-time goal-scoring record with 132 goals in 338 games in two spells between 1949 and 1958. And how many first-team games would Bernard Robinson have played but for the war? His City career stretched from 1931 to 1949, playing at right-half and right-back a total of 380 times.

Was there ever a better City centre-forward than Welsh international Ron Davies, sold amid public outcry to Southampton in 1966 for a paltry £55,000 after scoring 66 goals in 126 City appearances? And one man remembered with special poignancy every year is centre-half and former captain Barry Butler, one of the heroes of 1959, who died in a car crash in 1966. City's Player of the Year trophy, introduced the following year, bears his name.

Carrow Road approaching the year 2000 is, of course, unrecognisable from the ground constructed in a two-month building miracle in the summer of 1935, when it was hailed in the EDP as a *"monument of local enterprise and achievement"*. Today's all-seater stadium, three sides of which have been rebuilt in the past twenty years, houses fewer than 22,000 fans, almost exactly half the ground attendance record set against Leicester in 1963.

And as the new Millennium dawns, it is also a very different Norwich City battling against a very different football world. Relegation from the FA Premiership in 1995 meant that the Canaries suffered a disastrous drop in status and income at the worst possible time – just before the Premier League's new £800 million-plus TV deal.

City, by contrast, were almost permanently derailed by debts of more than £7 million inherited from former chairman Chase's administration, a financial handicap still plaguing the club in 1999 as they fought on an unequal footing with their rivals to return to the company of English football's elite. Unable to achieve anything more than mid-table security in Division One in the last few seasons of the century, City have looked increasingly like second-class citizens in the era of the £40,000-a-week pay packet, with clubs on the Stock Exchange, TV domination of the game, a flood of overseas players and the increasing centralisation of power, wealth and playing talent in the hands of a few all-powerful superclubs.

So have City's golden years already passed? Or will the Canaries of the 21st century, with the backing of TV cookery queen Delia Smith and her publisher husband, Michael Wynn Jones, as majority shareholders, rise again to challenge the best that England and even Europe can produce? If the first 97 years of club history have taught us anything, it is to expect the unexpected from Norwich City.

The Canaries have, of course, been Norfolk's footballing giants over the century. But the county's other sides have had their moments too. Diss had an unforgettable day out at Wembley in 1994 when Norwich City veteran Peter Mendham scored the winner for the Tangerines in a gripping FA Vase final against Taunton, and Yarmouth dumped Third Division (South) side Crystal Palace out of the FA Cup in 1953 in front of almost 9000 spectators.

But, as befits the county's second most senior side, King's Lynn have had the lion's share of those memorable moments.

An embarrassing 0-11 reverse against Aston Villa in the FA Cup in 1905-6 hardly augured well for the coming century. Yet over the years the Linnets claimed three League scalps – Halifax, Coventry and Aldershot – and played at Goodison Park against Everton in 1961, going down, albeit bravely, 4-0. One book in 1994 even claimed that Lynn were, statistically, the most successful club in the FA Cup's history ahead of – irony of ironies – Everton.

The days when an early-Fifties FA Cup tie against Exeter could attract 12,937 spectators were long gone by the Sixties and Seventies when gates dwindled to a few hundred. The club that could claim in 1956 that Football League status was a real goal was reduced to a notorious players' strike in 1992, managerial disputes and contemplating the one-way drop down to Jewson League status.

But a bold initiative by the club saw Peter Morris appointed as manager, a move which paid off handsomely when Lynn won promotion to the Beazer Homes Midland Division. By the time of the last full season of the century the dour but effective Morris had left, and Lynn began their campaign in disastrous style but ended it chasing the leaders.

A Conference place is a real possibility for early in the new century and then, who knows? Perhaps the fifty-year league dream will become a reality, and the sleeping giant will be, at last, finally awake.

**Has any football club had a more dedicated servant than Mick Wright? The facts speak for themselves: an astonishing 1152 appearances for King's Lynn – a British record for one club. Wright joined the Linnets on loan from Northampton in 1961 and his career lasted into the Eighties, including more than 100 goals. He scored the winners against Chelmsford and Coventry to take Lynn to their most famous match of the century – an FA Cup tie against mighty Everton. His quiet no-nonsense attitude to the game won him wide respect. Asked in November 1979 about his attitude to the game on the eve of breaking the appearance record, he said simply: "I'll never tire of football, although one day football might tire of me."**

**DAVID ARMSTRONG was born at Thorpe St Andrew Rectory in 1936, and was introduced to the delights of Lakenham – where his father had been a regular habitué since 1893 – as a babe in arms, although his conscious following of Norfolk had to await the resumption of cricket after the Second World War. A former schoolmaster at Beeston Hall School, he served as the Norfolk CCC Secretary between 1967 and 1985, and is currently Secretary of the Minor Counties Cricket Association.**

In looking at Norfolk cricket in the twentieth century it may, perhaps, be helpful to set the scene in context by looking first, very briefly, at events before 1900.

In 1831, four years after its foundation, the reputation of the Norfolk County Cricket Club had reached such a peak that the New Sporting Magazine described it as *"now the next Club to the Marylebone"* - although there were, of course, at that time no formal means of measuring cricketing standards - and three years after this, with the celebrated Fuller Pilch making 87 not out and 73 in what is believed to be the first county match to have been played at Norwich Norfolk beat Yorkshire (who could muster but 37 and 97 in their two innings) by 272 runs.

Twice going out of existence, from 1848 to 1862, and again from 1871 to 1876 from which date, world wars apart, it has operated continuously, the club began its Lakenham Cricket Festival - still an important item in the local sporting and social scene - in 1881 while in 1885, in scoring 695 against MCC at Lord's Norfolk set up what was, at that time, a record score for the world's most famous cricket ground. It says much for the hardiness of the cricketers of those days that Norfolk customarily met the far distant Durham, both home and away; in one of these encounters, in 1897, the formidable Charlie Shore achieved the remarkable feat of capturing all ten wickets in an innings, his figures (at Lakenham) being ten for 50; for good measure he took six for 22 in the second innings.

It was just before the turn of the century that the status of the various counties was formalised between First and Second Class and, despite their great deeds of the 1830s, Norfolk found themselves placed in the latter category. They were founder members, in 1895, of the Minor Counties Champions, in that inaugural year, with Durham and Worcestershire. Despite the presence in the side in 1898 and 1899 of Albert Relf, who later went on to play in 13 Test matches, Norfolk failed to make any particular mark in the years remaining to 1900.

Norfolk's initial, shared success was followed by three outright titles before the First World War; in 1905 and 1910 under the captaincy of the Rev G B Raikes and in 1913 under Michael Falcon who the previous year, in his first season in charge, had seen his side

**Early years: Norfolk county cricket's title-winning side of 1910.**

head the table with seven outright victories, and a win on first innings in the course of their eight matches. Unfortunately it proved impossible to arrange a championship play-off which would have been against an equally formidable Staffordshire team which included the legendary Sydney Barnes who had - uniquely for a Minor County cricketer, played for England in all six Test matches that summer.

G B Raikes, one of several clergymen to play for Norfolk in the years preceding the First World War, was a remarkable sportsman; he had played for Norfolk from 1890 to 1897 and gained his Blue at Oxford for both cricket and Association Football in 1894 and 1895. In 1896 he gained four full International caps as goalkeeper for England. From 1900 to 1902 a clerical appointment took him to Hampshire, with whom he enjoyed no little success, being second in the batting averages in his first season. He returned to play for, and captain, Norfolk in 1904.

The year 1906 was remarkable for the debut of both Michael Falcon and Geoffrey Stevens; while neither covered himself with glory in his first appearance, the selectors were more than vindicated the following season when each of them scored a maiden County century to start a great Norfolk career. Falcon, who became an all-rounder of more than local repute, actually captained the side both before the First World War and - in the unusual circumstances which prevailed in 1946 - after the Second. Geoffrey Stevens, who played until 1930, distinguished himself as a forceful batsman and a prehensile slip fielder. Twice he scored a double century, the first of these coming in the successful Championship Challenge Match against the much-fancied Berkshire in 1910, the visitors returning home much chastened, having lost by an innings and 150 runs.

The period between the wars went, surprisingly, unrewarded in terms of titles; surprisingly because Michael Falcon's side in that era must have been almost of first-class standard. In 1922 Norfolk headed the table, but lost the Challenge Match, against Buckinghamshire at Lakenham, by eight runs despite an innings of 98 by Geoffrey Colman while in 1933 they were again at the top of the table; they were challenged, and beaten at Lakenham by Yorkshire II (who included Len Hutton in their ranks) but it was later discovered that an administrative error had erroneously put Yorkshire in second place, instead of Wiltshire. It being, by now, October it was too late for a new Challenge Match to take place and the title was left "undecided".

The latter part of this inter-war period was the era in which the Edrich brothers followed the Rought-Rought brothers into a side which could boast as many as six Oxford or Cambridge "Blues" - Falcon, two Rought-Roughts and M R Barton who captained Surrey after the war, together with Tristan Ballance and David Walker (the former a cunning left arm spinner and the latter arguably the best batsman ever to play for Norfolk) both of whom were to lose their lives in action. With the exception of the abortive Challenge Match against Yorkshire the team went undefeated from 1933 to 1936, finishing first, third, third again and second in those years.

It took some time for Norfolk to re-establish themselves as a force following the Second World War. Michael Falcon, who at the age of 57 headed the batting averages, saw the county through its vital first post-war season, but the loss of stalwarts such as Ballance and Walker in action, together with Geoffrey and Eric Edrich who had followed their brother Bill into the first-class game, proved a fearful handicap. John Edrich and Peter Parfitt each found his way into the side before, all too soon, graduating to the first-class game, Edrich playing in 77 tests and Parfitt in 37.

However, when Bill Edrich retired from the first-class game and returned in 1959 to captain his native county - who had, in the preceding three seasons, failed to win a match - things took a dramatic turn for the better. Bill, who played cricket for Norfolk from 1932 to 1936 and again from 1959 to 1971 (having in the interim made his name with Middlesex and England, for whom he played 39 Test matches, and with the Royal Air Force, being awarded the DFC) was a distinguished

**Michael Falcon, who held the unique record of having captained his county cricket team from before the First World War until after the Second, was a man of many parts indeed, having been also Member of Parliament for East Norfolk and High Sheriff of the County. There were many in the Twenties who considered Falcon unlucky not to be in the England team. He had gained a "Blue" at Cambridge as a batsman, his serious bowling beginning only in his last year at the university; but although he scored no fewer than 22 centuries for Norfolk it was his bowling for which he was famed. Twice he routed the Australians with six for 67 at Eastbourne in 1921 and seven for 42 at Holyport in 1926. For Gentlemen v Players in 1924, at the Oval after taking seven for 78 in the first innings, he shared with Arthur Gilligan in a last-wicket stand of 134 in an hour. For Norfolk, in a career which stretched from 1906 to 1946, he scored 11,340 runs and took 727 wickets. He later served the Club as Chairman and finally as President; he died in 1976.**

**Norfolk stars: A Fifties EDP picture of future England players John Edrich and Peter Parfitt.**

member of a well-known cricketing family. His three brothers and a cousin also played first-class cricket.

Making his way into the Norfolk side as a 16-year-old, he gained particular prominence with an innings of 111 for his county against the South Africans at Lakenham in 1935. Joining Middlesex, he scored 1000 runs before the end of May in 1938 and forced his way into the Test team. His early matches at this level were unsuccessful, but the authorities persevered with him, and he put early disappointments behind him with a fine 219 in the "Timeless Test" at Durban in 1938.

After his retirement from first-class cricket he returned to captain the Norfolk side; this colourful character is remembered with great affection by those involved with Norfolk cricket at that time. For Norfolk, in all matches, he scored 8308 runs and took 417 wickets. He died in 1986, following a fall at home. A stand at Lord's Cricket Ground is named after him.

His skill and tactical awareness, together with his love of adventure and abhorrence of negative cricket, paid immediate dividends. Well supported by a side which included batsmen such as Ted Witherden (1031 runs in ten matches in 1959), Nigel Moore who had been desperately unlucky not to secure a "Blue" at Cambridge in a side containing six future test players, Henry Blofeld, the evergreen Peter Powell, the young Clive Radley and later Graham Saville, a formidable attack spearheaded by Peter Walmsley, Andy Corran, Arthur Coomb and, later, Richard Jefferson, who enjoyed a variety of support in the spin department - not least from the captain - Edrich took his side to seventh in his first season, and to the top of the table the following year.

Disappointingly the Challenge Match, against Lancashire II at Lakenham, saw the side sadly outclassed at last; it is not every challenging team which can call upon bowlers of the eminence (and Test Match experience) of Roy Tattersall and Malcolm Hilton!

The retirement of Bill Edrich in 1971 brought a difficult period of transition. Despite the stalwart efforts of players such as Tracey Moore, David Pilch, Quorn Handley, Robin Huggins, Steve Plumb and Doug Mattocks success was thin on the ground. The former Yorkshire and England player, Ken Taylor, who had taken a teaching post in Norfolk, was a welcome, if all too brief, addition to the side, while his former Yorkshire colleague, Phil Sharpe, later joined and then captained the county, taking them to the runners-up position in 1981. More recent honours have been the Holt Cup title in 1986 and the MCC Trophy in 1997 under Paul

**Bill Edrich, one of the county's finest-ever cricketers, leads out the Norfolk team in a 1967 match.**

Newman who also took the side to the leading position in the championship Eastern Division in 1996 only for his team to be outplayed by Devon in the final, while in 1997 his team so nearly caused a major sensation in the NatWest trophy having reduced Warwickshire to a desperate 25 for six at Edgbaston.

There is still much good cricket to be seen at Lakenham, with players such as Carl Rogers, Steve Goldsmith, Carl Amos, David and Mark Thomas, under Newman's leadership, providing entertainment of the highest order.

Boxing in Norfolk in the early 1900s was very different to what it is today. Bare-knuckle scraps, often fought to a finish, were still taking place in open fields and in the courtyards of the county's many inns.

These were attended by a small, well-informed crowd known as The Fancy. The rewards for the boxers, or pugilists as they were then called, were small, but the betting on the outcomes was heavy.

Side-stakes were wagered by the boxers' backers and their generosity, and "nobbins", coins thrown into the roped off area passing for a ring, in appreciation of a pleasing fight, helped to swell the boxers' purses. These bouts were frequently broken up by the police. Much more acceptable were boxing booths, huge tents erected on fairgrounds or at race meetings, where resident boxers took on all-comers. Contests were organised and well controlled and the boxers wore gloves.

Many boxers learned their rough trade in these arenas, including Jem Mace, without doubt Norfolk's greatest-ever ringman. Although known as the Swaffham Gypsy, Mace was born in Beeston-next-Mileham in 1831. British champion, he toured the world in the latter half of the nineteenth century. He retained his boxing skill to an advanced age and was generally regarded as the last of the really great bare-knuckle pugilists and the father of scientific boxing with gloves.

When he returned to England after retiring

**DICK FUTTER was born in Botolph Street, Norwich, in 1924. He joined the Norwich Lads' Club at the age of 14, and started to write about boxing three years later when he was invited to become Eastern Counties correspondent for Boxing News. Demobbed after Royal Navy service in 1946, he rejoined Boxing News and also became a freelance reporter for Weekly Sporting Review. These undertakings were interspersed with being a Master of Ceremonies at various amateur and semi-professional promotions. In 1951, he followed Walter "Straight Left" Day as boxing correspondent to Eastern Counties Newspapers, contributing under the *nom-de-plume* "Ringsider". His column still appears weekly in the EDP and Evening News. He is a vice-president of the Norwich Lads ABC and the Norwich & District Ex-Boxers' Association.**

**Arthur 'Ginger' Sadd was born in Norwich in 1914. A product of the Norwich Lads' Club, he boxed professionally from 1932 to 1951 and had 216 recorded contests. He won the Eastern Area welterweight title in 1935 when he outpointed Seaman Jim Lawlor. He held the Eastern Area middleweight title from 1937 until 1949. In 1939, he fought Jock McAvoy for the British middleweight title, losing on points over 15 rounds. Three weeks later, in Bournemouth, he beat Freddie Mills, who later became light-heavyweight champion of the world. In title eliminators, he fought Bert Gilroy, Dave McCleave and Ernie Roderick. Other champion opponents of his were Don Cockell, Albert Finch, Vince Hawkins, Dick Turpin, Pat Butler, Harry Corbett and Harry Mason. A Sergeant PT Instructor during the Second World War, he was wounded in the Normandy campaign. On his retirement, 'Ginger', a lorry driver, returned to the Lads' Club as a trainer and gave many years of service to boxing, recognised when he was made a member of the Uppercut Club in London. He died in 1992.**

he lived in Norwich, where he was landlord of the Swan public house, and when he attended boxing tournaments people queued up to shake his hand. He died in 1910, and was buried in Anfield Cemetery, Liverpool. As boxing gained respectability, and with the clouds of war gathering, boxing was encouraged in the Services.

At that time one of the Army's most prominent boxers was Bandsman Jack Blake of Yarmouth. A professional from 1910 to 1922, Blake began his boxing while a serving soldier and was middleweight champion of India before returning to England to eventually take on Bombardier Billy Wells of Mile End for the British heavyweight title at the London Palladium on March 3rd 1914. Giving away quite a lot of weight, he was, not surprisingly, knocked out in four rounds. Before that bout he was unbeaten.

Two years later he got a crack at the British middleweight title. This was against Pat O'Keefe of Bromley at London's National Sporting Club, and he won on points over twenty rounds. He held the title for twenty months before being knocked out in the second round in a return fight against O'Keefe at the same venue.

In his time the fighting Bandsman beat British light-heavyweight champion Harry Reeve of Stepney, but never got a shot at that title. He also beat another one-time holder of the British middleweight title, Jack Harrison, and he also defeated Sam Palmer, Harry Croxon, Young Johnson and the famous Dixie Kid. In all he had 64 contests, winning 49.

Blake's last fight was at the Yarmouth Hippodrome in 1921 when he knocked out Arthur Cameron of Fulham in the fourth round.

After his retirement he became a referee and for more than forty years he was a swimming instructor at the Yarmouth Bathing Pool. He died in 1961 at the age of seventy.

Boxing was now a major spectator sport and professional tournaments were held regularly in Norwich, Yarmouth and Lynn. Gyms were springing up all over the county. Usually these were in the back rooms of public houses, but, in 1925, the magnificent Norwich Lads' Club was opened in King Street. The city's youngsters flocked there and boxing was the club's topmost sporting activity. The club was the brainchild of the Chief Constable of Norwich, John Henry Dain, and many boxers who later become professionals had good reason to be grateful to him.

Not least among them was Arthur 'Ginger' Sadd. Professional from 1932 to 1951, he was an excellent, scientific boxer and was in demand by promoters all over the country.

The Thirties, late Forties and Fifties were the golden times for professional boxing in Norfolk — and Sadd dominated for most of that era. The old Norwich Corn Hall in Exchange Street was the county's Mecca. Dan Webb promoted regularly there before the Second World War and Cliff Butler succeeded him in the immediate post-war years.

Sadd was their main attraction. Whenever he appeared the hall was packed. He fought the best boxers at his weight in the country, his major achievement being his British middleweight title fight against Jock McAvoy, who, at the time, was reckoned to be the best 11 stone six pound fighter in the world. Sadd took the fearsome Rochdale Thunderbolt to a contentious 15 rounds points decision.

Before "Ginger" arrived on the scene, Jack Forster was the big favourite. Born in Marlingford, Jack moved to Norwich when he was 15 and boxed professionally from 1927 to 1938. He, too, fought McAvoy, and lasted the full 12 rounds. Like Sadd, he fought the best and his aggressive performances gained him a big following. Sadd ruled supreme until Joe Beckett of Hempnall relieved him of the Eastern Area middleweight title at Norwich in 1949.

Beckett won on points, but in the previous year Sadd beat him in eight rounds. Joe was an excellent, all-action fighter and was much in demand by promoters, his go-forward, crash-bang style making him popular wherever he appeared.

When they retired Beckett became a second at the Yarmouth Hippodrome and Sadd became an instructor at the Norwich Lads Club. For the better part of his career Sadd was managed by Walter Day, who

**One of the EDP's classic sporting photographs came in 1992 with Bill Smith's study of Herbie Hide's euphoric celebration at beating Conroy Nelson for the WBC International heavyweight title.**
**Hide, real name Herbert Maduagowu, was born in Nigeria in 1971. Educated in Norfolk, he joined the Norwich Lads' Club as a 15-year-old and was encouraged to box by instructors Chris Scott and Dick Sadd. In 1989 he reached the final of the Amateur Boxing Association heavyweight championship, losing on points. He turned professional the same year. Before winning the British title in 1993 with a fifth-round triumph over Michael Murray, he won a World Boxing Organisation Penta-Continental title. The following year he became the WBO's heavyweight champion of the world for the first time when he stopped Michael Bentt. In his first defence he was knocked out in the sixth round by Riddick Bowe in Las Vegas. He regained the title in 1997 by knocking out former champion Tony Tucker in two rounds at Norwich Sport Village, and defended it against Damon Reed and Willi Fischer, before crashing to a second-round knockout defeat against Ukrainian Vitali Klitschko in June 1999.**

**NORMAN GREENWAY, who lives on the Suffolk/Norfolk borders, has been actively involved in motor racing since the Fifties, both as a commentator and journalist. Starting his commentating career at Snetterton in 1958 he was a regular at Goodwood, Brands Hatch and Silverstone before returning to Snetterton in the early Eighties. He was a Grand Prix commentator for BBC Radio 2 throughout the Seventies and early Eighties. He regularly covered motorsport for the Eastern Daily Press and BBC Radio Norfolk as well as writing for Motoring News. He has been involved in motor racing PR and promotion work for the past 25 years. In 1999 he published a biography of Jim Russell.**

handled some of the county's top talent, including Bert Buxton, Charlie White, Jackie Hammond, Len Dunthorne and Russell Wilson. Former boxer Chucky Robinson later rivalled him, managing Clive Campling, Kenny Taylor, Johnny Pipe and Len Jarvis among others.

Later, George Blazeby, Jimmy Carter, Tony Webster and Roy Taylor were managed by Freddie King of Yarmouth. Norfolk also had some admirable trainers. Pudding Clarke and Dillo Cann were wonderful characters, but Jim Huggins stood above all others. To Jim boxing was an exact science. He was among the first trainers who believed boxers had to be prepared mentally as well as physically and over the years he trained most of Walter Day's boxers.

In the Fifties Cliff Butler staged very successful shows at the Yarmouth Hippodrome, but the advent of television changed the boxing scene in this area irrevocably. There were other promotions, but it was not until Herbie Hide and Jonathan Thaxton began to make their mark in shows at Norwich Sport Village that the sport's professional side again took hold.

Hide twice won the World Boxing Organisation's version of the world heavyweight title, beating Americans Michael Bentt and Tony Tucker.

Thaxton, a light-welterweight, has won WBO and IBF titles, but his most sensational win was his first-round knockout of the then British champion Paul "Scrap Iron" Ryan in a non-title bout.

Over the border in Lowestoft Seaman Jim Lawlor, George Pull, Bob Firmin and Mickey Thompson were bill-toppers before the Second World War, while, in more recent times, Mark Hawthorne won the 1997 ABA lightweight title.

As we end the century, there is a strong amateur boxing community in Norfolk, with dinner tournaments being held steadily in Norwich, Gorleston, King's Lynn, East Tuddenham, Dereham and North Walsham.

Norwich Lads, Lynn Friars, Yarmouth Kingfisher, Norwich Broadside, Aylsham Youth and Dereham are the leading clubs. All are under the jurisdiction of the Norfolk ABA, whose officials supervise at contests all over the country.

In common with most of the country (Brooklands excepted), motor racing in Norfolk started after the Second World War. Farmer Fred Riches owned the land around the Snetterton airfield and managed to get a one-year lease from the Ministry of Defence. Meanwhile publican Oliver Sear had started up the Aston Martin Owners Club and passing Snetterton one day he thought that it would be ideal for club events.

The outcome was a meeting with Fred Riches and a long association was started. Oliver then arranged a long lease with the MoD. They formed the Snetterton Motor Racing Club but the first meeting, which was held in 1951, was organised by the AMOC. Very soon Snetterton was hosting rounds of National championships including the very popular 500cc FIII single seaters.

Jim Russell, who was to become Norfolk's first International driver, was fascinated by these rapid little FIII cars when he visited Snetterton for the first time in 1952. Very quickly he bought his own car and entered the fray to such good effect that he was British Champion three years running. In 1957 he started the world's first racing drivers' school at Snetterton. The school stayed for thirty years introducing students from all over the world to the delights of Norfolk. It was only in 1988 that the school eventually located to Donington Park. Still going strong, there are now many branches around the world. Oliver Sear eventually took over complete control of the circuit until he sold out in the mid-Sixties to Grovewood Securities (later to become Motor Circuit Developments) who also owned Brands Hatch, Oulton Park and Cadwell Park.

Another local star was Jack Sears who concentrated on saloons, GT and sports cars. Jack, who had moved to Ashill in 1953, had been interested in motor sport and had done some speed trials and hillclimbs. His first race was at Snetterton in 1954 and over the next dozen or so years he regularly raced at his home circuit and all over the world in a variety of cars. Probably one of the most versatile drivers anywhere, he was quick and spectacular in whatever he drove. No one who saw his drifting style in an Austin Healey 3000, which he only drove in 1959, will forget it.

Jack has the distinction of being the first-ever British Saloon (now called touring) Car Champion in 1958. He went on to repeat this feat again in 1964. The versatile 'Gentleman Jack' has driven a host of cars — MGTC, Cooper MG sports, Jaguar XK120, Lister 2-litre MG, Ford Galaxie, Tommy Sopwith's Jaguar 3.8, Cortina GT (he was the first ever winner in that car), Lotus Cortina, Austin Healey 3000, Ferrari GTO, Shelby Cobra and others. Double British Saloon Car Champion Jack was also a member of the World GT Championship-winning Shelby Daytona Cobra team. He is still heavily engaged in motor sport through his involvement with the British Racing Drivers Club and the RAC.

He now has the satisfaction of watching his son David's career. After attending the Jim Russell Racing Drivers' School (where else?) David drove successfully in Formula Ford, Formula III and sports cars (recording an excellent third place at Le Mans) before starting his own racing team based at Griston. It did not take him long to progress from the lower formulae up to Formula 3000, which is the next stage below Formula 1 and provides the sporting race at most Grand Prix. His Super Nova Formula 3000 team has won three of the last four Championships.

In 1966 Colin Chapman decided to move his racing car business from Cheshunt up to Hethel. This move was to provide a launching pad for many other motorsport concerns over the following years. Within a couple of years the advent of Formula Ford led to the production of a Lotus model in that category. Mike Warner, Dave Baldwin, Jo Marquart, Derek Wild and Gordon Huckle, who had all been heavily involved in the design, production and sale of the highly successful Lotus 61 FF car, decided it was time for a move.

They all left in 1970 and set up a race car company at Griston called GRD (Group Racing Developments) to produce FIII and sports cars. Meanwhile Jim Russell also became involved in the same business producing a very popular Russell-Alexis FF car.

Lotus were on the crest of a wave over the next few years and although they lost the brilliant Jochen Rindt, his successor, Emerson Fittipaldi, who had won the 1959 FIII Championship under Jim Russell's guidance, proved more than capable to take over and become the Lotus World F1 champion in 1972.

Around that time Jim's brother-in-law, Ralph Firman, who had been Emerson's mechanic in FIII, launched his own race car construction business across the road from Snetterton. His Van Diemen Formula Fords have won every FF

**Snetterton has been the home of Norfolk motorsport since the last war. In this Good Friday 1971 picture we see some of the modified roadgoing saloons ready for a race.**

**Jim Russell was born and brought up in Downham Market where his very successful family-run Mercedes dealership still operates. Jim has lived in North Suffolk for many years. Introduced to motor racing at the surprisingly late age of 32 he was soon a main contender and became British Champion three years running — 1955, 1956 and 1957. He also set six world records for 1000cc sports cars in 1955 driving at Montlery. He moved up to race in European FII and was all set to win the championship when his career was brought to an end by a life threatening accident while he was competing in the 1952 Le Mans 24 hour race.**
**He started the world's first racing drivers school at Snetterton in 1957. It has become acknowledged as the world leader, still going strong with many overseas branches after 43 years. He was the technical advisor for the film Grand Prix, training all the stars at Snetterton and supplying the 'mocked-up' GP cars. If all that were not enough he ran a horse stud for many years at his home.**

Championship worldwide as well as the majority of the annual Formula Ford Festivals since they started. The first three Festivals were run at Snetterton in the early Seventies but were moved by MCD to Brands Hatch in 1976.

The existence of the Jim Russell Racing Drivers' School and Van Diemen has meant that many of today's top drivers, including Ayrton Senna, Eddie Irvine, Mauricio Guglemin, Robert Moreno, Raul Boesel, and many others, started their careers at Snetterton. After GRD cars had been driven successfully by the likes of Roger Williamson and future World Champion Alan Jones, Mike Warner called it a day and Jo Marquart joined Watton's Ted Savory to design and produce his Modus cars.

This time it was Tony Brise who gave the car most of its successes and when Modus closed its door, Jo went into business in the old GRD factory with the highly respected engineer Nick Jordan. They produced yet another successful car, the ARGO FIII car driven to great effect by Belgian Thierry Tassin, Colombian Roberto Guerrero (another future Formula 1 and Indycar star) and David Sears.

During the Sixties Snetterton hosted many International meetings when Grand Prix drivers such as Graham Hill and Jim Clark appeared. They were, of course, the days before more stringent safety measures applied. In the early Seventies the Tour of Britain visited Snetterton. This was a mixture of racing and rallying which went all over the country.

It ran for three years and on two occasions the Snetterton races were run in the dark, for the first time in this country. In 1979 the idea of a 24-hour race developed. It was realised that Snetterton was the only circuit which could host such and event and, after the writer had persuaded Willhire to be sponsors, it became a reality the following year and ran successfully for over a decade.

At first no one thought that a saloon or sports car could last for 24 hours so the first two events allowed three car teams — one racing, one ready to go and one being worked on! As it became apparent that the cars could last the distance, the rules were changed to make the event open to single teams! It was in one of these Willhires, as they were universally known, that the Brundle team emerged. Father John with sons Martin and Robin contested and won their class in a Toyota. Probably the first and only such family combination to win a race anywhere. Martin then went on to become a single seater and sports car star, moving up to become Norfolk's first-ever Grand Prix driver. In sports cars Martin has few equals and in 1988 he also became Norfolk's first-ever World Sports Car Champion.

For a short while Norfolk boasted a second Grand Prix team when Keith Wiggins, who had run a successful team from Formula Ford, through FIII and Formula 3000, into Grand Prix racing, entered the Formula 1 scene. Unfortunately Pacific Grand Prix failed due to a shortage of the necessary large amounts of cash which have become absolutely essential for survival in the world of Formula 1.

Over the years many motor racing connected companies have emerged around Snetterton. Glen Waters, ex-Lotus and GRD, has run his own team for years. Nick Paravanni's Competition Fabrications and Peter Denty, who lovingly restores the older racing cars, are just a few.

There have, of course, been many other drivers associated with Snetterton. One who is remembered very affectionately by many people is Archie Scott-Brown to whom a plaque on the Snetterton scrutineering bay is dedicated. He only had one hand but won many races, especially in the Lister sports cars which, like Archie, came from Cambridge. One of the Jim Russell School's first stars was Mike McKee from Norwich who regularly raced at Snetterton during the late Fifties and early Sixties. John Aley was famous for his exploits in a Mini with its distinctive JRA85 number plate.

For a very long time Snetterton has been the busiest testing circuit in the country, even though there are now fewer major meetings. During more recent years it has been the Touring Car Championship which has become the premier event at the circuit,

**Martin Brundle started in motorsport at 12 years of age in a grass track car. Soon he was successfully racing 'hot rods' on short ovals. He moved into circuit racing with a Toyota then into Formula Ford 2000 single seaters and drove for Norfolk in the BMW County Championship. He spent a season in saloon cars, partnering the great Stirling Moss. Next he secured a F111 drive in 1982 sponsored by BP. This brought him a Grovewood Award.**
**1983 saw the titanic FIII struggle with Ayrton Senna which went to the last race before the Brazilian marginally won the Championship. They both moved up to Formula I for 1984 and although Martin consistently performed well, very often in uncompetitive cars, wins eluded him.**
**Not so in touring cars and sports cars however. His many wins in the European Touring Car Championship driving a Jaguar XJS led to him being appointed lead driver in their sports car team in 1985. By 1988 he was dominating the series and became the World Sports Car Champion. In 1990 he joined the very exclusive band who had won the Le Mans 24 Hours Race. Although he continued to race in Formula 1, still getting plenty of podium finishes, he changed direction for 1997 by proving that he was a natural in the television commentary box alongside Murray Walker.**
**Still very much a racer, he is the lead driver for the Toyota sports car team at Le Mans this year. Martin still lives in West Norfolk where he is a co-director of the family motor business.**

bringing with it the queues to get in ad large crowds which were frequent during the Sixties. With that and a healthy club scene things look good for motor racing in Norfolk into the millennium.

*"Speedway,"* wrote the EDP's Colin Chinery, *"is the enigma of British sport, that which uses its own deathbed as a trampoline."* That 1967 appraisal has rung true, with a dizzying cycle of boom and bust this century - and rather more of the latter than the former. Norwich and Yarmouth have seen speedway come and ago (and in Norwich's case, twice) since the sport's arrival in this country in the Thirties. Lynn speedway, happily still with us, has come back from the brink on several occasions in its 34-year history. For every glory night, such as Lynn's superb 1977 capture of the KO Cup there have been plenty more of disappointment.

Yarmouth's small track was ideal for the young Billy Bales, who thrilled thousands of holidaymakers every meeting with his daring leg-trailing style. The stocky rider, who went on to ride for Norwich Stars, captured the British Junior Championship aged 18. But the Caister Road venue's fate was sealed by a savage entertainment tax and it closed in the early Sixties. Norwich speedway at The Firs stadium was destined to last just a few years longer.

The city's 25,000-capacity speedway stadium saw many classic meetings when it re-opened in 1937 after a brief unsuccessful start. Under the patronage of the wily Australian Max Grosskreutz, the sport took off. Riders such as Sid Hipperson, whose superb leg-trailing technique was only stopped by the introduction of shale tracks, Ted Bravery, Aub Lawson and Bob Leverenz were firm favourites.

But the greatest was the young Swede Ove Fundin, who raced to four world titles during his nine years at Norwich. On October 31st 1964 it was all over when the circuit staged its

**Seeing Stars: King's Lynn Stars line up for the cameras on the eve of the 1974 season. Standing, left to right, are team manager Alan Littlechild, Bob Humphreys, Eddie Reeves, Barry Crowson, Malcolm Simmons and David Gagen (then on loan to Boston). Seated on the machine is Terry Betts, the Lynn skipper, and either side of him are Ian Turner (left) and Ray Bales.**

last meeting. Within a year the circuit which had first staged grass-track meetings as far back as the late Twenties was bulldozed. It was left to an irrepressible cockney, Maurice Littlechild, to revive the sport. 'Maury' - described by his co-promoter Cyril Crane as "speedway crazy" - took over a ramshackle greyhound stadium in the shadow of Lynn's beet sugar factory and turned it into The Firs Mk II. The team colours were the same, the terracing, the lights - even the turnstiles were bought from the old Norwich track.

And Norwich rider Terry Betts came out of retirement - at the ripe old age of twenty - along with several former teammates, to win that very first Saddlebow Road meeting for the Lynn Stars on May 23rd 1965. The popular Betts went on to dominate Lynn speedway for 14 years, notching up more than 6600 points. But it was left to the brilliant, yet ultimately wayward, Michael Lee to bring the greatest glory to Lynn with his triumph in the 1980 World Final, with Stars teammate Dave Jessup second. The stadium closed for a year in the late Nineties, prompting fears that, this time, the sport would never return. But Lynn did come back, albeit with a new name (the Knights), to open yet another new chapter in the topsy-turvy 63-year history of Norfolk speedway.

Like all sports, horse racing has changed substantially through the last 100 years or so. From little more than a cottage industry, big business is now at the helm, with the major owners, breeders and race courses getting richer and more dominating, and the smaller ones fighting hard to survive.

The county of Norfolk is just a bit player in the game compared with its wealthier neighbour across the Waveney. Yarmouth and Fakenham, the only two courses in the county, can barely hold a candle to Newmarket. The county does not even have one point-to-point course since the demise of racing at Costessey, just outside Norwich. At the start of the century race meetings were held in many of the county's towns. These were very rough and ready affairs, bearing a close resemblance to the first point-to-points, when horses set off on a course defined sometimes only by church towers.

The horses were all locally-owned, and no-one bothered whether they were from pure thoroughbred stock or cross bred. Most were provided by the farming fraternity and were used as hunters during the hunting season. Years ago massive crowds turned up at Mousehold in Norwich for the races. Similar affairs were held at Dereham on the Neatherd, on Bungay Common, at New Buckenham and at several towns in West Norfolk including Swaffham.

They were the forerunner of National Hunt racing, and were rough unsophisticated affairs, but attracted huge crowds - these were the days before television and when people took any enjoyment they could. The county boasted several point-to-point courses. The Dunston Harriers was the last hunt to organise its own point-to-point course in the county on a special point-to-point course, and having left the permanent course at Hethersett it constructed a special course once a year at Costessey around the golf course.

The West Norfolk Hunt still holds its own annual meeting at Fakenham racecourse with fences smaller than the National Hunt fences specially constructed; but some point-to-point purists think this is a bit much as one of the fences has to be jumped three times. But as the golfers at Costessey rightly insisted that the course stayed further and further away from the greens and fairways, so the Dunston was forced out and now holds its point-to-point meeting in Suffolk.

But the county's two courses, at Fakenham and Yarmouth, still attract loyal followings, even though history shows that both have had to fight for survival with attacks coming from two very different directions. At Yarmouth racing started more than 280 years ago on the south Denes when innkeepers persuaded the town council to lease them land to hold races, but these were little more than donkey derbies. Records also show that pig racing was also a feature!

In the Twenties racing moved to the North Denes and a new course was built and those in charge had the foresight to build one with a straight level mile, Yarmouth's greatest asset and the main reason that top trainers in the country send their promising two-year-olds to the coast. The straight level mile is an ideal introduction for young horses having their first look at a racecourse, and the Cecils and Stoutes of this world are regular visitors with their good young horses. Many go on to take part in and win major races.

But later in the century the rows started and racing became a political battleground and only survived by the skin of its teeth. In 1982 the landlord, Yarmouth Borough Council, discussed closing it. The political division was neat, Labour on the one hand wanting it closed. They wanted to dig up the hallowed turf and build council houses. In the red corner was dour Scot and staunch Labour politician Harry McGee, no lover of the sport of the wealthy. In the blue corner was Michael Carttiss, later to become a Conservative MP. Labour claimed the course was run at a loss, Conservatives claimed it was vital for the tourist industry.

The council divided evenly and racing was only preserved on the casting vote of the mayor, Gordon Chapman. There were other predictable rows, with the council attacking the cost of providing lunches for the stewards "a public disgrace".

Later racing on one day was abandoned

**RICHARD WATTS was born at Dereham and lived there for the first twenty years of his life. Norwich School-educated, he joined Eastern Counties Newspapers straight from school, and, apart from nine years working in publicity in London, has lived in the county all his life. He has been covering racing for the EDP for 18 years. His first visit to a racecourse was at the age of 17 when a friend's mother took a car load. In the last race the group of young lads, barely old enough to bet, all backed the favourite. The person who took them backed a 10-1 outsider called Salmon River, which duly romped home. "I can't understand you boys not backing it," she said, "after all, you all like fishing." His love of racing increased ever since, especially National Hunt courses. But his betting success has remained unchanged...**

**The sport of kings: Another race under way at Fakenham.**

when fire engines putting out a blaze in some nearby gorse drove across the course making large ruts which would be dangerous to galloping horses and caused the following meeting to be abandoned. The row over compensation dragged on for some time.

In a more amusing incident a filly escaped from the course and galloped along the sea front towards Caister. Her trainer Gerry Blum stopped a taxi and with the immortal words "follow that racehorse" tanked along the seafront after her. Two youngsters eventually stopped her and held her to the trainer's relief. The course is in desperate need of a new grandstand – the two existing ones are of the type knocked down by many other courses years ago. Each year the council makes improvements – better stabling and accommodation for the lads, a new watering system which has been of huge benefit as the course used to suffer from firm going and consequent small fields during dry spells, and recently a remodelled unsaddling enclosure. But the elusive new stand seems as far away as ever.

Ron Laxon, who worked for the council, was for many years a sound manager keeping the course on an even footing and dealing with the thousand and one queries in a highly competent manner. He trod the difficult ground between politicians and the racing industry with very great care and skill.

The main meeting remains the three-day festival in September which has a Listed Race and some good contests for two-year-olds. The future, as it probably always will be with Yarmouth, looks difficult to predict as some in the town still doubt the worth of racing.

Fakenham is at the other end of the racing spectrum and has faced similar battles for its future, though from a slightly different quarter. For Fakenham is very much a countryman's course, National Hunt not Flat, racing though the bitterest months of the year, very little straight with horses always seeming to be on the turn.

They have been racing at Fakenham for more than 100 years, starting just as a point-to-point course for the West Norfolk Foxhounds, and running their first proper National Hunt meeting in 1905.

But here again it has been a struggle for survival towards the end of the century. For whenever racing faces a cash crisis the Jockey Club always turns to the smaller courses as a way of saving money. In the 1966 season the course was threatened with closure, and the latest threat came in 1991. For the 1992 season they actually had £32,000 less Levy Board money, but to their eternal credit the directors agreed that prize money and going would not suffer.

Through much of the last thirty years Fakenham was blessed with the services of one Pat Firth, manager, clerk of the course and the man responsible for founding the now hugely successful caravan site which brings in thousands for the course each year. For Pat there was only one way of doing things and that was the right way. He was a racing traditionalist, having been clerk of the course at most of the great courses in the country. Integrity was his watchword. He retired in 1997, and the course is now in the more than capable hands of David Hunter, ex-army, superb horseman but with a flair for innovation which will attract more people as well as keeping the traditionalists happy - no mean feat at a place such as Fakenham.

National Hunt horses have a far longer career than flat horses, and one of the joys is seeing the same horses back time and time again. Once a horse shows a liking for a tight little course such as Fakenham their trainers keep sending them back. Owners also show an extraordinary loyalty to the course, old-fashioned, traditional, full of character.

Fakenham horses, because of this, become more like old friends. Many return time and again, but never even get placed. Fakenham owners are often more interested in the sport than in the prize money.

After the war Major Eldred Wilson owned a horses called Essandem which was a prolific winner at Fakenham and has a race named after him. Major Wilson was tenant of a large farm on the Royal estate and had the task of breaking all the Queen Mother's young racehorses for many years. He was also a director of the course for many years.

Then there was that old warrior, Prince Carlton. Owned and trained by Mrs Beryl Bloom of Kimberley, near Wymondham, he too now has a race named after him. A grand little animal, he managed to scoot round the bends while bigger animals had steering problems and there was a time when he was in his prime when he could beat anything any trainer would send over three miles.

But there is one area where the county can hold its head high. Norfolk has two superb studs, the Royal Stud at Sandringham and Shadwell, just outside Thetford, owned by Sheikh Hamdan al Maktoum. The statue of Persimmon stands outside Sandringham, but more recently the stud will be remembered for Shirley Heights, the winner of the Derby and the sire of a Derby winner. At one time he was one of the finest stallions in the country.

Shadwell is a study in equine luxury. Some of the sheikh's best stallions are or have been based here including the wonder horse Nashwan and the first stallion to be installed, Green Desert. The stud seems certain to continue to produce a long line of Blue Riband winners.

**Ted Pillar, a name known to trainers, jockeys and race-goers alike, was the groundsman at Yarmouth for many years. He took over the job on October 1st 1944 from his father and retired in October 1993. He did all in his power to keep the straight mile up to scratch, and on his retirement many paid warm tributes to his unseen work in providing an ideal course for racehorses. Had he been there when the new watering system was introduced, one suspects the course would have done even better.**

**ALAN MALLETT, the EDP's sailing correspondent, was born in Norwich and educated at Town Close, Diocesan College (Cape Town) and Greshams School. He qualified as a Chartered Accountant in 1964. He started sailing in the mid-Fifties and joined Frostbites and Horning SCs in 1959. He began a distinguished career in local sailing circles by serving as Broads Area secretary for the Enterprise Class in the Sixties. He is currently Vice Commodore of Norwich Frostbite SC. He is also the author of three books on shipping history, on which he regularly broadcasts, and in 1997 was invited to act as guest lecturer on a voyage from Cape Town to Cardiff. He is currently Chairman of Coltishall Parish Council, where he and his dog Monty are familiar figures.**

Sailing was a privileged preserve a century ago, clearly defined in club titles headed by 'Yacht' Clubs, below them the 'Sailing' clubs. Foremost was the Royal Norfolk and Suffolk Yacht Club, based just over the county boundary in Lowestoft. The social distinction is now blurred, a Yacht Club catering predominantly for gentlemen owning large yachts, crewed by paid hands, and often steered by a professional waterman.

Naturally, the owner collected the kudos and silverware following victory, and his name was inscribed on the trophy. There remain trophies which, according to the deed of gift, are awarded to the boat rather than the helm although this is now generally disregarded. On the Broads, local gentry patronised the principal events, joined by farmers and leading business and professional men, and boatyard proprietors. Much of the Norfolk coastline being inhospitable, sea sailing was restricted to the creeks of North West Norfolk where over the years several clubs grew and prospered.

Despite emphasis on larger craft three relatively small keelboat classes emerged during the first decade, of which Linton Hope's Broads OD and Ernest Woods' Yare and Bure have proved durable with more than 150 still sailed. The contemporary Norfolk Dumpling Dinghy featured a single lug-sail and was very popular throughout the Twenties. One or two have survived. It was succeeded by the Norfolk Dinghy in 1931 from Herbert Woods' drawing board which, at a "ready to sail" cost of £65 proved an instant winner.

Throughout the century the name of Clabburn has been synonymous with Broadland sailing. By 1903 Norwich solicitor W L Clabburn was already a name to be reckoned with, and for the next sixty years could justly claim to be the leading light on the Broads. A formidable competitor in the YBOD and Broads OD classes, he was one of the first Norfolk Dinghy owners, and founder Secretary of Norfolk Broads YC when that club was established in 1938, setting the standards by which the club has since been run. He died in 1963.

His son Jimmy, who died at the age of 87 towards the end of May 1994, devoted his life to sailing, particularly in the Norfolk Dinghy class and the YBODs. His distinguished record of more than sixty years afloat included innumerable successes and service which included Commodore of both clubs, culminated when he won the Gold Cup in a thrilling race on Wroxham Broad in 1990 for

**River cruisers, including 251 Silver Queen (centre) reach Reedham during the 1996 River Yare Navigation Race.**

the fifth time, despite arthritis. Today the family reputation is maintained by his sons Ken, John, and James, and grandsons Louis and Alistair. Gearing themselves up for the next century are Ross, son of James, and Tom, son of John, both now in their early teens. The family reputation appears secure for the future.

The Fifties and Sixties saw a boom attributable to increased affluence accentuated by technological advances in boat and sail design and construction. Lighter dinghies, including several National 12 dinghies designed by Leslie Landamore, attracted a new generation. Jack Holt, of Wraysbury, did more than any other individual to introduce sailing to the masses. His "Hard Chine" Enterprise designed for home construction appeared in 1956, and was introduced by David Hastings to Horning. Numbers rose by more than 1000 a year to 10,000 by 1964 and now exceed 20,000. Few are now sailed locally but the class has a secure niche in history. Club membership rocketed and the present management of several clubs is in the hands of those introduced to sailing through the Enterprise, and Holt's later and even more successful creation, the Mirror dinghy.

At the start of the century, reefer jackets, collars and ties and the like were *de rigeur*. As late as the Fifties, Frostbites sailing Norfolks at Whitlingham in mid-winter wore tweed jackets, collar and ties, mostly smoking, sitting up on the gunwale in a clearly stiff breeze but none actually sitting out, and not a lifejacket to be seen.

The proliferation of classes and numbers has crowded regattas. Whereas forty years ago a Wroxham dinghy series involved around twenty Norfolks, twenty Enterprises, and perhaps ten Wayfarers in three class races, today starters comprise ten to 15 each of Norfolks, Wayfarers, and Optimists, plus a number of Toppers and Splashes, with perhaps the odd Mirror or Laser thrown in. When one adds thirty to 35 Cruisers, 12 BODs, 35 YBODs, and twenty Yeomans, planners are faced with accommodating something like double the numbers the programme was originally intended for, on a broad which has certainly not grown! Similar problems face other clubs and regattas. Once a summer activity, sailing is now a year-round sport, thanks partly to Norwich Frostbites, founded in 1933 as the country's first winter sailing club, essentially as a club run on the least expensive basis. It has remained so.

At national level Gerald Sambrook Sturgess was one of the Royal Yachting Association's most able legislators, and an authority on the Racing Rules. Round the World sailor Josh Hamer started sailing at Norfolk Broads YC Sailing School, and Olympic triallists of the post-war period included Jimmy Clabburn and Ian Mackintosh. Today's prospects include Josie Gibson in the 420 class. Leslie Landamore's contribution to boat design has been notable while several generations of the Jeckells family have made sails for boats of all designs sailed world-wide, and continue to do so.

Norfolk's fine record at speed sailing should not be overlooked. In that marvellous sporting year of 1972, Timothy Colman (later, of course, to become Lord Lieutenant and be knighted) was at the helm of 60ft outrigger catamaran Crossbow when it became the first sailing boat to be timed at more than 30mph (26.3 knots). In Crossbow and her successor, Crossbow II, Sir Timothy broke the record again and again.

Now, a Norfolk crew is readying itself to enter the record books once again. Bootiful – christened in honour of main sponsor Bernard Matthews' famous slogan – has been designed to challenge the current record of 46.52 knots (53.36mph), held by an Australian crew.

As Norfolk sailing enters a new century, the overall picture is one with which we may justly be proud.

**Mike Evans started his sailing career just after the war with Norwich Sea Scouts, and rapidly graduated to crewing and sailing National 12 dinghies at Norwich Frostbites and Wroxham. In 1958 he won the Enterprise National Championship followed in 1961 by the Sir William Burton Trophy and National 12 Championship, defending the latter successfully a year, and adding the Endeavour Trophy (Champion of Champions Trophy) for good measure. In 1973 Mike was elected a member of the Royal Yachting Association Council, and 11 years later led the British Sailing team at the 1984 Los Angeles Olympics. This was followed by election as Chairman of the RYA. Mike followed his RYA chairmanship by becoming Executive Director of the International Yacht Racing Union in which capacity he took charge of sailing in the Seoul 1988 and Barcelona 1992 Olympics, and was rewarded on his retirement in 1995 with the Silver Olympic Award. He remains an authoritative and industrious member of the Broads Authority Navigation Committee, and the Norfolk & Suffolk Yachting Association.**

# CHAPTER 15

# *Transport*

**COLIN CHINERY**

On the evening of Saturday February 28th 1959, a train headed across the Fens to Norfolk. It was in every way a Railway Special. For the Norwich City supporters aboard, still celebrating that afternoon's 1-1 FA Cup Quarter Final draw with Sheffield United, the Final and Wembley beckoned. Up on the footplate Billy Watts also had a final on his mind. But for driver Watts the end of the line was not the Empire Way but Melton Constable. After 66 years years of the Midland & Great Northern, he was taking the last train from Peterborough home to Melton and to history.

At the close of the twentieth century, Melton Constable has a brooding, some might say despairing air, perhaps the nearest East Anglia has to compare to a Klondyke gold-rush town. There is little to suggest to the visitor that here is a once a proud railway town, the centre point of a company whose network arched from Peterborough to Great Yarmouth, and from Norwich to Cromer. Returning there earlier this year, Amy Pearce, brought up in Melton, the daughter of an M & GN driver, broke down. "Whatever has happened to Melton?" she sobbed to a friend.

In 1881 the parish of Melton had a population of 118, but with the coming of the M & GN it had grown by the late 1890s to a thousand, the "Little Crewe" of Norfolk. In 1936 the M & GN was taken over by LNER, its engineering works closed, five hundred men lost their jobs and Melton went into steep decline. As driver Watts headed back that night in 1959 he knew "Little Crewe" had reached the end of the line.

The railways came comparatively late to Norfolk, the first line (Norwich Reedham Yarmouth, 1844) arriving 24 years after the opening of George Stephenson's Stockton to Darlington. The next year Norwich was linked to London via Ely and Cambridge, and from 1849 by Victoria Station to Ipswich. Two years earlier King's Lynn had been connected to London.

All manner of fantastic schemes and improbable partnerships, and aborted or short-lived ventures such as the Norwich and Spalding (which never reached further east than Holbeach) testify to the universal and mostly reckless speculative railway mania of the age. Even so by the middle of the century only the North Norfolk coast remained unconnected to the system. When in 1862 all track was taken into the Great Eastern, it seemed Norfolk had been absorbed into a rail monopoly. But by the next decade independent lines were developing, notably in the west of the county, the genesis of what in 1893 was to become the Midland and Great Northern.

So the twentieth century system in Norfolk began with two independent operators, and closed with three, Anglia, West Anglia, and Central Trains. Between these epochs was a 58-year period when - aside from the 13 years up to 1936 when M & GN operated in a curious detachment - the county was served first by the London and North Eastern Railway (LNER) formed out of the 1923 grouping, then from 1948, British Railways, later re-styled British Rail.

Britain's railways are an incomparable repository of popular nostalgia, a theme park of the national consciousness through which the aristocratic 'Castles' and 'Kings' of the Great Western, the majestic maroon locos of LMS, and the apple green expresses of the LNER steam on through the dappled sunlight

**The age of steam returned to Norfolk main line rails in March 25th 1996 – albeit for only a day. The locomotive 70000 Britannia, which pulled the Broadsman passenger train between London and Norwich for many years, returned for a day trip via Cambridge and Ely. Peter Swinger, chairman of Britannia Locomotive Company, said: "The old girl was working as well as ever and it was marvellous to bring her back to what is really her spiritual home."**

to the accompaniment of 'Coronation Scot'.

Yet in strict commercial truth the great age of the railways was almost over within a few years of the close of the First World War, first stopped and then thrown back by the rapid advance of the bus and road haulier which brought door-to-door flexibility and a frequently cheaper alternative. Up to the First War, Norfolk's roads had been rudimentary, the few buses mostly operated by the GER. A rail passenger from Lynn could travel to Norwich via Swaffham, Dereham and Wymondham, or strike out to Wisbech, Sutton Bridge, or Thetford. He could entrain to Hunstanton, Sheringham and Mundesley as well as Yarmouth and Lowestoft. If he had the time, he could take in Harleston, Bungay and Beccles via the London main line at Tivetshall. But by the late Sixties, only Sheringham, Yarmouth and Lowestoft were open.

Forty years earlier - dating ironically from around the formation in 1923 of the 'Big Four' - LNER, LMS, GWR, and SR - road surfaces started to improve and motoring was made more comfortable. Pneumatic tyres were introduced in 1927, and main roads tarred by 1930 (when speed limits were raised from 20mph) and secondary routes by 1938. Along these bright highways sped motorised freight transport, and rail's deserting passengers in car and coach. From the Twenties the rail system was mounting a limitless rearguard action, with the operating companies complaining with justice that Government policy favoured road as against rail. Little was to change.

The financial return for the M & GN for example, peaked long before, in 1906 (by when Blakeney was the only sizeable Norfolk town more than five miles from a station) returning a net profit of £41,000 on 950,000 locomotive miles. After 1914 the fare takings were no longer there. While the net profit increased to £54,000 in 1927, this was realised on more than two million loco miles, its value eroded moreover by wartime inflation.

To the perceptive, the bells were sounding their dread toll. Many lines lost their passenger services between 1927 and 1931, the narrow-gauged Halesworth to Southwold line closed in 1929, shortly followed by the Mellis and Eye, and the Stoke Ferry branch. In the shadow of the Second World War, passenger services

**William Marriott (1857-1943), engineer, traffic manager and Patriarch of the M & GN, was born at Basle in Switzerland, where his father was professor of English at the University. Apprenticed as a draughtsman with Ransomes and Rapier in Ipswich, and later as a civil engineer in London, he came to Norfolk in 1881, working on line construction including the greater part of the Stalham to Melton Constable. Marriott was manager and then locomotive manager of the Eastern and Midland Railway from 1883-93, and then for the M & GN, latterly as engineer and traffic manager. He retired in 1924 and died in 1943.**

were withdrawn from the Forncett-Wymondham line. A few years earlier in Kent, a schoolboy called Richard Beeching had left the sixth form of Maidstone Grammar School.

Of what this portended, nothing could have been foreseen in that first decade of the century when the Great Eastern and the M & GN were still in their prime. Known among its railwaymen as 'Swedey', the Great Eastern Railway was a remarkable combination of - at its London end - probably the most intensive suburban steam service in the world, and here in East Anglia the ultimate in rural meanderings. While it had nothing to compare with the glamour of the great 'named' expresses of the prestige routes such as The Flying Scotsman or the Cornish Riviera Express, the GER by the start of the century had become noted (especially the Continental boat trains) for the excellence of its rolling stock and service on a few publicised lines.

In those golden Edwardian summers, Yarmouth was reached from London in two and a half hours, and Lowestoft in little more. Following its connection to Yarmouth over Breydon Water in 1903, the Suffolk port and resort had an unbroken connection across Norfolk and the Fens to the Midlands.

But the pride of the Great Eastern in the Edwardian years was the 'Norfolk Coast Express'. Leaving Liverpool Street at 1.30pm with a scheduled non-stop run to North Walsham - 131 miles - in two hours 40 minutes, it reached Cromer at 4.25pm.

This remarkable, uninterrupted run had been made possible by the introduction of "stopless" watering troughs at Ipswich and Tivetshall, and the Wensum Curve at Norwich which made it possible to avoid Thorpe Station. Each summer from 1897 to 1914, Cromer had an each-way Liverpool Street service of two hours 55 minutes.

Called at first "The Cromer Express" it acquired its more famous and enduring name in 1907, a special corridor train of between 12 and 15 coaches of varnished teak complete with a restaurant car. Until 1914, before the First War laid it to rest, never to be revived, the Norfolk Coast Express, like the Cromer Express was invariably hauled by a class of locomotive that was to become another East Anglian rail legend, a 4-4-0 Claud Hamilton, which had made its debut 14 years earlier.

Lord Claud Hamilton was one of the towering figures of the region's railways, chairman of the Great Eastern for thirty years up to its grouping into LNER in 1923 (the Hamilton Dock at Lowestoft was named after him). It was Hamilton, and even more C H Parkes (who gave his name to Parkeston Quay, Harwich) who gathered up what had been a ramshackle undertaking, turning it into a railway of outstanding efficiency. The other titan of the Norfolk Iron Road - though an employee, unlike Hamilton who was also the son of the Duke of Abercorn - was William Marriott, Engineer and Traffic Manager of the Midland & Gt Northern Joint Railway.

Formed in 1893 by the Great Northern and the Midland Railway companies, the M & GN was inheritor of 170 miles of mostly single, small operator track. An immensely personalised railway of considerable enterprise and invention, and running at right angles westward from the Great Eastern, it inspired among its passengers and dark-green liveried staff a partisanship probably unsurpassed in the history of Britain's railways.

Marriott one of those energetic and self-assured visionaries who were a feature of Victorian industrial Britain, ran the 'Joint' in a highly personal style that could only enlarge on its already distinctly individual character.

The railway historian Adrian Vaughan of Barney recalls a characteristic incident. With the wife of an employee about to give birth, word was sent to Marriott that she was in trouble and should be moved to the Norfolk and Norwich Hospital without delay. Marriott immediately summoned an engine, drew a carriage from the sidings, cleared the track and got her to hospital. For some 'Joint' men however, Marriott's paternalism crossed the point where it ceased to be admirable and became insufferably interfering. "He was a man who believed in a very strict low-church evangelical religion," says Vaughan. "He was worried that if you let people off the lead they all turned to drink and that neither they nor the railway would be safe. You were not seen coming out of the Hastings Arms at Melton if you knew what was good for you." But as Adrian Vaughan adds, such figures must be taken in the round, and the Marriott who kept an eye on the Hastings Arms was also the Marriott who founded the Melton Railway Institute where young employees could take day release classes. A man of his time and as M & GN as Melton itself, William Marriott is one of the outstanding figures of twentieth century Norfolk.

In the west of the county, other, more conventionally outstanding figures alighted on to the platforms of a Great Eastern country station; the Royalty of the Western World. This was at Wolferton on the now-extinct Lynn-Hunstanton line. With the purchase of Sandringham House in 1862 by the Prince of Wales, later Edward VII, a link was formed between the Royal Family, Norfolk, the Great Eastern and its successors. A tiny principality of sandstone heights, woods and the distant marshes, Wolferton in its heyday received every member of the British Royal Family, who would then be driven up through the rhododendron-banked lanes to Sandringham House two miles distant. Between 1884 and 1911, 645 Royal trains steamed in and out. Continental deities, including the last Kaiser of Germany and the ultimate Czar of Russia came and went, and two British monarchs, George V in 1936 and George VI in 1952 began their last journeys here on their way to burial at Windsor.

Sandringham in turn was to give its name not only to a locomotive, but to an entire class, the 4-6-0, B17, which from its introduction in 1928 to mass liquidation in the wreckers' yards in 1960, was to be one of the most familiar and distinctive in East Anglia. With its nameplates celebrating great houses such as Blickling, Elveden, and Woodbastwick Hall, the 'Sandies' gave a regional touch at once grand and homely, while soccer club names – including of course Norwich City – were a delight to followers and schoolboys alike.

It was a 'Sandringham' that as often as not, hauled the named 'East Anglian', the first titled train to emerge in the region since the demise of the 'Norfolk Coast Express'. Introduced in September 1937 chiefly as a businessman's train, it covered London to Norwich in two hours 13 minutes, with a stop at Ipswich. It was hauled at first by the only two streamlined locomotives to regularly work the line, the B17s 'East Anglian' and 'City of London', specially adapted with casing similar to the Gresley A4 Pacifics such as the record-breaking 'Mallard'. Public interest was centred largely around the splendour of its rolling stock, and it soon acquired for LNER a reputation for comfort and luxury second only to the famous 'Coronation Scot'.

**Princess Anne waves goodbye to Norfolk as the Royal train leaves Wolferton station in January 1963.**

But fondly regarded by train spotters, and evocative of the Steam Age as they are, the B17 'Sandringhams' were less popular with the men who drove them. "They used to bruise your ribs," recalled ex-fireman Rod Fowkes of Ipswich. "Rough, rocking and bruising," mused Alan Baker of Norwich, fireman and driver, who suffered two cracked ribs on one B17 run.

Baker's fifty years on the railways reaches from the echo of the Great Eastern and M & GN, to electrification. Born within sound of the London main line at Lakenham, he joined LNER in 1944 as a 14-year-old greaser at City Station. On his first day he was given a tin hat and a gas mask. For the railways it had been a valiant but debilitating war. "Too much traffic

**Alan Baker: "There was a belief that now we were nationalised things would get better... Things started to go wrong, lines were closing."**

and not enough men," remembers Alan Baker. "The overworked engines used to wheeze and clank and groan, and sometimes fall to bits." It could take eight hours to get from Norwich to March.

City Station, near the site of the present Barn Road roundabout on the inner ring road, was an M & GN terminus. Opened in 1892, the station buildings were destroyed in the April 1942 blitz, to be replaced in 1946 by a pre-fab. After the uncertain post-war years, City was closed to passenger traffic in 1959, a casualty of the M & GN's demise, freight traffic stopped in 1970 and three years later the track was removed. Suggestions that the line to Drayton should be converted to light railway were ignored, and it now forms part of the poignantly-named Marriott's Way amenity trail.

But until 1959, if by then fading fast, City station was the M & GN beacon in a predominantly Great Eastern city (GER's second Norwich station, Victoria, on the site of the present Sedgewick building, "Victoria House", was closed to passengers in 1916, made redundant by the convenience of Thorpe). But while LNER may have absorbed the latter in 1923 and the 'Joint' in 1936, the old and often fierce tribal loyalties remained. "The old Great Eastern men were nearly as bad as the Great Western men," said Alan Baker. "If you were a GE man there was no railway like yours. Midland men were the same. It continued for years. We all reckoned that if you went to Melton and wanted to go in for coal or anything like that, all the M & GN men would jump on their engines and start shunting so you couldn't get in. And that's what it used to seem like! But it was all good fun." This robust demarcational spirit survived the 25 years of LNER, as well as the 1948 nationalisation. Suitably, one of LNER's last enactments was in October 1946, when the 'East Anglian' ran for the first time since the war, with the original and gleaming varnish and chromium on six coaches purpose-built by LNER's chief mechanical engineer, the legendary Sir Nigel Gresley.

Then in September 1948, nine months after nationalisation, a second 'named' train was introduced to the region. Decorated with milk churns and sheaves of oats, wheat and barley, 'The Norfolkman' made its inaugural run, leaving Liverpool Street at ten in the morning before returning from Norwich at 5pm for the two hour twenty minutes trip to the capital.

An EDP editorial - written almost certainly by Eric Fowler - welcomed the facility but not the name. There is no generic name for Norfolk men, expounded the editorial, and Norfolkman *"illegitimate, ugly, and we trust stillborn"* was no true son of the county. The newly-constituted British Railways was unmoved.

The prospect of nationalisation had led railwaymen to entertain high expectations. "There was a belief," recalled Alan Baker, "that now we were nationalised things would get better. We were promised better wages, conditions. We were shown pictures of the lovely new engines we were going to have. We were going to be the cat's whisker! Like hell we were! As footplatemen we got shiny topped caps and that's all we did get." By the early Fifties the dream had collapsed. "Things started to go wrong, lines were closing," he said. Facing what they saw as an unsympathetic and sometimes secretive and remote management, the rail unions became increasingly militant.

In Norfolk the first of the post-war line closures were the Heacham to Wells, and Wroxham to County School in 1952, followed the next year by the Cromer to Mundesley, Tivetshall to Beccles, Thetford-Bury, and Yarmouth Beach to Gorleston. Throughout Britain, there emerged a pattern of contraction, with the network at times seeming to carry as much rumour, suspicion and resentment as traffic. "We all thought it was political sabotage," said Baker. Disillusionment soured morale, and the old spirit was going. "It knocked enthusiasm out of the men, and a lot left."

Then in 1954, what for Norfolk was to prove a seismic event broke out with the first rumours of closure for the M & GN. Branch lines had gone, but here was a main line, an artery of towns and resorts, and a Norfolk institution. Vehement and stony-faced were the denials of officialdom. And when a few years later the EDP revealed that closure plans were definite, British Railways dismissed the reports as "premature".

But in 1958 BR's executive, the British Transport Commission, finally owned up. The line, it claimed, was losing as much as a million pounds a year, and had for many years "been kept in operation to provide occasional convenient facilities for a comparatively few people, many of whom can and do generally use road transport, and all of them can be provided for by alternative public services".

Raymond Meek of Briston, archivist of the 300 member-strong M & GN Circle says that British Rail in effect massaged the books shortly before closure announcement by transferring the freight business to the old Great Eastern line via Dereham and Wymondham. Phyllis Youngman remembers BR painting M & GN stations including Whitwell and Reepham, Lenwade and Drayton only weeks before shutting them. At South Lynn, BR even contrived to erect a new steam locomotive shed only months before the withdrawal of steam and the shutting of the M & GN. "'Muddle and Get Nowhere' was the cruel and totally inappropriate nickname," said Raymond Meek. "In fact it should stand for 'Missed and Greatly Needed.'"

If local reaction was often bitter and heartfelt, BR moved rapidly to conclude the obsequies. On February 28th 1959, Phyllis Youngman's late husband Percy, the last chief inspector at Melton Constable and a third generation M & GN man, closed the network, leaving just the section between Melton and Cromer. "Percy never ceased to his dying day to be unbelievably bitter about that," recalled

**A classic EDP picture of a stoker at work on one of the county's lines. Contraction and closure was the fate of many local railways in the Fifties and Sixties.**

**Dr Richard Beeching: Reviled for closing many of Britain's smaller lines – but the writing had been on the wall for years.**

Adrian Vaughan. 'My railway' he would say." Little more than 24 hours later BR men were out lifting the track at Sutton Bridge. Whatever the operating figures - and as was the case in in every closure, the details were not revealed - the end of the M & GN brought the passing of a way of life and reduced villages and communities to isolation. As the Norfolk writer, the late Jane Hales put it, *"in the scattered countryside people felt as far off from Norwich as Naples"*. By the next decade it was possible to drive a car along lengths of the old line without knowing that a railway ever existed, while other stretches had reverted to nature or yielded to the plough.

The end of the M & GN was the beginning of the end for other Norfolk lines, starting that same year with the Beccles - Yarmouth South Town. If the Beatles and Rolling Stones represent one strand of the decade that was to follow, for the railways the beat was down down all the way. Cliff Richard might extol the pleasures of a Summer Holiday but it was becoming increasingly more difficult to reach it by train. And if Dr Richard Beeching, who had left ICI in 1963 to run Britain's Railways is to be associated with a hit, It's My Party would seem as suitable as any, though the ensuing tears were assuredly not his.

With the publication of Dr Beeching's report on March 27th 1962, the writing was on many a track. Since Beeching was to become a rather demonised figure, it is perhaps surprising to recall that the leader of ASLEF, the footplatemen's union, hailed his report as "a very able document" representing "an entirely honest attempt to rationalise the railway system of this country". Had it been less ruthless "it would have been less honest". Such was to become Beeching's reputation however that today he is occasionally damned for the demise of the M & GN, closed four years before he arrived at BR headquarters.

Even so for Norfolk, which had already lost a third of its track between 1949 and 1959, Beeching was to spell the end for the Dereham-Wells, Melton-Sheringham (a former M & GN link), Thetford-Swaffham, and North Walsham-Mundesley (1964), Lynn-Dereham and Magdalen Road-Wisbech (1968), Lynn-Hunstanton, Wymondham-Dereham (1969), and Yarmouth South Town-Lowestoft (1970). Its links with the Rev W Awdry, creator of Thomas the Tank Engine notwithstanding ( he was a former vicar of Emneth), Wisbech lost its passenger rail link in 1968, the largest town in England to be so isolated.

Among station closures, those at Swainsthorpe, Flordon, Forncett, Tivetshall and Burston in 1968 meant there was now no stop between Norwich and Diss. This had been foreshadowed in the second Beeching plan, published in 1965, four years after the last of the regular steam-hauled passenger services. Farewell Britannia, Lord Hurcombe and John Bunyan, adieu Honingham Hall and Huddersfield Town, the end for Audley End. A heavy heart for Coeur de Lion and Hartebeeste, and henceforward learn to love the diesel. It was the late and near-legendary Bill Harvey, Shedmaster at Thorpe Station 1947-1972, who masterminded the introduction of the Britannias in 1951, Festival of Britain year, and as the Norwich-based railway historian Richard Joby recalls, Harvey who brought the best journey time to London down by twenty minutes to two hours. Bill Harvey was also the first shedmaster in Britain to run (1962 onwards) an all-diesel fleet. "Every time, he rose to the occasion, introducing successful services," said Joby. "He was a wholesale enthusiast, with a total dedication to his craft."

We pity our fathers, wrote the American Ralph Waldo Emerson, *"for dying before steam... as cheated out of half their human estate."* Now we may pity our children for being born after its demise. Dr Beeching had looked into the future however, and was in no doubt as to how it would best work. There would be a concentration on intensive volume trunk routes from which stopping services would be eliminated (it might be seen as indicative of Britain's penchant for narrow, short-term planning that their social and environmental role, for example in easing road and city centre congestion, was not considered). Beeching Two allocated East Anglia one trunk route, the Norwich-London,

**A photograph taken during the last days of steam at Norwich.**

though happily the seemingly doomed East Suffolk line was included in this blueprint for 1984. This owed much to the campaign of Gerard Fiennes of Aldeburgh, former general manager and board member of Eastern region, abruptly sacked by BR in 1967 after the publication of his book I Tried to Run a Railway. Fiennes remained a critic of the transport system, challenging official costings for threatened local lines as "inaccurate" and leading the campaign that was to keep the East Suffolk in service.

Like the Lowestoft-Ipswich link, other "branch" lines had operated under recurring rumours of closure, and were to do so through to the early Nineties. This culture of decline was contested vigorously by among others, the Railway Development Society, which has always had a strong East Anglian presence. But in 1967 British Rail introduced "Paytrains" - a creation of Gerard Fiennes - on the local diesel railcar services. Along with station closures, single-tracking, automatic level crossings and signalling, conductor-guards can be seen as part of a radical cost-cutting strategy that arguably saved many local routes. Even so the often rudimentary facilities that survived - for example unsheltered platforms too short for the trains - were resented. Such was BR management's reputation for cynicism and guile that there were those who suspected it was part of a plan to alienate passengers and so prepare the way for closure. In fact by 1974 paytrains - some by now operating on romantic-sounding lines such as "The Wherry" (Norwich-Yarmouth-Lowestoft)

**The Norfolk Norfolk Railway arose out of the ashes of part of the old Melton Constable to Cromer Beach branch line section of the M & GN. Enthusiasts initially bought the three-mile section from Weybourne to Sheringham and have since extended services to the outskirts of Holt. The granting of the second of two Light Railway Orders cleared the way for public services from July 1975. The line has grown into a much-loved tourist attraction.**

and "The Broads" (Norwich-Sheringham) were attracting new customers. "A major breakthrough in the uphill drive to win the public back to local railways," enthused Norwich divisional manager, Gordon Clarke.

It became discomfortingly obvious however that East Anglian passengers were stuck with BR's hand-me-down rolling stock. But in 1985, by when some of the two-carriage units were 25 years old, BR began introducing new half million-pound 158 class units named "The Sprinter", and beyond for the Nineties, a new generation of local and cross-country trains, air-conditioned, more commodious and capable of 90mph. In 1992 East Anglia's local services were re-organised into a new operational arm, Regional Railways Central, "Barmouth to Yarmouth". There was no doubt by now that British Rail was viewing its local services very positively. The improvements were obvious, and taken in hand with the completion of main line electrification (Norwich-Ipswich 1987, and Lynn-Ely 1992) there was a rail optimism unparalleled in living memory.

The separation in 1992 of BR's local and main line operations had put the Norwich-Liverpool Street service into a new organisation, Anglia InterCity. It was to be a brief affair. The following year the industry's long-promised if perplexing privatisation was finally embodied in the Railway Act, and in April 1994, the British Rail Board became in effect a holding company for a national network of 25 independent companies awaiting their franchisees. Enter Anglia

The age of the trams was over almost as soon as it had begun. Norwich's last tram ran on the Newmarket Road to Cavalry Road service on December 10th 1935, the electric tramways having started in 1900. Yarmouth's trams stopped running in December 1933, and Lowestoft's services ran from 1903 to 1931.

Norwich's trams created headaches virtually from day one. Trying to run a tram line system through the city's historic streets created many traffic hold-ups - a fact which only worsened with the growth in motor traffic. The Eastern Counties Omnibus Company bought a controlling stake in the trams in 1933 and announced they would close.

The greater flexibility of petrol-driven transport drove out tram systems in East Anglia as it had done throughout the country. Ironically, there have been many calls over the years for a light rail system to be reintroduced - but the huge initial capital outlay (one 1995 estimate was £100 million for Norwich alone) has thwarted any plans.

But the Norwich, Yarmouth and Lowestoft services were not the only ones.

The other tram service in the area ran until as late as 1966 - and inspired a character in one of the most famous series of children's books published this century.

The Wisbech and Upwell Tramway seems a curious idea now, a six-mile track which ran from Wisbech to Outwell Basin.

But the principle was interesting: the Great Eastern Railway wanted to experiment with a light rail service for villages which would then feed into the main line. The tramway ran from 1883 until 1966, and its distinctive box-shaped engines stuck in the memory of a certain Rev W Awdry who lived at nearby Emneth.

The tramway lives on... in the guise of Toby the Tram Engine.

**Electrification was a multi-million pound vote of confidence in the Norwich-London and Lynn-London lines in the Nineties.**

Railways (since January 1997 a subsidiary of GB Railways Group) which as well as Norwich-London, runs all the local operations in Norfolk and Suffolk with the exception of the Norwich-Ely section, owned by the Birmingham-based Central Trains. West Anglia Great Northern Railway operates King's Lynn-London, and Great Eastern lines south of Ipswich.

Next year Central will be introducing Britain's newest train, the 100mph class 170 diesel 'Turbostar' to its Norwich services, while in this final year of the century, Anglia Railways is investing £26 million in a fleet of new trains, extending the Norwich-London service to half-hourly frequencies, and restoring through services between London, and Yarmouth, Lowestoft and Sheringham. Other developments include stopping trains at Stratford to serve the Millennium Dome and Eurostar services, a cross-London link with other parts of the country, and a proposed East-West link from Norwich to Oxford.With passenger volumes rising substantially, and expected to increase by a further thirty per cent in the next ten years, is it fanciful to believe that a renaissance for rail travel is under way?

A septuagenarian motorist taking a car on to the Norfolk road network in the summer of 1950 would have found it as familiar as at the turn of the century. Almost all followed tracks made by cattle or early inhabitants long before the Romans arrived with their un-Norfolk attachment to linear road construction. Ninety-three-year-old Eileen Bromhead of Mundesley recalls the county highways of the

Twenties, narrow, twisting and stony-surfaced. In Norfolk said Mrs Rosalind Harris, 91, who lived in the inter-war years at the family home, Rackheath Hall, many of the country roads had crowns raised to drain surface water into adjacent ditches and dykes. Like Mrs Bromhead she remembers the emptiness of the roads and the pleasures and mutual courtesies of motoring. "If you suffered a puncture - which was fairly frequent - a passing motorist would be certain to stop and help with the wheel changing."

Up to 1939 the only significant innovation was the construction of the Norwich outer ring road. Even after a war which had shut roads across airfields and the Stanford battle area, and seen much of the remaining network pummelled by military traffic, the picture remained one of patchwork improvements, highlighted by some trunk widening and straightening of the more notorious convulsions.

In August 1949 Whitehall published a plan to give Norfolk and Suffolk a trunk road system at once speedier, safer and more comfortable. But in February 1955 Norfolk was omitted from a £147 million four-year plan for Britain's roads. However much County Hall engineers might protest that the network was inadequate (car ownership for example, had doubled to more than 75,000 between 1939 and 1953) the Ministry gave Norfolk a low priority. In fact by 1958 - while the M1 was being constructed - the Government had been systematically cutting back on funding for road works in the county; "the biggest scandal we have," growled one councillor. Into the sixth decade of the twentieth century, the A11 still squeezed and meandered through the narrow streets of Wymondham and Thetford, and it took the release of track following the closure of the M & GN network in 1959 to give Norfolk a small, delayed bonanza of straight roads. The A17 Lynn to Sutton Bridge and the A47 Dereham bypass through Scarning and Wendling are two beneficiaries, and other examples are at Holt and North Walsham. The first major new 'county' road was the Lynn eastern bypass, 1966 (the Norwich inner ring road was opened in 1971) and by 1991 north on the A149, the Dersingham/ Ingoldisthorpe/ Snettisham bypass was built partly on the former track of the Lynn-Hunstanton railway.

But it was the principal link with London, the A11, which was the most striking reminder of the county's backwater trunk road system. And it was not until 1979 that Whitehall unveiled a £28 million plan for dualling half of the length between Norwich and Newmarket. Yet despite a 1983 target date, only a small section at Cringleford had been completed the next year. Such was the background to the "Dual the A11" campaign, launched by the EDP in 1984. Perhaps no other Norfolk newspaper campaign has received such extensive and impressively heartfelt support; councils, MPs, communities, business, trade unions, tourism, motoring and road safety organisations all took up the banner. The campaign was carried to the floor of the Commons and pressed in Whitehall ministries. Not everyone in Norfolk supported the call - environmentalists, fearing that Roads to Prosperity would prove to be Highways to Hell, and sections of the public

**For every Norfolk road project built – such as the Lynn southern bypass, above – there were many others left on the drawing board, much to the frustration of campaigners, such as supporters of a Long Stratton bypass (below).**

transport lobby were critical - but there was no doubting its impact, not least on Government ministers.

In May 1985 the Attleborough bypass was opened, but with only one, short section dualled, and no proper run-offs for the roads that crossed.Three weeks later a lorry collided with a coach at the point where the dualled and single sections met, and three people were killed.

The following year one and a quarter miles of dualling south of Barton Mills were opened, and in 1987 the Hethersett bypass. It seemed that after Attleborough,Thetford would be the next victim of Whitehall funding/design myopia.The original plan had been for a single -carriageway road with a crawler lane in the central third section. But after vociferous protests, Whitehall relented and announced that a third of the 4.7-mile bypass would be dualled.While Road Minister Robert Atkin was cutting the tape in November 1989, workmen were out dualling the remaining sections, opened a year later. As with Attleborough, it is hard to explain Whitehall's preference for cheap-ticket, built-in obsolescence save in terms of an historic perception of Norfolk as a low-priority county.

While the 5.4-mile Wymondham-Besthorpe bypass was spared these false and hazardous economies, construction was long delayed as a result of a campaign by environmentalists. A smaller but intense protest had threatened the Dersingham/ Ingoldisthorpe/ Snettisham bypass at the end of the Eighties. There the issue was the fate of what came to be known as the Dersingham Micro Moth. At Wymondham it was a colony of great crested newts. The Department of Environment agreed to spend £150,000 to create a new breeding habitat for the endangered amphibians, and not without continuing 'green' protests, the bypass opened in March 1996. Elsewhere in Norfolk bypasses were being opened, including Dickleburgh and Scole, Blofield and Acle, Tilney, Narborough (undualled), Downham, and most impressive of all, the 14-mile, £95 million Norwich Southern bypass in 1992. Indeed since the start of the decade it seemed there had been an unstoppable roll, the Government in 1990 pledging the dualling of the A140 from Norwich to the A45 near Ipswich. Four years later it was the A47 from Yarmouth to Peterborough that was being targeted for dualling.

But abruptly later that year, Government cutbacks killed off more than half Transport Secretary John MacGregor's road building plans for 1995. Worse was to follow. In November 1995 the Government withdrew 77 motorway and trunk road schemes, a spending cut of a third, and reduced spending by the County Council also took its toll. The Norfolk casualties included six by-passes - among them Wroxham - and three schemes on the A47. While the A11 was still to be dualled from Norwich to the M11 - the next improvement is to be completed before 2003 - but similar plans for the A47 "would not be forthcoming" said the Roads Minister. As for dualling the A140, that had long disappeared from the road map. Even so the following March publication of hitherto secret Government papers revealed that all routes into Norwich would be "chronically congested" by 2015 unless there was an expansion in road building.

The Labour Government that came to office in May 1997 was not minded to begin it. Of 140 national schemes under review, only 37 emerged intact in March 1999, among them the dualling of the A11. But for the A47, long the Cinderella trunk road, ministers could promise nothing better than a "transport corridor study". In fact since May 1995 the A47 has been part of the Trans European Network, but despite its status of one of Europe's key economic roads - and critical to the economy of Yarmouth and to a lesser extent Lowestoft - Government policy contains no commitment to its significant improvement. From the Acle Straight in the east to the Hardwick roundabout at Lynn - surely the carbuncle on the face of East Anglia's road system - the future of the A47 seems to be one of, at best, piecemeal improvements, and perpetual frustration. Meantime the maintenance backlog on the county's existing 5898 miles of roads - the result very largely of

New era dawns as bypass opens

**The EDP reports on September 11th 1992 that the Norwich southern bypass is finally open.**

**Passengers on the number 26 Eastern Counties bus from Hellesdon had one of the century's most memorable trips at 3.30pm on March 3rd 1988. Their bus started disappearing down a former chalk working in Earlham Road, Norwich, creating an image which grabbed headlines all over the world. But the incident brought misery to businesses and residents who were faced with more than a year of disruption while investigations and repairs to the road were carried out.**

years of Whitehall under-funding – had climbed to £95 million. The most recent available figures (1994) showed that Britain spent £81 per capita on road maintenance and construction, compared with a Continental average of £125. Typically one might say, Norfolk's allocation per kilometre, at £1330, is well below the national average of £1954. In five to ten years, said planning and transportation chairman Eddie Littler in 1998, Norfolk could be on the onset of "very severe problems".

Norfolk's director of planning and transportation, Martin Shaw says that while it is clear the A11 will be dualled within the next decade, "it is also equally clear there may be no other significant improvements to the strategic road links between Norfolk and the rest of the country". The remaining trunk roads will remain in essentially their present state, though there will be a handful of new bypasses where there are issues of safety and environment, Long Stratton being the strongest case on the county's trunk roads.

Shaw says it is arguable that Norfolk is now "relatively speaking more remote than it was in the Fifties, given the lack of a dual carriageway link to the national motorway network. Norwich is now the only city in the country with a population of more than 100,000 not linked by a dual carriageway to the national motorway box.

"The great trunk route improvement age is all but over. The comprehensive improvement of the A47 for example, linking Norfolk to the East Midlands has long been abandoned. National transport policy has undergone a sea change supported by all parties, and Norfolk has been affected by its timing." For the future, national hopes are pinned on attempts to reduce the growth of total demand and to encourage a switch to public transport, walking and cycling.

**STEVE SNELLING**

It was an inauspicious beginning for a revolutionary mode of travel that would ultimately make the world a far smaller place. Norfolk's first, thrilling aerial display was drawing to a close by the seaside. Only one circuit remained for the frail-looking Bleriot monoplane when near-disaster struck. The wood and wire machine bounced across a field at Tom Cook's Crowhall Farm on the edge of Gorleston and soared into the sky only for the engine to suddenly cut out at 150ft. One of the spectators watched the drama unfold on that August day in 1910. *"The airman was not sufficiently high to turn,"* he recorded, *"and had to descend at once with a strong wind behind him. The machine, at great speed, ran the whole length of the field into a hedge, smashing the wings and the propeller..."*

Incredibly, the pilot clambered out of the wreckage none the worse for his ordeal in what must go down as Norfolk's first air accident. Even more remarkably, the splintered "wreck" was airborne again within a week and thrilling the crowds at Norwich. Bentfield Charles Hucks, the first British airman to successfully "loop the loop" and the man credited with bringing aviation to the county, was to become the dominating personality in the pioneering days of powered flight in Norfolk.

Yet few who witnessed those early joyrides and astonishing feats could have imagined the extraordinary advances that would propel aviation from the preserve of the daredevil amateur and the wealthy few to one of the safest modes of global transportation for the masses. Norfolk's place in the story of flight is a small yet far from insignificant one, dominated by one company, two wars and the rise and spectacular fall of the British airship.

It was the First World War which generated the first rush of airfield construction. The strips were all grass and most of the accommodation consisted either of tents or prefabricated huts. Only a few survived the peace to become permanent RAF bases. Significantly, however, the war was also responsible for laying the foundations from which civil aviation was eventually to take wing. So far as Norfolk was concerned this unexpected peace dividend was centred on two wartime air stations, the former Royal Naval Air Service base at Pulham St Mary and the Royal Flying Corps training field at Mousehold, on the eastern fringes of Norwich.

During the Twenties, Pulham became one of

**A suitably American-style send-off for the first direct flight from Norwich Airport to the United States, which took place on May 1st 1997 when 240 passengers travelled on a Boeing 767 to Orlando, Florida.**

the world's most important aeronautical test beds. The station had already played host to some remarkable aerial visitors, including the R34 which landed in Norfolk in July 1919, at the end of its historic double Atlantic crossing and the semi-rigid SR-1 which completed the first direct flight between Italy and Britain a few months earlier. And, at a time when optimism about the future of the airship as a trans-continental passenger carrier was running high, Pulham was at the forefront of airship development, a magnet for some of the

**"With us," said Wing Cmdr Ken Wallis in an EDP interview, "aeroplanes are a family vice." The pilot from Reymerston followed in the footsteps of his father and uncle to be an air pioneer, becoming world-famous for his championing of the autogyro. He is the most famous autogyro pilot in the world, having claimed almost two dozen records and featured in the thrilling air chase in the James Bond film You Only Live Twice. The many and varied capabilities of the aircraft have even seen him used in the hunt for the Loch Ness Monster and the fugitive peer Lord Lucan. The former wartime bomber pilot went into the new century in his mid-eighties still as full of enthusiasm as ever for his tiny aircraft. "Flying an autogyro gives you a special intimacy with the air and the ground," he once said. "It's the best low-flying aircraft there ever was."**

country's best and bravest aeronauts. It was a heyday which survived the loss of the R38 over the Humber and the drama of the R33, torn from its mast by a gale and swept backwards across the North Sea before its skeleton crew regained control, only to succumb to the fireball which engulfed not only the R101 but the entire airship programme in the autumn of 1930.

The impact of the disaster was felt not only in Pulham, but in the engineering works of Boulton & Paul, the Norwich aircraft manufacturers, who had designed and constructed the girder framework for the country's largest-ever aerial leviathan. The R101 contract represented a coup in 1925 which underlined the city firm's growing prestige in a highly competitive market. Originally noted for its iron and woodworking, Boulton & Paul had diversified, along with car manufacturers Mann Egerton, as a result of war exigencies into aeroplane construction. Most of the aircraft delivered to the battlefronts were built under licence. But by the end of the conflict the company, under the guidance of the designer John Dudley North, had begun to produce its own aircraft, which were wheeled out and tested from hangars constructed on the edge of Norwich's Mousehold aerodrome.

Despite a failed attempt to scoop the trans-Atlantic prize ultimately claimed by a Vickers Vimy flown by Alcock and Brown (the Norwich bid ending in a crash on Mousehold), Boulton & Paul went on to build an enviable reputation for its high performance twin-engined medium bombers, of which the best-remembered was probably the Sidestrand. Other successes included the P15 Bolton, the first all-metal aircraft delivered to the RAF, and the Overstrand, before the company sold off its aircraft department in the mid-Thirties.

Production switched to a new factory built in Wolverhampton, where the first aircraft to roll out was the last to be designed at Norwich, the Boulton & Paul Defiant.

By then, a new era in the county's aviation history had dawned with the establishment of the first Norwich Airport, officially opened in June 1933, by the then Prince of Wales. Championed by former Lord Mayor Robert Bignold and Archie Rice, who six years earlier had launched the Norfolk and Norwich Aero Club, Mousehold's municipal airport drew airliners, air taxis as well as aerial photography aircraft to its grass strip.

Operated by club members, the airfield, which had already drawn such distinguished aviators as Amy Johnson, Bert Hinkler and Alan Cobham with his flying circus, flourished, but success was quickly overshadowed by the gathering clouds of war. The airport was closed, the club suspended and, as if to rub salt into the wounds, one of the Luftwaffe's first bombs to fall on Norwich destroyed the clubhouse. A post-war revival at Mousehold was short-lived. The last fixed-wing aircraft took off from the airfield in 1946 and, although an experimental helicopter mail service used the field, it remained under-used until the decision was made in 1949 to cease flying. With the closure, civil aviation in Norfolk slipped into one of its periodic troughs, kept alive only by amateur flying groups, glider enthusiasts and the establishment during the mid-Sixties of heliports at Yarmouth and Ellough to serve the rapidly expanding offshore industry.

Norwich's revival at Horsham St Faith came a little later as part of a far-sighted joint venture by city and county councillors. In 1969, thirty years after being opened as an RAF base and twenty years after the demise of Mousehold, the unveiling of a new passenger terminal at the city's second airport signalled a fresh chapter which continues to this day. Officially opened on May 30th 1970 by Roy Mason, the President of the Board of Trade, Norwich Airport has blossomed by way of Air Anglia, Air UK and KLM UK into one of the regional success stories of civil aviation.

As it approaches a new millennium with a new name, a newly-refurbished terminal and a new range of holiday destinations, Norwich International, officially renamed in May 1999, is soaring on a flightpath of growth marked by record passenger levels, reaching almost 330,000 in 1998. Civil aviation has flown a long way since the days when the intrepid Bentfield Hucks brought the thrill of flying to an expectant Norfolk public.

## CHAPTER 16

# *Discovering Our Past*

The twentieth century has seen the greatest expansion yet of our knowledge about the lives of our Norfolk forefathers. The scientific application of techniques ranging from the use of computers to simple and meticulous observation - all with the support of dedicated professional and amateur help - has enabled us, as we move into an new millennium, to build a better idea of Norfolk's story than ever before. But there is much, much more yet to be discovered.

The Norfolk landscape we live in has been fashioned by man over the last few thousand years. Even the surviving areas of ancient woodland are the product of medieval land management where ground was carefully set aside and fully exploited to provide timber for building materials, fuel and for woodland crafts. The vast expanse of drained marshland between Acle and Yarmouth, although seemingly wild and empty, was by the early nineteenth century a highly regulated piece of water management with drainage dykes and windpumps making full use of the grazing potential of this former Roman estuary.

At King's Lynn engineers even managed to divert the course of the Great Ouse during the nineteenth century. Since the Neolithic period the people of Norfolk been having a lasting impact on the county we live in. This impact should be seen as the result of complex interactions between human ambitions, soils and the natural topography.

The nineteenth century was a great period of antiquarian curiosity when people interested in the past first really woke up to what was around them. The first Norwich and Norfolk Museum was set up in 1825, and from the beginning, the collections contained archaeological material.

The Norfolk and Norwich Archaeological Society was founded in 1846, and the 1840s and 1850s were an active time, when antiquarians were busy opening prehistoric burial mound, or "barrows", at a rate of at least 24 excavations each decade. The Archaeological Society flourished, and its annual report for 1900 records that during the year the society had organised visits to seven churches, three great houses, one castle and one other building. Thanks to the antiquarian clergy, the study of ecclesiastical architecture and the chronology of building styles was the antiquarians' main enthusiasm. Buildings were subjects they could understand. To many, churches and castles were archaeology.

By the end of the century, antiquarian perceptions of the archaeology of Norfolk were still sketchy in many respects. Some of our major monuments, such as the Roman town at Caistor St Edmund or the Roman forts at Burgh Castle and Brancaster, had by then been correctly identified, while other monuments were not understood and many had not yet been recognised. In particular, the appreciation of earthworks was still in its infancy, with the pre-Roman Iron Age forts at Warham and Thetford being labelled as Danish (Viking) encampments. Deserted medieval villages as a class of monument, for instance, were hardly recognised before the Fifties.

Much energy had been spent during the nineteenth century on the wholesale "opening" of prehistoric burial mounds - with disastrous results. At least 85 barrows had been dug into over the century, and high standards of recording being set by archaeologists in some parts of Britain were not being copied here. Soil layers were rarely noticed, records were sparse, and many of the objects antiquarians found either crumbled to the

**DR PETER WADE-MARTINS decided at the age of 12 that he was going to be an archaeologist after visiting the Roman town at Caistor. He started investigating medieval villages in Norfolk when he was 18 in 1962, and received his first government grant to organise a rescue excavation on a deserted village near Mileham in 1965/6. From 1967 to 1972 he ran the excavations on the Anglo-Saxon and medieval settlement in North Elmham Park. At the same time he carried out a detailed study into the origins of villages in central Norfolk. From 1973 he was Director of the Norfolk Archaeological Unit, and then County Field Archaeologist in the Norfolk Museums Service from 1978 to 1999. Having just taken early retirement from the service, he is currently taking on a managerial role for the Norfolk Archaeological Trust.**

**William Clarke (1877-1925) led the move to properly record the traces of prehistoric man in East Anglia. Though he was born in Yorkshire, his parents were Norfolk people, and his early years were spent at Thetford. He joined the Norwich Mercury as a reporter in 1897 and, after war service with the Norwich Cyclist Volunteers and Army Pay Corps, he joined the EDP's literary staff. A passionate champion of Norfolk archaeology and natural history, an obituary of him claimed: "Probably no county has ever had a more devoted student."**

touch or soon disintegrated in private collections.

Antiquities were, as Sir Mortimer Wheeler was to put it, being dug from the earth "like potatoes". A selection of the more robust finds was being gathered in the Norwich Castle Museum which was opened in 1894. A careful catalogue of this material, with accession numbers, was prepared by the great Norfolk historian and antiquarian, Walter Rye, and was published in 1909. The practice of digging into barrows and removing the contents without proper record continued well into this century; it is distressing to realise that at least a further 46 largely unrecorded and unpublished barrow excavations took place between 1900 and 1950. One easily forgets how recently standards have changed.

The region has nevertheless often been the originator of significant developments in archaeological practice. In 1908 local prehistorians met in the rooms of the Norfolk and Norwich Library to inaugurate *"an East Anglian Society for the study of all matters appertaining to prehistoric man"*. They were keen to encourage the recording, mapping, publication and preservation of monuments. The movement to create the Prehistoric Society of East Anglia was led by W G Clarke, author of In Breckland Wilds (1925), and the society fed on the great enthusiasm then current for collecting flint implements from the light soils of Breckland. But times moved on, and in 1935 this movement burst from its chrysalis to be become the national Prehistoric Society, which has since developed an international reputation for prehistoric studies.

The next major player was Rainbird Clarke, the son of W G Clarke and Curator of the Castle Museum from 1951 to his sudden death in 1963. From the Thirties onwards, initially for the Ordnance Survey who were building up a record of antiquities shown on their maps, Rainbird started to build a systematic card index of archaeological discoveries. His cards survive, and they have formed the basis of the modern computerised County Sites and Monuments Record (SMR). Through Rainbird's pioneering work, we have one of the oldest and largest SMRs in the country, with 32,296 separate records as at April 1999. This, increasingly, forms the basis for academic research and for heritage conservation policies in Norfolk.

Field archaeology, as opposed to museum archaeology, was not established as a profession until the early Seventies. Up until then museum archaeologists such as Rainbird Clarke had to run their excavations in their holidays, and on a shoestring, with the support of an enthusiastic inter-disciplinary group of mainly volunteers, the Norfolk Research Committee based at the Castle Museum.

Things changed when the Department of the Environment made grants to encourage the formation of archaeological units to undertake rescue excavations. The national "Rescue" movement was a great response to the outcry which began in the late Sixties over the enormous destruction to our archaeological heritage caused by the redevelopment of town centres and the wholesale (grant-aided) levelling and ploughing of monuments to increase productivity in the countryside.

The Norfolk Archaeological Unit was the first county-based unit to be formed in Britain, in April 1973. The Oxfordshire Unit started that October and the Suffolk Archaeological Unit followed in April 1974. The Norfolk Unit joined the county museums service in 1978. These units provided a national framework for the first time for archaeologists to study, record and publish research on a significant scale. The Norfolk and Suffolk units soon joined together, with the support of a regional co-ordinating committee, the Scole Committee, to launch the East Anglian Archaeology publication series. This was later widened to include Essex. Norfolk has since contributed 53 volumes of archaeological research to this series making the results of excavations and fieldwork, and to a lesser extent the study of historic buildings, widely available.

Strong policies for conserving the county's archaeology were first introduced into Norfolk's Structure Plan in March 1988 as follows: *"Development which would affect sites of outstanding archaeological*

**Rougham Deserted Village, one of the many earthwork sites being conserved under the Norfolk Monument Management Project.**

*importance will only be permitted in exceptional circumstances.*

*"On other sites of archaeological importance and where there is no overriding case for preservation, development will not normally be permitted unless agreement has been reached to provide for the recording and, where desirable, the excavation of such sites"*

The next breakthrough occurred in 1990 with the release by central government of a Planning Policy Guidance Note, No 16 Archaeology and Planning, known as PPG 16. This transformed overnight procedures for protecting archaeological evidence threatened by development. For the first time planning authorities had clear guidelines on how to deal with development threats to the historic environment.

From then on, in essence, the polluter paid. When a development was likely to damage archaeological evidence, the planning authority could take steps to ensure that the significance of the site was fully evaluated first, and could then withhold a decision until the results of evaluation were available. A planning consent could then be issued with conditions attached specifying precisely what further archaeological works were required before development could begin. In practice, this has injected considerable sums of new money from the development industry into archaeology throughout Britain.It has also led to a considerable amount of work in areas where no systematic excavation has been seen before.

Archaeologists now have the right of access, and in theory the resources, to record sites properly before they are destroyed. In practice, however, compromises have been necessary in order avoid "archaeological blight" over some urban areas where profits from development are marginal and where there are considerable political pressures for developments to proceed.These compromises have been over the size of excavations, not over whether they should take place. In time, though, market prices for property should

**Rainbird Clarke (1914-63), the son of W G Clarke, was Curator of Norwich Castle Museum from 1951 to 1963. He was the first to record systematically archaeological discoveries and their locations in Norfolk back in the Thirties. He started the card index for the Ordnance Survey, but over the next thirty years he built up his index as a comprehensive archive of the county's archaeology. This has since become the foundation of the county's computerised sites and monuments record. His book, East Anglia, published in 1960 was the first modern systematic account of the archaeology of the region.**

increasingly reflect likely archaeological costs, and the developer's case for not being able to afford the archaeology will be reduced.

The excavation on the Millennium Library site in Norwich, where all the area to be developed not previously damaged by the deep basement for the previous library built in the Sixties, is being fully and properly recorded. This is a clear and much-publicised example where the full consequences of PPG 16 have been accepted and implemented by all the parties involved.

Certainly, it is a far cry from the early Seventies when the Norfolk Archaeological Unit sometimes had to go on its metaphorical bended knee to the developer even to have access to a building site to watch the archaeological evidence being destroyed. The writer remembers well being refused access by developers to carry out excavations on a number of important sites at that time. The "Rescue" movement of the Seventies has since achieved most of its objectives.

In 1994, there was another PPG, No 15 Planning and the Historic Environment. For historic buildings, this set out the same evaluation and recording procedures as for below-ground archaeology. It is fair to say that historic building conservation officers have been slower to jump at the chance to require evaluations and to specify full recording of buildings prior to their alteration or conversion. Fewer adequate evaluation reports on historic buildings have been deposited with the Sites and Monuments Record, although, one hopes that this is only a matter of time.

The twentieth century has seen many advances in how we perceive the past, but perhaps the most significant has been a real appreciation of how ancient and profound the changes to the landscape have been. This understanding has developed with the growth of "landscape archaeology" as a discipline. The origins of this discipline lie in the realisation that the whole landscape is, in essence, archaeology. Every feature, be it a village street, a building or a hedgerow has its own antiquity, its own story to tell, and can often be much older in origin than was previously thought. The landscape as a whole is ancient and of great interest.

Archaeology is not just about dramatic discoveries such Iron Age gold torcs or Roman villas, however important they may be, and the gradual acceptance of this concept has been the most significant breakthrough for archaeology in the twentieth century. As our understanding of Norfolk's man-made heritage has developed by leaps and bounds over the last hundred years, several techniques have played a significant part in moving this process forward.

The first of these is improvements in our study of old maps. Old maps of different parts of the county survive in surprising numbers from the late sixteenth century onwards, and sometimes they can be linked to yet older written descriptions of manors or parishes. Maps should always be the starting point of any investigation by a landscape archaeologist. One of the most exciting discoveries made from maps came when Tom Williamson at the Centre of East Anglia Studies, UEA used early nineteenth-century Tithe Award maps of the Dickleburgh area. When he published his research in 1986 and 1987 he convinced most observers that the hedgerow pattern in the area appears to be early Roman or even Iron Age in origin. By looking at the hedgerow lines on the Tithe maps and by discounting those which appear to be of recent origin, he was then left with some four-fifths of the total. These form a rectilinear pattern running on a north-south axis which is quite clearly older than the Caistor to Scole Roman road which follows the modern A140.

This has encouraged archaeologists to look at the whole Norfolk landscape afresh to see how much else could be ancient and even be prehistoric in origin. It is sad, though, to reflect that so many of the hedgerows on the lines now identified as being possibly prehistoric were removed by post-war farm modernisation before their importance was appreciated.

The next technique, which is closely allied to the study of early maps is aerial photography. The Norfolk Museums Service

now has the largest and most comprehensive county-based air photographs collection in the country with some 85,000 pictures, and the ongoing aerial survey programme run by the service has led to some breathtaking discoveries.

Full appreciation of the potential of this technique dates from the inter-war years. There was a sensation when an air photograph by the RAF of the street pattern within the walls of the Roman town at Caistor St Edmund near Norwich was first published nationally following its publication in the EDP in 1928 and consequent urgent calls for it to be recorded from the air. Under dry conditions the streets showed as parched lines in the growing barley crop. The main north-to-south and east-to-west streets can be seen in the picture running between the four gateways through the Roman defences. A network of other streets and some buildings are also visible. The next year the great prehistoric monument, the Arminghall Henge near Norwich was similarly discovered by Wing Cmdr Insall. This timber henge built in the third millennium BC was as important to East Anglia then as Stonehenge was to Wessex.

When the Norfolk Archaeological Unit was formed in 1973 high priority was given to the creation of a county air photography programme. This has been run by Derek Edwards ever since with many notable successes, particularly in dry summers when growing crops reveal so many buried secrets. There were 196 recorded Bronze Age ring-ditches, the crop-marks left after burial mounds have been levelled, in 1975. Thereafter numbers have risen steadily as flying has continued: 549 in 1977, 899 in 1982 and about 1100 in 1987. Since then we have lost count!

The discovery in 1996 of the crop-mark of a complete outline of a Roman villa near Swaffham, with its underfloor heating system,

**One of the classic images of aerial photography, this RAF picture of Caistor St Edmund taken in the summer of 1928 clear shows the typical grid layout of a Roman town. The picture prompted enormous national interest. Earlier in the summer the EDP had published a series of articles (example below) and letters highlighting the cropmarks.**

ROMAN CAMP OF CAISTOR

WHITE LINES IN GROWING CORN.

A REMARKABLE PHENOMENON.

(BY PERCY A. NASH, ARCHITECT.)

All who take an interest in the period of the Roman occupation of Britain (c. A.D. 43-407) should not fail to view this camp as soon as possible. It is about three miles south of Norwich. The unmistakable evidence of the Roman layout of the camp is remarkably conspicuous owing to the fact that its whole tableland is now covered with growing corn, the surface of which, as seen from the high land above, on the Ipswich Road, is marked out with a chequer of straight white lines on the green surface of

**Derek Edwards, pictured by a Cessna 150 at Swanton Morley Airfield, is one of very small band of photographers who specialise in taking pictures of archaeological sites and the remains of ancient landscapes from the air. Since 1973 he has spent 672 hours in the air taking 41,000 pictures of the Norfolk landscape. In the process he has found thousands of previously unrecorded archaeological sites, some of which are illustrated in this chapter. His photographs now form the core of the Norfolk Aerial Photographs Library. A selection of his aerial views can be found in the two volumes of Norfolk From The Air, published by the Norfolk Museums Service.**

**One of his discoveries was this superb example of a classic aisled Roman villa, pictured on a flight near Swaffham on June 26th 1996. The pattern of the building is shown by the crop marks, which are formed when plants grow poorly over walls or foundations, or more strongly over buried pits or ditches.**

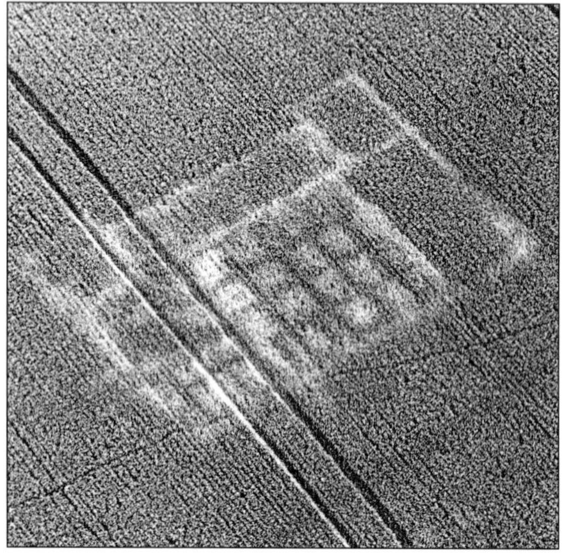

are just what dreams are made of. This building would have been occupied by a wealthy family from the local aristocracy able to control a large farming estate. The main central room had hypocaust underground heating ducts, and the projecting side wings would have included bedrooms, a kitchen and servants' quarters. The villa may well have been two-storied.

And the discovery in the same year of the complete crop-mark of a Roman fort at Saham Toney was equally breathtaking. The fort was probably constructed in the AD 60s as part of a major campaign to suppress the Boudican revolt in Norfolk. It was constructed at a strategic location close to where the Roman road, Peddars Way, crosses the Blackwater River. Peddars Way is clearly visible running through the fort, and at the entrance it passes across three ditches. The two inner ditches were probably palisade trenches for a timber rampart and the third was an open defensive ditch running outside the rampart. The clear relationship of the fort to the Roman road and the distinctively shaped "playing card" corners show the fort is Roman even without ground observation; such is the power of air photography. There are many other examples of dramatic discoveries from the air, but these are a sample.

The next two closely-related techniques of fieldwalking and metal detecting were not developed as disciplines until the Seventies. Isolated finds, some of them quite exciting such as flint arrowheads and Roman brooches, have been picked up from the surfaces of ploughed fields for centuries. But the systematic process of methodically walking up and down ploughed fields in parallel lines and at regular intervals when the soils surfaces have been well weathered, so that objects can be more easily seen, is relatively new.

The technique aims to record accurately the distribution of pieces of broken potsherds, worked flints and the occasional metal object and thereby to build up maps of human activity period by period. Where this work has been particularly successful it has been possible to produce period distribution maps of settlements, or at least indications of human activity, from prehistoric to medieval over a whole parish or a group of parishes.

The early pioneer of fieldwalking in Norfolk was a farmer, John Owles, who assiduously collected finds from his farm which covered the parish of Witton in north east Norfolk. For more than twenty years from 1960 he collected objects of all periods from his ploughed fields, and because he was not selective, the distribution of artefacts he recovered is likely to be an accurate representation of human activity over several thousand years. The work was not entirely systematic, and he left others to publish the results, but

his main achievement was to show to others what could be accomplished.

As Andrew Lawson's report on Witton concluded: *"The result of John Owles' collection is a staggering range of artefacts from Mesolithic microliths to Post-medieval porcelain."* This was in an area where very few finds had previously been recorded,so his discoveries helped us to realise just how rich the archaeology of Norfolk is,and that finds on this scale need not be limited to Breckland.

The writer then took the process a stage further with selective fieldwalking in Launditch Hundred, to the north west of East Dereham, between 1967 and 1970 around village greens and isolated churches. But the first complete block of Norfolk to be fully and methodically studied and published was at Hales, Loddon and Heckingham in south east Norfolk.

It was particularly interesting that those involved, in this project, notably Alan Davison and George Fenner, were, like John Owles, all amateur archaeologists. Norfolk has been especially successful at promoting close working relationships between active amateurs and professionals. Fieldwalking, which requires very long hours working in exposed conditions in all weathers during winter months, is ideal for the dedicated amateur. Few professionals have the time on top of their everyday workloads to produce worthwhile results over such extensive areas. This activity also requires a self-sufficient strong-willed personality able to go out in almost all weathers; it requires people who will go on and on when others dive for warmth and human company. Fieldwalking is, with a very few notable exceptions, the prerogative of the loner.

**At first view this might just seem an ordinary picture of some Norfolk fields. But look closer in the top left hand field... the curved mark by the road turns into a darker straight-line crop mark in the field to the bottom left. The mark continues in the field bottom right, running up to the bend in the road. Those curved corners give away that this is a previously undiscovered Roman fort. The soldiers had camped here, near Saham Toney, probably during the campaign in the AD60s to stamp out the Icenian revolt.**

**John Owles (1914-96) with his collection at Witton Hall in 1982. In 1960 he discovered a flint blade on a field on his farm at Witton. Armed with his new-found enthusiasm for archaeology, he spent the next twenty years searching his fields and collecting and recording objects of every period from prehistoric to modern. He demonstrated that, even in this part of Norfolk where few artefacts had previously been found, the ploughsoil can be a rich archaeological resource.**

What clearly emerged from the distribution maps produced by Alan Davison was that the areas of settlement, and by implication other forms of land use, were quite different in the Roman, Anglo-Saxon and medieval periods. The way man has exploited the landscape down the centuries has constantly changed. The maps from this project supported Tom Williamson's work on the field systems around Dickleburgh; both showed that the land, even on the heavy clays, was much more intensively settled in prehistory than we had expected.

The science of fieldwalking was later refined by Andrew Rogerson, a professional archaeologist in the Norfolk Museums Service, who carried out a more intricate study of the parish of Barton Bendish in West Norfolk entirely by himself over 139 days, much of it in his spare time, between 1983 and 1990. Andrew had already been involved with identifying the pottery from the Hales and Loddon project and must currently be the person in Norfolk most competent at identifying and dating small pottery sherds from the ploughsoil. It is a great skill few people have. The Barton Bendish survey was an epoch-making feat of personal endurance, backed up in this case by Alan Davison's documentary research. It revealed the settlement patterns of a parish during the Iron Age, Roman, Anglo-Saxon and medieval periods down to a level of detail not previously seen. This work was a very significant piece of research which extends our knowledge of the archaeology of the county to bounds undreamed of by our Victorian predecessors. Andrew has since gone on to complete a PhD thesis using similar techniques on his home parish of Fransham in central Norfolk, and the results of this work in a final publication are eagerly awaited. By far the most extensive piece of fieldwalking in the county has been organised as part of the ambitious Fenland Survey Project, a joint undertaking with Cambridgeshire, Lincolnshire and Suffolk, funded by English Heritage. Between 1981 and 1988 a group of Fenland Project officers walked 250,000 hectares over the four counties, or sixty per cent of the available land area of the Fens, although not in the same intimate detail as Barton Bendish. In Norfolk the project officer was Bob Silvester who found hundreds of new sites, dating back over the last 6000 years.

In Fenland extensive areas of waterlogged prehistoric archaeological deposits, until recently well preserved and buried in deep peat are being increasingly swept away by man's attempts to make these rich lands more productive.

The 1994 summary volume of the Fenland Survey by David Hall and John Coles is a moving read:

*"Today much of the peat fen lies like a desiccated corpse, a thin skin of peat stretched over the skeleton in some places, the bare bones of bedrock exposed in others. Its arteries, which once carried life to those limbs and organs, are detached now, and the water is dragged hurriedly along channels now raised above the drying frame.*

*"In time, the peat fen will disappear, and a reminder of ancient days and human endeavour will pass from our view. The relics of the earliest times will remain only as dried-out fragments, archaeological curiosities, in a land incapable of our comprehension. Only through the efforts of historians, prehistorians, and environmentalists are we able to describe Fenland lives over past millennia. The traces of those lives have survived only in fragments, and in conditions far removed from those where they once lay."*

The waterlogged Fenland has been a great archaeological databank of extraordinary richness containing so much well-preserved evidence of man's past. How to preserve what is left of these buried prehistoric landscapes, especially in the peat, is one of the great challenges facing today's archaeologists as the new millennium begins. We cannot do it alone, and it requires a concerted effort from all those concerned with landscape conservation in the region. The obvious solution is to re-flood some areas of Fenland where the archaeological potential remains high and at the same time re-create wetland habitats for wildlife. This is our only hope, and it seems perfectly feasible at a time of increasing

The century's most stunning archaeological discovery in Norfolk was the gold and silver torcs excavated at Snettisham in the early Nineties and now on display in the British Museum. This picture shows one of the torcs in the process of being excavated. Such headline-grabbing finds are extremely rare and do not reflect the unspectacular but vital work which goes on on a day-to-day basis.

FOR U.N.

ANOTHER FIND AT SNETTISHAM

November 24th 1950, and the EDP reports one of the first torc discoveries ploughed up at the Snettisham site.

emphasis on agri-environment schemes and the need to curtail food surpluses within British agriculture. Current discussions under the "Wet Fens for the Future" project, or some other similar scheme, may provide the best way forward. Having funded the original archaeological survey work, a stronger lead from English Heritage at this stage, in what is a national issue, is much needed now. No discussion about Norfolk's wetland can be complete without mention of the Broads. This area is a largely unexplored resource, compared with the Fens, and there is much scope for future work here.

Few techniques have revolutionised our understanding of Norfolk as a whole more than metal detecting. This is because so many active people are involved. Again, this work is usually performed as a hobby by amateurs. To produce useful results requires considerable skill. Born out of an enthusiasm for experimenting with ex-army mine detectors after the Second World War, the hobby was having a significant impact on the number of archaeological discoveries being made in the county by the late Seventies.

While the county's archaeologists have been busy this century identifying, recording and where possible, preserving Norfolk's below-ground heritage, there have been many dedicated people trying to perform a similar function for above-ground structures.

The great twentieth-century drive by councils to re-plan our towns and cities has had as its aims laudable objectives such as clearing slums and easing traffic congestion.

But it was quickly recognised that plans which called for wholesale clearances of particular areas risked destroying buildings of special merit which deserved restoration not demolition. It was one such proposal which prompted the formation in 1923 of the Norwich Society which has since achieved an enviable record of saving much which would otherwise have been lost.

It was the city council's proposal to modernise and widen the fourteenth-century Bishop's Bridge which galvanised wine merchant Walter Randall Rudd (1852-1927) and solicitor Basil Cozens-Hardy (1885-1976) to set up a meeting between archaeologists and architects, from which the Society was born. The society successfully persuaded the Ministry of Works - the forerunner of English Heritage - to 'list' the bridge and thus preserve it.

The society also fought a dogged and ultimately successful battle over a number of years to have the decaying Elm Hill fully restored.

Despite its existence, many historic buildings have been lost since then through decay, indifference, planning or enemy action. But the society can be proud of its many success stories in preserving buildings which would otherwise be just a memory.

**Elm Hill, one of Norfolk's best-loved streets. But the Norwich Society had to fight a long-running battle to save the area from neglect and redevelopment.**

The EDP summed up its role in a 1939 editorial: *"The Society is not a mere reactionary; an opponent of all change, which wants to keep old Norwich as a kind of museum piece. Rather, it seeks to be a skilled critic constantly reminding the city that it has a character to keep, as well as material gains to make."*

Much the same philosophy could be said to apply to the King's Lynn Preservation Trust, which has had a oustanding record since 1958. For many led by Lady Evershed, its successes include Hampton Court plus many other properties, including some in Pilot Street, King Street and Priory Lane. It has now taken on its biggest challenge yet: Clifton House.

'Preservation' is something of a misnomer as it implies the properties are left as empty museum pieces; in fact the trust aims to give them a new life as housing or offices. Its secretary, now chairman, Tony Williams, once summed up its role: "The bottom line is that if you've lost a building you can never replace it. That's the argument for fighting as hard as you can to keep as many as you can."

Yarmouth can claim the oldest conservation group in the county, the Yarmouth Historical Buildings Company (now Trust), set up to rescue the threatened Tollhouse in the last century. Other buildings saved by the group include the Greyfriars and Merchant's House. The preservation of the Fishermen's Hospital was another major success for conservation.

The traditional uneasy relationship between councils and conservation societies has now disappeared. Both work together, recognising that a built heritage is worth handing on to future generations.

Our Victorian ancestors would not have believed it possible to invent a machine which could detect metal objects buried unseen in the ground. It must be remembered, though, that most objects such as coins and brooches found in this way lie only in the top few inches of the soil. An object needs to be large to be found below that depth.

While archaeologists all over Britain were turning their backs on detectorists in the Seventies and Eighties and describing them as "vandals" and "treasure hunters", Norfolk's archaeologists recognised the contribution that responsible use of detectors could make to our understanding of the county's past. Here detectorists were encouraged to record the positions of their discoveries on maps and then to bring the objects and the information into a museum for study and identification.

This approach was led in the mid-Seventies by Tony Gregory, then an archaeologist in the Castle Museum, who saw the need to treat the hobby sympathetically. As a result, twenty years on, two members of museum staff are now working full time on detector finds from the county. About 20,000 objects a year are recorded, and more than a third of all the new information added to the County's SMR comes from metal detecting

The impact metal detecting has had on our understanding of Norfolk's past can be measured in a number of ways. Much information about the Iron Age comes from coins. Up to 1991 the number of recorded Iron Age coins in Norfolk was about 300. Since then a further 450 have been recorded, almost entirely as a result of detecting. Likewise, there has been a veritable explosion in the number of recorded Anglo-Saxon cemeteries, which are very distinctive sites for the post-Roman period; recorded Saxon cemeteries have risen from 57 in 1973 to 90 in 1999, an increase of more than half.

Viking settlement studies have greatly benefited from metal finds, which were the subject of a detailed study by Sue Margeson before her untimely death in 1997. There was a time when the Vikings were almost invisible in the archaeological record, but in the decade up to 1996 the numbers of Viking period finds increased ten-fold in East Anglia and Lincolnshire, with 200 new objects from Norfolk alone. Unlike the few very rare and elaborate swords and pieces of horse equipment from the military elite recorded in the past, the new material is relatively poor, well-worn and from both men and women. They were the everyday items from relatively poor farmers probably displacing Anglo-Saxon peasants in an early form of "ethnic cleansing" about which we hear nothing in the records. It is interesting how such a small group of finds is changing our understanding of settlers

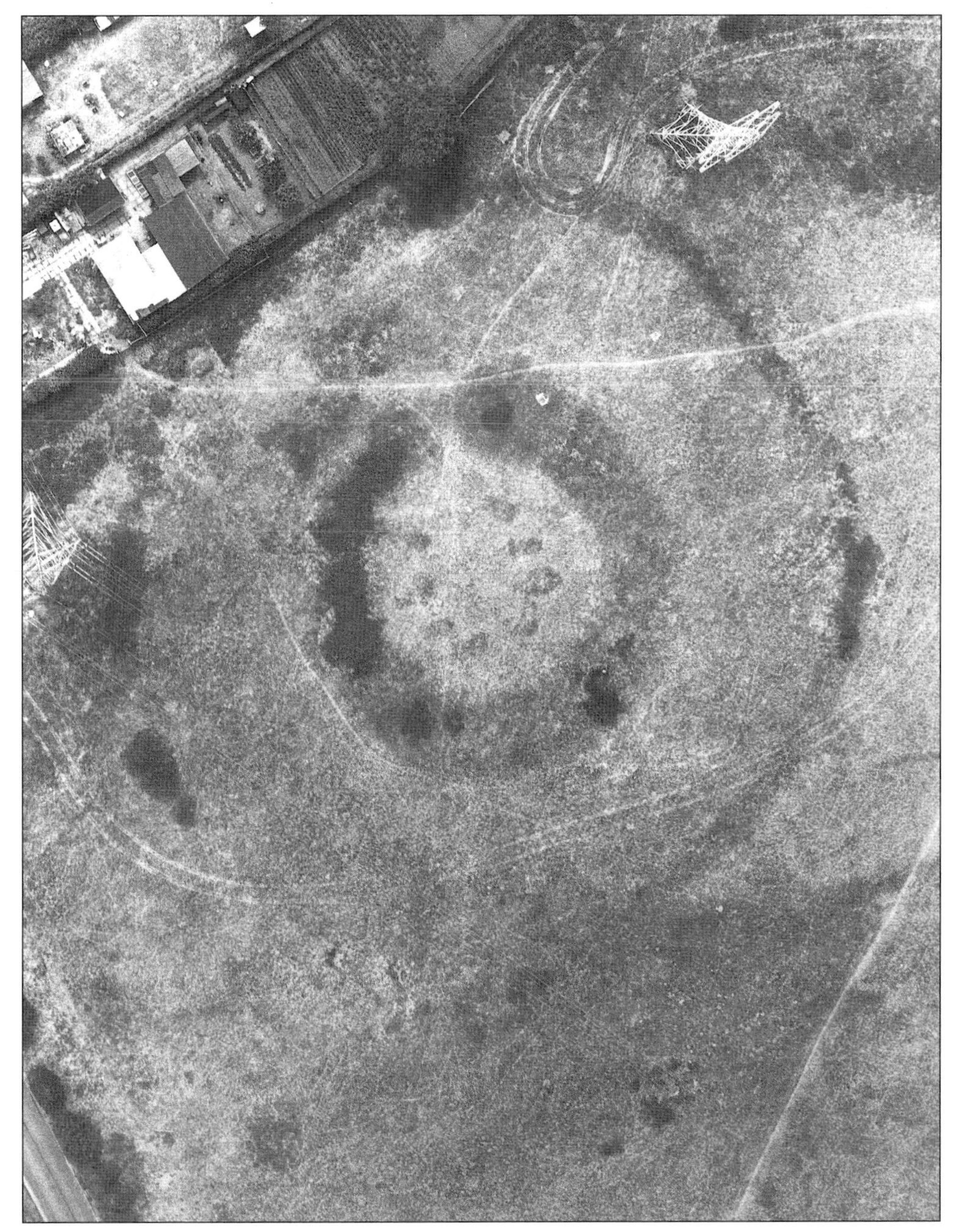

**The Arminghall Henge near Norwich was first discovered through aerial photography in 1929. This picture, taken in June 1996, clearly shows the double line of the ditches and the horseshoe-shaped collection of post-holes within them.**

**Andrew Rogerson has been active in field archaeology in Norfolk since he first joined the Norfolk Archaeological Unit in 1973. His fieldwalking projects at Barton Bendish and Fransham have demonstrated how field recording and documentary research, when combined, can greatly enhance our appreciation of the rural landscape.**

**Most of the ordinary archaeological work goes on very much behind the scenes, illustrated in these "before and after" photographs which show the painstaking work needed to clean loom weights from the medieval Coslany excavation in Norwich.**

whose distribution had previously only been recorded through place-names.

Scandinavian place-names, like those ending in *-by* (Scratby and Hemsby), had previously been our only clue to the nature of this settlement. While there is a strong concentration on Scandinavian place-names in the Flegg area north of Yarmouth, they are nevertheless widespread in the county. The distribution of Viking finds is similarly widespread.

It is still the popular belief that archaeologists spend most of their time digging up "things". This perception is regularly reinforced by the media who use photographs of excavators holding up objects to camera - a pot, a coin or a bone. While individual objects can on rare occasions make a real contribution to our understanding of a site, as happened when a Viking gold ingot associated with metalworking activity did turn up on the library site - as reported in the EDP on February 23rd 1999 - that is unusual.

Indeed, there are often times when negative evidence can be crucial. For it is the totality of the evidence - the layout of structures, the stratigraphic sequence of layers, the environmental data (such as preserved seeds and animal bones) and the artefacts which together make up the picture on which any judgement of an excavation depends.

Excavation is, by definition, destructive, and that destruction is usually only acceptable if the site is recorded with great care and the results are made available through archive reports and publication. The profession has a long tradition of not completing and publishing reports, and one of the worst examples in Norfolk was the late Professor Donald Atkinson's 1930-33 excavations of the Roman town at Caistor St Edmund. For some parts of his excavations little more than a few photographs remain. None of us would want to see that happen again. A big effort over the last few years has ensured that Norfolk's backlog of unpublished excavations has been almost cleared, and, it is important that no further backlog is allowed to accumulate. There have also been a number of remarkable new excavations published, mainly in East Anglian Archaeology. Up until 1987, when the statistics were last analysed, there had been 1123 excavations in Norfolk, which represents a considerable level of human endeavour. The earliest recorded excavation too place in 1451, when "hill diggers" dug into a mound in Bunwell and recovered treasure worth £100. That was quite a lot of money then, and the diggers must have unearthed a very rich burial.

There was an increase in antiquarian activity in the 1840s and 1850s which coincided with the formation of the Norfolk and Norwich Archaeological Society. It also saw the start of the Victorian enthusiasm for restoring churches. Since 1900 there has been a steady rise, only interrupted by the Second World War.

Numbers were boosted by the successful excavation programmes organised by the King's Lynn Archaeological Survey from 1963 to 1971, and a similar programme in Norwich from 1971 to 1978, although the publication of the Norwich excavations following the untimely death of the Norwich Survey director, Alan Carter, has been a struggle.

In the nineteenth century it was the opening of burial mounds and the recovery of objects for private collections which was popular. In the Eighties and Nineties of this century resources have been focused on rescue-led excavations within medieval urban centres in response to new shopping and office schemes. The figures for the whole of these decades have not been analysed, but they are likely to have shot up as the full impact of new planning guidelines took hold.

During a chapter such as this, one has to ask which excavations have made the greatest contribution to knowledge and which have created most public interest. They are not necessarily the same. Gold always catches the headline, and one has to admit that the discovery, and excavation by the British Museum, of the Iron Age gold torcs at Snettisham must come out as the top headline grabber of the century. Yet, it could be argued that these objects of precious metal are not telling us much new about Norfolk. They

**The early Sixties decision to clear the ancient Grime's Graves site of its birch covering was not without its opponents. But the work revealed the full extent of this startling and unique Norfolk site which it is estimated produced up to five million flint axe roughouts during its working life.**

demonstrate the wealth of the region in the Iron Age, based on the fertile soils of the region. But this is already well attested throughout prehistory and history. It is actually the technical skill of the gold and silversmiths which must hold our attention.

No two archaeologists would come up with the same list of their top six excavations, and some would say that it is a rather artificial exercise anyway, since the importance of an excavation can be assessed differently according to what answers you are looking for. In making the choice, the scale of the work has usually been an important factor, for there is a simple rule of thumb that applies with both settlement and cemetery excavations: the larger the area examined the more informative the results will be.

This is because spatial relationships between structures is often crucial, and it is a simple fact that the larger the hole you dig the more you are likely to find in it. It is also necessary to consider whether the results have been adequately assessed and published.

In the end, the writer's list would begin with the Grime's Graves Neolithic/Early Bronze Age flint mines near Brandon. Probably more excavations have taken place on this absolutely extraordinary site of European significance in Breckland than any other in Norfolk, because flints have always interested antiquarians. There have been major programmes organised by Cannon William Greenwell in 1868-1870, AE Peake in 1914, Leslie Armstrong over many seasons between the wars, Roger Mercer in 1971-72 and the British Museum from 1972-1976.

There are at least 360 mine shafts spread over nine hectares which were in production roughly between 2900 and 1900 BC, although

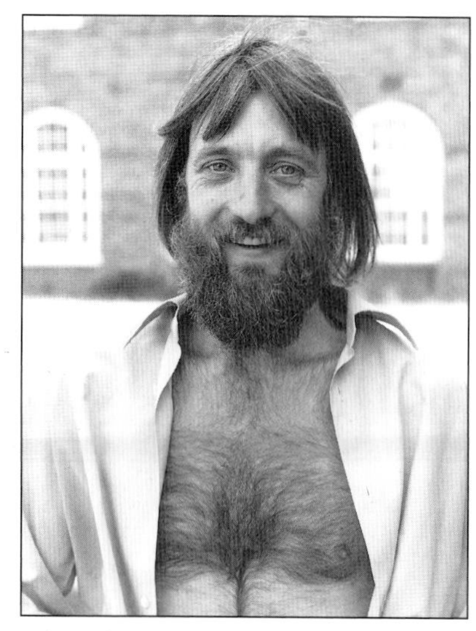

**The ultimely death of Tony Gregory (1948-91) robbed British archaeology of a remarkable spirit. Tony was a specialist in the Iron Age and Roman periods, but he was much more than that. During his 11 years in Norfolk from 1974 he led our thinking on how to work closely with metal detectorists, which ensured that all manner of important discoveries were added to the county's Sites and Monuments Record. As a lecturer and broadcaster, he inspired many people in all walks of life to have a lasting interest in the rich archaeological heritage of the county.**

there may not have been more than one or two open at a time. They were dug to reach the exceptional seam of flint nodules, known now as "floorstones" because that is this level at which the miners stopped digging downwards before sending out horizontal galleries.

It is interesting that Grime's Graves floorstone flint implements seldom seem to turn up on occupation sites in Norfolk. The reason is that the floorstone contains a beautiful lustrous black flint which fractures evenly, and the flint was used to produce high quality axes, discoidal knives and arrowheads which were roughed out in very large numbers on site before being traded in an unfinished state well outside the region.

The 12-metre shaft excavated in 1971-2 was one of the deeper mines, and it has been calculated that more than 1000 tons of overburden were removed to reach about eight tons of floorstone nodules, which could have been turned into 10,250 axes. Over the thousand or so years the mines were being exploited, an astonishing 2.5 and five million axe roughouts may have been produced. So trade routes from East Anglia were clearly well used over the later Neolithic and Early Bronze Age periods.

Another extremely significant site is the Arminghall Henge, a late Neolithic/Early Bronze Age henge which was discovered from the air in 1929. It was excavated impeccably, for the time, by Graham Clarke in 1935. The crop-mark showed the outlines of a wide circular ditch, 27 metres across, containing a horseshoe-shaped outline of eight very large post-holes, two of which were excavated and the rest were left undisturbed. The opening in the horseshoe faced the opening in the ditch. This ditch was surrounded by an outer bank and ditch.

The excavated post-holes had contained massive oak posts almost a metre wide and sunk 2.2 metres into the gravel. They had been erected by being slid down ramps into the ground before being stood upright. The lack of domestic refuse in the soil within the circle confirmed that this was not an occupation site, and that it was almost certainly ritual. At about 3000 BC this sacred structure was in its heyday with its very tall massive oak uprights, perhaps carved and painted like Indian totem poles, making an imposing sight.

The uprights may have been joined together at the top, as at Stonehenge, but this is by no means clear. Although the oaks could not have lasted more than a century or two, there is a cluster of burial mounds in the vicinity which continued in use for much of the Bronze Age, showing that this sacred prehistoric site, near the confluence of the Tas and Yare rivers, continued to dominate people's perceptions of the area long after the henge had disappeared.

A third site was "Boudica's Palace" off Fison Way, Thetford, which was excavated in the field which now forms the angle between the Thetford Bypass and the Mundford Road. Tony Gregory brilliantly excavated a massive 4.5 hectares between 1980 and 1982 to expose a Late Iron Age/Early Roman tribal and religious centre which was nicknamed "Boudica's Palace" even before he had finished. This was seen as a crop-mark in 1980 and was very close to the find-spot of the Thetford Treasure, a hoard of late Roman gold and silver jewellery and spoons, which came to the attention of the archaeological world in the same year. Nearby there was a building site where several thousand late Roman coins had been found in 1979, but not archaeologically recorded.

The structural sequence culminated in the early- to mid-first century with the construction of a large rectangular ditched enclosure surrounded by nine rows of extraordinary fences of closely-spaced timbers. Tony Gregory suggested that these lines of timbers, which survived as no more than stains in the sandy subsoil, might represent some sort of artificial grove; Celtic religious sites were often located in woodland clearings. These fences were in turn contained within an outer ditched enclosure. The great inner open space contained five large circular native-style buildings located at the end furthest from a massive ceremonial gateway approached through the strange "woodland" of parallel fences.

One can only guess what tribal ceremonies took place within this sacred ground in front of the "palace" buildings, but it is interesting that some of the items from the Thetford Treasure were dedicated to the native god Faunus, a woodland deity. It is suspected that a religious tradition was maintained on the site long after the original royal presence had been lost. The distribution of late Iron Age coins and decorated metalwork in the region is very much focused on this part of Breckland, indicating that Fison Way could indeed have been the tribal centre of the Iceni. It was a from a combination of clever excavation and the results of metal detecting in the region that a perfectly plausible explanation for this amazing site has emerged.

We now know of some ninety recorded Anglo-Saxon cemeteries in Norfolk, thanks in particular to metal detecting, but only Spong Hill has been fully excavated. On this low gravel hilltop Catherine Hills, Kenneth Penn and Robert Ricket ran an excavation which lasted for ten summer seasons from 1972 to 1981. During that time no fewer than 2300 pottery cremation urns, dating from around

**The evocative reconstruction by Sue White of "Boudica's Palace" at Thetford, which was brilliantly excavated by Tony Gregory. Modern archaeological techniques have given us a greater understanding than ever before of what life was like for our Norfolk ancestors.**

**No survey of the century would be complete without mentioning the Norfolk archaeologist who made the most celebrated discovery of the twentieth century. Howard Carter (1874-1939), son of a Swaffham artist, first went to Egypt in 1891. His excavations in the Valley of the Kings reached their historic climax on November 26th 1922 when, watched by his patron Lord Carnavon, he broke through the last barrier to the tomb of Tutankhamun. "Can you see anything?" Carnavon asked. "Yes, wonderful things," came the reply...**

AD 450 to 600, were carefully excavated from just beneath the ploughsoil.Then the contents of each urn had to be emptied and measured so that the position of the cremated bone fragments and grave-goods could be recorded.

The broken fragments of each urn were then cleaned and stuck together so that the urns could be photographed, drawn and classified according to shape and decoration. In addition, there were 58 inhumation burials of similar date in a distinct part of the cemetery. There is much of considerable interest from this site, but the evidence for the earliest of these Germanic settlers and the links with their Danish and North German homeland are particularly important.

The catalogue of the cremation burials ran to five volumes of East Anglian Archaeology. The cremated human bone fragments were analysed in a separate volume, and there were separate reports on the inhumation graves, Neolithic and Bronze Age occupation and also the Iron Age, Romano-British and Anglo-Saxon settlement evidence. This was an extraordinary achievement, with the last report published in 1995. All we need now is a final cemetery discussion volume.

The human resources needed to take the Spong Hill project thus far have been enormous, and one wonders if it will attempted again for a very long time. With this quantity of data, it is almost impossible to single out particular results in a few lines. No cremation pyre was found, which led to the conclusion that the dead were cremated near their homes and then brought for burial already in their urns, possibly from quite a distance.

One urn lid has created considerable interest, because it was formed in the shape of a person sitting on a chair. It is believed to be the only three-dimensional representation of a human figure from the Early Saxon period in this country. Despite the need for political correctness over gender issues these days, when he was found he was automatically called "Spong Man"!

Thetford was the location for another significant site excavation, but this time from the Late Saxon period. Thetford is unusual in having so much Late Saxon urban archaeology not disturbed or built over until this century, which makes it of national importance. Parts of the pre-Conquest town close to the Brandon Road were excavated by Brian Davison from 1964 to 1966 and Phil Andrews from 1988 to 1989. Late Saxon and Viking Thetford was a large and prosperous town, located on both sides of the river and clustered close the crossing point where the Bell Hotel is today.

The south side, where these excavations took place, is thought to have been a tenth-century expansion of the original settlement to the north. The first Brandon Road excavation of the tenth-century town was immensely innovative at the time. Brian Davison demonstrated a new approach to excavation by using a mechanical digger to expose around.1.2 hectares of the Saxon and Viking town in advance of London Overspill development.

He uncovered the lines of flint-surfaced streets, the post hole patterns of a wide range of timber houses, rubbish pits and pottery kilns. Other crafts were indicated by industrial waste and tools such as antler and bone carving, metalworking, carpentry and textile manufacture. Two underlying phases of Roman and Early Saxon occupation were also found. This was the first time that post hole pattern indicating the outlines of timber buildings had been exposed on any scale in the county, and the excavation showed the full potential of large-scale open area excavation in Norfolk. The nearby Redcastle Furze site was dug by Phil Andrews more than twenty years later to the west along the Brandon road. This was significant in two respects. Firstly, it allowed the theories about the origins and development of Thetford to be advanced further. But secondly, it also showed how a number of advances in excavation techniques and in the recording and analysis of the artefacts and environmental evidence had taken place in the meantime which helped to move the Thetford story forward.

The Anglia Television site near Norwich Castle provided important evidence about the city's Late Saxon period and excited considerable public interest. Part of the old cattle market was excavated by Brian Ayers in 1979 before the construction of new offices for the television company over what had once been the north east castle bailey. Because the site was being developed by Anglia, there was considerable public interest, and work on the site was regularly filmed.The excavators found below the levels of the bailey the complete plan of a Late Saxon timber-built church with its surrounding graveyard. The church seems to have been demolished in the eleventh century to make way for the castle bailey.This ties up with Domesday Book which records that a part of the town had to be cleared at the time for the construction of the castle.

There was a sequence of three Late Saxon timber buildings on the site, probably all churches, with the earliest dating from the tenth century. The final church had a clear outline with a nave and a smaller eastern chancel and a possible doorway at the west end. Outside the west door there was a large post-hole, possibly for a ceremonial cross. Near the centre of the nave there was a pit for casting a church bell, and to the west there was a soakaway, probably for a font. In the chancel there was an altar base.

Clustered around the church were 130 burials, aligned west-to-east, as Christian burial usually are. Some of the skulls were supported on small pillows of flints. The bones tell us much about the Late Saxon urban population of Norwich, even though the sample was relatively small. More than half of the burials were of children, emphasising the high infant mortality rate of the period. Of the adults, 46 per cent of the males and two-thirds of the females survived to between 35 and 45 years of age. Few people lived beyond 45. Several children died of rickets (vitamin D deficiency).

The bones as a group show a poor state of health, with several widespread pathological conditions attributed to dietary deficiencies. One surprise was a skull with strong negroid characteristics. How she reached Norwich we do not know, but early slave trading is suspected. The writer had previously excavated another negro skeleton from a context of similar date at North Elmham.

This was a gem of a site, revealing so much about early church architecture, urban topography and the pre-Norman population of Norwich. From 1989 to 1991 there was another, much larger, excavation carried out in advance of the Castle Mall development, and the final publication of these results should immeasurably increase our understanding of Norwich. Other excavations could so easily have been included in our survey, such as John Wymer's excellent 1984 excavation of a barrow at Bawsey, Trevor Ashwin's recent research on prehistoric sites along the Norwich Southern Bypass or Jonathon Coad's impressive 1972-7 study of Castle Acre Castle.

This chapter has focused mainly on the progress of archaeological research in Norfolk, and some of the illustrations have featured examples of the more dramatic discoveries in the county. The level of archaeological research reflects the fact that the "Rescue" movement led to a great increase in funding from central government for excavations in the Seventies, and PPG 16 has created an even greater increase in funding from developers in the Nineties. But we have yet to see any big upsurge in funding for site conservation.

**The huge excavation of cremation urns at the North Elmham site of Spong Hill from 1972 to 1981 provided a wealth of material about the Saxon period. Among the many discoveries was the quirky urn lid pictured below, which was instantly christened "Spong Man".**

**The Worthing Helmet, now on display in the Castle Museum, was discovered in August 1947 in the Wensum during dredging operations. It dates from the later Roman period.**

Raising funds for any monument conservation scheme, in comparison with rescue work, has been very hard work indeed. The writer has been involved in the archaeology of Norfolk since the early Sixties, and throughout that time considerable sums have been spent on rescue archaeology compared with what has been available for conservation schemes.

However, we may be about to see a change in emphasis now that English Heritage has completed a national Monuments at Risk Survey, the MARS Project, which has demonstrated just how severe damage from agriculture has been since the war. We will see.

It is likely, though, that conservation projects will be limited to a relatively small number of sites. There is still little hope that the continuing widespread damage from ploughing and subsoiling on arable land can be reduced in the foreseeable future.

Despite the shortage of funds for conservation work, we can still feel quite proud with what Norfolk is achieving in three distinct areas.

The first is the development of the Norfolk Archaeological Trust. This trust was founded by Basil Cozens-Hardy in 1926, in the same year the Norfolk Naturalists'Trust was formed. Since then the aim of the Archaeological Trust has been mainly to acquire and conserve historic buildings. However, during the Nineties it has taken on a new lease of life and has acquired through bequest and purchase most of the Roman town at Caistor St Edmund. The trust has opened the site to the public, and a series of illustrated panels along the walks around the monument provide an effective on-site interpretation scheme.

Since then it has acquired and similarly opened the Tasburgh hillfort for public access. More recently it has acquired the fine Roman fort at Burgh Castle and the surrounding land which is rich in evidence for Roman settlement. Better public access and a site interpretation scheme are currently being considered for this site as well. It is hoped that the Trust will further expand its work as opportunities permit.

Secondly, Norfolk is unique in running a Monuments Management Project aimed at conserving every earthwork site of significance in the county, whether or not they are yet legally protected as Scheduled Ancient Monuments. Large numbers of important sites are not yet scheduled, and with the slow progress English Heritage is making with its scheduling programme it will be at least twenty years before their work is completed in Norfolk.

The Monument Management Project, supported by the Norfolk Museums Service, the County Council, English Heritage and farming and wildlife organisations is working ahead of the scheduling programme to ensure that every farmer who manages a monument will have a visit by 2001 and that conservation measures will be in place wherever these are thought necessary.

Linked to this is the Norfolk Earthworks Survey which will ensure that all the earthworks of Norfolk of any quality will be surveyed and recorded at a scale of 1:1000 by March 2000, and the results are then to be made available as a volume entitled The Earthworks of Norfolk in the East Anglian Archaeology series.

**Warham Camp near Wells, one of the fine examples of Norfolk's heritage which can be visited by the public. The Iron Age fort was described as a "Danish encampment" in the nineteenth century, but modern work has revealed its true origin.**

In conclusion, one can say that the archaeologists of Norfolk, both amateur and professional, have been pretty active over this last century, building on the enthusiasm and discoveries of their predecessors.The strength and continuity of Norfolk's archaeological institutions have served the county well through difficult times. An understanding of the archaeology of a county helps people have a sense of place.

And Norfolk people do care about their past, sometimes passionately so. As this chapter went to press, the news and letter columns of the EDP were filled with comments and debate about conservation work at - and the ultimate future of - the Bronze Age timber circle uncovered on the beach at Holme and dubbed - colourfully but inaccurately - "Seahenge".

The better people understand and appreciate their archaeological and built heritage, the more they enjoy it, and the safer that heritage will be for the future.

## Postscript

# *Norfolk in 2050*

**TREVOR HEATON**

The Child is father of the Man, wrote Wordsworth, and in the same way the future is the child of the past. In concluding our survey of the eventful last 100 years it is thus perhaps fitting to peer into our crystal ball and make some predictions about the years ahead.

What kind of Norfolk have we passed on to the next century? A county no longer isolated from the rest of the country, a place which, in the words of Norfolk's most senior planner, joined the South East in the mid-Eighties. A place where villages have lost schools, shops, jobs. Where bypasses and business parks cover what was once pastures. Where the rich Norfolk dialect has had to fight a rearguard action against the constant stream of "furrin" accents and culture. Paradise Lost? Well, perhaps.

But we have also said farewell to the worst of the grinding poverty and the spectre of the workhouse which haunted thousands of working people. We live longer and generally healthier lives. Where a weekly trip to the nearest market town and an annual seaside visit was the best most people could look forward to, it is now possible to travel all over the world via Norwich Airport. The humblest houses have consumer goods which would have astounded a Norfolkman from 1900.

The way we live our working lives has changed dramatically in the last few years. The average villager these days is no longer a worker on a local farm but an office worker commuting into Norwich or one of the big towns. But the internet and other technology will change that still further. Will the high street of 2050 have, for example, banks, building societies or travel agents when all these services are being offered on the net or via the telephone? The EcoTech site at Swaffham may bring in a new area of green industries with low environmental impact. And the increasingly global nature of the business community has affected Norfolk as it has everywhere else. Many of our biggest employers have decision-makers elsewhere in the country or the world. And what of Norwich Union, the county's business giant? Will it stay independent - or will some American megabank swallow it up?

Travelling to work may become a rarity, fuelled by the proliferation of on-line facilities at home and an increasingly draconian attitude to cars in towns and cities. At the very least a compulsory park and ride could be in operation in Norwich, King's Lynn and Yarmouth, perhaps even the long-vaunted light rail network could spring up in Norwich.

Our precious man-made and natural heritage will have more protection than ever before. The casual destruction of our archaeological and built heritage in earlier decades has been largely stopped through a combination of legislation, pressure groups and above all public awareness. Archaeology will be seen increasingly as an integral part of the planning and development process and there will be a steady rise in the number of excavations carried out. As the next century unfolds we will realise that our knowledge of the county is only a fraction of what we know in 1999. New technology will help us understand the lives of our forefathers better than ever before.

Our historic buildings have more protection than previous generations, and techniques of repair and conservation have never been higher. This will ensure, for example, that the majority of well-preserved Anglican church buildings will still be used for

**Norwich's massive Riverside redevelopment is typical of the confident spirit of investment which is in the county as the century ends. As well as the new hospital and Riverside developments, Norwich – and Norfolk – is also looking forward to the construction of the £60 Millennium Project to replace the fire-ravaged Norwich Central Library. The project will have a library, business and learning centre, multi-media auditorium, visitor centre and restaurants. Work began on June 2nd 1999 and is scheduled to be completed in early 2001.**

worship in 2050 - perhaps under the spiritual guidance of Norfolk's first woman bishop.

As for nature, there has never been greater awareness of the need to conserve our rich heritage. Of course there have been many bad aspects of this century, including the loss of so many hedgerow habitats. But we can think of the many success stories such as the fine work of local conservationists and the fightback of species such as the otter. Trying to build that elusive compromises between development pressures, the needs of farming, and the environment will continue to exercise our minds.

But nature itself may have the last word. The World Wide Fund for Nature has predicted the loss of half the world's coastal wetlands by 2080 due to rising sea levels and global warming. It predicted the loss of many areas such as the grazing marshes around Cley. Sea defences built after the 1953 disaster are showing their age and need replacing, but even that might not be enough.

The sea has seen its fisheries badly drained, its waters polluted and its seabed dredged over the last century. The challenges of the next fifty years are great indeed. The effect of the creation of the Wash and most of the North Norfolk coast as a SSSI (Site of Special Scientific Interest) remains uncertain. In addition, the proposals for the same area to become a SAC (Special Area of Conservation) under the EU Habitats Directive will mean the UK government now has a responsibility to protect this marine environment.

Unless the Common Fisheries Policy is changed by the EU, any country will be able to fish right up to our shores, with obvious implications for fish stocks. But stricter pollution controls by 2050 will have long stemmed the flow of household and industrial wastes into the North Sea.

Fishing in North Norfolk will still be around in 2050. The only question mark hangs over who will be taking part in it. Fishing remains a tough job, with no nine to five routine in a cosy office and a warm car ride to work. Sons from fishing families have been drifting away into less risky work ever since the start of the century. By the year 2050 there could be a trend for fewer boats going further for their quarry.

The future of the Yarmouth area is bound in with the need to improve road communications and the success of its proposed outer harbour project. Both are need for the port to be able to offer quick, efficient turn-rounds of cargo from visiting ships and rapid distribution to the rest of the country. Such investment will help the area cope with the run-down of the North Sea gas reserves by perhaps 2030. The gas fields which have led to the creation of so many jobs were predicted to have run out in 1991. But they are still here and industry experts believe there are massive reserves still untouched. Recovering them will need a massive investment in technology, but the will is there from the major companies.

The rapid expansion of the county's population in the last few decades is set to continue for the next few. Survey after survey proves that the English family's dream still remains a rose-encrusted country cottage. If the reality is a piece of suburbia grafted on to a Norfolk country town or village, then at least the dream has partially been fulfilled. The widespread use of teleworking may spark something of a renaissance in our villages, bringing in young families once again to keep services going.

But they will have to be well-heeled. The days when a Norfolk labourer's cottage would change hands for a few hundred pounds are long, long gone. The pressure on honeypot areas such as the Waveney Valley and North Norfolk coast will continue unabated.

The age profile of the population is set to change too. In Norfolk the number of elderly people is predicted to increase steadily, which will pose hard questions for providers of health and residential nursing care.

Turning to Norfolk art and culture, the county's dialect will find itself even more squeezed in our multi-media world. But the character of the county is something that all will aspire to keep. As Keith Skipper has observed: "Newcomers and visitors alike are bound to be bitterly disappointed if they see Norfolk turning soft and betraying its stubborn, one-paced, one-way reputation."

That multi-media world is also worrying some that art is losing out too. The fact that the Leonardo da Vinci Codex, sold by the Holkham Estate in 1980, now adorns the Seattle mansion of Microsoft billionaire Bill Gates may offer a warning. Just as many fretted in 1900 that the landscape painter would soon be rendered obsolete by the camera, so in 2000 some worry that the lovely term "oil on canvas" is losing out to the command "log on computer". But future creative souls will surely find new ways of building on the past and present to produce beguiling and original works of art.

And turning from art to sport, what of Norwich City? It seems likely that the existing Premier League, three-division Football League and access to and from non-League football is unlikely to survive much longer. The elite will move in the exalted circles of European Super League, perhaps even a World Cup League. In 1999 Norwich City asked the business community for £7 million backing to help make its proposed soccer academy the very best. But whether Norwich can really compete with the mega-rich Manchester Uniteds, Arsenals and Liverpools of this world is debatable. A British League consisting of regional divisions may be the best Norwich City fans can reasonably hope for.

The move towards regional assemblies could lead to the end of county or even district councils, which can only weaken our sense of local identity. The East of England Regional Chamber, which met for the first time on March 12th 1999, could be the taste of things to come. And it is perhaps even more significant that it met in Bedford.

The 75 miles or so from Yarmouth to Walpole Cross Keys represented a huge self-contained world to our forefathers. Many only became fully aware of the outside world when called up to fight on distant battlegrounds. Even today there are people who have hardly been out of the county in their lives. It is hard to see that insularity surviving another generation. We have become increasingly aware of our place in East Anglia, in Britain, in Europe, in the world.

In that context holding on to a sense of

Norfolkness will be the hardest task of the next few years.

And, after all, what is "Norfolkness" anyway? To some it is the lonely beauty of the North Norfolk marshes; the sight of a wherry sail; the massed voices of the Barclay on a Norwich City cup run; the taste of the first Cromer crab of the season; the heart-stopping beauty of a field of poppies; the rich country voices of Swaffham market; evensong on a warm autumn evening in a Norfolk country church; the fluttering of a swallowtail butterfly in a warm breeze at Strumpshaw Fen. Norfolkness is something that is essentially indefinable because it is has a different meaning for every lover of the county. Yet perhaps it is precisely because it is so difficult to define that makes it so rare and precious.

The only certain thing about the future is that it will be different, and different in all kinds of unexpected ways. People in 2050 will look back on our time as a time of innocence, a golden age, in the same way we stare nostalgically at pictures of previous decades. Norfolkness may be a little harder to find in fifty years' time, but if we can succeed in passing on our love of this great, historic, beautiful land of ours then perhaps we will be leaving our finest legacy of all.

**At the twilight of the twentieth century, we can reflect on the tremendous changes which have been wrought in our daily lives, and ponder those to come in the next 100 years.**

Producing a project of this size has been of necessity a team effort. I have been fortunate in having available the services of a wide variety of people both inside Eastern Counties Newspapers and outside who have given unstintingly of their time, expertise and enthusiasm. To them all I express my sincere thanks.

They are: David Banks, editorial secretary Julie Barfield, editorial assistant Linda Barrington-Smith, Denis Browne, Richard Bunting, Dave Cartledge, Rosemary Dixon, Derek Edwards, Stephen Godfrey, Michael Gooch, Barry Hartley, Annette Hudson, Ken Hurst, John Hutchison, Steven Jennings, Clive Jones, Martin Kirby, Ian McIntyre, David Newham, Norfolk Museums Service, Gill Pattinson, Frances Pearce, Philip Preston, Steven Riseborough, Martin Rodwell, Bill Smith, Steve Snelling, Diane Townshend, Peter Waters, Dennis Whitehead and Joy Wright.

Trevor Heaton

Picture sources:
Eastern Counties Newspapers Library (photographer's name in brackets): Facing title page (Simon Finlay); 10 (Daniel Hambury); 11 (bottom picture: D Hambury); 13 (Brian Waite); 15 (Tony Kemp); 19 (Graham Corney); 20; 21 (D Hambury); 23 (Sam Robbins); 25 (S Finlay); 26, 28-9 (Bill Smith); 32, second top (John Hocknell); 33; 35 (top); 36; 38; 39 (B Smith); 40; 41 (J Hocknell); 43; 44; 45 (Dennis Whitehead); 47 (J Hocknell); 48 (Simon Lunt); 51 (J Hocknell); 52; 53; 55; 56; 57; 59; 61; 63; 65 (D Whitehead); 66 (S Finlay); 68 (J Hocknell); 70; 72; 74; 75; 77 (G Corney); 79; 80; 81; 82; 85; 87 (B Smith); 89 (Keith Whitmore); 91; 92; 93 (J Hocknell); 94 (B Smith); 95 (G Corney); 96; 98; 99 (Kieron Tovell); 100; 101; 113 (S Finlay); 121; 125; 126; 127; 128; 129; 131 (J Hocknell); 132 (S Lunt); 133 (B Smith); 136; 137 (John Folkes); 139 (Bill Darnell); 143; 145 (top: J Hocknell, right: S Finlay); 149; 150; 151 (J Hocknell); 152, 153 (Les Gould); 155 (B Smith); 161; 163 (D Whitehead); 166; 167 (B Smith); 168; 169 (B Darnell); 171 (S Finlay); 172; 173 (S Finlay); 175 (B Waite); 176; 177 (B Smith); 178; 179 (L Gould); 181 (Chris Gorman); 185 (G Corney); 187; 188, 190 (top), 193 (J Hocknell); 194 (S Lunt); 197 (S Robbins); 199 (B Waite); 200; 201 (G Corney); 207 (L Gould); 209 (B Darnell); 210; 213; 219; 221 (S Robbins); 223; 227 (L Gould); 228 (J Hocknell); 229; 233; 234 (Dick Jeeves); 235; 236; 237; 238; 239; 240 (S Robbins); 245; 247; 251; 255; 263 (B Smith); 264; 267; 268; 269; 270; 271; 272; 273 (S Finlay); 274 (Steve Adams); 275 (Alan Howard); 277; 278; 280; 281 (B Smith); 283; 285 (B Waite); 286; 288 (S Lunt); 289; 290 (S Lunt); 291; 293; 295; 296 (S Robbins); 297; 298; 299; 300; 301; 302 (B Smith); 303 (top, J Hocknell, below, Sam Robbins); 305; 307 (S Adams); 308 (Sarah Hunt); 310; 312; 318; 320 (top, G Corney); 324; 329 (B Smith); 331.

Anglia Television: 156, 157, 158.

David Armstrong collection: 276, 279.

Ken Arnott collection: 190 (bottom).

British Museum Library: 317.

British Sugar: 135.

Created Images (Rod Scott): 165.

English Heritage, National Monuments Record: 313. Crown copyright material is reproduced by permission of English Heritage acting under licence from the Controller of Her Majesty's Stationery Office.

Norman Greenway collection: 284.

Trevor Heaton collection: 111 (main picture); 141.

Adrian Hoare collection: 253.

Holkham Estate: 186.

Alan Howard Photography: 237.

R Lawson collection: 261.

M and GN Circle archive: 294.

Tony North collection: 257.

Mike Page: 31, 231.

Mary Rae: 97.

Norfolk Library and Museums Service: 108, 109, 111 (inset picture), 117, 118, 249 (George Swain), 323 (illustration: Sue White), 325. Norwich Castle Museum: 83, 84, 86, 320 (middle and bottom), 326. Norfolk Aerial Photography Library (All pictures by Derek Edwards except p16, George Swain; p314, top, David Wicks; P325, bottom, Mick Sharp): 17, 311, 314 (bottom), 315, 316, 319, 321, 322, 327.

Norfolk Wildlife Trust: 30, 32 (top, and bottom two pictures), 34, 35 (F W Oliver), 42.

Pat Ramm collection: 258

Dick Rayner: 122.

Vince Re: 259.

Royal Air Force: 250.

Charles Roberts collection: 144, 147.

Keith Skipper collection: 71, 73, 76, 78, 230.

Steve Snelling collection: 106, 110, 112, 115, 119, 244, 248, 260.

Le Strange archive: 189.

True's Yard Museum, North End Trust, King's Lynn: 107, 215 (Steve Worfolk), 217.

Wartime Watton Museum: 243.

Trevor Westgate collection: 205.

**Chapter 1: Population**
Richards, Dr P, 1990. *King's Lynn* (Phillimore).
Crosby, A, 1986. *A History of Thetford* (Phillimore)

**Chapter 2: Nature**
Ellis, E A, 1998. *A Tapestry of Nature* (EDP Classics)
Dymond, D, 1985. *The Norfolk Landscape* (Hodder & Stoughton)
Stone, E, 1986. *Ted Ellis - The People's Naturalist* (Jarrold)
*The Norfolk Broads Plan* (Broads Authority)

**Chapter 3: Royal Norfolk**
Hepworth, P, 1978. *Royal Sandringham* (Wensum)
Jenkins, S C, 1987. *The Lynn and Hunstanton Railway and the West Norfolk Branch* (Oakwood Press)

**Chapter 4: Norfolk Art and Culture**
Aldiss, B, 1993. *Remembrance Day* (Harper Collins)
Bagshaw, R, 1997. *A Norfolk Chronicle* (George Reeve)
Blyth, J, 1903. *Juicy Joe, A Romance of the Norfolk Marshlands* (Grant Richards)
Cook, O, 1956, 1980. *Breckland* (Robert Hale)
Collins, I, 1990, *A Broad Canvas* (reprinted by Black Dog Books 1999)
Dorman, B, 1972. *Norfolk* (Batsford)
Earwaker, J, Becker, K, 1998. *Literary Norfolk* (Chapter 6 Publishing)
Fenn, I, 1976. *Tales of Norfolk* (George Reeve).
Grapes, S, 1958. *The Boy John Letters* (Norfolk News Co) also published by Wensum Books, 1974.
Haggard, L Rider (ed), 1935. *I Walked By Night* (Nicholson & Watson), reprinted by Boydell Press, 1974.
Ketton-Cremer, R W, 1944. *Norfolk Portraits* (Faber & Faber)
Mann, M, 1902. *The Fields of Dulditch.* Reissued by Boydell Press, 1976
Mardle, J, 1973. *Broad Norfolk* (Wensum Books)
Skipper, K, 1996. *Larn Yarself Norfolk* (Nostalgia Publications)
Spilling, J, republished 1998. *Giles's Trip to London,* (Jarrolds)
Taylor, D J, 1992. *Real Life* (Chatto & Windus)
Tolhurst, P, 1996. *East Anglia, A Literary Pilgrimage,* (Black Dog Books)
Williamson, H, 1941. *The Story of a Norfolk Farm* (Faber & Faber)

**Chapter 5: Faith**
*A Great Gothic Fane: A Retrospect of Catholicity in Norwich* (W T Pike)
Atherton, I et al (ed), 1996. *Norwich Cathedral: Church, City and Diocese 1096-1996* (Hambledon Press)
Blofeld, The Hon Mr Justice (ed), 1991. *Rural Church Buildings* (Diocese of Norwich)
Cornick, D, 1998. *Under God's Good Hand* (The United Reformed Church of the United Kingdom)
Cullen, T, 1975. *The Prostitutes' Padre: The story of the notorious Rector of Stiffkey* (The Bodley Head)
Ede, J, Virgoe, N and Williamson, T, 1994. *Halls of Zion - Chapels and Meeting-Houses in Norfolk* (Centre of East Anglian Studies)
Jewson, C J, 1957. *The Baptists in Norfolk* (Carey Kingsgate)
Mortlock, D P, and Roberts, C V, 1981-5. *The Popular Guide to Norfolk Churches* (three vols) (Acorn Editions)

**Chapter 6: The First World War**
Brew, A, 1995. *Boulton Paul Aircraft* (Alan Sutton)
Chatterton, E Keble, 1936. *Amazing Adventure: A biography of Cdr Godrey Herbert* (Hurst & Blackett)
Cole, C, and Cheesman, E F. *The Air Defence of Britain 1914-18* (Putnam)
Gliddon, G, (ed), 1988. *Norfolk & Suffolk in the Great War* (Gliddon)
Petre, F Loraine, *The History of the Norfolk Regiment, Vol II, 1914-18* (Jarrold & Sons)
Poolman, K, 1960. *Zeppelins Over England* (Evans Brothers)
Storey, N R, 1995. *Norfolk at War* (Alan Sutton)
Storey, N R, 1997. *The Royal Norfolk Regiment* (Sutton)

**Chapter 7: The Land**
Douet, A, 1995. *Breaking New Ground: Agriculture in Norfolk 1914-1972* (UEA PhD thesis)

**Chapter 8: Entertainment and the Media**
Joice, D, 1991. *Full Circle* (Boydell Press)
Peart, S, 1980. *The Picture House in East Anglia* (Terence Dalton)
Roope, F C, 1961. *Come to the Fair* (Showmen's Guild)
Temple, C R, 1990. *Grandfather's Norfolk* (Ian Hendry Publications)
Worfolk, S, 1992. *The Cinema in King's Lynn: From Bioscope to Wide Screen* (Stephen Worfolk)

**Chapter 9: Industry and Commerce**
Wade-Martins, Dr S, 1984. *A History of Norfolk* (Phillimore)
Cartwright, A R, Fitch, A, Robins, D L J et al (eds), 1961. *Norwich and Its Region* (British Association)
Various, 1993. *An Historical Atlas of Norfolk* (Norfolk Museums Service)
Holmes, K, 1992. *Start-rite 1792-1992: Two Centuries of Shoemaking* (Start-rite)

**Chapter 10: The Families**
Arnott, K, 1983. *Hunstanton: The Story of a Small Norfolk Seaside Resort* (Ken Arnott)
Barnes, P, 1993. *Norfolk Landowners Since 1880* (Centre of East Anglian Studies) (Full text of thesis accessible in Norfolk Local Studies Library)
Berry, V, 1979. *The Rolfe Papers: The Chronicle of a Norfolk Family 1559-1908* (Veronica Berry)
Birkbeck, H., 1993. *The Birkbecks of Norfolk* (Michael Russell)
Cornforth, J, 1998. *The Country Houses of England* (Constable)
Ketton-Cremer, R W, 1962. *Felbrigg: The Story of a House* (Boydell Press). Republished by National Trust, 1976.
Winkley, G, 1986. *The Country Houses of Norfolk* (Tyndale & Panda)

**Chapter 11: The Sea**
White, M, 1999. *A Century of Fishing* (M White)
Bentham, H, and Finch, R, 1983. *The Big Barges* (Harrap)
Castleton, F, 1990. *Fishers End* (Frank Castleton)
Various, 1946. *The Fisheries in Wartime* (MAFF)
Payn, R, 1998. *The Port & Pilotage at King's Lynn* (True's Yard)
Temple, C R, 1986. *Shipwreck* (Tyndale Press and Panda Publishing)
Vause, J, 1986. *U-Boat Ace, the story of Wolfgang Luth* (Airlife)
Worfolk, S, 1997. *The Worfolk Family* (S Worfolk)
Lee, K, Stibbons, P, and Warren M, 1975, reprinted 1983. *Crabs and Shannocks - the Longshore fishermen of North Norfolk* (Poppyland)
Eastern Sea Fisheries Joint Committee, 1994. *The First One Hundred Years 1894-1994* (Eastern Sea Fisheries)
Brooks, P, 1980. *Sheringham, The Story of A Town* (Poppyland)

**Chapter 12: Social Affairs**
Various, 1989. *Centenary, A hundred years of County Government in Norfolk* (Norfolk County Council)

**Chapter 13: Second World War and Aftermath**
Banger, J, 1974. *Norwich at War* (Wensum Books)
Bowman, M, 1995. *Low Level from Swanton* (Air Research)
Collis, R, 1992. *East Anglian Air War Fact-File 1939-45* (Norfolk & Suffolk Aviation Museum)
Hoare, A, 1997. *Standing Up to Hitler: The Story of Norfolk's Home Guard and 'Secret Army', 1940-44* (Reeve)
Rothnie, N, 1992. *The Baedeker Blitz* (Ian Allan)
Snelling, S, 1996. *Over Here: The Americans in Norfolk during World War II* (Breedon Books)

**Chapter 14: Sport in Norfolk**
Cuffley, D, 1995. *The Norwich City Story* (Breedon/EDP)
Bell, T, 1972. *On The Ball City* (Wensum Books)
Davage, M, 1994. *Glorious Canaries, Past and Present* (Norwich City FC)
Eastwood, J, and Davage, M. 1986. *Canary Citizens* (Almeida)
Greenway, N, 1999. *The Jim Russell Story* (Transport Bookman)

**Chapter 15: Transport**
Allen, C J, 1968. *The Great Eastern Railway* (Ian Allan)
Body, G, 1986. *Railways of the Eastern Region* (Patrick Stephens)
Clark, R H, 1967. *A Short History of the Midland and Great Northern Railway* (Goose and Son)

**Chapter 16: Discovering Our Past**
Ayers, B, 1994. *Norwich* (English Heritage)
Ayers, B, Heywood, S, Margeson, S (eds), 1996. *A Festival of Norfolk Archaeology* (Norfolk and Norwich Archaeological Society)
Meeres, F, 1998. *A History of Norwich* (Phillimore)
Wade-Martins, Dr P (ed), 1997. *Norfolk From the Air, Vol I* (Norfolk Museums Service) 1999. *Norfolk From the Air, Vol II* (Norfolk Museums Service)
Williamson, T, 1993. *The Origins of Norfolk* (Manchester University Press)